Party Competition

PRINCETON STUDIES IN COMPLEXITY

Series Editors
. . . .
SIMON A. LEVIN (Princeton University)
STEVEN H. STROGATZ (Cornell University)

Lars-Erik Cederman, *Emergent Actors in World Politics: How States and Nations Develop and Dissolve*

Robert Axelrod, *The Complexity of Cooperation: Agent-Based Models of Competition and Collaboration*

Peter S. Albin, *Barriers and Bounds to Rationality: Essays on Economic Complexity and Dynamics in Interactive Systems*. Edited and with an introduction by Duncan K. Foley

Duncan J. Watts, *Small Worlds: The Dynamics of Networks between Order and Randomness*

Scott Camazine, Jean-Louis Deneubourg, Nigel R. Franks, James Sneyd, Guy Theraulaz, and Eric Bonabeau, *Self-Organization in Biological Systems*

Peter Turchin, *Historical Dynamics: Why States Rise and Fall*

Andreas Wagner, *Robustness and Evolvability in Living Systems*

Mark Newman, Albert-Laszlo Barabasi, and Duncan Watts, eds., *The Structure and Dynamics of Networks*

J. Stephen Lansing, *Perfect Order: Recognizing Complexity in Bali*

Joshua M. Epstein, *Generative Social Science: Studies in Agent-Based Computational Modeling*

John H. Miller and Scott E. Page, *Complex Adaptive Systems: An Introduction to Computational Models of Social Life*

Michael Laver and Ernest Sergenti, *Party Competition: An Agent-Based Model*

Party Competition

AN AGENT-BASED MODEL

Michael Laver and Ernest Sergenti

PRINCETON UNIVERSITY PRESS

PRINCETON AND OXFORD

Copyright © 2012 by Princeton University Press
Published by Princeton University Press, 41 William Street,
Princeton, New Jersey 08540
In the United Kingdom: Princeton University Press,
6 Oxford Street, Woodstock, Oxfordshire OX20 1TW

press.princeton.edu

All Rights Reserved

Library of Congress Cataloging-in-Publication Data

Laver, Michael, 1949–
Party competition : an agent-based model / Michael Laver and Ernest Sergenti.
p. cm. – (Princeton studies in complexity)
Includes bibliographical references and index.
ISBN 978-0-691-13903-6 (hardcover : alk. paper) –
ISBN 978-0-691-13904-3 (pbk. : alk. paper)
1. Political parties. 2. Competition—Political aspects—Simulation methods.
I. Sergenti, Ernest. II. Title.
JF2051.L36 2011
324.2 dc22   2011005333

British Library Cataloging-in-Publication Data is available

This book has been composed in Sabon

Printed on acid-free paper. ∞

Printed in the United States of America

10 9 8 7 6 5 4 3 2 1

Contents

Preface   vii

Acknowledgments   xiii

Part One: Preliminaries   1

  1. Modeling Multiparty Competition   3
  2. Spatial Dynamics of Political Competition   15
  3. A Baseline ABM of Party Competition   28
  4. Systematically Interrogating Agent-Based Models   56

Part Two: The Basic Model   83

  5. Benchmarking the Baseline Model   85
  6. Endogenous Parties, Interaction of Different Decision Rules   106
  7. New Decision Rules, New Rule Features   132

Part Three: Extensions and Empirics   157

  8. The Evolutionary Dynamics of Decision Rule Selection   159
  9. Nonpolicy Factors in Party Competition   183
 10. Party Leaders with Policy Preferences   206
 11. Using Theoretical Models to Analyze Real Party Systems   228
 12. In Conclusion   258

References   267

Index   275

A link to the following material is available at http://press.princeton.edu/titles/9604.html
   Appendix: Additional computational results.
   NetLogo computer code for each modeling chapter (chapters 5–11).

Preface

THIS IS A NEW BOOK ON AN OLD SUBJECT: the contest between political parties in regular, free and competitive elections, a contest that underpins most working definitions of representative democracy. Given the vast volume of words already written on this subject, why on earth do we need a new book on it? The answer, in essence, is that we now have access to a new technology that allows us to investigate hoary old intractable problems in exciting new ways. Party competition, as we will see, is a complex dynamic system. Huge advances in information technology, and, more importantly, in programming environments that exploit this, allow us to take the rigorous investigation of this complex system beyond age-old "pencil and paper" techniques of classical formal analyses and into a modern era in which we have access to massive computational power when pencil and paper fail us.

This is not necessarily a good thing. A flawless and elegant classical formal proof can be beautiful to behold. No new technology will ever change this. Its aesthetic beauty, furthermore, is typically the product of formidable intellectual prowess, creativity, and deep insight. Moving beyond sheer intellectual aesthetics, however, into the real world in which we are substantively interested, we face a crucial trade-off. Any theoretical model of the real world is, axiomatically, a simplification of it. Indeed the whole point of modeling is to simplify and generalize rather than merely to describe the world in every minute detail. The key intellectual decision that faces us is *how much* we should simplify and generalize, and we find ourselves on a continuum. Starting from the complex reality that ultimately fires our interest, we can almost always simplify and generalize our description of this until we have specified our problem in a way that renders it tractable using the most rigorous analytical techniques that are currently at our disposal. As we do this, we progressively gain rigor and lose realism. The typical intellectual dilemma, familiar to every serious scholar, is that rigorous analysis can be disappointingly unrealistic, while realistic descriptions of the parts of the world that interest us can be disappointingly intractable using currently available techniques. Such disappointments are part and parcel of intellectual life.

Nonetheless, intellectual progress does indeed happen. This often happens following the discovery of new technologies and techniques that can be applied to previously intractable old problems. Statistical analysis for the social sciences, for example, has been completely transformed in recent decades by the development of methods that rely on techniques of computational simulation that would have been inconceivable before the era of modern computer power. The old pencil and paper statistical models are still as valid as they ever were, but they are for the most part too simple to address the types of problem in which most people are really interested. Given current computational techniques and processing power, scholars no longer have to settle for these simple methods. New technology has thereby changed the trade-off between rigor and realism.

The same is true for the formal theoretical analysis of complex dynamic systems such as multiparty competition. For many years, the rigorous investigation of party competition has been dominated by pencil and paper techniques of classical formal analysis. The gold standard has been the flawless and elegant classical formal proof, also strived for by the world's greatest mathematicians and theoretical physicists. New technology has also changed the trade-off between rigor and realism in this field of the social sciences. One example of how this has happened has been the emergence of the "agent-based modeling" (ABM) approach to analyzing social interactions. This relies heavily, for its rigorous application, on formidable computing power put to work by exciting new programming environments. We discuss ABM in more detail in chapter 1. What is important here is that this approach models ways in which large numbers of autonomous agents interact with each other in complex dynamic settings.

This type of social interaction is of course what we usually find in the real world; no self-respecting formal theorist has ever denied it. Before the recent availability of heavy-duty computational techniques, however, the intellectual trade-off that was typically made was to simplify descriptions of the social interaction under investigation so radically as to specify a very small number of autonomous decision-making agents (often only two) interacting in a very sparse setting (often static rather than dynamic). This paid a huge, obvious, and well-understood price in realism. The payoff was in rigor, as the problem under investigation could be subjected to pencil and paper techniques of classical formal analysis, such as game theory.

It is now a plain fact that the parameters of this trade-off have changed, following the emergence, thanks to new technology, of heavy-duty computational ABMs. As has already happened in statistics, new technologies bring new benchmarks for intellectual rigor. Rigorously designed and analyzed computational experiments, however exhaustive, will never be substitutes for flawless and elegant classical formal proofs. But, and this is the crucial point, exhaustive computational work using ABMs can bring its own well-specified standards of rigor to the investigation of substantive problems that classical formal analysis cannot handle. This transforms the trade-off between rigor and realism by bringing a new standard of rigor, for computational as opposed to formal analytical work, into the equation.

Nobody should ever turn her back on a *flawless* and elegant formal proof that *realistically* applies to the problem at hand—to do this is just plain stupid. A sad fact of life, however, is that such proofs are rarely available for the problems that really interest us. The new way forward that has opened up is to use computational ABM, deployed as rigorously as we possibly can, to attack much more realistic descriptions of the problems that interest us than the less realistic ones that can be solved analytically. This is not an "either-or" decision. Some scholars will quite rightly choose to devote their intellectual energies to the ongoing search for new techniques of classical analysis that might crack open old intractable problems. Others will be more impatient, eager to attack intractable old problems using new technologies with their own new standards of rigor.

We are impatient. The point of this new book on an old subject is that most of what is really interesting to us about party competition has been set on one side as being intractable using classical formal analysis but is now wide open to us using techniques of computational ABM. What really interests us, and therefore motivates us to build models in the first place, is competition among many political parties, and potential new parties, for the support of voters who have diverse policy preferences that span many different and unrelated matters. We see party competition as an evolving dynamic process, in which the outputs of politics today are the inputs of politics tomorrow; we find it hard to imagine politics ever settling into a static "equilibrium" state. We see politics as involving many diverse and autonomous human decision-making agents who continuously adapt their behavior to what has gone before. We see different decision makers as being likely to attack the same political problem in very different ways. *This* is the type of politics we want to investigate. Our response to the inevitable trade-off between rigor and realism is that, for us, almost everything of substantive interest about multiparty competition is lost if we simplify this problem so drastically as to be able to generate classical formal proofs, but that computational ABM does offer us an exciting new way forward.

To give a small taste of what we have found by doing this, we have discovered that politicians who use "satisficing" decision rules in complex dynamic settings, leaders who are satisfied with a vote share that is above some comfort threshold, often do better *at winning votes* than competing politicians who search ceaselessly for higher voter shares. We have also found that politicians who factor their own private policy preferences into the policy positions they promote at election time often do better, *at winning votes*, than competing politicians who take account only of the policy preferences of voters. These were initially surprising and counterintuitive findings, but our computational results were rock solid, forcing us to think again about likely outputs of party competition in complex dynamic settings where different politicians use different types of decision rules. Crudely speaking, though we return to this in much more detail in what follows, if you find yourself in a complex dynamic setting that is analytically intractable for you, and even if decision making is completely costless, you may well be better off over the long run if you are satisfied with a "good" payoff than if you search tirelessly for the "best" payoff. The best may be the enemy of the good in complex dynamic settings. Similarly, in a complex dynamic world in which politicians may enter the fray to found new parties at policy positions where there is unsatisfied demand from voters, it may be better to keep party policy close to that founding position rather than to move all over the map in search of higher vote shares. At least there is evidence of sufficient voter demand for a political party at that founding position, which is more than can be said for many other policy positions.

Before we can draw theoretical inferences such as these from the results of computational experiments, those results do need to be rock solid, as rock solid in their own distinctive way as the inferences that can be drawn from classical formal proofs. In designing and executing the computational work we present in this book, we are motivated by the view that a fair number of the ABM results that have hitherto been published in the social sciences have yet to take account of the need for standards of rigor that are analogous to, while nonetheless different from, those that apply to classical formal analysis. We therefore devoted a lot of time to researching, specifying, and deploying standards for our own computational work that allow our results to be "taken to the bank" in the same way as those of classical formal models. We have made all our computer code, experimental designs, and model specifications publically available. If you rerun our code using the same design and the same specifications, you will get the results we publish here. You might say we should have specified the model or analyzed the results differently, but that is a bona fide intellectual debate you could equally engage in with a classical formal modeler. One objective of this book, therefore, is to set a high methodological standard for computational work using ABM. Since we had extensive access to the Harvard-MIT high-performance computing cluster, we set higher standards of precision in our analysis than other sane individuals might well have been satisfied with. We wanted to show that it is indeed possible to get rock-solid results with these techniques. Furthermore, computers will continue to get faster at a very rapid rate, so that what may seem like a lot of computing today will seem trivial in a few years. In a decade or less, ordinary decent civilians will have the

Preface • xi

equivalent of today's high-performance cluster sitting on their desk, and waiting eagerly to be unleashed on the type or work we present in this book.

The widespread availability of massive computing resources, combined with techniques of ABM that can deploy these to good effect, have generated a subversive new intellectual technology. This puts the power to model complex political interactions in the hands of people who are untrained in classical formal analysis—a twin-edged sword.

On one hand it is an extraordinarily good thing that smart and serious people whose first interest is in politics, not in the rigorous techniques of classical formal analysis, now have in their hands a tool that, correctly deployed, allows them to investigate interesting political problems in a more rigorous way. This is why we have deliberately used a simple, intuitive, and easily accessible ABM programming environment, NetLogo, and have made all our code available on our website in the hope that readers will explore and improve our models. Standards are still developing in this field, but it seems clear that NetLogo is emerging as one standard for simple and intuitive ABM programming. This is more important than many people realize, since the ability of scholars to read, understand, run, and modify other scholars' code will be an important feature of any emerging intellectual community. There will always be smart and experienced people who want to push the limits and specify problems that are too complex for any common platform such as NetLogo. But NetLogo is surprisingly powerful when you look into it, and for people coming to this field for the first time, our sincere view is that "if it's too complicated for NetLogo, it's too complicated." While they were eventually deployed on a high-performance computing cluster, every one of the programs used in this book was developed and tested, and the initial sketch analyses performed, on a standard laptop computer. Going beyond this, you can do an AWFUL lot of computing if you acquire a cheap second machine and leave it running 24/7 in the background. For all of these reasons, ABM is intellectually empowering, and there is nothing in the least bad about that.

On the other hand, a new technology like ABM is liable to be used by enthusiastic tyros, early adopters, and thrill seekers who neither know nor care whether classical formal analysis works for the particular problem that interests them. They may therefore waste a lot of effort developing a computational solution to a problem that is amenable to classical formal analysis. Not only is this distressing aesthetically, but it ignores the fact that formal proofs are always best when they are available. Computational techniques should be brought to bear on interesting problems when formal proofs are neither available nor reasonably likely to be available in the foreseeable future.

Given all of this, the twin *methodological* aims of this book are (1) to engage classical formal modelers by setting new standards of intellectual rigor for specifying and exercising ABMs in a manner analogous to classical analysis, then bringing these to bear on interesting but hard problems; and (2) to show people who want to use ABMs that they must do this in a rigorous way if they want to be taken seriously by scholars in the wider intellectual community.

The modeling technology is of course important, but the *substantive* problems are what really motivate us. This is a book about party competition. It is about dynamic and evolutionary processes of multiparty competition when the preferences of voters span many different matters. Given the analytical intractability of this problem, it models a situation in which real politicians may use one of many different decision rules to make choices in the same situation. It takes account of the fact that political parties are *endogenous outputs* of the process of party competition, not inputs to it that are *specified exogenously* by God or Nature. It moves on to look at what happens when voters value nonpolicy "valence" attributes of candidates for election, and when these candidates care about their own policy preferences as well as about winning votes.

All of this is what interests us, and as we have said, we are impatient. We prefer to show readers how the techniques of ABM can give us significant intellectual purchase on these problems right now rather than waiting, perhaps forever, until techniques of classical formal analysis can take them on.

One thing is absolutely certain for us. As has already happened with statistics, the *potential* analysis of interesting, important, but complex social interactions has been fundamentally changed by new technology, and this genie will never climb back into the bottle. Whether or not scholars *choose* to attack hard and important problems using computational techniques like ABM, there is now a clear choice to be made. This choice can no longer be ignored, and our purpose in this book is to map out one way in which it might be exercised.

Acknowledgments

THIS BOOK HAS BEEN a long time in the making. Many people have sat patiently through conference and seminar presentations and have offered volumes of helpful advice and encouragement. Though some venues may have slipped our minds, we know for sure that aspects of the argument in this book have been presented at seminars at Trinity College, Dublin; European University Institute, Fiesole; London School of Economics; University of Bologna; New York University; University of Iowa; Columbia University; University of Michigan; Emory University; MIT; Yale University; Duke University; and Florida State University and at the following conferences: 19th International Joint Conference on Artificial Intelligence, Edinburgh (July 30–August 5, 2005); Conference on the Dynamics of Party Position Taking, Binghamton (March 23–24, 2007); Annual Meeting of the American Political Science Association, Chicago (August 30–September 2, 2007); Arrábida Workshop on Complexity and Political Simulation, Arrábida, Portugal (July 8–9, 2008); Conference on Vote Maximizing Strategies of Political Parties, Washington University in St. Louis (November 5–7, 2009). Our heartfelt thanks are due to the discussants and participants at all of these venues for the many helpful comments we received. Many of these comments have influenced the words in this book.

We would also like to thank Gary King for hosting one of us at the Institute for Quantitative Social Science at Harvard University, during which time most of the methodology that we deploy in this book was hammered out. In addition, the Institute graciously allowed us to make use of their computer clusters, on which all of the analyses in this book were conducted. Special thanks also to Bob Kinney and the entire Remote Computing team at the Institute for helping us get started on the computer clusters and their continual support throughout.

This book's findings, interpretations, and conclusions are entirely those of the authors and do not necessarily represent the views of the World Bank, its executive directors, or the countries they represent.

PART ONE

Preliminaries

CHAPTER ONE

Modeling Multiparty Competition

We hold these truths to be self-evident:

- *Politics is dynamic.* It evolves. It never stops; It is never at, nor *en route* to, some static equilibrium. Politics evolves.
- *Politics is complex.* Political outputs today feed back as input to the political process tomorrow.
- *Politicians are diverse.* In particular, different politicians attack the same problem in different ways.
- *Politics is not random.* Systematic patterns in political outcomes invite systemic predictions, making a political "science" possible.

Politics in modern democracies is largely the politics of representation. It concerns how the needs and desires, the hopes and fears of ordinary citizens affect national decision making at the highest level, doing this via public representatives who are chosen by citizens in free and fair elections. Representative politics is to a large extent about party competition: about how a small number of organized political parties offer options to a large number of voters, who choose at election time between alternative teams of public representatives. Party competition is therefore a core concern for everyone, be they professional political scientist or ordinary decent civilian, who cares about politics in democratic societies.

We believe that party competition is a complex and evolving dynamic process that can be analyzed in a rigorous scientific manner. More precisely, we analyze the dynamics of *multi*party competition, by which we mean competition for voters' support among more than two parties, opening up the possibility that no single party wins a majority of votes cast. Figure 1.1 plots some observations of multiparty competition in the Netherlands over the period 1970–2005. The left panel shows positions of the three main Dutch parties on a left-right scale of party ideology, estimated from their party manifestos.[1] The right panel shows support for these same parties in the Dutch electorate, estimated using Eurobarometer surveys.[2] While some of the plotted "variation" in party sizes and

---

[1] These parties are the Liberals (VVD), the Christian Democrats (CDA), and the Labour Party (PvdA).
[2] The Comparative Manifestos Project and the Eurobarometer survey series, the sources of these data, are discussed at some length in chapter 11 below. Several smaller parties represented in the Dutch legislature have been omitted in the interest of clarity.

4 • Chapter 1

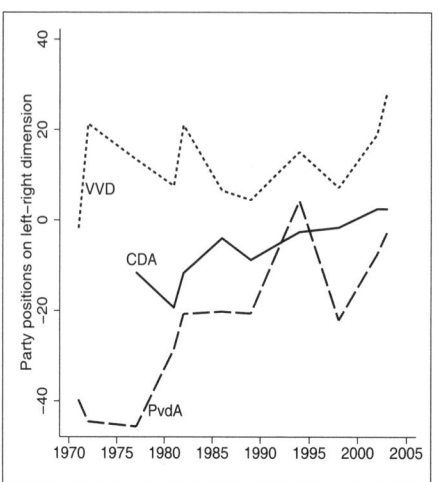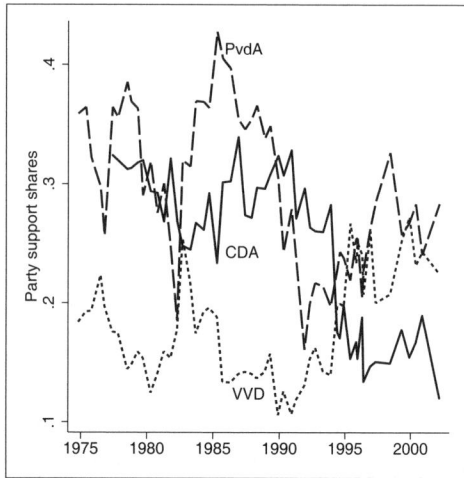

Figure 1.1. Dynamic party competition in the Netherlands, 1970–2005.

policy positions is surely the result of measurement error, by no stretch of the imagination was the Dutch party system "flatlining" in steady state during the period under observation. It was clearly a dynamic system and, as a result, there were frequent changes in the partisan composition of Dutch governments. These dynamics are clearly a central concern for all political scientists analyzing Dutch politics during this period, be they theorist or country specialist. Equivalent plots can be generated for any party system in which we might be interested.

We Need a New Approach to Modeling Party Competition

Formal models of party competition have been an abiding preoccupation of political scientists since the early 1960s. A vast body of existing work has added hugely to our understanding of party competition. Our own *substantive* interest, however, and we believe the substantive interest of most people who want to understand party competition in democratic societies, concerns crucial features of party competition that these models typically assume away as a price to be paid for analytical tractability. We ourselves are interested in party competition among many more than two parties. We are interested in "multidimensional" political environments in which politicians and voters care about more than one type of issue. We see politics as a continuously evolving dynamic process that never settles at some static equilibrium, to be perturbed only by random shocks. Pursuing these interests poses formidable theoretical challenges.

We show in chapter 2 that dynamic models of multiparty competition, especially when voters care about a diverse set of issues, are analytically intractable. They are not just "difficult" to solve, they *cannot* be solved using conventional analytical techniques.

The *analytical* intractability of the relevant theoretical models does not make us any less interested, *substantively*, in dynamic multiparty competition. Indeed, this very intractability gives us an important and liberating theoretical insight. If analysts cannot use tractable formal models to find optimal courses of action in this setting, then *neither can real people making real decisions about real party competition*. These people still need to make decisions about what to do. If no formally provable best-response strategy is available, real humans must employ informal decision rules or heuristics.[3] To preview a decision rule we investigate extensively in this book, a party leader might decide to move party policy toward the position currently advocated by some larger rival party, on the grounds there must be more voters who prefer this rival's policy position. We find that this decision rule (which we call Predator) is sometimes very, very good and sometimes perfectly horrid. It is certainly not a "best" response in any conceivable situation but, in the analytically intractable setting of dynamic multiparty competition, it is one of many potentially good rules that politicians may use in certain circumstances when they set party policy positions.

Agent-Based Modeling

Analytical intractability of the decision-making environment, and the resulting need for real politicians to rely on informal decision rules, suggests strongly that we use *agent-based modeling* to study multiparty competition in an evolving dynamic party system. Agent-based models (ABMs) are "bottom-up" models that typically assume settings with a fairly large number of autonomous decision-making agents. Each agent uses some well-specified decision rule to choose actions, and there may well be considerable diversity in the decision rules used by different agents. Given the analytical intractability of the decision-making environment, the decision rules that are specified and investigated in ABMs are typically based on adaptive learning, rather than forward-looking strategic analysis, and agents are assumed to have bounded rather than perfect rationality (Gigerenzer and Selten 2001; Rubinstein 1998; Simon 1957). ABM is a modeling technology that is ideally suited to investigate outcomes that may emerge when large numbers of boundedly rational agents, us-

---

[3] We use these terms interchangeably in what follows.

ing adaptive decision rules selected from a diverse portfolio of possibilities, interact with each other continuously in an evolving dynamic setting (MacGregor et al. 2006).

Putting a particular ABM to work by manipulating its parameters and observing the associated outcomes typically involves *computing* the outcomes of these interactions if the underlying model is analytically intractable—as is usually the case. Such computation, does not, of its essence, involve *electronic* computers. One of the most influential early ABMs analyzed housing segregation by scattering black and white chips and then moving them around on what amounted to a large chess board (Schelling 1978). This model was computational in the sense that an abacus is a computer, implemented by moving pieces around a chessboard. As originally published, it did not rely on using an *electronic* computer.[4] Scatter a number of black and white chips at random on a chessboard; these chips represent people of different color. Assume people have some view about the color of their neighbors; say, for example, they are unhappy if fewer than a quarter of their neighbors are the same color as them. The modeled behavior is simply that unhappy agents move to a randomly chosen close-by empty square that makes them happy. A model "run" begins with chips scattered at random. With an equal number of black and white chips, the typical person will find that 50 percent of neighbors are the same color and will be happy to stay put. There will however be some people in the random scatter who find that fewer than a quarter of their neighbors are the same color; they will move to a square that makes them happy. Everyone is given a chance to move, and to move again, using this rule until there is no unhappy agent who wants to move. The results are striking and unexpected. Even if everyone merely wants at least a quarter of their neighbors to be the same color, modeled population movement typically results in a steady state in which on average about 60 percent of a typical agent's neighbors are of the same color. If we change the key model parameter and assume people to be unhappy, and to move, when they are in a local minority (fewer than 50 percent of neighbors are the same color) then people find that on average 88 percent of neighbors are the same color in the typical steady state that emerges. The deep substantive insight from Schelling's ABM is that intense spatial segregation can arise when people do not seek this at all, but simply prefer not to be in a small minority. More generally, this model shows very nicely that simple decision heuristics can interact to generate complex and unexpected "emergent" patterns of social behavior. This is the core insight of agent-based modeling.

---

[4] A version of this model implemented in NetLogo for electronic computers can however be found in the NetLogo models library.

All good things come at a price. The price paid for using computational as opposed to formal analytical models, and thus for using agent-based modeling, is that computation involves calculating model outputs for particular parameter settings. An analytical result, if it is general, is a beautiful thing that is good for all valid parameter settings. Strictly speaking, computational results are good only for those parameter settings that have actually been investigated. Inferences about parameter settings that have not been investigated—and thus more general theoretical inferences we might want to draw from the model—are, in effect, interpolations. This is one reason why we never use computational methods when analytical results are available for the substantive problem that interests us.

The distinction between analytical and computational methods should not be overdrawn, however. A longstanding set of observations that compare models of computation with systems of formal logic, collectively known as the "Curry-Howard isomorphism," shows us that computer programs and formal proofs are in essence the same thing (De Groote 1995). Both take a set of explicit premises and manipulate these, using some system of formal logic, to prove theorems based on these premises. Consider, for example, the area, A, of a circle with radius r. It is well known that we can prove analytically the proposition: $A = \pi \cdot r^2$ for *any* positive real r. We can also prove $A \approx \pi \cdot r^2$ for *any given* positive real r by various computational methods. With *infinite* computing power at our disposal, we could prove $A \approx \pi \cdot r^2$ for *any* positive real r.[5] This would not be an "elegant" proof according to most standards of elegance, but now we are talking about aesthetics. With less-than-infinite computing power, we can sample a huge number of positive real values of r, compute A, and show in every single case that $A \approx \pi \cdot r^2$. We can draw the *statistical* inference, at a specified level of confidence, that $A \approx \pi \cdot r^2$ for any positive real r. If for some reason it happened that we could not prove analytically that $A = \pi \cdot r^2$, then this computational/statistical inference would be immensely valuable to us. If we wanted to increase our confidence in this inference, we could simply do more computing and sample more values of r. Of course, we could never be *perfectly* confident in this conclusion. We can show that $A \approx \pi \cdot r^2$ when r = 2.0000001 and 2.0000002; you could claim it is possible $A \neq \pi \cdot r^2$ when r is set between these values, at

---

[5] The approximation arises because π is a transcendental number that cannot be stored to any arbitrary level of precision in a digital computer. However, a number very close to π can be stored as a high-precision floating point number. For the same reason, the area of any circle calculated using the classical formula $A = \pi \cdot r^2$ can be *written down* as a real number only using an approximation that deploys some arbitrary level of precision specifying the number of decimal places we are prepared to use.

2.00000015. Strictly speaking, this would be true.[6] We could however show statistically, with access to enough computing power, that the *probability* of this exception is extraordinarily small. Furthermore, we could drive down this probability to as low a level as makes you feel happy—simply by doing more computing.

This is an issue we take very seriously indeed in this book since we do want our computational results to have effectively the same scope and precision as those derived from analogous analytical work. We address this by specifying careful procedures for systematically varying parameter settings, and rigorous methods for estimating model outputs of interest associated with these settings. If we carefully design and execute our computational work in this way, then the scope and precision of our results depend only on the volume of computation we are willing and/or able to deploy. Since we want our own results to have the same scope and precision as typical results from formal models in this field, we are both willing and able to deploy a huge amount of computing power, taking advantage of the Harvard-MIT Data Center's high-performance cluster in order to do this. An important consequence of this is that we are confident that the computational results we present in this book can be "taken to the bank," in the formal statistical sense that, if we were to do very much more computing, or if many other people were to repeat our procedures, essentially identical results would arise. Thus, while this is a book above all about the substantively fascinating topic of multiparty competition, it is also an exercise in how to use computational methods in general, and ABMs in particular, in a way that allows us to draw confident general conclusions.

To summarize, the substantively important real-world problem that interests us is the dynamics of multiparty competition. Theoretical models are no more than intellectual tools designed to help us understand substantively important real-world problems. The technology of classical formal modeling is not a good tool to help us understand the dynamics of multiparty competition, since the resulting models are analytically intractable, with consequences for analysts and more importantly for real humans making decisions in these settings. In contrast, the empowering new technology of agent-based modeling is well suited to investigating problems that are of great substantive interest to us. Impatient for results and problem focused as we are, this book is about how agent-based modeling helps us think systematically about the dynamics of multiparty competition. We start simple and build an increasingly complex model of party competition that deals with a range of substantive matters we have

---

[6] Although our advice to you in this case would be that you should get out more.

wanted to think about for a long time but had not really been able to think about in a systematic way before the emergence of ABM.

PLAN OF CAMPAIGN

Chapter 2 sets up the core problem in which we are interested. To demonstrate that this problem is analytically intractable, we use compelling results from a subfield of geometry that deals with "Voronoi tessellations" (or tilings) and has powerful applications in many disciplines. Largely unnoticed by political scientists, this work addresses a problem of "competitive spatial location" that is directly analogous to the problem of dynamic competition between a set of political parties competing with each other by offering rival policy programs. One result from this field is that the problem of competitive spatial location is intractable if the space concerned has more than one dimension (we return below to discuss the meaning of a "dimension" in models of party competition), implying that there are no formally provable best-response strategies for this. This is an important and widely recognized justification for deploying computational methods, and the study of Voronoi tessellations is a major subfield in *computational* geometry.

Chapter 3 specifies our "baseline" ABM of dynamic multiparty competition, which derives from an article published by one of us (Laver 2005). This assumes that each voter has in mind some personal ideal "package" of policy positions and supports the political party that offers the policy package closest to this. The dynamic system at the heart of our model is as follows: voters support their "closest" party in this sense; party leaders adapt the policy packages they offer in light of the revealed pattern of voter support; voters reconsider which party they support in light of the revealed pattern of party policy packages; and this process continues forever. This recursive model describes policy-based party competition as a complex system, and our baseline model specifies three decision rules that party leaders may deploy when they choose party policy positions in such a setting. These rules are Sticker (always keep the same position), Aggregator (move policy to the centroid of the ideal policy positions of your current supporters), and Hunter (if your last policy move increased your support, make another move in the same direction; or else change heading and move in a different direction). These rules model, in a simple way, an "ideologically intransigent" party leader who *never* changes party policy, no matter how unpopular this might be; a "democratic" party leader who always adapts the party position to the preferences of *current* supports; and a "vote-seeking" party leader who is always looking for *new* supporters and does not care what policies must be chosen in order to do this. These decision rules were specified in Laver (2005); the innovation in this chapter concerns our assumptions about the preferences of voters. Rather than assuming a single coherent voting population with a perfectly symmetrical multivariate normal distribution of ideal policy positions, we now assume that electorates comprise a number of distinct subgroups. Combining subgroups into an aggregate voting population, we produce an aggregate distribution of ideal points that is no longer perfectly symmetric. This more generic assumption about voter preferences makes a big difference to what our model predicts.

Chapter 4 develops our methods for designing, executing, and analyzing large suites of computer simulations that generate stable and replicable results. We start with a discussion of the different methods of experimental design, such as grid sweeping and Monte Carlo parameterization. Next, we demonstrate how to calculate mean estimates of output variables of interest. In order to do so, we must first discuss, among other things, stochastic processes, Markov Chain representations, and model burn-in. As we see below, we are especially interested in three stochastic process representations: nonergodic deterministic processes that converge on a single state, nondeterministic stochastic processes for which a time average provides a representative estimate of the output variables, and nondeterministic stochastic processes for which a time average does not provide a representative estimate of the output variables. The estimation strategy we employ depends on which stochastic process the simulation follows. Last, we present a set of diagnostic checks, used to establish an appropriate sample size for the estimation of the means. More observations obviously lead to more precise estimates. However, given a fixed computational budget, in terms of computer processing time and storage space, as well as the opportunity costs of not executing other simulations, we want to gather enough observations to allow precise estimates, but no more than is needed.

We report our benchmark results in chapter 5. Perhaps the most striking of these concerns the "representativeness" of any given configuration of party policy positions and uses a second result that comes from the Voronoi geometry of competitive spatial location. A set of n points arranged so as to generate a "centroidal Voronoi tessellation" (CVT) is an "optimal representation" of the space in which these points are located. By this we mean that the *aggregate* distance between all points in the space and their closest generating point can never be less than when the n generating points are arranged in a CVT (Du et al. 1999).[7] If we think that voters are

---

[7] The analogous problem in digital imaging is to find the most representative set of n points (party positions) to represent a much more detailed image comprising m points (voters). More generally, a CVT can be seen as a "best" simple representation of any spatially structured dataset.

more satisfied at election time the closer their own ideal policy is to the policy position of their closest party, then this implies that the electorate as a whole is most satisfied when party policy positions are arranged in a CVT. Since the "representativeness" of any party system is an important matter, both normatively and in terms of practical politics, the notion of an optimal representation gives us an important benchmark for assessing evolved configurations of party policy positions. A robust conjecture in computational geometry, concerning what is known as Lloyd's Algorithm (Lloyd 1982), is very relevant in this context. If all party leaders use the Aggregator rule for setting party policy positions, continuously adapting party policy to the centroid of *current* supporters' ideal points, then Lloyd's Algorithm tells us that the set of party policy positions will converge on a steady state that is a CVT. *Party positions in all-Aggregator party systems thus evolve to configurations that are optimal representations of the space.*[8] Other configurations of party policy positions will generically imply suboptimal representation, in this precise sense.

Thus far we have treated the set of competing political parties as exogenously given to us by God or Nature. We move beyond this in chapter 6 and define a model of endogenous party "birth" and "death" (Laver et al. 2011; Laver and Schilperoord 2007) that has the implication that *the set of surviving political parties is endogenous* to the system of party competition. We now also model competition between party leaders using different decision rules, extending work on this using computer "tournaments" (Fowler and Laver 2008). All of this requires us to extend our model to define a de facto survival threshold for political parties; an updating regime that specifies how voters feel about the party system today, given what happened today and how they felt about the system yesterday; and a distinction between "campaign ticks" of the model, during which party leaders make choices that do not have long-term consequences for their survival, and "election ticks" that do have a bearing on party survival. The resulting more realistic model of party competition with endogenous parties is *evolutionary*, describing a *survival-of-the-fittest* environment in which more successful parties survive and less successful parties do not.

Up to this stage in the argument, we have extended, improved, and generalized previously published work based on three simple decision rules: Sticker, Aggregator, and Hunter. We break completely new ground in chapter 7, defining new "species" of vote-seeking decision rule (Predator and Explorer) and specifying both these and existing rule species in terms of a set of parameterized rule "features," including satisficing and speed of adaptation. Predator rules, specified in a flawed form in Laver (2005)

---

[8] In this context it is very important to note that there is typically no unique optimal representation.

and redefined by us here, in essence attack the closest more successful party by moving their policy position toward it. Explorer rules are generalizations of "hill climbing" algorithms. Explorers randomly poll positions in some local policy neighborhood during campaign ticks—moving on an election tick to the best position they found during the campaign. The net result of these extensions is that we now consider competition between party leaders who may choose from one of 111 different decision rules—or, strictly speaking, parameterizations of rule-agent pairings. This dramatically expands the state space of our model and forces a major modification in the method we use to estimate characteristic model outputs. We find that which particular vote-seeking rule is most effective depends critically on parameters of the competitive environment. Chapter 7 reports another result we feel is particularly important, concerning what happens when *satiable* and *insatiable* vote-seeking party leaders compete with each other. We find well-defined circumstances in which satiable leaders, who do nothing until their party vote share falls below some "comfort threshold," systematically win higher vote shares than insatiable leaders, who always seek more votes no matter how many they currently have. This is a good example of the classic "exploitation-exploration trade-off" in reinforcement learning (Sutton and Barto 1998). Insatiable party leaders always explore the space in search of more votes, whereas satiable leaders exploit their good fortune whenever vote share is above their comfort threshold. This is the type of insight that can be derived only from a *dynamic* model of party competition.

In chapter 8, we extend our survival-of-the-fittest evolutionary environment to take account of the possibility that new political parties, when they first come into existence, do not pick decision rules at random but instead choose rules that have a track record of past success. We do this by adding *replicator-mutator dynamics* to our model, according to which the probability that each rule is selected by a new party is an evolving but noisy function of that rule's past performance. Estimating characteristic outputs when this type of positive feedback enters our dynamic model creates new methodological challenges. Having addressed these challenges, the simulation results we report in chapter 8 show that it is very rare for one decision rule to drive out all others over the long run. While the diversity of decision rules used by party leaders is drastically reduced with such positive feedback in the party system, and while some particular decision rule is typically prominent over a certain period of time, party systems in which party leaders use different decision rules are sustained over substantial periods. More generally, we continue to find party leaders choosing from a diverse rule set in this evolutionary setting. We find no evidence whatsoever of evolution toward the dominance of a single decision rule for setting party policy positions.

Moving beyond the assumption that voters care about only the party policy positions on offer, chapter 9 models the possibility that they also care about perceived "nonpolicy" attributes of political candidates: competence, charisma, honesty, and many other things besides. These characterize what have become known as "valence" models of party competition. Voters balance utility derived from each candidate's nonpolicy valence against utility derived from the candidate's policy position. The contribution of valence models has been to explain why all parties do not all converge on regions of the policy space with the highest densities of voter ideal points. Higher valence parties tend to go to regions of the policy space with higher voter densities, while lower valence parties are forced to steer well clear of these parties and pick policy positions in regions with lower voter densities. We replicate and extend the findings of traditional static valence models, with one important twist. Over the long run, lower valence parties tend to die and higher valence parties tend to survive, a finding that suggests a reappraisal of valence models as currently specified. These essentially static models show a snapshot of the party system at a given time; but the tendency of low-valence parties to disappear in an evolutionary setting suggests that these snapshots are not dynamic equilibriums that can be sustained over time.

Moving beyond voters who care about more than policy, we look in chapter 10 at party leaders who care about their own private policy preferences as well as about winning votes. In the spirit of our existing model of endogenous party birth, we take the preferred policy position of a party leader as the founding policy position of his or her party. In an intriguing echo of our findings on satisficing in an evolutionary setting, we find that party leaders who care somewhat about their own policy position may do somewhat better *at winning votes* in competition with party leaders who care exclusively about vote share. This may arise from the fact that, in an evolutionary setting, *the ideal points of surviving party leaders are endogenous*. Each surviving party leader was once a new entrant into the system at a policy position for which there was demonstrable voter "demand." Leaders who stay close to this founding position continue to satisfy the demand that originally caused the party birth. They thereby also, effectively though not intentionally, forestall new party births in this region of the policy space.

Having specified theoretical models of multiparty competition in the first ten chapters of the book, we investigate empirical implications of these models in chapter 11, comparing model predictions with changes in observed party policy positions and vote shares in ten real European party systems. Confronting theoretical models with empirical data is a central part of the definition of political science as a "science," highlighted by the influential Empirical Implication of Theoretical Models project. This is easy to say but hard to do well, and it is even harder for dynamic models that have many parameters whose values are not directly observable in the real world. We face serious problems of model *calibration*, of finding parameter settings for our theoretical models that plausibly correspond to those in the real party systems for which we can observe empirical observations. Calibration problems are compounded in this case by an acute shortage of high-quality time series data on party system outputs of interest. Given all of these problems, the best we can hope for is to find "plausible" model calibrations generating predictions that are close to reality. This is of course not a full-dress scientific test of our model, which is not feasible given the lack of good time series data on party policy positions, combined with the lack of reliable independent data for model calibration. We prefer, however, to be honest about the calibration and data problems that arise with any dynamic model of multiparty competition rather than, dishonestly we feel, making "assumptions" about model calibration that will give us lovely empirical results but that are, in effect, assumptions chosen to give those lovely results. What we call the "auto-calibration" of our model, searching for model calibrations consistent with accurate predictions, does allow us to conclude that the model *can* be calibrated to generate accurate predictions and that the calibration values associated with good predictions do have good face validity.

Putting all of this together, our fundamental interest in this book is in multiparty competition, seen as an evolving dynamic system. Our fundamental intellectual objective is to explore some of the puzzles about this that can be addressed using techniques of agent-based modeling. Substantively, while readers are the ultimate judges of this, we do feel that agent-based modeling empowers us to tackle interesting and important questions that cannot be addressed so fruitfully using the techniques of classical analytical modeling. Methodologically, we do feel that carefully designed and executed computational work can generate results that have a scope and precision equivalent to those generated by more traditional techniques.

Our sincere hope is that we open an intellectual window for at least some readers, who will take the ideas and suggestions in what follows and improve them beyond all recognition.

CHAPTER TWO

Spatial Dynamics of Political Competition

Spatial Models of Political Competition

Politicians compete with each other in many different ways. They trade on personal popularity; they attack the integrity and character of their opponents. They exploit, or are victims of, biased coverage in the news media. They hire advertising agencies to manipulate these same media. They practice dark arts and dirty tricks. Political competition in any given setting has many idiosyncratic features that are not at all amenable to general explanations. If we want to understand the close-in detail of any particular political system, we do best to ask people who have particular local knowledge and/or insight—"gurus" who specialize in the exceptional features and minutiae of the domestic politics of interest.

Notwithstanding this, key features of political competition look remarkably similar in different domestic settings. Politicians make promises about the policies they will implement if elected. Voters have views about the different policy promises on offer and choose public representatives, at least in part, on the basis of these promises. Naïve voters may take these promises at face value. More sophisticated voters may treat them as signals from which to draw inferences about what, given what politicians *say* they would do, they actually *will* do if given the chance. All of this characterizes party competition in many different domestic settings. This characterization of democratic politics, as competition among politicians for the support of voters on the basis of the public policies they offer, underpins the account of party competition we consider in this book.

"Spatial" descriptions of the preferences of key decision makers are widely used by political scientists modeling in a wide range of different settings, from elections and legislatures, to government formation, to international organizations, to the U.S. Supreme Court, and many other things besides. References to "left" and "right," and to changing policy "positions," are part of day-to-day political discourse and not just terms of art for political scientists. Spatial models based on this way of describing politics have provided such a fruitful basis for rigorous thinking about political competition that this approach is now seen as "the workhorse theory of modern legislative studies" (Cox 2001) and has generated a diverse and vibrant literature. The seminal presentation of the spatial modeling approach, building on earlier work by Harold Hotelling and Duncan Black, is Anthony Downs' book *An Economic Theory of Democracy* (Hotelling 1929; Downs 1957; Black 1958, 1948). Adams, Merrill, and Grofman provide an excellent survey of this vast literature, which we do not attempt to review here, while Austen-Smith and Banks offer a comprehensive technical treatment (Adams et al. 2005; Austen-Smith and Banks 2000, 2005). The conclusion that attracted most attention to Downs' book, especially from scholars with an interest in the United States, was that, if only one dimension of policy is important and if there are only two disciplined vote-seeking political parties, then these parties will both tend to offer policy positions that approach the "center" of this policy dimension, seen as the preferred policy position of the median voter.

More than fifty years of sustained intellectual effort has extended and refined this simple model in many different ways. At least theoretically, it now comprehends more parties; more than one policy dimension; strategic voters; politicians who care about policy, not just about maximizing votes; activists; party financiers; anticipations of downstream government formation in multiparty systems; the actual or anticipated "entry" of new parties into the fray; the nonpolicy "valence" of political parties; and many other things besides.

STRUCTURES IN VOTERS' PREFERENCES

Ultimately, spatial models of party competition are grounded in assumptions about the preferences of voters, whose support politicians compete to attract.[1] Voters may have preferences on a huge range of different matters, many of which are interrelated in any real setting. Given these interrelationships, we often find it easy to predict a voter's unknown preferences on one matter from her preferences on other matters, about which we do have some information. Imagine someone who you know is strongly in favor of abortion on demand, legalization of marijuana, voluntary euthanasia, gay marriage. Imagine you need to predict this person's views on capital punishment. You will probably predict she is *against* capital punishment, and you will probably be right. Nothing inherently links this variegated bundle of issues together, but, as a matter of empirical fact, preferences of real voters do tend to correlate strongly across different

---

[1] We use the term "voter" in this book to describe someone who has the legal right to vote, regardless of whether or not this person actually casts a ballot at any given election. We do not, in this book, get into an analysis of voter turnout.

issues in this bundle (Converse 1964). In general, knowing someone's views on certain matters vastly improves your ability to predict her views on others, even on matters that may seem logically unrelated.

Given this strong *empirical* relationship between voters' preferences on different aspects of public policy, we can usefully describe the structure of policy-based political competition with reference to a small number of underlying "dimensions." We treat voters' correlated attitudes across some bundle of issues as if their attitudes on all issues in the bundle are correlated to the same, underlying and unobservable, "latent" dimension. By far the most familiar of these latent dimensions in popular political discourse is the *left-right* dimension, dating at least from the days of the French Revolution. A single underlying policy dimension, however, is often not enough to let us say what we want to say about the structure of voters' preferences on all important aspects of public policy. Two voters may both be "on the right" on economic policy, for example, favoring low taxes and minimal state intervention in the economy. But they may disagree radically on state intervention on matters such as abortion, gay marriage, or gun control. A second "liberal-conservative" policy dimension is needed before we can adequately characterize how the views of these voters differ. There are many other matters, such as environmental policy or justice between generations, which divide voters in ways that can be described only using a third dimension. Foreign policy may require a fourth dimension, and so on.

Figure 2.1 shows party policy positions in Germany in early 2003, estimated using an expert survey (Benoit and Laver 2006). Positions are plotted on two dimensions: a "left-right" dimension of economic policy and a "liberal-conservative" dimension of policy on abortion, gay rights, and similar matters. Seen this way, German politics looks at least two-dimensional. Compare the positions of the Free Democrats (FDP) and the PDS, which evolved from the former East German Communist Party. These parties occupy the opposite ends of the economic policy dimension but have very similar liberal positions on the liberal-conservative dimension. Similarly, the Greens and the "radical right" Republikaner (Rep) are at opposite ends of the liberal-conservative spectrum but have very similar positions on economic policy. Figure 2.1 suggests there is no way to describe German politics adequately using a single latent policy dimension.

The richest possible description of the structure of political preferences in any population requires many different dimensions, but our task is to build *simple* descriptions of politics. We therefore balance our desire for rich and detailed descriptions that use many different policy dimensions, against our desire for simple descriptions that capture a lot of important information but also form the basis for systematic generalizations. Fortu-

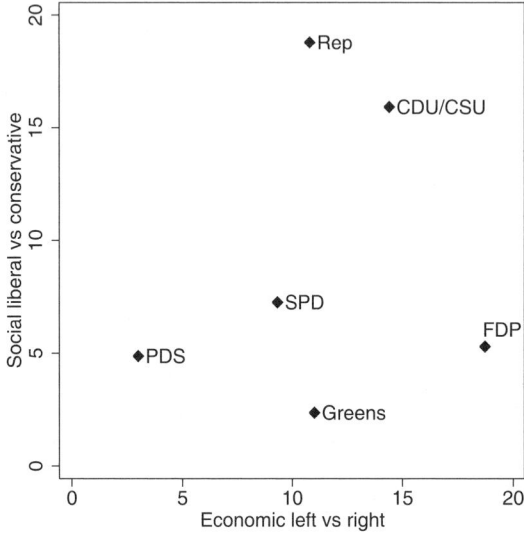

Figure 2.1. Two-dimensional party policy positions in Germany, ca. 2003.

nately, it often turns out *empirically* that the essential structure of voters' preferences can be captured using a small number of policy dimensions. Benoit and Laver, for example, find that two, sometimes three, independent policy dimensions are typically enough to capture most of the important information (Benoit and Laver 2006).

All of this means that, while the detailed substance of political competition varies in gloriously idiosyncratic ways from setting to setting, key features of its broad structure are fairly constant. Empirically, voters' preferences do always tend to correlate across large bundles of issues, which can be summarized using a small number of underlying policy "dimensions," though the precise content of these bundles differs from country to country. Taken together, these dimensions define a spatial "map" or "policy space" for policy-based political competition, akin to the map of German politics in 2003 we drew in Figure 2.1. It is this type of map that underlies "spatial models" of policy-based political competition. Different political environments clearly have different spatial maps. These differences are generated by empirical variations in the structure of voters' preferences as we move from place to place. In some places, for example, one underlying left-right dimension may be enough to summarize most of the important variation in voters' preferences. In other places, as we have seen, more dimensions may be needed.

Multidimensional Spatial Models of Political Competition

A large part of the intellectual progress made by the "workhorse" spatial model has been for settings where a single policy dimension provides a good description of voter preferences. These models have been frequently applied to empirical settings such as the United States where only two political parties are in serious contention. The spatial modeling approach has been both analytically tractable and substantively fruitful when applied to such simple cases. One-dimensional party systems are of course special cases of a more general multidimensional setting where an adequate summary of voter preferences may require more than one policy dimension. Results generated for the one-dimensional special case, furthermore, can be very "brittle." Tiny departures from unidimensionality can catastrophically undermine key inferences, which may depend critically on the dimensionality of the policy space.

An excellent example of this concerns famous theoretical results showing that *voting cycles*—whereby A beats B, B beats C, and C beats A—are generic with majority rule decision making in multidimensional spaces (McKelvey and Schofield 1987, 1986; Schofield 1983). Such cycles are *not* generic in one-dimensional spaces, something that vastly simplifies analysis of one-dimensional models. This is an excellent example of the "rigor versus realism" trade-off discussed in the Preface. Assuming that political preferences can be summarized by a single latent dimension may enable beautifully rigorous formal proofs, but the price paid for such "rigor" is using a premise that is known to be false. The resulting proof, however beautiful, does not actually apply to the problem in which we are interested. It may be a gorgeous intellectual work of art, but it does not do anything useful.

As we have stated quite clearly, we ourselves are both problem focused and impatient. Our interest is neither in beautiful models per se nor in the special case of one-dimensional, two-party political systems so extensively analyzed using formal models in the classic analytical tradition. We are interested in the more general case of competition among several (five, six, or more) political parties when the preferences of voters span many different matters and cannot adequately be summarized using a single dimension. If that was not hard enough, we also see party competition as an evolving dynamic process, one in which the set of political parties in contention is an endogenous output of politics, not an exogenous input to it. Scholars have been able to *describe* multiparty competition in such settings using the language of spatial modeling,[2] but the resulting spatial

---

[2] For stylistic reasons, whenever we use the term "multiparty competition," we mean *multidimensional* multiparty competition.

models have not proved amenable to tractable rigorous analysis. As we now see, this is because many aspects of multiparty competition, and especially dynamic multiparty competition, are *intractable* analytically. This in turn has profound implications for how real humans make real political decisions.

Geometric Models of Competitive Spatial Location

Voronoi Diagrams

Although this is not widely recognized by political scientists, multiparty competition in a multidimensional policy space is part of a much more general class of problems of "competitive spatial location." These problems belong to a subfield of geometry dealing with "tiling" or "tessellation." If we take any space—to keep things simple think of a two-dimensional Euclidean plane like this page—we can draw a set of lines that divide the space into regions. This is a tiling, or tessellation, of the space.[3] There is a special sort of tiling, known as a Voronoi diagram (or tessellation), that is associated with a particular set of "generating points."[4] A Voronoi diagram is a tiling (an exclusive and exhaustive partition) of the space into regions, known as Voronoi regions, such that each Voronoi region is associated with a unique generating point and any point in the region is closer to the region's generating point than to any other generating point. There is a special sort of Voronoi diagram, to which we return, known as a centroidal Voronoi tessellation (CVT). This is a Voronoi diagram in which each generating point is at the centroid of its Voronoi region, the point that minimizes the sum of the squared distances between itself and all other points in the region.

This may seem far removed from party competition, but think of the generating points as party policy positions and the set of points in each Voronoi region as actual or possible voter ideal points. The party policy positions generate a Voronoi tessellation that is an exclusive and exhaustive partition of the space. Each voter's ideal point is in some Voronoi region; voters' ideal points in a given Voronoi region are, by definition, closer to the policy position of this region's generating party than to any other party position. The "proximity voting" assumed in the classical "Downsian" spatial model of party competition implies that voters support the party with the policy position closest to their own

---

[3] More generally, a tiling in an n-dimensional space is created by hyperplanes, not the lines used in a two-dimensional space.

[4] Named after the Russian mathematician Georgy Voronoi (1868–1908), a student of Andrey Markov.

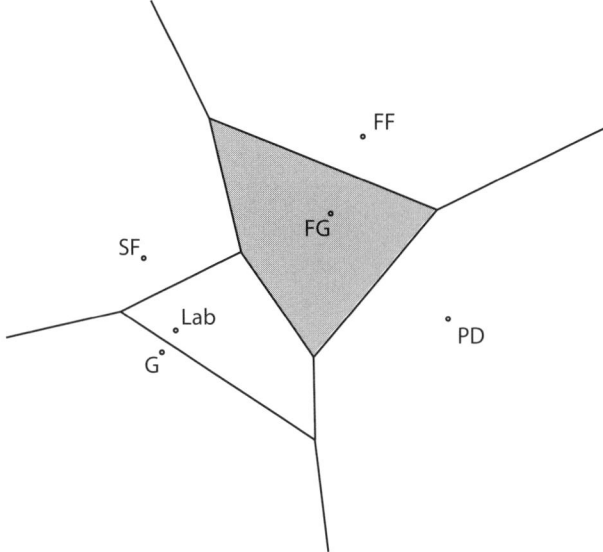

Figure 2.2. Voronoi diagram of Irish party system, ca. 2003.

ideal point. In a nutshell, each party's Voronoi region contains the ideal points of its Downsian supporters; each Downsian voter supports the party with the policy position generating the Voronoi region that contains her ideal point.

To take a concrete example, Figure 2.2 shows a Voronoi diagram of the Irish party system in 2003. Party policy positions are estimated from an expert survey (Benoit and Laver 2006). Positions on the horizontal axis concern economic policy (left to right in the conventional sense); those on the vertical axis concern the liberal (bottom) versus conservative (top) dimension of social policy. The six parties are Fianna Fáil (FF), Fine Gael (FG), Progressive Democrats (PD), Labour (Lab), Greens (G), and Sinn Féin (SF). The shaded region around Fine Gael's policy position, FG, shows where we find the ideal points of "Downsian" Fine Gael voters. Voter ideal points in this region are, by definition, closer to FG than to any other party policy position. Similarly, the regions around FF, PD, Lab, G, and SF show where we might find the ideal points of voters for these particular parties.

This geometric interpretation of the spatial model of voting is important because a huge amount of rigorous work has been done, over many years and in many different disciplines, on the geometry of Voronoi diagrams. Okabe et al. provide the benchmark survey of this work (Okabe et al. 2000) and note that the characterization of core analytical problems in terms of Voronoi diagrams has independently arisen in many different disciplines, to which we now add political science. Recent applications, among many others, are found in astronomy, physics, meteorology, biology, robotics, image enhancement, noise reduction, and computer graphics/display. Since potential commercial payoffs in some of these areas are huge, tremendous intellectual firepower has been deployed on Voronoi diagrams, which can be seen as "fundamental geometric data structure[s]" (Aurenhammer 1991). Of great significance for our own purposes, many Voronoi problems in multidimensional spaces, including as we see below the problem of competitive spatial location, have not proved amenable to closed-form analytical solutions. As a result, the study of Voronoi diagrams has evolved as a major subfield in *computational* geometry. This shows us very clearly why we need to use computational methods when we analyze multidimensional spatial models of multiparty competition.

Competitive Spatial Location

Figure 2.2 shows Irish party positions at a single snapshot in time. We are not interested in a snapshot, however, but in a *moving picture* of multiparty competition in which leaders may continually change party policy positions as they seek to fulfill their various objectives. We can describe dynamic multiparty competition using *dynamic* Voronoi diagrams (Aurenhammer 1991). Imagine that, starting from the configuration shown in Figure 2.2, FF made a policy move toward the center of the space, for example from FF_1 to FF_2 in Figure 2.3. Would this increase FF's vote share? The solid lines show the boundaries of Fianna Fáil's Voronoi region with party policy at FF_1; the dashed lines show these boundaries after it moves to FF_2. This move flips shaded sections of the diagram between Voronoi regions of four parties. FF *gains* lighter shaded areas in the center from FG and PD; it *loses* the darker area in the top left to SF and FG and the darker area in the top right to PD. If voter idea points were uniformly distributed across the space, the fact that the lighter areas are smaller than the darker areas implies that this centripetal move by FF would result in a *loss* of votes. However, for reasons we develop in chapter 3, we expect everyday social interaction to generate a situation in which voter ideal points are *not* uniformly distributed. Whether the lighter areas gained by FF's policy shift contain more voter ideal points than the darker areas lost by the same shift is entirely a function of the precise distribution of voter ideal points. If there are many more ideal

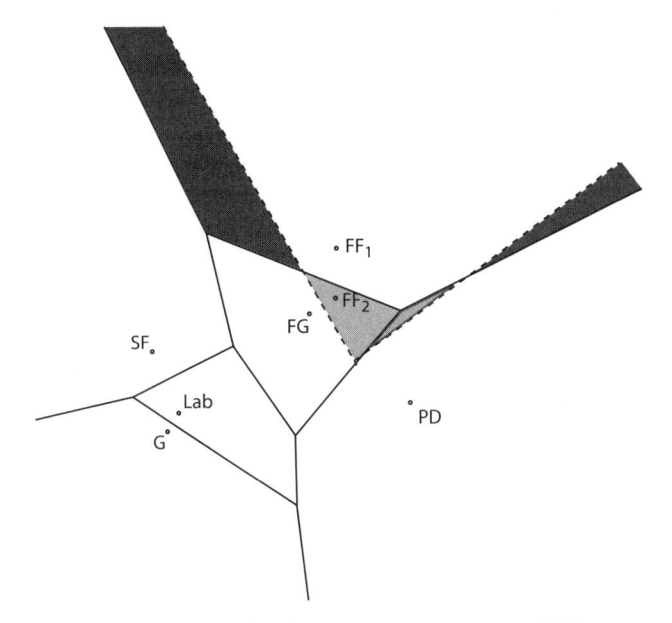

Figure 2.3. Voronoi dynamics of Irish party competition, ca. 2003.

points closer to the center of the space, making the lighter shaded areas much more densely populated, and far fewer in the outer regions, making the darker shaded areas much more sparsely populated, then this move toward the center could *increase* FF's vote share.

Figure 2.3 also shows that a small move in generating points (the policy shift from FF_1 to FF_2) exerts "scissor-like" leverage on Voronoi boundaries that can have big effects on the size of Voronoi regions containing the ideal points of party supporters. This is especially true when party positions are close to each other. In this case, tiny shifts in the FG and FF policy positions can radically shift the Voronoi boundary between these parties. This is in stark contrast to the situation in one-dimensional policy spaces, in which there is no such leverage. This "scissor" effect is an important reason why multidimensional party competition is quite different from, and generally more difficult to analyze than, unidimensional competition.

Something very close to the classical spatial model of party competition is encoded in the *Voronoi Game* of competitive spatial location. Each of n players has p points to insert into an n-dimensional space. Players insert points in sequence, each attempting to control the set of Voronoi regions with the largest volume.[5] Consistent with one-dimensional spatial models of party competition, the Voronoi Game has analytically provable best strategies for one-dimensional spaces. Consistent with the chaos results for multidimensional majority voting, the Voronoi Game does not have analytically provable best strategies for competitive spatial location in spaces of higher dimension. Even after reducing the game to a highly simplified two-player version played on a discrete graph rather than a continuous real space, it has been proved that, while particular examples can be solved, the general multidimensional Voronoi Game is *PSPACE* complete. That is, it is not just *difficult* to solve but *intractable*. There is no system of equations that can be resolved analytically to solve it and no upper bound on the time required to solve it computationally (Teramoto et al. 2006).

The Voronoi Game involves sequential insertion of new generating points, leaving existing points intact. To express this game in terms of dynamic multiparty competition, we describe a change in party position as the deletion of an existing point and the insertion of a new point. This allows us to see that party policy moves in a multidimensional policy space imply an (intractable) Voronoi Game:

1. Start with *n* points (the policy positions of *n* political parties).
2. For any putative party policy move, delete the current policy position, p_1, leaving *n-1* points in total.
3. Insert a new point p_2 as the position after the putative move. This is a Voronoi Game with *n-1* points.
4. There are now *n* points again; *p* has "moved" its position from p_1 to p_2.

We know from Teramoto et al. (2006) that the Voronoi Game played at stage 3 is intractable in a general setting. Thus the competitive spatial location involved in dynamic multiparty competition, which reduces to a Voronoi Game after deletion of the policy position at the time of the putative move, is also intractable in this formal sense. In stark contrast to the problem of competitive spatial location in a one-dimensional space, even simple-looking policy changes of party position, even in a two-dimensional space with rather few parties, generate intractable Voronoi dynamics.

---

[5] In a direct analogy with the original one-dimensional Hotelling model of competitive spatial location, a common practical application of the Voronoi Game is in the location of competing fast food franchises on a two-dimensional map. For a brief introduction to the two-player, two-dimensional version of the Voronoi Game, and computer applet implementing this, see www.voronoigame.com. The general problem of competitive spatial location is often referred to in this literature as the "Hotelling problem." We have not uncovered any reference in this literature to spatial models of party competition.

This, in a nutshell, is why the problem of competitive spatial location in a multidimensional space has been studied as a problem in *computational* geometry, and why we ourselves turn to computational techniques in what follows.

Decision Rules and Heuristics

Two crucial implications flow from analytical intractability of competitive spatial location in a multidimensional setting. One implication, though frankly we think of this as the boring implication, is *methodological*; it indicates a shift from classical formal analysis to rigorously designed suites of computer simulations. We do know from the huge volume of work reviewed by Okabe et al. (2000), that directly analogous problems in Voronoi geometry are amenable to computational investigation.

The second implication is the one that excites us; it is deep, interesting, and of crucial substantive importance for any theorist of political competition. *Analytical* intractability has huge *behavioral* implications. When there is no provable best-response strategy, real humans making real decisions in real multiparty competition must rely on informal decision heuristics. These are decision-making rules of thumb that can in practice be very effective but can never be proven formally to be best responses to any conceivable state of the world.[6] Our intellectual focus shifts from analytical ways to solve formal models to the behavioral decision rules that real people may actually use to "solve" the real problem that confronts them. This is a fundamentally empirical question about human behavior. It is quite possible that different humans use different rules in the same setting, so the choice of decision rules by real politicians is of interest to all who want to understand multiparty competition. Indeed, as we noted in chapter 1 when stating the self-evident truths that motivate us, we find it almost absurdly implausible to assume that all politicians making important decisions in complex settings use precisely the same decision rule.

Diversity of decision rules is well documented in relation to another spatial decision problem well known to be intractable for the general case. This is the Traveling Salesman Problem (TSP), "one of the most intensively studied problems in computational mathematics."[7] A salesman must visit a set of cities with locations described on a two-dimensional

---

[6] The term "heuristic" is given quite different meanings by scholars in different disciplines. To avoid ambiguity, we use the term "rule" or "decision rule" in what follows. By "rule" we mean a heuristic in the sense used by computer scientists—an algorithm designed to produce good results in complex settings.

[7] www.tsp.gatech.edu.

map. The problem is to find the shortest route that takes the salesman to every city. The number of possible routes is (n-1)!/2. This is a big number even when the number of cities is small; it explodes as the number of cities increases. With 16 cities, for example, there are 10,461,394,944,000 possible routes. The number of different routes between 100 cities is about 4.666×10^{155}. This problem cannot be smashed with feasible finite computing resources by investigating every possible route. It is typically possible *with a particular example*, if the number of cities is not too large, to find the shortest route using some algorithm or another. But it is effectively impossible to find an analytically provable best strategy for doing this in the general case with an arbitrary number of cities at arbitrary locations.

What is of key importance for us is that there are many different types of decision rules for traveling salesmen that typically come quite close to finding the shortest route. One example is the intuitive "nearest neighbor" rule: (1) start at a random city; (2) visit the closest unvisited city; (3) repeat (2) until all cities have been visited. This algorithm runs very fast indeed,[8] in comparison with most alternatives on most configurations of cities, and often performs well at finding something close to the shortest route. But particular configurations of cities can be constructed for which it performs disastrously. There are many alternative algorithms that also perform well for traveling salesmen (Hahsler and Hornik 2007), although, given fundamental intractability of the problem, none can be proven to work "best" in the general case. Especially interesting to psychologists is that, despite its intractability, many real humans quickly come up with good solutions to the TSP, even if these are not absolutely optimal.[9] The TSP is thus used in experiments designed to investigate how real humans make decisions in intractable settings (Dry et al. 2006). In such settings, different real humans typically use different decision heuristics to tackle the same intractable problem and hence come up with different solutions to it (MacGregor et al. 2006).

---

[8] The speed at which a decision rule runs on real data is a fundamental concern for theoretical computer scientists. It is strangely neglected by political scientists. Imagine, however, that a computer takes microseconds to evaluate one reasonably good rule but millennia to implement some more effective rule. If time is of the essence, as it so often is in the real world, then the faster algorithm is likely to win and the "better" algorithm is likely to lose. Substantial sums of real money are won on this basis every day in the chess corner of Washington Square Park in Greenwich Village, as chess hustlers beat chess masters against a lightning clock.

[9] By "very good" in this context we mean solutions with a route length for the salesman that is close to that of the optimal route for a particular solved case.

All of this has a direct bearing on how we model multiparty competition in multidimensional policy spaces. We know the underlying problem of competitive spatial location is intractable. We know that real humans come close to "solving" such intractable problems using informal rules of thumb. And we know that different humans use different rules of thumb to tackle the same intractable problem. The purpose of this book is to model multiparty competition using these insights, investigating interactions between party leaders who use (possibly different) rules of thumb to realize their objectives by manipulating party policy positions in this complex competitive environment.

CHAPTER THREE

A Baseline ABM of Party Competition

WE JUST SAW THAT PARTY leaders involved in the complex dynamics of multiparty competition face analytically intractable decision problems. This implies that real party leaders use informal rules of thumb rather than formally provable best response strategies. This *behavioral* assumption about party leaders motivates using agent-based models (ABMs) of decision making in complex dynamic settings. In the rest of this book, we develop and analyze an ABM of multiparty competition in multidimensional policy spaces.

Recent examples of such models include widely cited and seminal work by Kollman, Miller, and Page (1992, 1998, 2003). Building on this, Laver developed an ABM of party competition (Laver 2005). He assumed a two-dimensional policy space and two sets of agents: voters and party leaders. At the outset of the simulation, voters are given random ideal policy points drawn from a normal density function over the two-dimensional policy space. Voters do not vote strategically but choose the party advocating the policy position that is closest to their ideal point. Party leaders choose policy positions in this two-dimensional policy space using simple decision rules.

The complex system described by the Laver (2005) model is summarized in Figure 3.1. Following a random start that is essentially a model artifact, political competition cycles endlessly around the loop at the bottom of Figure 3.1. Voters adapt their party support to the current configuration of party policy positions. Leaders then adapt their party policy positions to the current configuration of voter support levels. Voters then readapt, and this process continues ad infinitum.

Laver specified four different decision rules for party leaders, each distilled from the substantive literature on intraparty decision making:

Sticker: never change position (an "ideological" leader)
Aggregator: set party policy on each dimension at the mean ideal point coordinates of current party supporters (a leader who responds perfectly to supporters' preferences)
Hunter: if the last move increased support, make the same move; else, reverse heading and make a unit move in a heading chosen randomly from the 180° arc centered on the direction now being faced (a leader who is a Pavlovian vote forager)

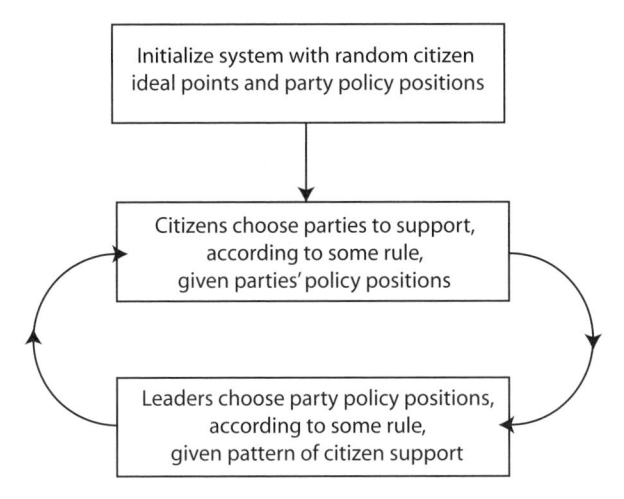

Figure 3.1. Complex dynamics of multiparty competition.

> Predator: identify the largest party; if this is you, stand still; else, make a unit move toward the largest party (a leader seeking votes by attacking larger parties)

The big news in Laver's 2005 paper was that the adaptive Hunter rule, despite its simplicity, was good at finding high concentrations of voter support. Furthermore, when several different party leaders use the same vote-seeking Hunter rule, Laver found that *party positions tend to stay away from the dead center of the policy space*, despite the fact that this is the place with the highest voter densities. Another important finding was that party systems in which all party leaders use the Aggregator rule quickly reach a deterministic steady state with no party movement at all. In competition for votes with other rules, however, parties using the Aggregator rule tend to fare poorly, occupying systematically more off-center locations and winning fewer votes.

In the rest of this chapter, we rebuild this ABM of multiparty competition from the bottom up. We go on in later chapters to add features to this baseline model that allow us to explore processes of substantive interest to us, endogenizing the birth and death of political parties, adding new decision rules and rule features, and investigating the effects of candidates' nonpolicy attractions for voters and the impact of having politicians who may care as much about their own policy preferences as they do about winning votes. Before we do any of this, we must be more systematic about how we characterize the preferences of voters.

CHARACTERIZING THE PREFERENCES OF VOTERS

Spatial models of party competition, as we have seen, are "spatial" in the sense that they describe voters' preferences on a wide range of issues using a small number of policy dimensions. This is substantively plausible because, *as a matter of empirical fact*, real voters' views on many different issues tend to be interrelated. Preferences on each of a substantial "bundle" of issues can be treated *as if* they were all correlated to a single underlying dimension. This "latent" dimension can be used in a parsimonious way to describe the empirical structure of voters' preferences on all issues in the bundle. For example, it is often possible to summarize voters' preferences on abortion, gay rights, stem cell research, capital punishment, and gun control in terms of a single "liberal-conservative" dimension of social policy. Once we know a voter's position on one of these issues, we can make a good prediction of her position on other issues in the same bundle. A set of latent dimensions such as this, together with information or assumptions about the distribution of voters' preferences on these, are fundamental primitives in all spatial models of political competition.

For most of this book we assume voters care only about the policy positions that are on offer at election time. (In chapter 9 we modify that assumption to model voters' evaluations of candidates' nonpolicy attributes.) We assume that each voter's preferences can be characterized by an ideal policy position in some n-dimensional policy space and a "loss function" that describes how different policy positions are evaluated, given how far these positions differ from the voter's ideal point.[1] This means that a crucial feature of our model is a description of the distribution of voters' ideal points. We assume that ideal points, whether in the overall voting population *or in well-specified subpopulations*, are normally distributed on policy dimensions of interest. This is in line with common practice. For example, Downsian one-dimensional models of party competition typically assume ideal point distributions that are bell shaped (Downs 1957). The normal distribution is bell shaped and occurs naturally in a huge variety of settings. Another reason for assuming a normal or bell-shaped distribution is that an n-dimensional Euclidean real space extends to infinity in all directions, but we typically do not think that some real voters have "infinitely extreme" ideal policy positions. This is an important restriction on possible distributions of voter ideal points. For example, it excludes the possibility that ideal points are *uniformly* or *arbitrarily* distributed, since these distributions imply we are just as likely to find someone with an infinitely extreme ideal point as

---

[1] In the language of Humphreys and Laver (2010), ours is a "strongly spatial" model—one that makes spatial assumptions about the *cognitive processes of real agents*.

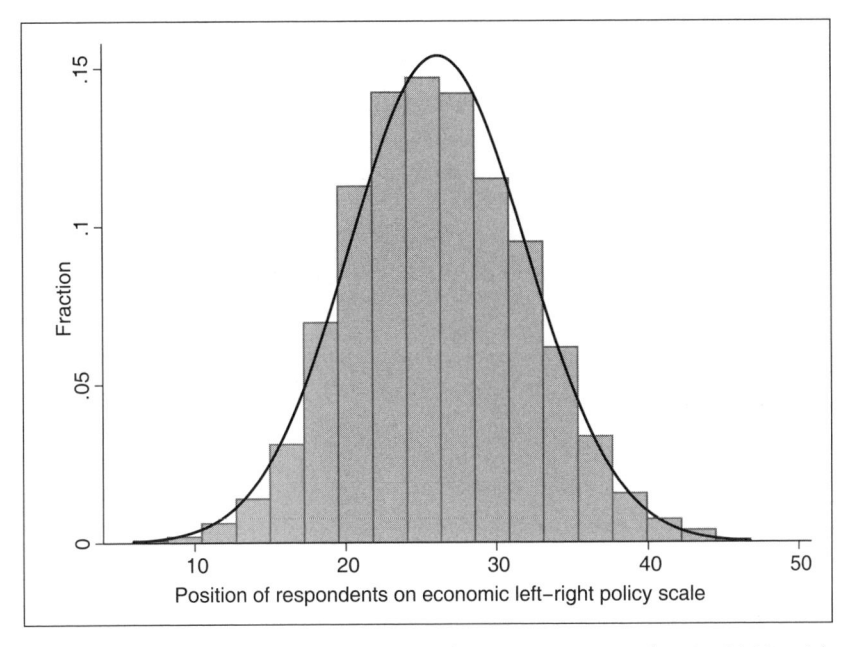

Figure 3.2. Density of Irish voters' attitudes on economic policy in 2002, with normal curve superimposed.

someone closer to the center.[2] Precluding infinitely extreme voters thus implies that densities of voter ideal points asymptotically approach zero in every direction as policy positions become more extreme. This implies distributions that are in this sense "bell shaped," at least at the extremes. We show in the appendix to this chapter that normal distributions of voter ideal points do not have to be imposed as "brute force" assumptions but may evolve endogenously on the basis of standard models of social interaction.

The justification for assuming normal distributions of voters' ideal points is not purely theoretical. It is also based on findings about distributions of policy preferences in real voting populations. Figure 3.2 shows the density of preferences, on a left-right dimension of economic policy, of 2,605 Irish survey respondents in 2002.[3] A theoretical normal curve is su-

---

[2] We return shortly to define the origin or "center" of a policy space.

[3] This scale was built, using data from the Irish National Election Study (INES), by aggregating each respondent's answers on seven different questions that probed attitudes on economic policy. These included agreement or disagreement with statements such as "income tax should be increased for people on higher than average incomes" and "business

perimposed and matches the empirically observed distribution of public opinion very closely. We can plot similar bell-shaped distributions of Irish survey respondents' positions on two other policy scales—one measuring liberal versus conservative attitudes on social policy, the other measuring attitudes on environmental policy. In each case, the empirically observed distribution of survey respondents' preferences closely resembles a normal curve.[4] More generally, when we measure the policy positions of populations of real humans on particular policy dimensions, we often encounter ideal point distributions that are essentially bell shaped. In short, the assumption of normal distributions of voters' ideal points is, for both theoretical and empirical reasons, nothing like as "special" as it might seem at first sight; normal distributions of public opinion can, and do, evolve in a range of plausible ways.

As we noted above, the models in this book are implemented for two-dimensional policy spaces. We assume, when specifying distributions of voter ideal points in particular populations or subpopulations, that the spatial distribution of ideal points has a bivariate normal density. For the sake of simplicity, we assume that standard deviations of ideal point locations are the same on both dimensions, with ideal points uncorrelated between dimensions; policy dimensions are taken to be "orthogonal" in this sense. This is a standard assumption in most implementations of the classical spatial model, giving us an assumed distribution of voter ideal points that is perfectly symmetric about its center.

A Coordinate System for Describing Ideal Points and Policy Positions

Any particular coordinate system for describing positions in a real Euclidean space is essentially arbitrary. A particular realization of any spatial model, whether computational or empirical, nonetheless requires some scale for specifying policy positions. In what follows, we use the distribution of ideal points as the basis of such a scale, describing party policy positions in terms of standard deviations, σ, of this distribution. Without loss of generality, we set the mean of the ideal point distribution at zero and the standard deviation at one. We thereby define the origin of the coordinate system of our policy space as the centroid of the set of population ideal points. We describe a policy position as being at (x, y) if it is at the position of an ideal point that is x standard deviations (of the distribution of population ideal points) from the population centroid

and industry should be strictly regulated by the State." A full description of this scale can be found in Appendix E3.

[4] See Appendix E3.

on the x dimension and y standard deviations from this on the y dimension. Any other coordinate system for describing party positions can be transformed into our system, but ours has the advantage of describing party positions explicitly in terms of the distribution of voters' ideal points. *Every party policy position can thereby be described in terms of the ideal point of some actual or possible voter.* Policy "positions" have no absolute meaning and must be described in relation to something; the distribution of voter ideal points is a natural benchmark.

Asymmetric Ideal Point Distributions Arising from More Than One Subpopulation

While we find bell-shaped distributions of public opinion in many different settings this is not always the case empirically, and it is certainly not the general case. An important issue for any decision maker, furthermore, is the possibility of getting stuck at some local maximum. In seminal work on ABMs of party competition by Kollman, Miller, and Page, some party leaders use "hill-climbing" rules, for example, polling voters in the local environment of their ideal point and moving in the policy direction that yields the greatest local improvement in voter support (Kollman et al. 1992, 1998).[5] Having climbed to the top of some local voter density hill, however, a party leader using a hill-climbing rule is unlikely to climb down the other side. This is true even when we know, from an all-knowing external vantage point, that this local hill is but a tiny bump on the population landscape. This decision rule may therefore perform poorly at maximizing party support. The relative effectiveness of different decision rules may be very different when spatial distributions of ideal points are asymmetric and multimodal.

For this reason, we generalize our description of voter preferences and assume the overall voter population to be the sum of a set of well-defined subpopulations. Think substantively of these subpopulations as, for example, ethnic, religious, economic, linguistic, or regional groups. We now modify our description of the distribution of voter ideal points to allow for populations that are aggregations of two subpopulations. While this is far from the most general possible case, it does generalize our description of the voting population in two important ways. First, it accommodates the possibility of *local maxima* in ideal point distributions. Second, generalizing the unrealistic assumption that the overall distribution of voters' ideal points is perfectly symmetrical about the origin, ideal point

---

[5] The catch-22 of hill climbing in the context of multiparty competition, of course, is how parties would know which voters to poll, as being in their ideological neighborhood, without first polling them. We do not torment ourselves with this conundrum here.

densities are typically *asymmetrical* about any given point in the policy space when the overall population is an aggregation of two distinct subpopulations. As we shall see, such asymmetries are important features of the environment for party competition and make a substantial difference to the outcomes we predict.

Even confining attention to two subpopulations, each with a bivariate normal distribution of members' ideal points, there may be an infinite number of possible ideal point distributions. There are three basic ways in which two distinct normally distributed subpopulations can differ: they can differ in their relative sizes, the means of their ideal point distributions, and the variances of these distributions. Since we confine ourselves to pairs of subpopulations with ideal points distributed in a Euclidean policy space, matters are simplified by the fact that all policy distances are invariant to rotations of the space. This means that we can, without loss of generality, take the line joining the centroids of two subpopulation ideal point distributions and rotate this to define it as the x-axis. We interpret this substantively as the *main axis of policy disagreement* between the two subpopulations of voters—the main axis of political competition in the political system under investigation.

In what follows, therefore, we consider two subpopulations with ideal point centroids that are separated on this axis of disagreement, which we specify as the x-axis. In addition, we set subpopulation ideal point variances equal. This enables research designs that explore the political effects of having increasingly "polarized" subpopulations, with ideal point centroids that are increasingly far apart on the x-axis. We do this, in the computational work we specify in chapters 5 and 6 below, by investigating the effects of a range of parameter settings for aggregated voter subpopulations. Using our baseline symmetrical bivariate normal distribution with means (0, 0) and standard deviations (1, 1) as a point of reference, we set standard deviations of each of the two subpopulations, l and r, at (0.5, 0.5). We investigate subpopulations with relative sizes, n_l/n_r, that are sampled from a uniform distribution on the interval [2.0, 1.0] and with ideal point means, $\mu_r = -\mu_l$, sampled from a uniform distribution on the interval [0.0, 1.5].

Table 3.1 describes aggregate populations generated by examples of two distinct subpopulation ideal point distributions parameterized within these ranges. The top three rows describe ideal point distributions arising from the aggregation of two equal-sized subpopulations ($n_l/n_r = 1$); the lower three describe aggregate populations in which the left subpopulation is twice the size of the right ($n_l/n_r = 2$). If these distributions are plotted,[6] it transpires that, with relatively unpolarized subpopulations

---

[6] These plots can be found in Table E3.4 in the electronic appendix.

TABLE 3.1
Summary Measures for Ideal Point Densities in Six Sample Populations
Aggregated from Two Subpopulations ($\sigma_l = \sigma_r = 0.50$)

n_1/n_2	$\mu_r\ (=-\mu_l)$	$\mu_{\text{x-pop}}$	Median$_{\text{x-pop}}$	$\sigma_{\text{x-pop}}$
1.0	0.5	0.0	0.0	0.707
1.0	1.0	0.0	0.0	1.118
1.0	1.5	0.0	0.0	1.582
2.0	0.5	−0.166	−0.218	0.687
2.0	1.0	−0.334	−0.662	1.067
2.0	1.5	−0.500	−1.162	1.500

($\mu_r = 0.5$), the aggregate population has a *unimodal* distribution of ideal points, though this distribution is asymmetrical, being "stretched" along the *x*-axis of primary policy disagreement. In sharp contrast, for the most polarized pairs of subpopulations we investigate ($\mu_r = 1.5$), subpopulation ideal point centroids are now so far apart that there is almost no overlap between subpopulations. Plots of aggregate population ideal point densities are, on these parameterizations, in effect plots of two distinct subpopulations. Intermediate examples ($\mu_r = 1.0$) generate two distinct but overlapping subpopulations that combine to form bimodal distributions for the population as a whole.

When we randomly sample parameters for the distribution of voter ideal points in this way, we not only generalize the model to comprehend asymmetric and potentially multimodal distributions but also introduce a very important new challenge for party decision rules. These now encounter many different ideal point distributions with unknown parameter settings rather than one single distribution to which they can adapt. Robust decision rules will perform well in the range of different environments we now specify. In contrast, more "brittle" rules may perform better than robust rules in certain specific settings, but not in any possible setting that might be encountered. This is perhaps the most important reason to model party competition using a large variety of different asymmetric distributions of voter ideal points.

Using asymmetric distributions of voter ideal points that aggregate two distinct subpopulations has the *theoretical* advantage of specifying more general ideal point distributions that are nonetheless well parameterized. It has the great *substantive* advantage that, anticipating empirical work we report in chapter 11, we find it relatively easy to calibrate observed party support shares to observed party policy positions in real party systems using parameterizations of the two-subpopulation model of voter ideal points that we specify above. While this does not mean that our two-subpopulation model of voter ideal point densities is "correct" in some sense, it does at least mean that it is consistent with what we observe.

Smooth *Densities of Voter Ideal Points*

Rigorous and exhaustive computational interrogation of dynamic models requires that these models be *parsimonious*, with as few parameters as is consistent with substantive realism. We therefore make an important modification to the Laver (2005) ABM and its extensions,[7] which treat each *voter* as an independent decision-making agent. Reported simulations typically involve one thousand voters; each voter in each simulation is given an ideal point randomly drawn from the symmetric bivariate normal density distribution specified above. Different repetitions of the same model run, even with identical parameter settings, generate different results because each repetition uses a different random draw of ideal points.[8] Given the stochastic components in the model, using many different random draws of ideal points for every vector of parameter settings means we must repeat simulation runs many times, *for each random draw*, if we want to ensure that run results are not a product of some particular random ideal point draw. This increases our computational budget by an order of magnitude.

We address this by replacing a *finite* population of voters, with ideal points drawn randomly from an underlying density function, with an effectively infinite population of voters characterized by the underlying density function itself. Since party support shares no longer depend on details of a discrete random draw of ideal points, the same configuration of party policy positions always generates the same configuration of party support in a given type of population. Our approach thus characterizes the population as a density function, not as a set of autonomous agents. This is directly analogous to the "electoral landscapes" used by Kollman, Miller, and Page and by de Marchi (Kollman et al. 1998; De Marchi 1999).

---

[7] Laver and Schilperoord (2007) extend the model to include endogenous political parties, while Fowler and Laver (2008) add a more rigorous examination of competition between different decision rules.

[8] Another way of looking at this is to see the seed of the pseudo-random number generator used for each run as a model parameter.

Voters' Evaluations of Different Policy Positions

Metrics for Measuring Policy Distances

Given a "common" policy space that can be used to describe voter ideal points, party policy positions, and the relationships between these, we must now specify how we assume voters to evaluate different policy positions when deciding which of these they prefer. If voters care only about policy, then the "policy distances" between their ideal points and the party policy positions on offer are crucial quantities in any spatial model. We are accustomed to living our daily lives in local regions of natural spaces that we treat as Euclidean, thinking of a straight line as the shortest distance between two points, expressing our ideas on Euclidean planes such as sheets of paper or computer monitors. It is hardly surprising, therefore, that human theorists tend to have in mind, albeit often implicitly, the notion that real people use a Euclidean metric when they measure *cognitive* distances in a *policy*, as opposed to a *physical*, space.

The Euclidean metric defines the distance between two points in a two-dimensional space using the well-known Pythagorean formula.[9] However, there is no good reason, theoretical or empirical, to believe this is an accurate description of how real people think about policy, given the infinite number of possible metrics (including the plausible "infinity metric")[10] that they could use when measuring policy distances. One cognitive metric that has been subject to empirical investigation over a long period by psychologists, and has explicit behavioral justification in certain real settings, is the "city block" or "Manhattan" metric (Attneave 1950; Shepard 1991; Gärdenfors 2000). The cognitive justification for using a city block metric in the context of political competition is that, when considering two voters with ideal points on two unrelated policy dimensions, one voter's perception of her difference from the other might, *as an empirical generalization about how real people actually think about politics*, be better described as the sum of their policy differences on each dimension,[11] not the square root of the sum of the squares of these differences. Humphreys and Laver show that it can make a big difference to

---

[9]
$$d_2((x_1, x_2), (y_1, y_2)) = \sqrt{|x_1 - x_2|^2 + |y_1 - y_2|^2}$$

[10]
$$d_\infty((x_1, x_2), (y_1, y_2)) = \sqrt[\infty]{|x_1 - x_2|^\infty + |y_1 - y_2|^\infty}$$

According to the infinity metric, the distance between two policy positions is their distance on the dimension on which they most differ.

[11]
$$d_1((x_1, x_2), (y_1, y_2)) = |x_1 - x_2| + |y_1 - y_2|$$

key theoretical results to assume voters perceive policy distances in terms of the city block metric, as opposed to making the orthodox Euclidean assumption (Humphreys and Laver 2010). Moreover, Eguia argues axiomatically that assuming Euclidean as opposed to city block preferences implies making some odd assumptions about how real people think about risk (Eguia 2009).

Having switched from formal analysis to computation, we are not constrained to make behavioral assumptions simply because these generate analytically tractable models. Liberation from the need to choose unrealistic but analytically tractable assumptions is, indeed, a signal virtue of the computational approach. For the purposes of the present book, however, we maintain theoretical continuity with previous scholars and use a Euclidean metric for measuring policy distances. We do not want to distract attention from our key results by raising the possibility these are driven by what would currently be the unorthodox choice of a city block metric to measure policy distances.[12]

Loss Functions for Measuring Individual Voter Utility

Having considered how real people *perceive* the "distance" between two different policy positions, we turn now to the closely related matter of how they *feel* about this perceived distance. When voters choose to evaluate the positions of two political parties competing for their support, for example, we could assume they favor the closest party, in the sense we just defined this, and that their preferences are single peaked. This amounts to a fairly weak assumption about how real people think about politics—that each voter has some "ideal" policy position and that the utility she anticipates from some putative policy outcome is monotonically decreasing in the distance between this outcome and the ideal point. If we model voters' decisions as being based solely on policy, there is often no need to be more specific about which precise function describes how voters' utility declines as policy distance increases—we need to know just that the closer alternative is seen as better. There are, however, circumstances in which we do need to be more precise. We may want, for example, to model decision making that combines evaluations of policy positions with other, nonpolicy, elements in the value of some particular

---

[12] It is also important not to underestimate the fundamental reconsideration of party competition that is implied by shifting assumptions to the city block metric. For example, moving "toward" some other position takes on a whole new meaning in a city block space. There are arguments in the philosophy of geometry, furthermore, that real humans find it difficult to visualize non-Euclidean spaces. This is an issue for *human analysts* who plot and interpret spatial maps of policy positions, though it is never argued that *real voters* actually visualize policy distances when making their decisions.

outcome or to model how voters choose between risky alternatives. There are infinitely many mathematical functions that decrease monotonically in the distance between two points—"loss functions" in common scholarly usage. The assumption of a particular loss function is, once again, *a behavioral assumption about how real people think*. Once again, this choice is in practice often motivated more by analytical convenience than behavioral realism.

The most common assumption we find, in a wide variety of published work on many different matters, is of *quadratic* policy loss (Adams et al. 2005). On this assumption, voter utility declines as the square of the distance between the policy position being evaluated and the voter's ideal point. The assumption of quadratic loss is common whether the model is analytical (Schofield and Sened 2006; Ansolabehere and Snyder 2000; Groseclose 2001; Adams et al. 2005; Adams 2001; Hinich and Munger 1994) or computational (De Marchi 2003; Jackson 2003). As Adams, Merrill, and Grofman point out (Adams et al. 2005: 17) an alternative plausible assumption about voter utility involves *linear* policy loss. Setting analytical tractability aside, there is at least one *substantive* argument for quadratic loss, based on the assumption that real voters tend to be risk averse. Faced with a choice between the certainty of a middling outcome b and a fair lottery between a good outcome a and a bad outcome c, the empirical claim is that most people are risk averse in the sense they prefer the certain alternative to the fair lottery, despite the fact that both appear on the face of things to have the same expected payoff. For voters who are risk averse, bearing risk has a cost in itself. If voters are assumed to be risk neutral *about policy choices*, then this implies a linear loss function. If they are assumed to be risk averse, and empirical research on both referendum dynamics and "economic" voting seems to imply this assumption may be behaviorally realistic, this implies a "concave" loss function, of which simple quadratic loss is a tractable example. Given what we take to be a consensus that real voters tend to be risk averse when they make important political choices, as opposed to being risk neutral or risk seeking, we assume a quadratic loss function when defining the utility $U(i, j)$ of a policy at j for a voter with an ideal point at i:

$$U(i, j) = -d(i, j)^2 \tag{3.1}$$

DECISION RULES FOR VOTERS

We now turn to the decisions made by voters when choosing which party to support. This is an important matter on which, given fundamental intractability of dynamic multiparty competition, we depart substantively from many classical analytical models of party competition. In these classical models, especially those that assume a small number of parties and voters' preferences well described using a single policy dimension, it is natural to consider the possibility that voters might make *strategic* calculations. Such calculations could imply supporting not the party with the policy position closest to the voter's ideal point but the party for which an added vote would maximize the voter's expected utility—given its policy position, given the policy position of all other parties, given a forecast of the behavior of all other voters, and given a forecast of the eventual policy outcome, conditional on different election results. These severe conditions show us why the analysis of strategic voting is most developed with reference to party systems with first-past-the-post elections, a small number of parties, and a single salient policy dimension. In such settings, the assumed rules of the game are that the party with more votes than any other "wins" the election and then instantly implements all of its policy promises. Given these assumptions and some estimate of the ideal positions of all other voters on the one salient policy dimension, it becomes feasible to consider the possibility of strategic voting. This remains far from straightforward if all voters are assumed to make the same strategic calculations, possibly dissembling about their "true" preferences as part of this process, but it is a feasible analytical objective. However we have seen that, when we add more parties and more salient policy dimensions and consider the dynamics of electoral competition, the resulting models of dynamic party competition are analytically intractable. Crucially, they are intractable for real voters since it is not possible formally to "solve" for party policy positions and consequent election results, conditional on a profile of voter preferences. This makes strategic voting, in the classical sense, infeasible.

The problem of designing an effective strategic voting rule runs much deeper than analytical intractability of dynamic multiparty competition. The norm in multiparty systems with proportional representation, the typical case, is for no party to win a legislative majority. This means that coalitions of parties, at either the legislative or executive level, are needed to sustain a government in office and implement any policy position. Axiomatically, more than one government may emerge from a given election result in which no single party wins a majority. This in turn means that every strategic voter needs to anticipate the government formation process before she can forecast how an election result maps onto a government and hence a policy outcome (Kedar 2009). This process is in itself quite complex, and has been the subject of considerable theorizing and empirical research (Laver and Schofield 1998; Laver and Shepsle 1996). Any human voter considering strategic voting must thus append a (inevitably complicated) model of government formation, not to mention a model of downstream policy implementation by coalition cabinets, to an already intractable model of dynamic multiparty competition. This seems to us to stretch the notion of "rational" strategic voting in national elections so far beyond the limits of credibility—in the context of dynamic multiparty competition—that it implies preposterous assumptions about how real voters actually think. For all of these reasons we assume, in the tradition of the classical Downsian model, that voters use a nonstrategic "proximity" voting rule when deciding which party to support.

There is more to the assumption of proximity voting than complexity of any strategic decision facing voters. Another important argument treats voting as a form of "expressive" behavior. Expressive voters *get more utility from the very act of voting for things they like* than from voting for things they do not like, regardless of the downstream strategic implications of this (Brennan and Hamlin 2000; Brennan and Lomasky 1993; Schuessler 2000). The argument for expressive voting is that rational voters in large populations know with near certainty that their individual votes make no difference whatsoever to the eventual result. Strategically instrumental voters in large electorates will thus typically not vote at all if there is any cost whatsoever associated with voting. On this argument voters who vote, and we observe that many voters who we think of as rational do indeed vote, must do so *for reasons that are not strategically instrumental*. The expressive voter, in these terms, derives *intrinsic* satisfaction from supporting particular political parties. Looked at in this way, a Downsian "proximity" voter gets most satisfaction from supporting the party policy position closest to her ideal point and feels increasing pain if she votes for parties whose positions are further away from this.[13]

Our baseline decision rule for voters is thus that they support the party with the closest policy position—the party whose position generates the Voronoi region in which their ideal point is located.

CHARACTERIZING THE PREFERENCES OF PARTY LEADERS

Having characterized the preferences of voters and specified a decision rule for voting in light of these, we turn our attention to party leaders.

---

[13] We have come across no theoretical account of "expressive" strategic voting, whereby the voter derives pleasure from the very act of making complex strategic calculations, over and above *or even despite* the downstream consequences of strategic voting. In our experience, however, there are economists and political scientists who actually think like this. Thus the core distinction is between voters who get some value out of voting as an act of self-expression and those who see voting as an instrumental way to change the odds of receiving some downstream benefit.

We first draw attention to an important question we beg by defining the problem in terms of "party leaders." In the spirit of both game theory, strictly applied, and agent-based modeling, we do not treat any self-evidently collective entity such as a "political party" in anthropomorphic terms, as if this were a discrete agent with a single collective brain. Our prime concern is with decision makers, and we thus focus our attention on party leaders. In effect we assume *either* that decisions for each party we model are taken by a single leader *or* that there is some leadership cohort of individuals with identical preferences who can be modeled *as if* they were a single leader. This sets aside the interesting and important matter of *intraparty* politics between politicians with conflicting preferences. We relish the prospect of returning to this in future work.

Earlier, when we specified the decision rules used in the Laver (2005) model and its extensions, we conflated two distinct things. The first concerns the *preferences* of party leaders; the second concerns the *decision rules* these leaders use when trying to realize these preferences. Stickers were presented as ideological party leaders who care only about their party policy position and not at all about their party's vote share. Aggregators were presented as "democratic" party leaders who care only about representing the preferences of current party supporters and not at all about either vote share or any particular policy position. Hunters and Predators were presented as party leaders who care only about vote share. The distinction between Hunters and Predators is important in this regard. Both types of party leaders care only about party vote share, but they use different decision rules when trying to increase this.

We now clarify the distinction between the preferences of the party leader and the decision rule she uses. Consider the vote share of party p (labeled v_p) and three policy positions of possible interest to the leader of party p. These are the ideal point of the party leader (labeled i_p), the current party position (labeled j_p), and the optimal representation of the ideal points of party supporters (labeled k_p). Having assumed a Euclidean distance metric for agents' perceptions of policy differences, we specify k_p as the centroid of the ideal points of current party supporters. A substantive interpretation of the rationale for the Sticker rule is that a leader who is a Sticker cares only about i_p, without regard for v_p or k_p and uses the rule of thumb of setting j_p at i_p. A leader who uses a Hunter or Predator rule may care only about v_p; she uses some rule to set j_p, seeking to maximize v_p without regard for i_p or k_p. A leader using an Aggregator rule may care only about moving to k_p, without regard for v_p or i_p. In light of this we specify a general utility function for party leaders,

$$U(v_p, i_p, j_p, k_p) = (1 - \varphi_1 - \varphi_2) \cdot v_p - \varphi_1 \cdot d(i_p, j_p)^2 - \varphi_2 \cdot d(j_p, k_p)^2 \quad (3.2)$$

where φ_1 and φ_2 are trade-off parameters specifying the relative contributions of the party leader's ideal point, and the centroid of supporter ideal points, to the utility of the party leader, and $\varphi_1 + \varphi_2 \leq 1$.[14] One possible implication of this utility function is that party leaders using the Sticker rule do so because, for them, $\varphi_1 = 1$ and they are concerned only with having party policy at their ideal points. They achieve this by setting $j_p = i_p$. Similarly, party leaders using the Aggregator rule may do so because, for them, $\varphi_2 = 1$ and they are concerned only with setting a party policy that is an optimal representation of current supporters' ideal points. They achieve this by setting $j_p = k_p$. Finally, leaders using the vote-seeking Hunter or Predator rules may do so because, for them, $\varphi_1 = \varphi_2 = 0$; their utility derives solely from their party's vote share. There are many alternative parameterizations of this general party leader utility function, but in what follows we concentrate on these "ideal types" of party leader. We return in chapter 9 to consider party leaders who are also concerned both with their party's vote share and with their own ideal policy position, investigating the behavior of leaders who have utility functions such that $0 < \varphi_1 < 1$.

Decision Rules for Party Leaders

In light of the utility function for party leaders specified above, our baseline model of party competition involves three decision rules, defined and investigated by Laver (2005) and discussed briefly above.[15] These are Sticker, Aggregator, and Hunter.

Sticker

The simplest rule is Sticker: publish a policy position and never change this.[16] As we have just seen, the Sticker rule is an obvious choice for a party leader for whom $\varphi_1 = 1$, who maximizes utility when party policy

---

[14] Note that, while the specified utility function for party leaders is conceptually accurate, any realization of this in a model generating numerical values for $U(\cdot)$ requires an additional "scale" parameter, δ, applied to v_p. This is in effect an exchange rate that gives a common *numeràire* allowing expected utility derived from policy loss to be compared with expected utility deriving from vote share. This is not a model artifact but a real substantive matter, since these sources of utility are denominated in different "currencies"—policy distances and votes. At no point in this book will we make interpersonal comparisons of politicians' utility that, for obvious reasons given the above, and more generally, are deeply problematic.

[15] We return in chapter 6 to consider the Predator rule, which we redefine in the light of pathological behavior by agents using the rule as defined in Laver (2005).

[16] NetLogo code to the Sticker rule is thus:
```
to stick
end
```

is set at her ideal point. On March 4, 2008, for example, in a speech announcing his withdrawal from the U.S. presidential primary, Mike Huckabee said: "[W]e've kept the faith. And that for me has been the most important goal of all. I'd rather lose an election than lose the principles that got me into politics in the first place." Casual observation suggests that Huckabee is not unique in being doggedly unwilling to adapt stated policy positions for reasons of political expediency, and thus that we do indeed observe Stickers in the real political world. Over and above this substantive justification, Sticker is a theoretically interesting component of any portfolio of decision rules under investigation in a dynamic setting precisely because it is fundamentally static. The performance of any dynamically responsive decision rule can be measured relative to the performance of a static Sticker benchmark. Dynamically responsive decision rules should, if they are to be seen as effective, perform at least as well as the static Sticker rule.

Aggregator

The Aggregator rule sets party policy at the centroid of current supporters' ideal points.[17] This is a heuristic that is suitable for use, as we have seen, by a party leader who is concerned above all else to represent the views of current party supporters—for whom $\varphi_2 = 1$. We can also think of such a leader as a "benevolent social planner." This does not require knowledge of any particular citizen's ideal point but in effect assumes the party leader has some internal system (a general meeting of supporters, or an unbiased representative sample of these, or some other internal polling process) that allows her to estimate the aggregated preferences of party supporters. Alternatively, we could assume party rules to mandate that party policy positions are set at the centroid of current supporter ideal points by some unmodeled but binding "democratic" internal procedure. Empirically, furthermore, we do find real political parties (many Green parties, for example) with internal procedures designed to represent the wishes of supporters in party policy platforms.

---

[17] Note that, when all points in a set are weighted equally, the centroid of the set is the average of these points. NetLogo code for the Aggregator rule is thus:

    to aggregate
        let xbar (sum [votes * pxcor] of patches with [closest-party = myself] / mysize)
        let ybar (sum [votes * pycor] of patches with [closest-party = myself] / mysize)
        setxy xbar ybar
    end

Hunter

Most traditional spatial models of party competition assume that party leaders are vote seekers (for whom $\varphi_1 = \varphi_2 = 0$). Hunter is a decision rule based on Pavlovian learning that is designed for vote seeking in the analytically intractable context in which we are interested. If a Hunter's move at time *t*-1 was rewarded by an increase in vote share, then it makes a unit move at time *t* in the same direction as the move at *t*-1.[18] If not, a Hunter reverses direction and makes a unit move on a heading randomly selected within the half-space now being faced.[19] In a nutshell, a party leader using a Hunter rule keeps moving party policy in the same policy direction as long as party vote share keeps increasing; otherwise she makes a random policy move in the opposite direction. Hunter is a straightforward "win-stay, lose-shift" algorithm of the type investigated by scholars interested in adaptive learning (Nowak and Sigmund 1993). Substantively, Hunter encodes the behavior of a party leader who relentlessly forages in the policy space, always searching for more votes and never being satisfied—changing policy in the same direction as long as this is rewarded with more votes, but casting around for a new policy direction when the previous policy move was punished with falling or static support.

CHARACTERIZING KEY OUTCOMES OF POLITICAL COMPETITION

There are many "outcomes" of any evolving system of multiparty competition, most of which are difficult to characterize in a systematic way. At any given time, for example, there is a spatial "constellation" of party policy positions and sizes. As with the constellations we see in the night sky, we can try to describe these, but the shapes we see may be in the eye of the beholder and systematic characterization is problematic. Nonetheless, the whole point of modeling party competition is to generate outputs that can indeed be described and analyzed in a systematic way. In what

---

[18] For stylistic reasons we often refer in what follows to, for example, a "Hunter Party" or a "Hunter," by which we mean a "party with a party leader who uses the Hunter rule."

[19] We specify this unit move, given our coordinate system, as 0.1 standard deviations of the baseline distribution of voter ideal points. NetLogo code for the Hunter rule is thus:

```
to hunt
    ifelse (mysize > old-size) [jump 1]
        [set heading heading + 90 + random-float 180 jump 1]
    set old-size mysize
end
```

follows, therefore, we specify four types of metric that characterize substantively important outputs of multiparty competition. These deal with the number of surviving political parties, the typical policy positions of surviving parties, the extent to which the current configuration of party positions represents the preferences of voters, and the number of different decision rules in use by surviving party leaders.

Effective Number of Parties

It is easy to count N, the absolute number of surviving political parties. This is clearly an important output of multiparty competition, especially if we endogenize the birth and death of parties. However, N-party systems can differ in important ways. For example the parties may have roughly equal levels of support, or support may be concentrated on a single political party. An index of the "effective" number of parties, ENP, defined by Laakso and Taagepera, compares the extent to which party support is concentrated on a small subset of parties in a system, or is distributed evenly between them (Laakso and Taagepera 1979). This index is substantively intuitive because, when all parties are of perfectly equal size in an N-party system, then $ENP = N$. When all votes are concentrated on a single party, then $ENP = 1$. As support becomes more evenly distributed among parties, ENP approaches N.

Eccentricity of Party Policy Positions

It is difficult to be systematic about the "shape" of different party policy configurations. We can however measure the *policy eccentricity* of any given party as the distance of its policy position from the centroid of voter ideal points.[20] This gives us a simple summary measure for any configuration P of political parties, as the mean policy eccentricity of the parties (labeled E_p). When interpreting the mean policy eccentricity of any configuration of parties, we need a sense of the eccentricities of voter ideal points underlying this. Figure 3.3 plots eccentricities of one hundred thousand voter ideal points, drawn at random from our baseline standardized bivariate normal distribution. Mean voter ideal point eccentricity is 1.25 and the median is 1.18. Contrary to casual intuition, few voters are at the precise policy centroid, since this is a single point location. Considering voter density *contours* that describe concentric circles of increasing circumference around this centroid, the number of voters with a given eccentricity increases as we move away from the center,

---

[20] In a Euclidean space such as we use here, we can rotate any configuration of points without changing interpoint distances, so policy eccentricity is invariant to the rotation of party positions. This would not be true, for example, in a city block space.

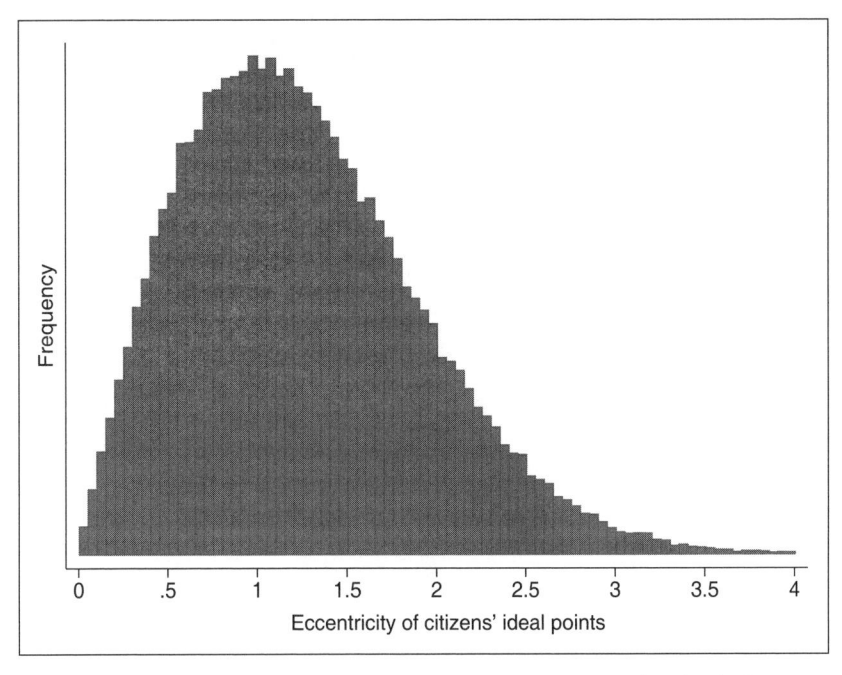

Figure 3.3. Eccentricities of one hundred thousand simulated ideal points drawn randomly from a bivariate normal distribution with mean 0 and standard deviation 1.

peaking at an eccentricity of about 1.00 standard deviations away, after which the density of voters declines as ideal point eccentricity increases. Looking at things another way, median voter eccentricity in this baseline distribution of ideal points tells us that half of all voters have ideal points less than 1.18 standard deviations from the voter centroid, while half have ideal points further away than this from the centroid. This gives a sense of scale to our measure of party policy eccentricity.

"Representativeness" of a Given Party Configuration

It is self-evidently important to measure how well any evolved configuration of party positions represents the policy preferences of voters. There are several ways to think about what we call *representativeness*, and what Golder and Stramski, in their extensive review of this matter, call "congruence" between ideal points and policy outputs (Golder and Stramski 2010). First, there is a "one-to-one" congruence between some summary of voter ideal points (for example, the ideal point of the median voter on some policy dimension) and some summary of policy positions on offer (the position of the eventual government on this dimension, for example). Second there is a "many-to-one" congruence between the full set of voter ideal points and some summary of policy positions on offer. Finally, there is a "many-to-many" congruence between the full set of ideal points and the full set of policy positions arising from party competition (the set of elected legislators' ideal points, for example).[21]

Here, we use a many-to-many measure of the extent to which the configuration of party positions represents the set of voter ideal points. We see each voter ideal point as "represented" at the time of the election by the ideal point of her closest party; we specified how voters feel about this in expression 3.1 above. This gives us a natural measure of representation, R_p, as the mean quadratic distance of all voters from their closest party. If n is the number of voters and $d(i_v, j_{vp})$ is the Euclidean distance between the ideal point of voter v (labeled i_v) and the policy position of her closest party in configuration P (labeled j_{vp}), then:

$$R_p = -\frac{\sum_v d(i_v, j_{vp})^2}{n}$$

Higher values of R_p imply a more representative configuration of party policy positions. This measure has a theoretical maximum of zero, in the unlikely event there is a party policy position at the ideal point of every voter. In the general case with more unique voter ideal points than distinct party policy positions, R_p is constrained to be negative.

This measure fits perfectly with the notion of "optimal representation" in Voronoi geometry, which as we have seen encompasses an account of competitive spatial location. Given a set of p population points (voter ideal points) defined in a space and a set of n generating points (party positions), the set of generating points is an optimal n-point representation of the population points if this minimizes the sum of the squared distances between population points and generating points. The allows us to exploit the analytical result that a set of n points is an optimal n-point representation of a p-point population if it generates a centroidal Voronoi tessellation (CVT) of the population points, in which each generating point is at the centroid of its Voronoi region (Du et al. 1999). This tells us that *representativeness of any party system is maximized when party policy positions are configured in a CVT*, a very useful result indeed.

This insight gives us access to another result of substantive and normative significance in the context of dynamic multiparty competition.

---

[21] Any measure defined to characterize these different types of congruence is subject to the assumptions about cognitive metrics and loss functions that we just discussed.

A widely used computational procedure for *finding* a CVT from an arbitrary starting configuration of generating points is Lloyd's Algorithm (Lloyd 1982). This recursive algorithm is simple: (1) generate a Voronoi tessellation of the space; (2) move each generating point to the centroid of its Voronoi region; (3) go to (1). There are formal proofs in the computer science literature that a CVT can be found using Lloyd's Algorithm for any arbitrary *one-dimensional* space and starting configuration of generating points (Du et al. 1999). In multidimensional spaces, it has been found that Lloyd's Algorithm does converge on a CVT, in finite time and for any arbitrary level of precision. This has been used in a wide variety of heavy-duty computational applications, never failing but never being proved formally (Okabe et al. 2000).[22]

Lloyd's Algorithm is important for students of dynamic multiparty competition because a setting in which all party leaders use the Aggregator rule is, precisely, a party system implementing Lloyd's Algorithm. Consequently, we know that party positions in an all-Aggregator system converge on a CVT of the policy space that maximizes representativeness of the configuration of party policy positions as we have defined this.[23] Intriguingly, this emergent phenomenon arises despite the fact that leaders of individual Aggregator parties never try to maximize overall representativeness of the party system, but simply try to represent the ideal points of their own current supporters.

Effective Number of Decision Rules

In most of the models of party competition we investigate in this book, the set of surviving parties is endogenous and the set of rules used by party leaders is diverse. This means that the diversity of the set of decision rules in use by the leaders of *surviving* parties is an important output of party competition.[24] In some settings, each surviving party leader may use a different decision rule; in others, all leaders may use the same rule. We therefore define a measure of the *effective number of rules* (ENR) that is directly analogous to the effective number of parties (ENP). If the aggregate vote share of all parties with leaders using rule r is v_r, then the ENR is:

---

[22] We can think of this as a "feral" de facto proof or, in the language of political science, a "folk theorem."

[23] In terms of computational method we also know from Lloyd's Algorithm that an all-Aggregator system reaches steady state, in finite time, for an arbitrary level of precision determined by the floating point precision of the computation. We make use of this helpful result when specifying run designs in chapter 4.

[24] For stylistic reasons we often refer to *rules* in what follows, rather than to parameterized rules or rule-agent pairings.

$$ENR = \frac{1}{\sum_r (v_r)^2}$$

If all party leaders use the same decision rule, then $ENR = 1$; if every leader uses a different parameterized rule, then $ENR = ENP$. Thus, for a given number of parties, the closer ENR is to 1, the closer is some single decision rule to dominating the party system.

Moving Forward

We used this chapter to specify our baseline model of multiparty competition and define a set of measures that characterize evolving dynamic systems of competing political parties. We move on in the next chapter to develop the methodological tools we need to investigate this model in a rigorous way. While this next chapter may seem something of a methodological interlude, we urge readers not to skip ahead to the substantive findings that emerge from our model later in the book. As we have seen, the complexity of our model mandates the use of computational methods. If we are to feel confident in the inferences we draw from our computational work, we must feel confident that these inferences are as rigorous, to all intents and purposes, as the inferences drawn from rigorous classical analysis. Only by giving careful consideration to the methodological matters we discuss in the next chapter can we feel confident that our results are just as solid, both logically and statistically, as conclusions drawn rigorously from traditional analytical models.

Appendix to Chapter 3: Endogenous Evolution of Normal Distributions of Voter Ideal Points

Although not a central feature of our core argument, we now show that our specification of normally distributed ideal points in voter populations and subpopulations is by no means the brute force assumption it might seem at first sight. It is easy to show that such distributions of voters *tend to evolve endogenously* from simple but plausible models of social interaction between voters. Imagine, for example, a *uniform* random distribution of ideal points in some policy space, such as the distribution shown in the left panel of Figure 3.4. Sketch a simple model of social interaction as follows. One voter, *a*, is picked at random from the set of all voters to have an interaction with another voter, *b*, also picked at random. Following this interaction, *a*'s ideal point follows a random walk, though this is very slightly biased in favor of moving *a*'s ideal point closer to *b*'s ideal

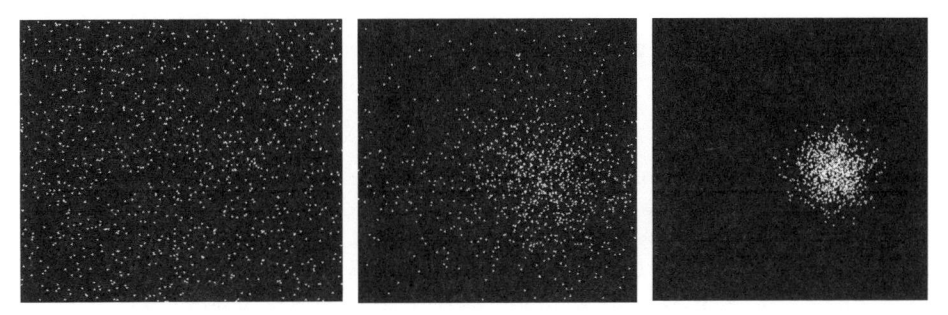

Figure 3.4. An emerging bivariate normal distribution of one thousand voter ideal points arising from random social interactions.

point, rather than further away from this. (We return shortly to discuss people whose views are unmoved by any social interaction.) In line with much of the social psychological evidence about social conformity and personal influence (Baylis 1996; Amorin Neto and Ström 2006), the rationale for this is that social interactions, all other things equal, are more likely to result in the views of those who interact moving closer together rather than further apart. If we iterate such a model continuously, then the pattern that evolves is that the set of ideal points tends to cluster and that, in line with the central limit theorem, their distribution tends to be binomial—approximating a normal distribution in large populations.

Watching such simulations in motion, we clearly observe the evolutionary process. An initial arbitrary scatter of ideal points, for example that in the left panel of Figure 3.4, at first just appears to follow a random walk as a result of the interactions between random pairs of voters. These random interactions also generate small local clusters of ideal points, however. After a period of time, some local cluster of voters emerges at random with sufficient critical mass to act as an attractor for other voters. We can see this beginning to happen in the middle panel of Figure 3.4, which shows a screen shot taken during a simulation run using a NetLogo implementation of our simple model of the evolution of voter ideal points. Random interactions between voters are now more likely to arise with voters in the denser local cluster, and this biases ideal point movement toward the cluster. The clustering process thereby becomes self-reinforcing. The centroid of the evolving distribution of ideal points then "locks in" on the attracting cluster, which is like a grain of sand in an oyster. The precise location of this centroid is entirely arbitrary. The local random cluster of ideal points that eventually emerges as being dense enough to attract other ideal points in the interaction process can arise anywhere at all in the policy space. Indeed, the same initial scatter of ideal points can evolve toward different distributions, given different random social interactions along the way. As the process of social interaction continues, the ideal points evolve to have a bivariate normal distribution, seen in the right panel of Figure 3.4. Strikingly, the emergent normal distribution of voter ideal points is a stochastic steady state—a dynamic equilibrium in which distributions vary periodically around a long-run stationary mean. Although alas this cannot be seen on a static page, *every ideal point in the right panel of Figure 3.4 is in continual motion, but the distribution of the set of ideal points remains the same.*

If we find it substantively unattractive to model social interactions that can result in distributions of voter ideal points with entirely arbitrary centroids, we in effect admit the possibility that these centroids should be substantively "anchored." One such anchor arises if we characterize some subset of voters as "fundamentalists" *whose ideal points do not change as a result of social interaction.* We may further assume that fundamentalists' ideal points are concentrated around some particular spatial location that is substantively important to them. Given the nonevolution of fundamentalists' ideal points, the existence of a very small fundamentalist hardcore can have a big impact on the substantive location of the centroid of any evolved ideal point distribution. Figure 3.5 shows evolved normal distributions of voter ideal points, of which a mere 3 percent were designated fundamentalists, with fixed ideal points drawn from a bivariate normal distribution centered on the origin. The remaining 97 percent were given arbitrary ideal points in a random start and subsequently adapted these on the basis of iterated random interaction. Having "seeded" the voter population with a very small set of inflexible fundamentalists, the centroid of the ideal points of the remaining voters evolves to a position very close to the mean ideal point location of those fundamentalists.

We can generalize this simple model by assuming voters are partitioned into subpopulations. The left panel of Figure 3.6 shows a random start with a uniform random distribution of voter ideal points in two subpopulations, colored white and gray. If we assume random social interactions take place *within but not between subpopulations*, then ideal points *in each subpopulation* evolve under our model of segregated social interaction to have distinctive normally distributed sets of ideal points.[25] The right panel of Figure 3.6 shows a screen shot of quite distinct normal distributions in the white and gray subpopulations, each distribution

---

[25] We by no means need to make such a strong assumption to derive the type of result we report here. Since our main focus in this book is not on endogenous ideal point distributions, however, we use the strong assumption, for didactic reasons, to make our point in the clearest possible terms.

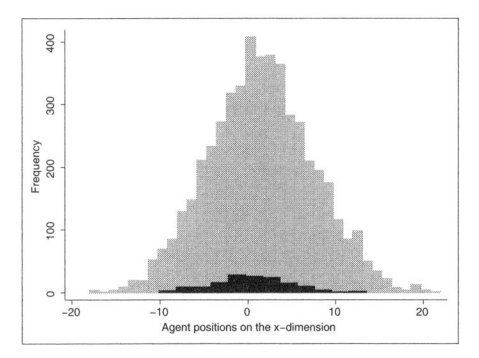

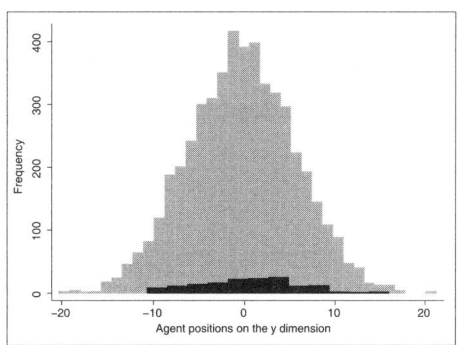

Figure 3.5. Distributions of voter ideal points on x- and y-dimensions, plotted in gray, following repeated random interaction from a random start in which 3 percent of voters were designated fundamentalists, plotted in black, with unmoving ideal points drawn from a bivariate normal distribution with mean (0, 0) and standard deviation 5.0.

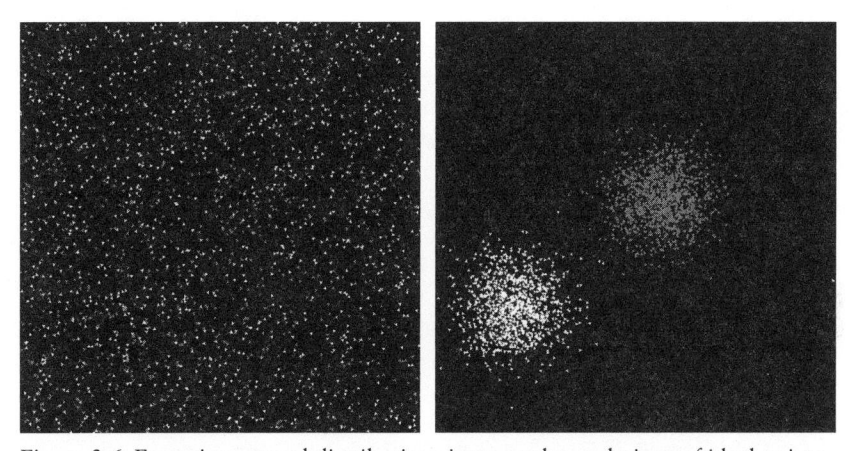

Figure 3.6. Emerging normal distributions in two subpopulations of ideal points.

evolving from the random start in the left panel of the same figure as a result of interaction within but not between subpopulations. Combining subpopulations into an overall voter population, the aggregate distribution of voter ideal points will be asymmetric and may be multimodal. Once again, the emergent ideal point distribution is a stochastic steady state with individual ideal points in continual motion, and subpopulation ideal point centroids are entirely arbitrary.

If we prefer to model subpopulation ideal point centroids as having substantive meaning, rather than being an entirely arbitrary result of

54 • Chapter 3

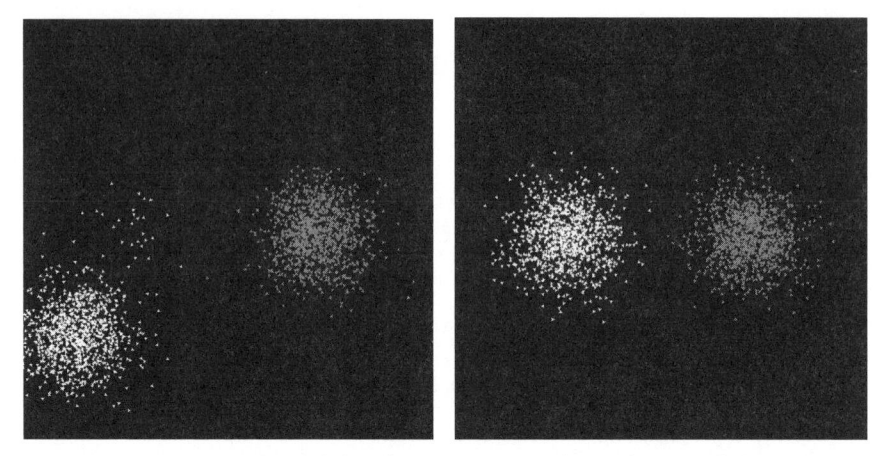

Figure 3.7. Emerging normal distributions in two subpopulations of ideal points, 3 percent of each subpopulation being fundamentalists whose ideal point centroids are at –20 (white) and +20 (gray) on the x-dimension.

random social interactions, then we can again add fundamentalists to our model. Assume that just 3 percent of each subpopulation are fundamentalists who never change their views as a result of social interaction and that the two sets of fundamentalists have distinctive positions on the x-dimension, with no difference between them on the y-dimension. White fundamentalists are on the left and gray fundamentalists are on the right. The left panel of Figure 3.7 shows an interim screen shot at a point in the simulation where the two subpopulations have evolved to have distinctive distributions of ideal points. This is not a stochastic steady state, however, because the unmoving fundamentalists continue to exert a "pull," as a result of the process of random social interaction, on the ideal point distributions of their respective subpopulations.

Thus, in the left panel of Figure 3.7, we can see the white fundamentalists away from the rest of the white subpopulation, with ideal points scattered in the center-right of the space. These never change position and are thus never drawn by social interaction toward the larger distribution of ideal points in "their" subpopulation. Indeed, the reverse happens; *the fundamentalists slowly but surely draw their subpopulation toward them* as they interact with other subpopulation members. The right panel of Figure 3.7 shows the same simulation many thousands of iterations after the interim state shown in the left panel. The evolved normal distributions of subpopulation ideal points are now centered on the centroids of their respective fundamentalists' ideal points. These distributions are now in stochastic steady states. All nonfundamentalists' ideal points are in continual motion, but the aggregate normal distributions of these remain essentially the same, with each subpopulation ideal point centroid centered on the ideal point centroid of its fundamentalists. *While we do not explore this here, we consider this general type of result to have huge implications for the evolution of public opinion in societies in which social interaction is strongly structured by ethnicity.*

This result does not depend on having 3 percent, or indeed any particular positive proportion, of fundamentalists. Any proportion will do, although the process can take a very long time if there are very few fundamentalists. In the end, however, just as a lone donkey can pull an ocean liner, albeit very slowly, by applying a continuous force in the same direction, even a small number of fundamentalists can eventually move a large subpopulation with which they interact. What we have reported here are essentially model sketches and doodles. We do not have the space to specify and investigate a full-scale model of the endogenous evolution of voter deal points, and this would indeed distract us from our core focus on decision making by party leaders. We leave this as a matter for future work, contenting ourselves here with demonstrating that normal distributions of voter ideal points are not the brute force assumptions they might superficially appear to be.

CHAPTER FOUR

Systematically Interrogating Agent-Based Models

WE HAVE SHOWN that dynamic multiparty competition is analytically intractable, both for third party analysts and for the real politicians involved. This led us to specify a computational agent-based model of multiparty competition, and we start computational investigations of this model in chapter 5. Before we can do this, however, we must settle several important matters of experimental design and methodology. *Experimental design* issues concern the particular simulations we specify, and why. *Methodological* issues concern how we estimate quantities of interest from the output of the simulations we specify. We want to be clear before we start any computation that we can rely with confidence on any estimate we derive from the computations we run.

EXPERIMENTS, RUNS, REPETITIONS, AND ITERATIONS

We first fix some terminology. A computational *experiment* is the direct analogue of a laboratory experiment. The objective is to vary one or more input parameters, holding all else constant, in order to investigate the effects of these parameters on outputs of interest. At least one input parameter, x, must vary to specify an experiment. This variation is achieved by observing outcomes of multiple model runs that have varying values of x. A model *run* is an execution of the computational model for a fixed vector of input parameters and is the basic unit of analysis in an experiment. The precise way in which input parameters are varied is a matter of *experimental design*, which we treat in some detail below.

Values of output variables for a particular model run are estimated by analyzing repetitions and iterations of the run. A *repetition* of a run is an execution of a run with a specific random seed. There can be n repetitions of a given run, each repetition using exactly the same input parameter settings but a different random seed.[1] For a given random seed,

---

[1] If a particular random seed is not specified by the analyst, the simulation program will generate one automatically, usually based on an algorithm conditioned on a high-precision reading of the computer clock time when the seed is required. Computers are deterministic machines and cannot generate "true" random numbers, which require an external physical source. True random numbers are available from many sources, for example www.random.org, which uses atmospheric noise to generate true random numbers. The pseudo–random number generators now used by

the pseudo–random number generator used by the program generates a particular sequence of random numbers that are used by the computer program implementing the experiment. Hence, for a model with a stochastic component, all repetitions of a run that have the same random seed generate the same output. Repetitions with different seeds (potentially) generate different outputs. An *iteration* of a repetition is a single execution of the main procedure of the model, excluding the setup procedure. The "length" of a repetition is thus defined as a number, t, of iterations. We examine repetitions, iterations, and estimation of run output variables in more detail below. Before doing so, we start by considering experimental design.

Experimental Design for Simulations of Party Competition

Analytical theorists typically set out to "solve" a model so that they can investigate its "comparative statics," characterizing the effect of changes in model inputs on outputs of substantive interest.[2] When the model is analytically intractable, and thus cannot be solved in a formal sense, it remains possible to conduct computational investigations of how model outputs respond to model inputs, holding all else constant. In these computational investigations, meticulous experimental design takes the place of rigorous formal logic in ensuring that everything has indeed been held constant, so that effect can be traced to cause, and that the full range of valid settings of model inputs has indeed been taken into account. There are two basic approaches to experimental design for such computational work: grid sweeping of parameters and Monte Carlo parameterization of the model in large suites of model runs. Both are designed to investigate the model in a disciplined way, allowing systematic characterization of how changes in model outputs are associated with changes in model inputs.

Grid Sweeping

The most straightforward way to design a computational analogue to analytically derived comparative statics is to engage in the "grid sweep-

---

computers are accepted as random for all practical purposes, however. As we will see, furthermore, the fact that they can be reproduced by using the same random seed is extremely useful for ABM purposes.

[2] Most definitions of comparative statics do not have the qualifier "of substantive interest." However there is often a trade-off between what we might think of as "model-driven" comparative statics that can be tractably analyzed but may be substantively uninteresting and "problem-driven" comparative statics that are of more substantive interest. The term comparative statics may be confusing in relation to a dynamic model, although essentially the same intellectual exercise can be conducted with dynamic models.

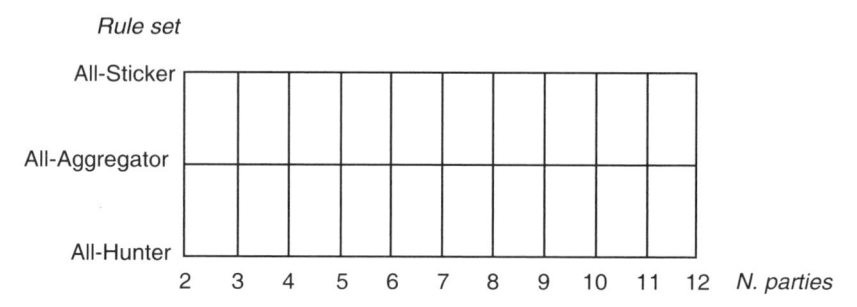

Figure 4.1. Parameter grid for benchmark runs on a symmetric population.

ing" of parameters. This approach is possible when there are very few free model parameters of interest, and especially when there are "naturally" arising values of these parameters. We illustrate this approach in Figure 4.1, which shows the parameter space for an experiment we deploy in chapter 5, designed to benchmark the performance of various decision rules.

Our aim in the benchmarking exercise of chapter 5 is to investigate the effects of different party decision rules on key party system outputs, such as the policy eccentricity of parties and the representativeness of evolved configurations of party positions. We want to set benchmarks that characterize what happens when all party leaders are Stickers, all are Aggregators, or all are Hunters. The vertical dimension in the parameter space shown in Figure 4.1 shows three different rule sets under investigation: all-Sticker, all-Aggregator, and all-Hunter. We also want to estimate key party system outputs for party systems of different sizes. We feel that an empirically realistic calibration of our model to real party systems of interest is to allow the number of parties, N, to take integer values between 2 and 12. Crudely speaking, we feel it is a waste of scarce time and resources to use our model to investigate 255 party systems. The horizontal dimension in the parameter space is therefore specified in terms of 11 evenly spaced integer values that calibrate our model to the class of multiparty systems in which we are substantively interested. The 3 rule sets and 11 party system sizes generate a two-dimensional graph, or grid, that specifies 33 different "natural" parameter vectors for our model—a three-Aggregator system, a five-Hunter system, and so on. This simple baseline model has no other free parameter. Our computational task is to derive robust estimates of model outputs of interest, for each point on the grid of input parameters.

Monte Carlo Parameterization

Computational grid sweeping is a natural analogue to analytical comparative statics when there are few parameters, and when parameter settings are in some sense "natural"—as when there can be one of a few small integer numbers of political parties. Grid sweeping, however, is not scalable. Adding new free parameters to the model, thereby adding dimensions to the model's parameter space, increases the number of grid points at an exponential rate. We investigate 11 "natural" settings of our number-of-parties parameter. Adding another such parameter would give us 121 parameter settings; adding a third would give us 1,331 settings; adding a fourth would give 14,641 settings; and so on. Another problem is that many model parameters are real numbers and do not have "natural" discrete settings.

Figure 4.2 shows two additional dimensions added to the parameter space of our model for another experiment that we investigate in chapter 5 where we generalize our description of distributions of voter ideal points, seeing this as an aggregation of two distinct subpopulations. We investigate the effects of having subpopulations with different relative sizes, n_l/n_r, and different degrees of polarization between the means of their ideal point distributions μ_r ($= -\mu_l$). Both of these new parameters are real numbers without discrete settings that are in any sense "natural." One way forward is to investigate a discrete set of arbitrary, evenly spaced, in-range values of these input parameters. Since we are interested in the effects of n_l/n_r within the range (1.0, 2.0), we could investigate the 11 settings listed on the vertical axis of Figure 4.2. Similarly, we could investigate the 16 settings of mean polarization, μ_r, listed on the horizontal axis. These two additional dimensions of the parameter grid generate 176 grid points. Compounded with the 33 grid points described in Figure 4.1, this gives us an expanded grid with 33 × 176 = 5,808 points in all. Note that there is nothing "natural" about the grid shown in Figure 4.2. There is no particular reason to pick 11 or 16 points in these ranges, rather than 3, or 30, and no reason to suppose that using grid points that are realizations of input parameters to one decimal point are in any sense natural, especially since the scaling of the input parameters is completely arbitrary. Indeed there is no intrinsic reason, especially in relation to a complex nonlinear model, to suppose model outputs arising from the set of on-grid model parameterizations is a fair summary of all possible in-range parameterizations, both on and off grid.

In light of all of this, we do not use grid-sweeping designs for most of our computational work in this book. We use an alternative design that not only is scalable but also removes the need to investigate arbitrarily

n_l/n_r

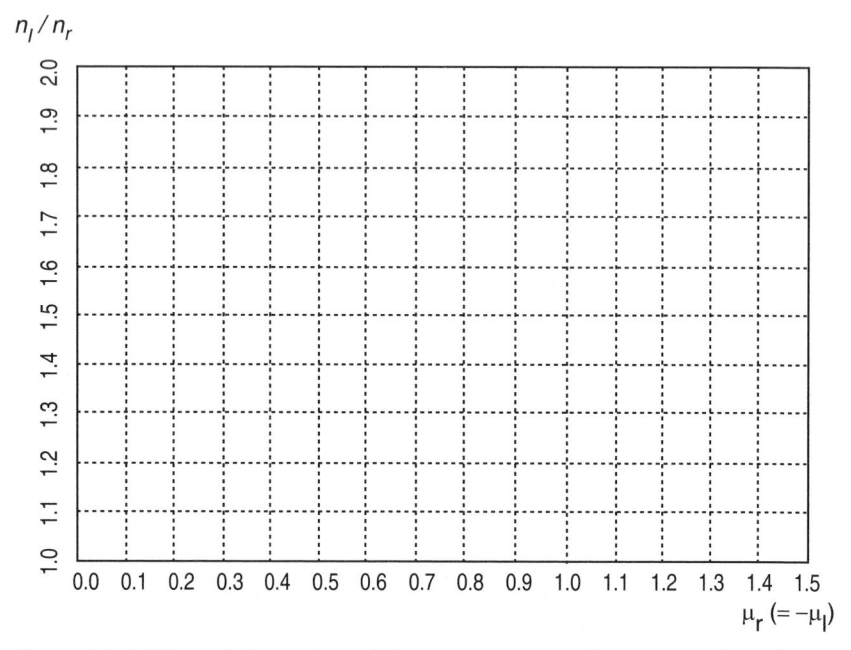

[Figure: graph with y-axis n_l/n_r from 1.0 to 2.0, x-axis $\mu_r (=-\mu_l)$ from 0.0 to 1.5]

Figure 4.2. Additional dimensions of the parameter space for benchmark model runs in which the voting population is an aggregation of two distinct subpopulations.

chosen discrete values of input parameters that are real numbers, as well as giving an equal chance for any in-range point in the parameter space to be investigated. We describe this experimental design as using suites of model runs with "Monte Carlo parameterizations." Quite simply, having specified what we take to be substantively relevant ranges of parameter values, we randomly sample precise parameter values for any given model run from uniform distributions within these ranges. Thus, given the parameter space in Figure 4.2, we parameterize any given model run with a point randomly chosen from this space. For example, in chapter 5 we design suites of one thousand model runs for the all-Sticker, all-Aggregator, and all-Hunter party systems, each model run involving picking a random point in the real parameter space shown in Figure 4.2 and setting the number of parties at a random integer in the range (2, 12).[3]

---

[3] All work with digital computers is ultimately discrete. What we can actually pick using programs for digital computers are floating point, as opposed to real, numbers. In this sense, the precision of the floating point numbers we can pick lays down a very fine finite grid on the parameter space. We follow the almost universal convention here of treating high-precision floating point numbers "as if" they were real numbers.

We estimate output quantities of interest from each model run, and our task is then to characterize the effect of changing one input parameter, holding all others constant.

Precise Estimation of Run Output Variables

Once we have determined the type and number of runs we want to execute, the next task is to estimate model outputs for each run of an experiment. The goal is to calculate a mean estimate for all output variables from all runs. We do this by calculating a mean for each output variable over several repetitions of a run or over several iterations of a single repetition of a run.[4] Before we proceed to a full description of the methods used to estimate means for output variables, however, we must first describe the output "data" we examine and some properties of the processes that generate these data.

Stochastic Processes

For any given repetition of a run, our model of party competition generates, at each iteration, a vector of values for all output variables. For example, the first run of the first benchmark experiment we examine in chapter 5 investigates a two-party all-Sticker party system. These input parameter settings are represented by the top-left corner of the grid in Figure 4.1. At each iteration of each repetition of such a run, our model generates values for the following variables: party1-x-coordinate, party1-y-coordinate, party2-x-coordinate, party2-y-coordinate, party1-vote share, party2-vote share, effective number of parties (ENP), mean policy eccentricity, and party system representativeness. We label this vector of output values as $y_t^{(n)}$, where y refers to the vector of values,

---

[4] Note that, by focusing on the mean of a distribution, much information about the distribution of a variable is ignored, such as the exact form of the distribution, its standard deviation, its skew, and so on. In what follows, besides the standard deviation, which is used below to normalize the standard error of the mean estimate, none of the other nonmean estimates are analyzed. Nor is an attempt made to determine the exact form of the distribution of the output variables. An alternative strategy might be first to determine the distribution of the output variable and then estimate the parameters of that distribution. This would be an excellent procedure to employ if one were analyzing one output variable that followed the same distribution across model executions. In the more general case, however, one is interested in characterizing several output variables, the distributions of which may change depending on the execution of the model. Attempting to determine the distribution for each output variable for each model execution and then estimating the parameters of these distributions would severely complicate our task and hinder comparisons across output variables and model executions.

n refers to the repetition number and t refers to the iteration number associated with this vector.[5] For example, if we execute one repetition of one run for ten iterations, we produce a series of ten vectors. These are $(y_1^{(1)}, y_2^{(1)}, \ldots, y_{10}^{(1)})$, where $y_1^{(1)}$ is the vector of output values from repetition 1 at iteration 1, $y_2^{(1)}$ the vector of values from repetition 1 at iteration 2, and so on. The exact values in these ten vectors depend on the random seed used for the repetition. Another repetition with a different random seed might produce a different series of ten vectors.

For each iteration, t, each vector $y_t^{(n)}$ represents a single realization of a *random vector*, Y_t, where Y_t represents all of the possible realizations of y at iteration t. $y_1^{(1)}$ is the realization of Y_1 associated with repetition 1, and the series $(y_1^{(1)}, y_2^{(1)}, \ldots, y_{10}^{(1)})$ is the realization of $(Y_1, Y_2, \ldots, Y_{10})$ associated with repetition 1. The series $(Y_1, Y_2, \ldots, Y_{10})$ constitutes a *stochastic process*, or a family of random vectors indexed by a time or iteration parameter t. Stochastic processes are distinguished by their *state space*, which describes the range of possible values for the random vectors Y_t; the index set associated with the time or iteration parameter t; and the dependence relations among the random vectors Y_t.[6] A stochastic process in which each of the random vectors of the process takes on some particular value with probability equal to 1 is a *deterministic process*. As we see below, deterministic processes are an important subset for our purposes.

A Markov Chain Representation

As Izquierdo et al. note, with most computational models, an execution of a model run can be represented as a time-homogenous Markov Chain, and it is useful to do this to clarify the dynamics of the run (Izquierdo et al. 2009). All of the runs that we examine in this book can be represented as time-homogenous Markov Chains, which we define presently.[7]

A *Markov process*, X_t, is a stochastic process in which the probability of any particular future behavior of the process depends only on the current state of the process and not on the past behavior or "history" of the process. Such a process is said to have the *Markov property*,

---

[5] The notation used here is based on Hamilton (Hamilton 1994: 43–47).
[6] Taylor and Karlin provide an excellent introduction to stochastic processes (Taylor and Karlin 1998).
[7] The model runs with replicator dynamics, which we examine in chapter 8, are a slight exception to this rule in that the matrix of transition probabilities changes once the replicator dynamics is turned on. As we discuss in chapter 8, we model these runs as being composed of two separate runs, a start-up run and a main run, both of which can be represented as stationary, time-homogeneous Markov Chains.

Methods for Interrogating ABMs • 63

$$\text{Prob }(X_{t+1} = j \mid X_t = i, X_{t-1} = i_{t-1}, \ldots X_0 = i_0) = \text{Prob }(X_{t+1} = j \mid X_t = i)$$

for all iterations t and all states of the process, $i_0, \ldots i_{t-1}, i$, and j. As with any stochastic process, the *state space* of the Markov process is simply the range of possible values the process can take. The *size or dimension of the state space*, s, is the number of possible states in the state space, and the *state space distribution vector*, π_t, is a $(s \cdot 1)$ vector that represents the unconditional probability distribution over the state space at iteration t. Quite simply, each element i of this vector represents the probability that the process will be in state i at iteration t.

A *discrete-time Markov Chain* is a Markov process with a finite state space, and a discrete time or iteration index set, $T = (0, 1, 2, \ldots)$. The *one-step transition probability* that X_{t+1} will be in state j, given that X_t is in state i is defined as:

$$P_{ij}^{t,t+1} = \text{Prob }(X_{t+1} = j \mid X_t = i).$$

A Markov Chain in which all of the transition probabilities are not a function of the time or iteration parameter t, that is, where $P_{ij}^{t,t+1} = P_{ij}$, is a Markov Chain with *stationary transition probabilities* or a *time-homogenous Markov Chain*. Simply put, the transition probability that a time-homogenous process is in state j at time $t+1$, given that it is in state i at time t, is constant over time.

Three components are necessary to define a time-homogenous Markov Chain: (1) an s-dimensional state space; (2) a $(s \cdot s)$ *transition probability matrix*, **P**, which presents all of the one-step transition probabilities of moving from one state to another,

$$P = \begin{matrix} P_{00} & P_{01} & P_{02} & P_{03} & \cdots & P_{0s} \\ P_{10} & P_{11} & P_{12} & P_{13} & \cdots & P_{1s} \\ P_{20} & P_{21} & P_{22} & P_{23} & \cdots & P_{2s} \\ & & \cdots & & & \\ P_{s0} & P_{s1} & P_{s2} & P_{s3} & \cdots & P_{ss} \end{matrix}$$

and (3) a $(s \cdot 1)$ *initial state space distribution vector*, π_0, the ith element of which represents the probability of being in state i at iteration 0.[8] This is simple and intuitive. There is a space of possible states of the world that can be generated by the model, there is a time-invariant matrix of transition probabilities that maps the state at t into the state at t + 1, and there is an initial state for the model.

---

[8] The notation used here is based on Ljungqvist and Sargent (Ljungqvist and Sargent 2004: 29–39).

From these three components, all subsequent *state space distribution vectors*, π_t, evolve by postmultiplying the transpose of the previous vector by the transition probability matrix: $\pi'_{t+1} = \pi'_t \cdot P$. In addition, we can derive any vector π_t based on the initial state space distribution vector, π_0, as follows: $\pi'_t = \pi'_0 \cdot P^n$. In a nutshell, we derive the state of such a model at time t by starting with the initial state and iteratively applying the matrix of transition probabilities that characterizes the model.

A state space distribution vector is *stationary* if it does not change with the passage of time: $\pi_{t+1} = \pi_t$. In most cases, the initial state space distribution vector, π_0, is not stationary. It is often defined to allow for a random start. Several iterations of the process are needed before the state space vector can become stationary. A process is said to be in *equilibrium* or to have reached *steady state* once the state space distribution vector has become stationary. We represent this stationary state space vector as π_∞ where the $\lim_{(t \to \infty)} \pi_t = \pi_\infty$ and where π_∞ solves $\pi_{t+1} = \pi_t$. The period of iterations before a process enters steady state is known as the *transient state*. We discuss the transient state in more detail below, when we treat *burn-in*. For the moment, we focus on steady state properties of a process.

All time-homogenous Markov processes tend toward at least one steady state. Of special interest are those processes that, regardless of the initial starting distribution vector, π_0, tend toward a unique distribution vector, π_∞. Those processes are known as *ergodic*. While a deterministic, time-homogenous Markov process may or may not be ergodic, all stochastic, time-homogenous Markov processes—that is, all Markov processes that contain a random component and have a finite state space—are ergodic (Eisenhardt 1989; Ljungqvist and Sargent 2004). As we see below, this implies that all runs of a model with a random component are ergodic.

We can think of any model run that can be represented by a time-homogenous Markov Chain as being divided into three distinct parts: (1) the run environment, (2) the run Markov process, and (3) the run output variables. The *run environment* consists of both the fixed computation rules of the model and the exogenously fixed settings of the run input parameters. The run environment determines the run Markov process. The *run Markov process* is a representation of the run dynamics using a Markov process. Like all Markov processes, it is composed of a state space, a transition matrix, and an initial state space vector. Finally, the *run output variables* are derived from the state of the Markov process.

In most cases, several Markov representations are possible. One must choose a vector of variables, X_t, to construct the Markov state space, such that the following two conditions are met. First, given the fixed run environment, one must be able to derive all of the output variables, Y_t, from a given value of the vector of state space variables, $Y_t = f(X_t)$. Second, the vector of state space variables, X_t, must satisfy the Markov property. One may of course define a Markov state space using a large set of variables.

It is often more fruitful, however, to choose only those variables that are required in order to meet the two necessary conditions.

For example, with the two-party, all-Sticker run, the environment would consist of the computational model in which, among other things, all three party decision rules, Sticker, Aggregator, and Hunter, have been specified, as well as the input parameters for the run, the distribution of voter ideal points, the number of competing parties, and the party decision rule being employed. This environment determines the run Markov process. With a two-party, all-Sticker run, it is sufficient to represent the process of the run with four variables: the x-coordinate of the first party, the y-coordinate of the first party, the x-coordinate of the second party, and the y-coordinate of the second party. The state space of the run would be all of the possible permutations of these four variables.[9]

Moreover, this combination of four variables satisfies the necessary conditions for a Markov process. First, given the exogenous run environment, all of the output variables can be calculated from these four state space variables. The position of each of the parties is simply the x-coordinate and y-coordinate of the parties. Each party's vote share is determined from the party positions and the specified distribution of voter ideal points. The same holds true for the aggregate measures. ENP, mean eccentricity, and representativeness can be derived from the party positions, the derived vote shares, and the run environment. Second, the vector of party positions satisfies the Markov property: the future behavior of the vector of state space variables depends only on the current state of the vector. This is because the Sticker rule dictates that the party should not change position. When all parties use this rule, none of the parties changes position. Hence the probability of all of the positions of all of the parties and, by extension, the state of the process at iteration t is conditional only on the positions of the parties or the state of the process at iteration t-1. In this case, as Stickers do not move, the probability is in fact equal to 1 that the positions will be the same as the positions in the previous iteration. Finally, the probability that some particular configuration of party positions occurs depends on the probabilities associated with the initial state space distribution vector, π_0, which is a function of the computation rules used to set up the model run and the run input parameters selected.

Run Burn-In: Theoretical Concepts

The Markov Chain representation of the model helps us understand the dynamics of each model run. With the exception of the all-Sticker runs,

---

[9] As was mentioned above, all output variables investigated are discrete, albeit to a very high level of precision, and the state space, though large, is finite.

a run repetition does not normally start out in steady state. Several iterations of a repetition are typically needed for the repetition to reach steady state. Recall that the run output variables, Y_t, are all functions of the state space variables, X_t. Once the vector of state space variables is within the steady state, so too will be the vector of output variables. The ultimate goal is to calculate mean values for each output variable, Y_t, in steady state. Methodologically, this means that none of the values of the output variables obtained during the transient state are of interest. We cannot use these to estimate mean values in steady state. They are therefore discarded as model *burn-in*, iterations of the run repetition before the process has reached steady state. It is, furthermore, important to distinguish burn-in for deterministic processes that converge on a single state from burn-in for stochastic processes that converge on a distribution of states.

Burn-in for a deterministic process that converges on a single state is straightforward. Recall that a deterministic process is a stochastic process in which each of the random vectors of the process takes on a particular value with probability equal to 1. Deterministic processes that converge on a single state do not contain a random component and tend toward a single state in the state space of the process, as opposed to a distribution over possible states in the state space. As we see below, such deterministic processes can tend toward different states depending on initial conditions. The point for now is that a deterministic process that converge on a single state has "*burnt in*," that is, has reached steady state, once all of the values of the state space variables no longer change. Thus, the burn-in procedure for deterministic run processes that converge on a single state is to continue to execute a run repetition until all of the values for the state space variables, and by extension all of the values for the output variables, no longer change. Once this occurs, we can record the values for all of the output variables as representative of the given run repetition.

Burn-in for a stochastic run process is more complicated. Theoretically, it is the same as for a deterministic process that converges on a single state. In practice, since a stochastic process tends to a distribution over several states rather than a single state, it is less easy empirically to determine when a process has entered steady state. There are two methods that we can employ. The choice of method depends on whether or not a time average of the output variables is an unbiased estimate of the true mean. Before we develop these two methods in detail, we must therefore discuss time averages.

Mean Estimation: Ensemble Averages and Time Averages

Assuming for the moment we have established that a process has burnt in, the next step is to calculate mean estimates for each of the output variables, Y_t, in steady state. We define $\mu_t^{(n)}$ as the expected value of Y_t for repetition n at iteration t. As we saw above, all stochastic processes in steady state are stationary. Hence, by the definition of stationarity, in steady state, for all repetitions n, the expected value of Y_t at time t is equal to the expected value of Y_t at time $t+1$, at time $t+2$, and so on: $\mu_t^{(n)} = \mu_{t+1}^{(n)} = \mu_{t+2}^{(n)}$, and so on. We can thus dispense with the time subscript and define $\mu^{(n)}$ as the expected value of Y_t for repetition n over all iterations t. With these definitions in hand, it is useful to represent the process of any output variable, Y_t, in steady state as the sum of $\mu^{(n)}$ and an iteration-specific serially correlated disturbance term, ε_t:

$$Y_t = \mu^{(n)} + \varepsilon_t.$$

We will have more to say below about the serially correlated nature of the disturbance term. For now, we note that repetition n is only one of many possible repetitions of a run. We can easily imagine that other repetitions of a run might be associated with different values for $\mu^{(n)}$. Hence, we model the realized $\mu^{(n)}$ for a given repetition as a random variable, drawn from a distribution with mean μ and standard deviation σ_μ, where μ represents the expected value of Y_t over all repetitions and all iterations.

Given stationarity, it is useful to remember that μ is the expected value of Y_t *at any iteration of the process in steady state*. For example, assume that a process is burnt in after 250 iterations. The goal is to answer the question, "What is the expected value of Y_t in steady state?" or, analogously, "What is the expected value of Y_t at iteration 251, iteration 252, and so on?" The most natural way to answer this question, that is, to estimate μ, is (1) to execute several repetitions of a run up until a prespecified iteration t within the steady state and then (2) to take the average of the realized values, $y_t^{(n)}$ of the output variable Y_t for each repetition at iteration t. This average is known as the *ensemble average* of Y_t at iteration t,

$$\text{Ensemble Average}_t \text{ of } Y_t \equiv \sum_{n=1}^{N} y_t^{(n)} / N$$

where N is the total number of repetitions of a run. In the limit, as the total number of repetitions approaches infinity, the ensemble average converges on μ:

$$\mu = \text{plim} \sum_{n=1}^{N} y_t^{(n)} / N$$

If, in addition to being stationary, a process is also ergodic, there is another method for estimating μ. This method entails using data from just one repetition of a run. It is thus the main method used in time series analysis, in which one has access to only one realization of a process. If a process is both stationary and ergodic, then it tends to a unique stationary distribution regardless of its initial starting distribution. This means that the expected value of Y_t for *any* given repetition, $\mu^{(n)}$, equals μ, the expected value of Y_t for *all* repetitions. With such a process one can also estimate μ using a *time average*—the average over all of the realized $y_t^{(n)}$ from a single repetition of the process,

$$\text{Time Average}^{(n)} \text{ of } Y_t \equiv \sum_{t=1}^{T} y_t^{(n)} / T$$

where T is the total number of iterations of a repetition of a run. In the limit, as the total number of iterations approaches infinity, the time average converges on the expected value of Y_t for repetition n over all iterations, $\mu^{(n)}$. Given ergodicity, this is also equal to μ:

$$\mu = \text{plim} \sum_{t=1}^{T} y_t^{(n)} / T$$

As we see below, it is often advantageous to estimate μ with a time average rather than an ensemble average.

Mapping the Steady-State Distribution, and the R-hat Statistic

Whenever we estimate μ, with either an ensemble average or a time average, we try to gather a *representative sample* of observations. This sample should include values derived from all states within the steady state of the process with non-negligible probability of occurring, and which have been sampled in rough proportion to the steady-state state space vector, π_∞. Colloquially, we say that the representative sample has "mapped out" the steady-state distribution, π_∞.

When we employ an ensemble average, we take the average over several repetitions of the output variable realized at a particular iteration. Given that the different random seeds used by the random number generator for each repetition generate sequences of random numbers that are independent and identically distributed (IID) at any given iteration, the resultant realized values of the output variables per repetition at a particular iteration are also IID. Hence, if we were to create a sample of twenty-five repetitions, we would expect that observed values would be randomly dispersed around the true mean of the output variable in rough proportion to the steady-state distribution vector, π_∞. As we see below when we discuss sample size determination, more repetitions, which lead

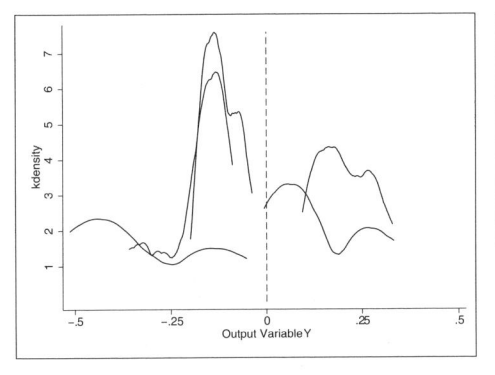

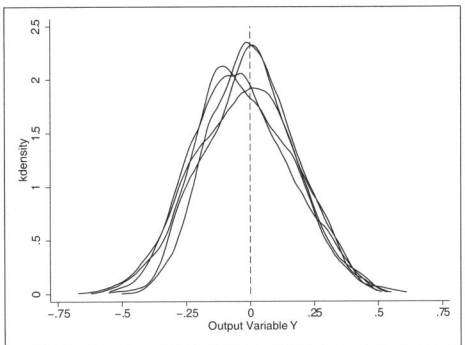

Figure 4.3. Kdensity plots with twenty-five (left panel) and five thousand (right panel) iterations for five different repetitions for a hypothetical variable with mean zero.

to more observations, would obviously be better than fewer repetitions in terms of the precision of the mean estimate. The point for the moment is that the ensemble average estimate, even when calculated with a small sample of observations, would still be roughly representative of μ.

The same normally cannot be said of the time average estimate. When we employ a time average, we take the average over realized values for several iterations of a single repetition. These observations are not IID. Rather, they are serially correlated, with above average values for an output variable following above average values and below average values following below average values. Depending on the degree of autocorrelation of the process, it may take some time for the process to map out roughly the entire steady-state distribution vector, π_∞. For example, in Figure 4.3, we plot output from five separate repetitions of a hypothetical ergodic run process with an output variable that we happen to know analytically has a mean of zero. The left panel presents the distribution of states that the process has mapped out after twenty-five iterations for each of the five repetitions, while the right panel presents the same distributions mapped out after five thousand iterations. As we can see from the left panel, if we calculate a time average of the output variable using any one of the five repetitions involving just twenty-five iterations, we get a mean estimate of y that is not representative of its true mean value. None of these repetitions has mapped out most of the steady-state states that occur with non-negligible probability. By contrast, a time average calculated with values from five thousand iterations is much more representative of the true value μ. As we see from the right panel, each of the repetitions has visited most of the steady-state states with non-negligible probability of occurring, and has thereby mapped out the steady-state distribution.

When we use a time average, therefore, we must be extra careful to ensure that enough observations have been gathered so that the process has had a chance to map out the steady-state distribution, π_∞. Fortunately, there is a statistic that we can use to make this determination. This is the "potential scale reduction factor" or "R-hat" statistic, proposed by Gelman and Rubin and generalized by Brooks and Gelman (Brooks and Gelman 1998; Gelman and Rubin 1992). This estimates the factor by which the scale of the current distribution of values arising from the iterations executed so far could be reduced if a run repetition were continued indefinitely. In the limit, R-hat tends to 1. For values of R-hat close to 1, the scale of the distribution cannot be reduced much further; the output variable will oscillate within the range defined by its mean and standard deviation. The R-hat statistic is calculated by executing several run repetitions and, for a given number of iterations, comparing between-repetition variance to total within-repetition variance from all repetitions, a technique similar to an analysis of variance test. The R-hat statistic approaches 1 as between-repetition variance becomes less important and is eventually completely dominated by within-repetition variance. Whenever we use a time average, we want to make sure that the distribution of obtained values has approximately mapped out the steady-state distribution. Using conventional criteria, we make this judgment when the R-hat test statistic is less than 1.05.

The reason for our focus on the time average is that it is often much more efficient to estimate μ by using a time average over one single long repetition than using an ensemble average over many short repetitions. This is because we can use only observations from any repetition after this has burnt in, and burning in one long repetition uses far less computing resources than burning in many short repetitions. As we see below when we discuss sample size, it will often be necessary to execute 1,000 repetitions to estimate μ with an ensemble average. All 1,000 of these repetitions must be burnt in. For example, if we determine that a run process is burnt in after 250 iterations, we will need to execute all 1,000 repetitions for at least 251 iterations. As the burnt-in observations must be deleted, that would entail deleting 250,000 observations. If, instead, we use a time average to estimate μ, we need delete only 250 observations. We will therefore want to use the time average whenever we can. As we see in the next section, however, this is not always possible.

Three Types of Run Process, Implying Three Estimation Methodologies

With the concepts of ensemble average and time average in hand, we can now examine the types of run process we encounter in this book and the methods we employ to estimate μ for each of these.

NONERGODIC DETERMINISTIC PROCESSES THAT CONVERGE ON A SINGLE STATE

By definition, all time-homogenous Markov processes tend toward a stationary state space distribution vector, or steady state. Since all of the processes we examine are time-homogenous Markov processes, they are all stationary. Within the group of *deterministic* time-homogenous Markov processes, we do however need to make two distinctions. First, not all deterministic processes are ergodic. Unlike general stochastic processes, deterministic processes do not contain a random component; there is therefore no guarantee they will converge on a unique stationary distribution, π_∞. Second, not all deterministic processes—ergodic or not ergodic—tend toward a single steady-state state. Some deterministic processes converge on a "steady state" in which the process oscillates among two or more states. In this book, all of the *deterministic* processes that we examine both are nonergodic and converge on a single state.

A nonergodic deterministic process that converges on a single state may converge on a different single state, depending on the random seed used in the simulation. In order to estimate μ for such processes, therefore, we must execute several repetitions of the same run. Each run repetition involves a different random seed, resulting in a different initial state space vector, π_0, and possibly a different steady-state vector, π_∞. Our procedure is to execute several repetitions until the process has reached steady state, collect final values for each of the output variables for the particular run repetition, and finally calculate an ensemble average of all of the collected values as an estimate of μ for each output variable of the run.

STOCHASTIC PROCESSES FOR WHICH A TIME AVERAGE PROVIDES A REPRESENTATIVE ESTIMATE OF μ

Given the presence of a random component, all stationary nondeterministic stochastic processes are also ergodic. The random component ensures that it is possible for a process to transition from one state to any other state within the state space of the process. The question that concerns us with a stochastic process is whether or not we can use a time average to calculate a representative estimate of μ. This in turn depends on three main factors: (1) how many post-burn-in iterations we collect, (2) the dimension or size of the state space of the process, and (3) the ease with which the process transitions from one state to any other state, in other words how large are the off-diagonal elements of the Markov transition probability matrix. For a given number of post-burn-in iterations collected, a time average may not be a representative estimate of μ if either the size of the state space is too large or the off-diagonal transition probabilities are too low. Of course, if we could collect an infinite sample of post-burn-in iterations, the size of the state space or the values of the off-diagonal transition probabilities would not be a problem. However, given any finite computational budget, we divide the stochastic processes we examine in this book into two categories based on whether or not, for a specified total number of post-burn-in iterations set by the budget constraint, a time average provides a representative estimate of μ.

Our procedure for stochastic processes for which a time average *does* provide a representative estimate of μ is as follows. We execute a single repetition, collect observations for each post-burn-in iteration, and calculate a time average of the collected values. As we see below, using the time average will entail that we first confirm that enough iterations have been executed so that the steady-state distribution vector has been mapped out.

STOCHASTIC PROCESSES FOR WHICH A TIME AVERAGE DOES NOT
PROVIDE A REPRESENTATIVE ESTIMATE OF μ

The last of our three run processes are stochastic processes for which a time average does not provide a representative estimate of μ. These processes, though ergodic, do not, over the course of a run of a prespecified length set by the budget constraint, pass through a representative sample of states that have a non-negligible probability of occurring. Instead, perhaps due to a large state space or low off-diagonal transition probabilities, the set of observed values for the output variables is confined to one part of the overall distribution.

The procedure we use to estimate μ in these cases is similar to the procedure we use with nonergodic deterministic processes that converge on a single state. We execute several repetitions until each repetition has reached steady state, collect final representative values for each of the output variables for the particular run repetition, and finally calculate an ensemble average of all of the collected values as an estimate of μ for each output variable of the run.

Empirical Burn-In

One major part of our empirical strategy remains to be specified. This concerns how to determine run burn-in empirically. As with mean estimation, establishing model burn-in depends on which of the three processes we are investigating.

With *nonergodic deterministic processes that converge on a single state*, the procedure is simple. As we mentioned above, deterministic processes do not contain a random component and tend toward a single state in the state space of the process. A nonergodic deterministic process that converges on a single state is considered burnt in once all of the values of the state space variables of the run repetition no longer change. Crudely put, it is burnt in when plots of all state space variables are flatlining.

Determining burn-in with stochastic processes is less clear-cut. We differentiate again between stochastic processes for which a time average provides a representative estimate of μ and those for which a time average does not provide such a representative estimate. With *stochastic processes for which a time average provides a representative estimate of μ*, our procedure for determining burn-in proceeds in four steps. First, we specify a Markov Chain representation of the run process under study. We specify the vector of state space variables and one or more variables that can be used to summarize the vector of state space variables. We refer to these as *summary variables*. Second, we identify those runs of an experiment which, based on their parameter settings, would require the most iterations to burn in. We focus on the extreme cases because we want to select a burn-in period that we use for all of the runs of the experiment. By using the extreme cases to determine burn-in, we ensure that all runs of the experiment will have burnt in after the selected period of iterations.

Third, for the runs selected in the previous step, we execute several test repetitions. Our goal is to estimate a time average for each of these repetitions. In order to calculate the time average accurately, we need to delete some of the initial observations as burn-in. However, burn-in is what we are trying to estimate. To get around this obstacle, we follow a procedure recommended by Gelman and Rubin (1992) and Brooks and Gelman (1998). Namely, with our test repetitions, we use only the "second halves" of the executed iterations. For example, if we execute a run repetition for one thousand iterations, we discard the first five hundred iterations and use only the second five hundred iterations to calculate the R-hat statistic and to estimate μ. We use this procedure to obtain representative estimates of μ.[10]

Fourth and last, with μ so estimated, we proceed to determine burn-in. We consider that a particular test repetition has burnt in after an iteration when the summary variables are within one standard deviation of μ for the variables. After having examined all of our test repetitions, we take the maximum burn-in value from the test repetitions and designate that number of iterations as the burn-in number of iterations for all runs of the experiment.

---

[10] The "second-halves" procedure recommended by Gelman and Rubin (1992) and Brooks and Gelman (1998) is a *sufficient* condition for burn-in. If the second halves have converged then the first halves must have burnt in. It is not a *necessary* condition, and in many instances is not efficient. It can waste many iterations of a run repetition. For example, below when we examine an experiment in which all parties employ the "Hunter" rule, we find that only fifty to one hundred iterations need be deleted due to burn-in, while using the second-halves procedure would require deleting one thousand iterations per repetition as burn-in.

74 • Chapter 4

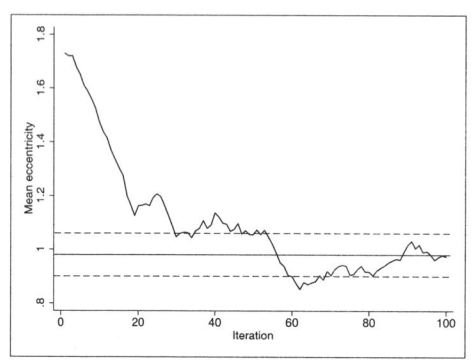

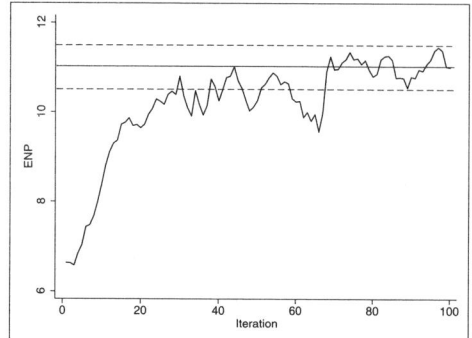

Figure 4.4. Burn-in for mean eccentricity and ENP, stochastic processes for which a time average provides a representative estimate of μ.

For example, when we run an experiment in which all parties employ the "Hunter" rule in chapter 5, we use mean party eccentricity and ENP as summary variables for the state space variables. Figure 4.4 plots both of these by iterations from one repetition of the most extreme run with the number of parties set at twelve. The mean (solid line) and standard deviation (dashed lines) of both variables were calculated using the second halves from two thousand iterations, the number required so that the R-hat statistics would be less than 1.05 for both mean eccentricity and ENP. As we see from the left panel of Figure 4.4, both mean party eccentricity and ENP moved to within one standard deviation of its mean after about seventy iterations. As we discuss in chapter 5, to err on the side of caution, we set burn-in at one hundred iterations for all of the all-Hunter experiment runs.

With *stochastic processes for which a time average does not provide a representative estimate of μ*, we continue to follow the first two steps of the previous procedure. Namely, we also create a Markov Chain representation of the run process and determine summary variables, and we examine those runs that we expect will take the longest to burn in. The difference here is that because either the state space is too large or the off-diagonal transition probabilities are too low, we are unable to map out completely the steady state probability distribution of the process with a single repetition and hence cannot use a time average as a representative estimate of μ with a relatively small number of iterations. Therefore, we must find another, less precise method for determining burn-in. The method we employ is a graphical method. We execute each of our test repetitions for many iterations and examine plots of each of our summary

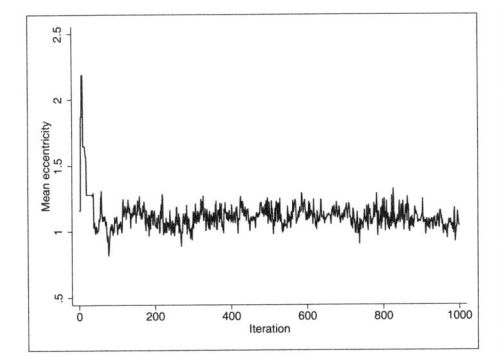

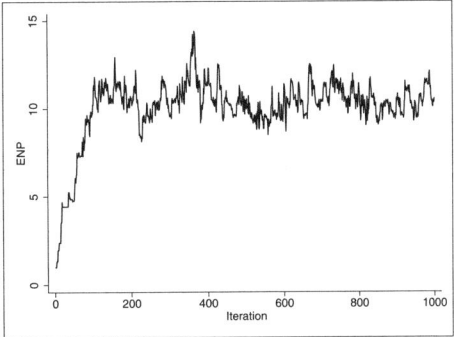

Figure 4.5. Burn-in for mean eccentricity and ENP, stochastic processes for which a time average does not provide a representative estimate of μ.

variables by iteration in order to determine when the process appears to have entered the steady state.

For example, the model we develop in chapter 7 generates a party system in which the number and identity of surviving parties, and the decision rules they use, are all endogenous. This generates a larger state space and may lead to lower off-diagonal transition probabilities. Figure 4.5 plots both of our summery variables, by iteration, from one repetition of the most extreme run.[11] Visual inspection of the plots reveals that this test repetition appears to have reached the steady state by around the two hundredth iteration.

Having examined all of our test repetitions, we take the maximum burn-in value from the test repetitions and designate that number of iterations as the burn-in number of iterations for all runs of the experiment.

Box 4.1 provides a summary of the three estimation strategies discussed in this and the previous subsection.

Run Sample Size

Having specified a method for determining burn-in and estimating μ, the next methodological decision is to determine how many observations per run should be gathered (1) to ensure that the mean estimate is representative of μ and (2) to obtain a satisfactory level of precision in this estimate.

We have already spoken about the possibility that an estimate may not be representative. It is possible that, due to a small sample size, the

---

[11] That is, a run in which the survival threshold τ, defined in chapter 6, is set at 0.05.

Box 4.1
Estimation Strategies

Non-ergodic deterministic processes that converge on a single state	
Burn-in:	Once the deterministic steady state has been reached
Iterations:	1
Repetitions:	More than 1
Mean estimate:	Ensemble average

Stochastic processes for which a time average provides a representative estimate of µ	
Burn-in:	The maximum number of iterations from several test repetitions, after which the run process has moved within one standard deviation of µ for each of the state-space summary variables of the process
Iterations:	More than 1
Repetitions:	1
Mean estimate:	Time average

Stochastic processes for which a time average does not provide a representative estimate of µ	
Burn-in:	The maximum number of iterations from several test repetitions, after which the run process appears to have entered steady state based on an examination of plots of the state-space summary variables of the process by iteration
Iterations:	1
Repetitions:	More than 1
Mean estimate:	Ensemble average

calculated mean estimate might be very different from the true mean μ. We focus now on *precision*, by which we simply mean the standard error of the estimate. The smaller the standard error around the mean estimate, the more precise this estimate is.

Although the method used to gather observations differs, depending on whether we employ a time average or an ensemble average, we may assume, as we shortly note, that all gathered observations are IID, and hence we may use the standard formula to calculate the standard error of the mean estimate. When we use an ensemble average, we take the average over several repetitions of the output variable realized at a particular iteration. Given that the different random seeds used by the random number generator for each repetition generate sequences of random numbers that are IID at any given iteration, the resultant realized values of the output variables per repetition at a particular iteration are also IID.

When we employ a time average, we take the average over realized values for several iterations of a single repetition. These observations are not IID. Rather, as we saw above, they are serially correlated, with above average values following above average values and below average values following below average values. Nevertheless, as Gelman et al. (2004) note, if we have mapped out the steady-state distribution, that is, if the R-hat statistic is less than 1.05, then we have collected a representative sample of observations. We do not need to worry about *how* the observations were obtained. Once we have mapped out the distribution, we can treat the observations of the sample as IID observations.

Hence, regardless of whether we employ a time average or an ensemble average to estimate μ, the formula for the standard error of the mean estimate is simply the standard deviation of the output variable divided by the square root of the number of observations, N, used to calculate the mean:

Standard Error of the Mean Estimate = Standard Deviation $(Y_t) / \sqrt{N}$.

With either the ensemble average or time average method, the goal is the same. We are interested in collecting enough observations to generate a representative sample and to increase precision to as high a level as we can get it, within the constraints set by our computational budget. The more observations we gather the more representative the sample will be and the more precise our estimate of μ. In the limit, as the sample size tends to infinity, we gather a perfectly representative sample and the standard error of the estimate will tend to zero, leading to a perfectly precise and representative estimate of μ. Given that the standard error decreases as a function of the square root of the sample size, however, we must increase the number of observations by a factor of four, for example, to reduce the standard error by a factor of two. There are thus diminishing marginal returns, in terms of precision, to increasing the sample size.

In fact, we face a problem closely analogous to the problem of choosing the "right" number of individuals to interview in a random sample survey. This is also a problem of budgeting finite research resources, subject to acceptable standards of statistical precision. Without any resource constraint we would execute all repetitions to infinity or execute an infinite number of repetitions, just as we would interview an infinite number of survey respondents. In the real world of constrained research resources, however, we always have a budget. We might decide that a well-designed random sample of one thousand survey respondents is "large enough" to estimate a single simple quantity of interest—the proportion of voters who think the president of the United States is doing a good job, for example. On the other hand, if we were lucky enough to have sufficient resources to interview fifty thousand individuals, given the diminishing returns to increasing the sample size, we might decide that conducting ten quite different five-thousand-respondent surveys was a much better use of our fixed survey budget than conducting a single fifty-thousand-respondent survey. This would be a statistically informed budgetary decision that the marginal level of extra precision derived from the larger survey was not "worth" the opportunity cost of forgoing nine other smaller surveys on matters of great interest to us—in essence that we would "waste" huge survey resources in search of the relatively small marginal increases in precision that the statistics of random samples tell us we would get.

We execute an analogous procedure in deciding how many repetitions and iterations to execute with a run. For each of our main output variables, we employ five diagnostic checks to ensure that we have collected "enough" observations. Some checks are more focused on controlling for the representativeness of the estimate, while others are more focused on precision. We list the checks in order of the extent to which they control for the representativeness of the estimate.

MAPPING (TIME AVERAGES)

This test focuses on the representativeness of the sample. As we saw above, whenever we employ a time average to estimate μ, we must first check that we have gathered enough iterations so that most of the steady-state states with non-negligible probability of occurring have indeed occurred and have occurred with the frequency given by the steady-state state space vector, π_∞. This will ensure that the calculated time average will be a representative estimate of μ. The diagnostic check we employ is the R-hat statistic described above. Specifically, we decide that enough iterations have been collected when the R-hat statistics for all output variables are at or below 1.05. This ensures that the entire steady-state state space distribution has been "mapped out" and the estimate of μ is representative.

CONVERGENCE ON KNOWN VALUES

In some cases we have an analytical expectation that one or more of our output variables will take on a particular value for a given run or set of runs. For example, with all the all-Sticker runs that we examine in chapter 5, we have an analytical expectation that the expected value of mean party eccentricity is 1.5. Given this knowledge, we want our mean estimate for mean party eccentricity to be statistically indistinguishable from this known value.

The diagnostic check that we use is a simple F-test that the calculated mean is not statistically different from the analytically known value. We examine the p-value of this test, where the p-value reports the probability of obtaining the mean estimate (and the value for the F-test statistic) given that the true mean is the known analytical value. To control for representativeness, we require that the p-value from the F-test from all mean calculations be greater than at least .10. In this way, we ensure that none of the mean estimates is statistically different from the analytically known quantity. Furthermore, if we want to ensure that the mean estimate is not only not statistically different from μ but also very close to μ, we could specify a higher threshold p-value for the F-test. For example, we could require that we collect enough observations, from either iterations or repetitions, that the probability of obtaining the mean estimate we obtain, given that μ is the true value, is greater than 0.90. We are thus free to decide on the level of representativeness that we would like to achieve.

POWER DIFFERENT FROM ZERO

In most instances, we expect that the true value of μ for most output variables is different from zero. When this is the case, we want to be sure that we have gathered enough observations so that a t-test typically rejects the null hypothesis of a zero effect. The probability of rejecting the null hypothesis of a statistical test, when the alternative hypothesis is true, is known as the *power* of the test. For a difference-from-zero t-test, the power of the test depends on the effect size, or the magnitude of μ in the present analysis; the significance level of the test; and the sample size. Hence, for our third diagnostic check, we perform a post hoc or post-estimation power analysis. We use the standard formula for calculating power with IID observations. Following usual practice, we fix the significance level at .05 for all variables. The effect size is simply the ensemble average or time average estimate of μ. We consider that we have collected enough observations when the power of the t-test is at least 80 percent or 0.80 for all output variables that we expect to be different from zero.

POWER DIFFERENT FROM PREVIOUS (GRID SWEEP)

Whenever we employ an experimental design in which we sweep an input variable along a grid, there is another check for statistical significance that we employ. With most cases, we have the expectation that μ will be different for different settings of the input parameter—that the input parameter will have an effect. In these cases, we would like, to the extent possible, the mean estimate for each output variable for one parameter setting to be statistically different from the mean estimate for adjacent parameter settings on the grid. To check this, we examine the power of a two-sample difference-in-means t-test. As before, we fix the significance level at .05 for all variables. We compare the mean estimate calculated for one setting of the input parameter with the mean estimate for the previous setting on the grid. We consider that we have collected enough observations when the power of the two-sample difference-in-means t-test is at least 0.80 for all output variables of interest and for all input settings, excluding the first setting, along the grid.

RELATIVE PRECISION: THE STANDARD ERROR TO STANDARD DEVIATION RATIO

Up to this point, to the extent we discussed precision, we described checks that estimates of each output variable of interest meet certain minimum conditions of precision. We have not discussed comparing precision across output variables within a single run, nor have we discussed comparing precision of a single output variable across more than two runs. To the extent possible, we would like to ensure that the level of precision we demand is roughly equivalent across variables and across runs.

In order to compare standard errors across variables and across runs, we must first normalize the standard errors to create a unit-less measure, such as a percentage. We do this by dividing the standard error for each variable by its standard deviation to create the standard-error-to-standard-deviation *ratio* measure. For example, if we fix the ratio at around 3 percent, we continue to gather observations for all variables and all runs until the standard error of the mean estimate is within 3 percent of its standard deviation for each variable. In so doing, we demand a level of precision from each variable that is appropriate given the observed variation of that variable. For instance, two variables could have the same mean but vastly different standard deviations: variable A might have a standard deviation of 1 unit while variable B might have a standard deviation of 4 units. If we impose a ratio of 3 percent, we would require that we gather enough observations so that the standard error is .03 for variable A and .12 for variable B.[12]

In practice, as we have seen, whether we use a time average or an ensemble average as an estimate of μ, we may assume that sample observations are IID if we have mapped out the distribution. Given that the formula for the standard error with IID observations is just the standard deviation divided by the square root of the number of observations used

---

[12] An alternative relative measure of precision proposed by scholars working in operations research is essentially to divide the standard error of each output variable by its mean estimate. This measure is known as gamma (Law and Kelton 2000). Unfortunately, it has several problems. First, and most important, it becomes unusable with variables with mean estimates close to zero. For those variables, the calculated gamma approaches infinity, regardless of the size of the standard error, and thus it cannot be used as a means of comparison. Second, for variables with similar variation, that is, similar standard deviations, but different means, the gamma measure requires greater relative precision for those variables with lower means than for those with higher means.

to estimate the variable, we can ensure that all output variables from all runs are estimated to the same level of precision simply by using the same number of observations with each mean calculation.

Box 4.2 summarizes the diagnostic checks we have presented, along with the appropriate decision statistic.

Box 4.2
Sample Size

Mapping (time averages)	When using a time average to estimate μ, have enough iterations been realized so that most of the steady-state states with non-negligible proability of occurring have indeed occurred and have occurred with the frequency given by the steady state state space vector, $\pi\infty$? That is, is the R-hat statistic less than 1.05?
Convergence	For those output variables for which we have sound analytical expectations, have enough observations been gathered (either repetitions or iterations) so that the mean estimates are not statistically different from the analytically known values? That is, is the p-value from an F-test comparing the calculated mean to the known value greater than .10?
Power zero	For output variables that a priori we do not expect to be zero or close to zero, have enough observtions been realized (either repetitions or iterations) so that the power of a t-test that the value is statistically different from zero is greater than .80?
Power difference (grid sweeps)	When performing grid sweeps, for a given level of fineness of the interval between the parameter settings of the parameter that is being swept, have enough observations been realized (either repetitions or iterations) so that the power of a t-test that two sample means from adjacent input parameter settings are different from each other is greater than .80?
SE/SD ratio	To ensure that all output variables have been estimated with roughly the same level of precision, have enough observations been realized (either reetitions or iterations) so that the ratio of the standard error of the mean estimate to the standard deviation is roughly the same for all runs and all output variables?

Conclusions

Our aim in this chapter was to specify methods and procedures that structure rigorous computational work using agent-based models. What we want to do is generate computational results with scope, reliability, and precision that are to all intents and purposes analogous to analytical results. This implies a series of decisions on careful design of computational experiments and rigorous estimation of outputs from these. Methodologically, we feel confident that our systematic consideration of the different types of Markov process that arise in the different types of computational experiments we conduct has resulted in experimental design, diagnostic, and estimation procedures that generate results that are as rigorous as can be achieved within any given computational budget. Since we have access to powerful computational resources, our computational budget is large, and the level of precision we can achieve in our results is consequently high. Without reiterating the precise procedures we specify above, we do thus feel confident that the simulation results we report in this book can be "taken to the bank." We mean by this that if anyone else were to run the same analyses using the same specifications, or if we were to rerun these deploying even more computer power, the results would be essentially identical to those we report in the subsequent chapters.

PART TWO

The Basic Model

CHAPTER FIVE

Benchmarking the Baseline Model

HAVING SET OUT OUR METHODS IN CHAPTER 4, we are now at last in a position to start investigating multiparty competition using the baseline model we specified in chapter 3. As we said when setting out our plan of campaign, we start simple in this chapter and build up to a more complex and realistic model of party competition in subsequent chapters. We need to understand the basic processes of dynamic multiparty competition in a simple setting before we move on to study complications such as endogenous political parties, diverse sets of decision rules, voters who care about more than policy, and politicians who care about more than votes. Our aim in this chapter is to analyze our baseline model of multiparty competition and develop benchmarks against which to measure future results.

Specifically, we begin here by modeling party systems with an exogenously fixed number of parties, all of which use the same decision rule. While current models of party competition in the classical analytical tradition do also typically deal with exogenously fixed sets of parties in which all parties use the same decision rule,[1] our ambition in this book is to go very far beyond this. We reign in our ambitions in the current chapter, however, in the interests of an orderly program of model development. The results we report below are useful for two main reasons. First, they provide a benchmark against which to evaluate results generated by the increasingly complex models we develop in subsequent chapters. Second, they provide a point of reference that allows us to compare results generated by our model to those generated by more traditional models of party competition. By the end of the book, in contrast, the substantive reach of our model will be so far beyond models in the classical tradition that there will be nothing to compare it with.

We first benchmark our model for the baseline assumption that voters' ideal points are distributed over the policy space with a perfectly symmetric bivariate normal density. This essentially replicates and confirms already published work (Laver 2005), always an important starting point for any scientific project. We then move beyond existing computational work to exercise our model under the new assumption about ideal point

---

[1] As we note in the next chapter there are classical formal models of "party entry" in very spare settings, in which the set of competing parties may be endogenous.

distributions that we specified in chapter 3. This leads us to investigate multiparty competition in the more general setting with distinct subpopulations of voters and consequently *asymmetric* aggregate distributions of ideal points. Before we do any of this, we specify design and estimation procedures for our computational work that build on the methodological conclusions we reached in the previous chapter.

EXPERIMENTAL DESIGN

We specify different designs for experiments with symmetric and with asymmetric distributions of voter ideal points—given the more complex parameterization of the model in the latter case.

Symmetric Populations

Our computational experiments for symmetric populations have the simple grid-sweeping design set out in Figure 4.1, since we are manipulating two model parameters, each with a small number of discrete and "natural" settings. We investigate the effects of three different rule sets (all-Sticker, all-Aggregator, all-Hunter) in party systems of eleven different sizes, ranging from two to twelve parties. This gives us a thirty-three-point parameter grid and hence a total of thirty-three model runs for the experiment.

Asymmetric Populations

The description of distributions of voter ideal points is now generalized to comprise aggregations of two subpopulations, each with normally distributed ideal points. This mandates a more general experimental design since the dimensionality of our parameter space is now considerably expanded to include two new parameters, as shown in Figure 4.2. The new parameters are the relative size of the two subpopulation, n_l/n_r, and their ideal point means, μ_r ($= -\mu_l$). Given the increased size of the parameter space, we use a design based on Monte Carlo parameterization. For each of the three rule sets under investigation, we run a suite of one thousand runs. Each run in each suite uses a Monte Carlo parameterization of our model that is specified as follows:

- the number of parties is sampled from a uniform distribution of integers on the interval [2, 12]
- the relative size of subpopulations, n_l/n_r, is sampled from a uniform distribution of real numbers on the interval [2.0, 1.0]
- the ideal point means μ_r ($= -\mu_l$), are sampled from a uniform distribution of real numbers on the interval [0.0, 1.5]

Run Design

The suites of runs for all-Sticker, all-Aggregator, and all-Hunter party systems all generate different stochastic processes, and for this reason, each requires a different run design.

All-Sticker Runs

Political parties in an all-Sticker system never change position. Since voters in our model do not change their ideal points, "nothing happens" in all-Sticker simulations once initial party positions have been generated. Immediately after the random scatter of party positions at the start of each run repetition, therefore, the repetition has reached a single deterministic steady state: no party will change position, none of the party vote shares will change, and none of the values for the aggregate measures, mean eccentricity, ENP, and representativeness will change. There is no transient state, hence no need for burn-in.

In addition, given that the steady state obtained for any particular run repetition depends entirely on the initial random scatter of parties (which in turn depends on the random seed used by the repetition), these run processes are nonergodic. Each all-Sticker run process, therefore, is a nonergodic deterministic process that converges on a single state. Our estimation procedure for the output means of interest, therefore, is to execute several repetitions, each with a single iteration, recording the value for each of the output variables at the first iteration as being representative of the repetition. We then calculate the ensemble average of the output values across the repetitions we perform. Using the diagnostics we developed in chapter 4 for this run procedure, we determined that one thousand repetitions per run were sufficient to ensure a representative estimate with the level of precision we desire.[2]

All-Aggregator Runs

There is no random component in the Aggregator rule: set party policy on each dimension at the mean preference of all current party supporters. An all-Aggregator run process is thus also deterministic. In addition, as we saw in chapter 2 and develop more fully below, we have the theoretical result from Voronoi geometry that party positions in all-Aggregator systems always converge on a centroidal Voronoi tessellation of the policy space. Each all-Aggregator run process therefore tends toward a single steady state. As with all-Sticker runs, different steady states are

---

[2] Section E5.1 in the electronic appendix gives details of the diagnostic tests that led to this conclusion.

possible, depending on initial conditions. As with all-Sticker runs, therefore, all-Aggregator processes are nonergodic deterministic processes that converge on a single state. Hence, we calculate the mean by taking an ensemble average of the steady-state values of the output variables from several repetitions. Unlike all-Sticker runs, however, all-Aggregator runs do not start out in steady state. Aggregator parties adapt away from their initial random starting positions, eventually settling after a series of iterations into a deterministic steady-state configuration.

Our design for all-Aggregator runs is therefore to execute several repetitions until each run repetition has reached steady state, collect final representative values for each of the output variables for the run repetition at which steady state is achieved, and calculate an ensemble average of all of the collected values as an estimate of μ for each output variable of the run. Using the diagnostics we discuss in chapter 4, we settled on a sample size of one thousand repetitions.[3] As we see throughout this book, one thousand observations are sufficient to satisfy the first four diagnostic checks with all of the theoretical simulations that we execute. Hence, with all simulations, we always collect one thousand observations to calculate mean estimates. In so doing, we achieve the same relative precision of 3.2 percent across all runs and all output variables analyzed in this book.

All-Hunter Runs

All-Hunter runs are more complex. First, the Hunter rule stipulates that, if the last policy move increased party support, the party should continue in the same direction, otherwise it should reverse heading and make a unit move in a heading chosen randomly from the 180-degree arc centered on the direction it is currently facing. This random component of the Hunter rule makes all-Hunter run processes stochastic and ensures that they are ergodic.

Given that the run processes are stochastic, determining run burn-in for all-Hunter runs is a more complicated matter. To facilitate the burn-in analysis, we create a Markov representation of the run process. One such representation is to define the state space at time t, using the set of variables that summarizes the x- and y-coordinate positions for all-Hunter parties at times t and $t-1$. Thus, the *vector of state space variables* at time t, X_t, comprises the configuration of party positions at *both* time t and time $t-1$, $X_t = \{P(t), P(t-1)\}$. For example, with an all-Hunter benchmark run with 12 parties, the vector of variables would comprise, for each

---

[3] Section E5.2 in the electronic appendix gives details of the diagnostic tests that led to this conclusion.

party competing, the *x*-coordinate at time *t*, the *y*-coordinate at time *t*, the *x*-coordinate at time *t–1*, and the *y*-coordinate at time *t–1*. This is a total of 4 × 12 = 48 variables. This combination of variables satisfies the necessary conditions for a Markov process. First, combined with information about the initial distributions of voter ideal points, all other output variables at time *t* can be determined from these variables. The vote shares at time *t* are determined by the party positions at time *t* and the distribution of voter ideal points. The heading for each of the Hunter parties at time *t* can be determined by comparing its position at time *t* to its position at time *t–1* and the change in its vote share from time *t–1* to time *t* (which itself is derived from the positions of all of the parties at times *t* and *t–1*). Last, all of the aggregate measures at time *t*, mean eccentricity, ENP, and representativeness, can be calculated using the party positions at time *t* and the distribution of voter ideal points. Second, the vector of state space variables satisfies the Markov property. The probability that the process will be in any state of the state space at time *t+1*, Prob (X_{t+1} = j), is conditional on solely the state of the process at time *t*, X_t. This is because (1) the probability of a particular configuration of Hunter parties at time *t+1*, P(*t+1*), is completely determined by the positions of the parties at times *t* and *t-1*, Prob(P(*t+1*)) = f(P(*t*), P(*t–1*)) and the (2) the positions of the parties at time *t* are already known, P(*t*) = P(*t*). Hence, the probability that the vector of state space variables will take on a particular value at time *t+1*, Prob (X_{t+1} = j) is completely determined by the vector of state space variables at time *t*, X_t.

Given this Markov representation of the process, we use two summary variables, mean eccentricity and ENP, to diagnose when the run process is burnt in. Both of these variables ultimately depend on the positions of all parties. When these parties have reached a stochastic steady-state configuration, the output variables mean eccentricity and ENP will also be in stochastic steady state. The next step is to determine whether or not a time average provides a representative estimate of μ for all of the output variables. In fact, we already examined this case in the empirical burn-in subsection of chapter 4. As we described there, one thousand post-burn-in iterations are sufficient to map out the steady-state vector for the summary variables, and hence a time average provides a representative estimate of μ for all output variables. Also, as we see with Figure 4.4, which plots each summary variable by iteration, one hundred iterations are more than enough to reach the stochastic steady state with the most extreme run with twelve competing parties.[4] Therefore, our procedure for estimating the mean of the output variables for the all-Hunter runs is to execute a single repetition per run, collect

---

[4] Runs with fewer parties required fewer iterations for burn-in.

one thousand observations starting from iteration 101, and calculate a time average of the collected values.[5]

Multiparty Competition in Symmetric Voter Populations

We are now finally in a position to run computational experiments using our baseline model of dynamic multiparty competition. We analyze the results of these computational experiments in the rest of this chapter. We begin with competition among parties for the support of voters whose ideals points have a symmetric normal distribution in the policy space. We move on to consider multiparty competition in settings where the distribution of ideal points is asymmetric, as a result of the existence of at least two distinct subpopulations of voters.

Evolved Eccentricities of Party Policy Positions

Figure 5.1 shows two sample screen shots from our simulation runs. The shaded area in the background shows the bivariate normal distribution of voter idea points; lighter areas have higher ideal point densities, darker areas have lower densities. The seven gray arrowheads in the left panel show the policy positions of a deterministic steady-state configuration of seven Aggregators. These party positions evolved, as a result of iterated decisions taken by party leaders using the Aggregator rule, from a set of seven completely random policy positions to a configuration of positions that are very evenly and symmetrically distributed in the policy space. Since all party leaders are using the Aggregator rule, we know from Lloyd's Algorithm that this steady-state configuration of party positions is a centroidal Voronoi tessellation and is therefore an optimal seven-point representation of the set of voter ideal points.

The right panel shows a snapshot of the positions of seven Hunters. These policy positions, again shown by gray arrows, are never at rest but are in continual motion with headings indicated by the arrowheads. This continual motion arises because each Hunter is "insatiable," to use a term we define more precisely in chapter 7. Whatever the state of the process, a Hunter always makes some policy move in search of more votes. This snapshot of a configuration in constant motion shows Hunter party positions that are unevenly distributed and closer to the center of the space than the Aggregator positions.

These configurations of party positions are typical, and Figure 5.2 plots typical policy eccentricities in our simulations of political parties

---

[5] Section E5.3 in the electronic appendix gives details of the supporting diagnostic tests.

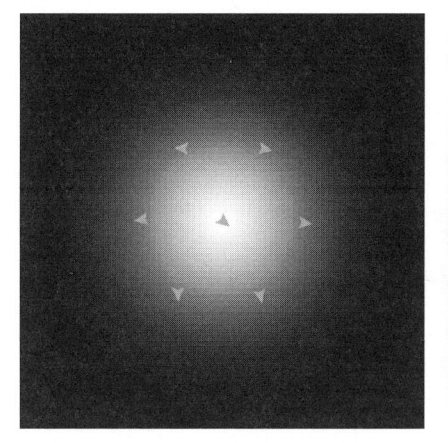

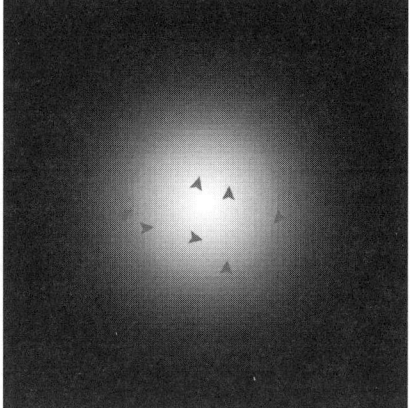

Figure 5.1. Screen shots of locations of seven Aggregators (left) and seven Hunters (right) in benchmark runs.

competing for votes in all-Sticker, all- Aggregator, and all-Hunter party systems.[6] Setting these results in context, recall from Figure 3.3 that mean policy eccentricity of *voters* in the baseline symmetric population is 1.25 and that we know analytically, given the algorithm for randomly scattering parties, that the typical policy eccentricity of random Stickers will be 1.50.

The conclusions we draw from Figure 5.2 are clear-cut and substantively important. Compared to parties in equivalent all-Aggregator party systems, vote-seeking parties in all-Hunter systems systematically choose more central policy positions. Party systems with two vote-seeking Hunters are somewhat atypical; parties tend to search for votes close to the centroid of voter ideal points (typically 0.2 standard deviation units away from this). When more parties compete for votes, confirming results reported in Laver (2005), Hunter parties typically compete for votes at locations that are fairly close to the voter centroid but very definitely not at it. The solid line in Figure 5.1 shows that parties in all-Hunter systems typically promote policy positions that are 0.75–0.95 standard deviations from the voter centroid, positions significantly closer to the center than the ideal point of the typical voter.[7] In all-Aggregator party systems with four or more parties, in contrast, party leaders tend to promote posi-

---

[6] Standard errors of all estimates are less than 0.002. The detailed estimates generating Figure 5.2 are reported in Table E5.4.

[7] Since our estimates are very precise, whenever we use the word "significant" in reporting results this also indicates statistical significance.

92 • Chapter 5

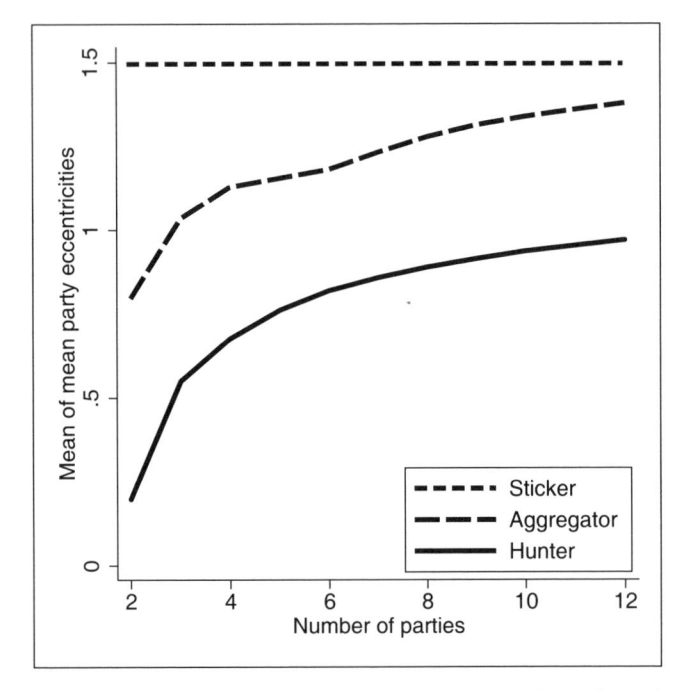

Figure 5.2. Mean party policy eccentricity, by decision rule and number of parties; benchmark runs in symmetric populations.

tions close to the mean policy eccentricity of the underlying voter population. Our simulations also show clearly that, whether in all-Aggregator or all-Hunter party systems, mean party policy eccentricity increases with the number of parties. When there are more parties, some of these tend to take more eccentric policy positions.

One of the seminal Downsian intuitions about party competition is that competitive spatial location by parties in *one-dimensional* policy spaces tends to result in centripetal position taking and a resulting convergence of parties on the center of the policy space. Given this, avoidance of the center of the policy space by vote-seeking Hunters, even though this is the location of the highest voter densities, is substantively striking; it is also a very robust result. To gain some intuition about this, we return to the geometry of dynamic Voronoi diagrams. Figure 5.3 builds on the example used in chapter 3, showing the Voronoi dynamics of a move by the Fianna Fáil party toward the voter centroid. The move is from FF_1 to FF_2, and the voter centroid is at x. As before, solid lines show the Voronoi diagram generated by the party configuration with FF_1. Dotted straight lines show changes in the Voronoi diagram resulting from the change in

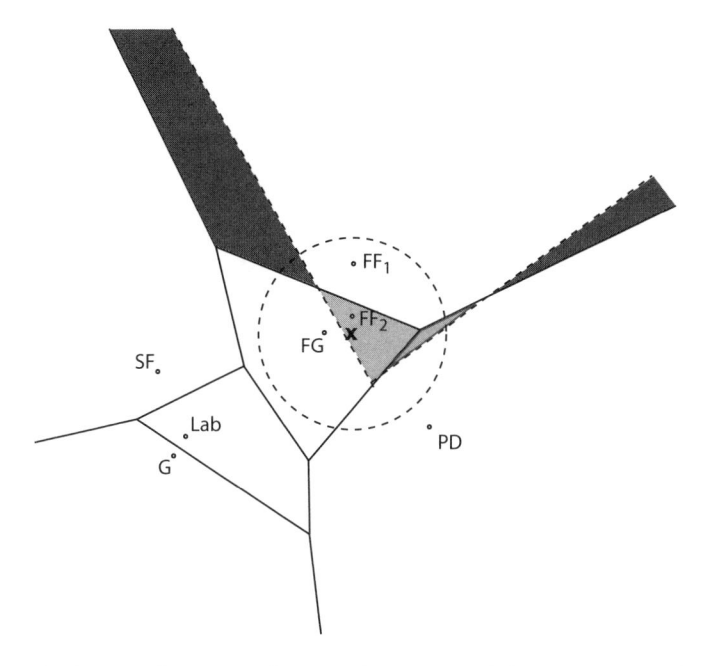

Figure 5.3. Voronoi dynamics of a move by FF toward the voter centroid at x.

Fianna Fáil policy. Note that FF_2 is closer than FF_1 to x, that is, the move is toward the voter centroid. The regions *added* to Fianna Fáil's Voronoi region as a result of this move are shaded lighter gray; the regions *lost* are shaded darker gray. Whether Fianna Fáil's move toward the center results in a net gain or loss of votes depends on the distribution of voters' ideal points

The dotted circle plots an ideal point density contour for this symmetric distribution. If ideal point densities outside this contour are very low, then Fianna Fáil's move toward the center would on balance win the party more votes. If the contour plots three standard deviations from the voter centroid, for example, FF_1 would be about two standard deviations from the voter centroid and there would be relatively few voter ideal points (less than 0.5 percent) outside the dotted circle. In this case, Fianna Fáil's move toward the center would be rewarded. Gains in densely populated regions inside the circle would greatly outweigh losses in sparsely populated regions outside this. In contrast, if the contour plots 0.5 standard deviations from the voter centroid, then FF_1 would be about 0.4 standard deviations from the voter centroid and about 62 percent of voter ideals would be outside the circle. Now, if Fianna Fáil moves from FF_1 to FF_2, gains of votes in the light gray regions would be far outweighed by losses in the dark gray regions. In this case, with Fianna Fáil relatively close to the voter centroid, *a move closer to the centroid would be punished by a net loss of vote share.*

More generally in this case, if the Fianna Fáil leader is using a Hunter rule and the party starts at an eccentric policy position, say two standard deviations from the voter centroid, and moves toward the center, then such a move will at first tend to be rewarded and the move will therefore be repeated. After a series of such moves party policy will be close enough to the centroid that a further centripetal move will be punished with a lower vote share. At this point, the Hunter rule implies reversing direction and moving away from the voter centroid.

Figure 5.4 gives a more general feel for the complex dynamics generated by vote-seeking multiparty competition in multidimensional policy spaces. It plots typical vote shares against policy eccentricities for each party, over the course of a burnt-in five-Hunter simulation run. The solid horizontal line shows the mean long-run vote share for each party. For five parties this is, axiomatically, 20 percent. The dashed lines show that each party's vote share is maximized, at about 22.5 percent, when it locates about 0.4 standard deviations from the voter centroid. Why then do these five vote-seeking parties typically locate, as we see from Figure 5.2, at 0.76 standard deviations from the voter centroid? Is this location not suboptimal for them?

The answer is no. It is arithmetically impossible for five parties to average 22.5 percent of the vote over the long run. The solid vertical line in Figure 5.4 shows that each of the five parties averages its long-run expectation of 20 percent of the vote when it is 0.76 standard deviations from the voter centroid. Since all parties use the same rule and thus expect the same average vote share over the long run, the *average* long-run positions for each of the five Hunters should be 0.76 standard deviations from the center, the location at which they all tend to get the five-party mean vote share of 20 percent. Figure 5.4 does show that a *single* Hunter can expect to do better than this if it locates closer to the center, but it also shows that this situation is not dynamically stable in the long run. If one vote-seeking party wins more than an average share of the vote, *then other parties using the same decision rule must win less*; their vote-seeking behavior will correct this situation over the course of dynamic party competition in the long run. Figure 5.4 shows us that perfect symmetry between the five Hunters means that they should, over the long run, tend to locate at 0.76 standard deviations from the voter centroid, and Figure 5.2 shows us that this is indeed the case.

We have taken some time working though this example because it gives us a clear sense of why we must think about party competition in very different ways when this is set in an intrinsically *dynamic* environment, in contrast to the static environment of the classical spatial model.

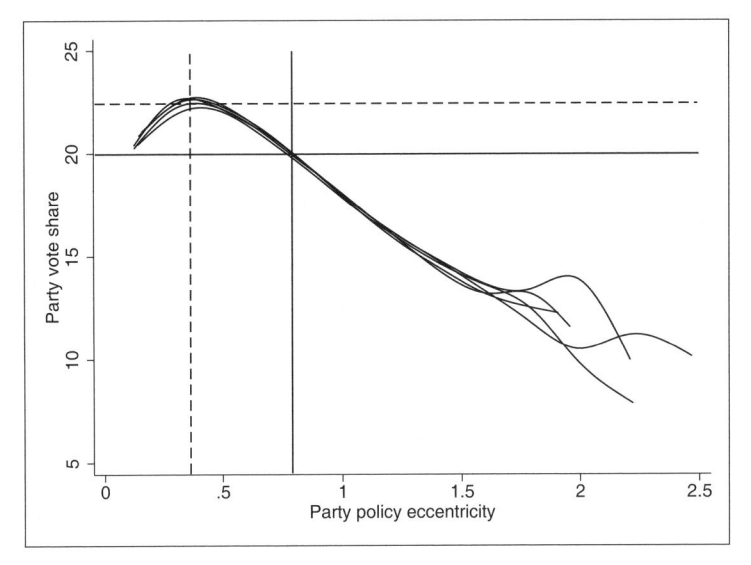

Figure 5.4. Median splines of party vote shares by policy eccentricities, burnt-in five-Hunter benchmark run. Plotted lines are twelve-band median splines and exclude cases where party policy eccentricity > 2.0.

Scholars in the classical formal modeling tradition have used many different assumptions to account for the commonplace empirical observation that vote-seeking political parties in real party systems *do not* tend to engage in "Downsian" convergence on the ideological center ground. Our ABM of dynamic multiparty competition, in contrast, shows us that observed nonconvergence of vote-seeking parties is indeed to be expected with multiparty competition in multidimensional policy spaces. No special assumption is needed to generate a model of party competition in which vote-seeking party leaders have a strong tendency to avoid the dead center of the policy space. Center avoidance by vote-seeking parties *arises directly from the Voronoi dynamics of competitive location in multidimensional policy spaces.* This substantively important intuition flows directly from our dynamic ABM of multiparty competition.

Effective Numbers of Parties

We noted when specifying our output measures that there is a distinction between the absolute number of parties engaged in party competition, which is fixed exogenously in these simulations, and the *effective* number of parties (ENP). The latter takes account of relative party sizes. For example, if five parties are in competition, then a setting in which all parties have equal vote shares implies an ENP of five, while one in which nearly

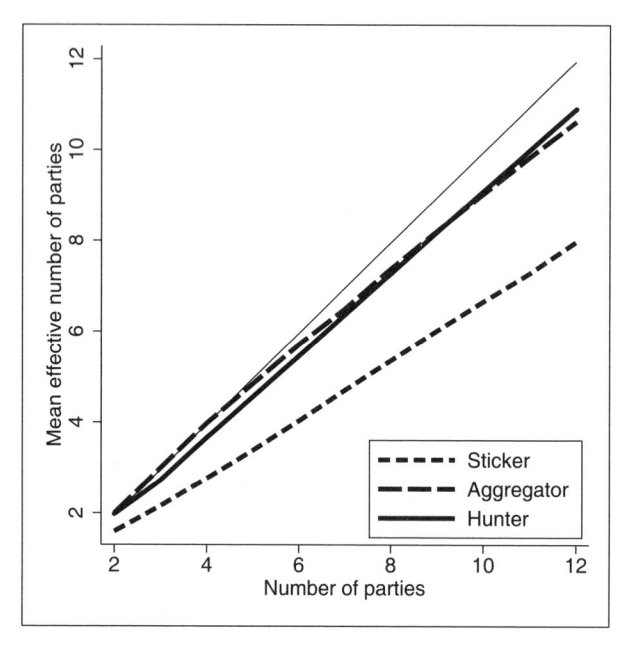

Figure 5.5. Effective and absolute number of parties, benchmark runs in symmetric populations.

all votes go to a single party implies an ENP close to unity. The more absolute and effective numbers of parties diverge, the more unequal the party vote shares. Figure 5.5 plots the relationship between the absolute number of parties and ENP.[8] The thin black 45-degree line highlights a striking pattern whereby ENP is always close to the absolute number of parties for all-Aggregator and all-Hunter party systems. These simulated party systems have a strong tendency to generate party configurations in which all parties are of roughly equal size over the long run. In all-Sticker party systems, in contrast, ENP differs significantly from the absolute number of parties because party sizes typically vary substantially

This is a striking pattern that shows another important intuition that arises from analyzing dynamic as opposed to static party competition. A dynamic party system in which all parties use the same adaptive decision rule for setting party positions and do not differ from each other in any systematic way should result, by symmetry, in a situation in which

[8] Standard errors of all estimates are less than 0.001 (Aggregators), 0.004 (Hunters), and 0.012 (Stickers). Detailed estimates generating Figure 5.5 can be found in Table E5.5 in the electronic appendix.

all parties tend *over the long run* to have the same levels of support. As we indeed find in our simulations, a *snapshot* of the dynamic process at any given point in time, such as that shown in the right panel of Figure 5.1, typically shows a situation in which parties have substantially different vote shares. But these short-run differences even out over the long run, unless there is some other, as yet unspecified, systematic difference between the parties.

This has another important substantive implication that becomes available to us only when we use dynamic models of party competition. If we observe systematic long-run differences in party sizes in some real party system, then this implies one of two things. Party leaders are not all using the same decision rule, with some rules more effective than others in finding votes in the same environment; or all things are not equal among parties using the same rule in the same environment. We analyze situations in which different party leaders use different decision rules in every subsequent chapter of this book. We return in chapter 9 to the possibility of systematic differences among parties using the same decision rule, considering effects of variations among parties nonpolicy electoral "valence."

Representativeness of the Configuration of Party Positions

Recall that we defined representativeness of a configuration of party policy positions in terms of the average closeness of voters' ideal points to the position of their closest party. We do not analyze government formation or downstream policy making; our concern here is with the representativeness of the configuration of party policy positions on offer at election time. Figure 5.6 plots representativeness of the configuration of evolved party policy positions, by number of parties and party decision rule.[9] We see two clear patterns. First, the upward slope of all lines shows that, whatever decision rule party leaders use, *representativeness increases with the number of parties in contention*. The more unique party positions there are, the closer any random ideal point is likely to be to some party position. Second, we see from the dashed line plotting representativeness in all-Aggregator party systems that, for any number of parties, *voters are significantly better represented when party leaders use the Aggregator rule than when they use Hunter*.

This computational finding comports perfectly with the twin theoretical results from Voronoi geometry, reported in chapter 3, that an *n*-Aggregator system reaches steady state when party policy positions are

---

[9] Standard errors of all estimates are less than 0.0001 (Aggregators), 0.002 (Hunters), and 0.005 (Stickers). The detailed estimates generating Figure 5.6 can be found in Table E5.6.

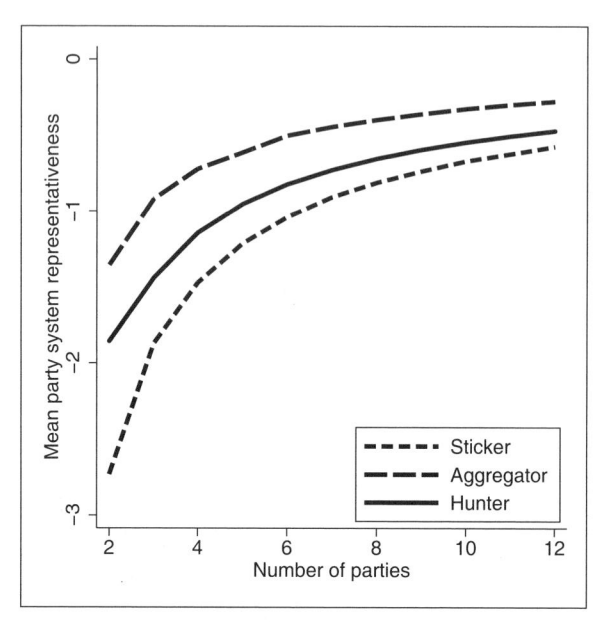

Figure 5.6. Party system representativeness, by decision rule and number of parties in symmetric populations.

at the centroids of their Voronoi regions; the resulting centroidal Voronoi tessellation (CVT) of the policy space is an optimal *n*-party representation of the set of voter ideal points. Leaders of individual Aggregator parties never seek to increase representativeness of the party system *as a whole*. Nonetheless, an all-Aggregator system in which each party leader seeks to maximize representation of her *own party supporters* evolves, given Lloyd's Algorithm, to a configuration of party policy positions that optimizes representativeness of the party system as a whole.

An equivalent number of Hunter parties will almost never be at the centroids of their Voronoi regions. Configurations of Hunter party policy positions will typically not be a CVT and representation will typically not be optimal. Strikingly, this means that the policy preferences of the voting population *as a whole* are not best represented by a set of political parties that compete for voters' support on the basis of trying to find the most popular policy positions. When parties do behave in this way, they tend to compete for support "too close" to the center of the policy space to maximize overall representativeness of the party system. On one view this might be seen as contradicting a standard normative justification for competitive elections, which is that competition among parties for votes will tend to result in representative election results.

The big picture in Figure 5.6, given Lloyd's Algorithm and the fact that CVTs are optimal representations, is that the line plotting representativeness of all-Aggregator party systems also plots *the optimal level of representativeness that can be achieved by party systems of equivalent size*. Voters, in short, are better served by a set of political parties whose prime concern is to satisfy *current* supporters rather than search restlessly for *new* supporters.

MULTIPARTY COMPETITION IN ASYMMETRIC POPULATIONS

Thus far we retrieved and consolidated results on dynamic multiparty competition with symmetric voter populations that were previously reported by Laver (2005). We did this using much more robust computational experiments, and we introduced a substantively important new measure of party system representativeness, with its implied notion of optimal representation. We now go well beyond this to analyze party competition in a more general setting with asymmetric and quite possibly multimodal distributions of voter ideal points. As we saw in chapter 3, these typically arise from aggregating distinct subpopulations of voters reflecting, for example, different ethnic, linguistic, or social groups. We use two subpopulations in the rest of this book. We experimented with more subpopulations and found that the important effects on model results arise from the departure from symmetric ideal point distributions that can be achieved with two distinct subpopulations. In our experience—though this could be a subject for future work—moving to three or more voter subpopulations adds many new parameters and thereby increases the computational budget by orders of magnitude, without adding substantive insight.

Experimental Design

As we saw in chapter 4 when discussing the difference between grid-sweeping designs and Monte Carlo model parameterizations, moving to two distinct subpopulations adds two new real-valued parameters that do not have "natural" discrete settings. These parameters are polarization of subpopulation ideal point centroids and the relative sizes of constituent subpopulations. As specified in chapter 3, we calibrate our computational work to the type of party system in which we are substantively interested by simulating party competition in settings where the relative size of subpopulations, n_l / n_r, is in the range [2.0, 1.0] and subpopulation ideal point means, $\mu_r = -\mu_l$ are in the range [0.0, 1.5]. Our experimental design therefore involves one thousand different Monte Carlo parameter-

100 • Chapter 5

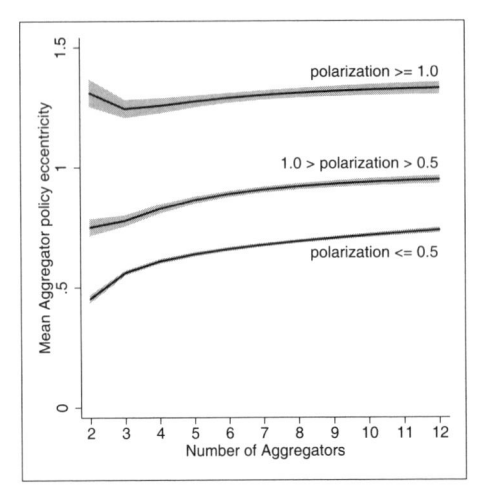

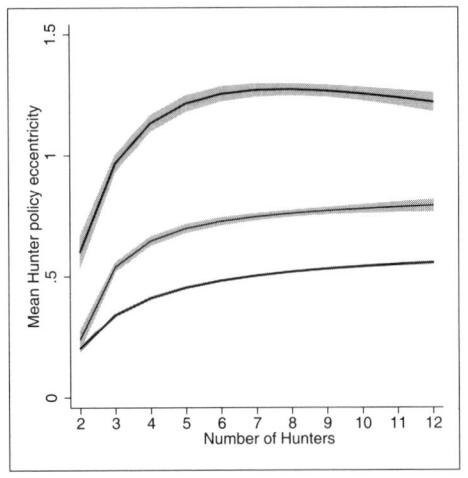

Figure 5.7. Mean party policy eccentricity, by decision rule, number of parties, and subpopulation polarization; asymmetric populations.

izations of the distribution of voter ideal points. For each of the one thousand model runs, values of n_l / n_r and μ_r are high-precision floating point numbers randomly drawn from a uniform distribution over the specified range. The method we employ to estimate the run output parameters is the same as the method used with the symmetric voter population.

Party Policy Positions

Figure 5.7 is analogous to Figure 5.2 and shows evolved party policy eccentricities, now with asymmetric distributions of voter ideals points, by party decision rule and number of parties. In contrast to Figure 5.2, which summarizes results for a single symmetric bivariate normal population, Figure 5.7 summarizes results from one thousand different Monte Carlo parameterizations of asymmetric populations, with different panels for all-Aggregator (left) and all-Hunter (right) party systems.[10] Each parameterization specifies a different level of polarization between the two subpopulations.[11] Given the highly nonlinear nature of many of the results we report in the rest of this book, we summarize these using

---

[10] Plots of party policy eccentricity against relative subpopulation sizes reveal no noticeable pattern and are shown in Figure E5.1 of the electronic appendix. Party positions in all-Sticker benchmarking runs contain no new information since they reflect simply the random positions that Stickers are assigned in simulations.

[11] Strictly speaking, we mean a different distance between subpopulation ideal point centroids.

fractional-polynomial prediction plots. The three bands in each panel of Figure 5.7 plot 95 percent confidence intervals around fractional polynomial fit lines summarizing model output for highly polarized (top), moderately polarized (middle), and relatively unpolarized (bottom) voter subpopulations.

Comparing the two panels of Figure 5.7, we see that Hunters continue to take significantly more central policy positions than Aggregators, as they did in symmetric voter populations. Comparing the upper bands in these two panels, however, we see that this difference is far less striking when voter subpopulations are highly polarized and the number of parties is relatively large. In polarized settings such as these, typical Hunter and Aggregator policy positions are relatively similar. The reason for this can be seen clearly in the right panel of Figure 5.7, which gives the big news from these simulations. *Party systems with four or more Hunters are very different from those with two or three.* Moving from two to three to four parties, the typical policy eccentricity of Hunter parties increases rapidly, leveling off dramatically as the number of parties increases beyond four. The reason why this happens can be seen easily by watching simulations in motion. With four or more Hunter parties in contention, we typically see two or more parties competing for support in each subpopulation. When this happens, Hunters tend to be punished for moving away from "their" subpopulation toward the center of the space, and thus tend not to do this. The right panel of Figure 5.8 is a screen shot of precisely this situation as it emerged in a four-Hunter benchmark run with two highly polarized voter populations—as before, lighter background colors show regions with higher ideal point densities. With only two or three parties, at least one voter subpopulation can "host" at most one party and this party cannot be punished for moving away from the subpopulation ideal point centroid, toward the center. We see this in the left panel of Figure 5.8, which shows a screenshot of Hunter positions in a three-party benchmark run. Once two Hunters are competing in one subpopulation, *there is nothing to deter the third Hunter from moving toward them.*

This striking pattern is documented systematically in Figure 5.9, which shows histograms of parties' x-coordinates, in both two- and four-Hunter systems, over benchmark runs for an asymmetric population with subpopulations of equal sizes and ideal point centroids at ±1.0. The left panel shows that, with only two Hunters in contention, both party leaders have a strong tendency to choose policy positions near the center of the x-dimension, *completely ignoring the two high-density subpopulation centroids of citizens' ideal points.* There is no punishment in this two-party environment for parties that choose policy positions far away from the ideal points of most voters and evolved Hunter policy positions are perversely unrepresentative. In stark contrast, with four Hunters in con-

102 • Chapter 5

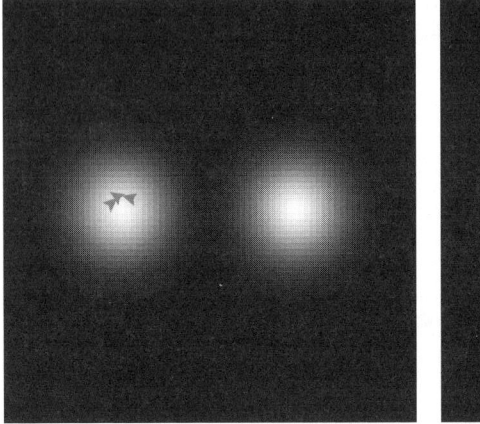

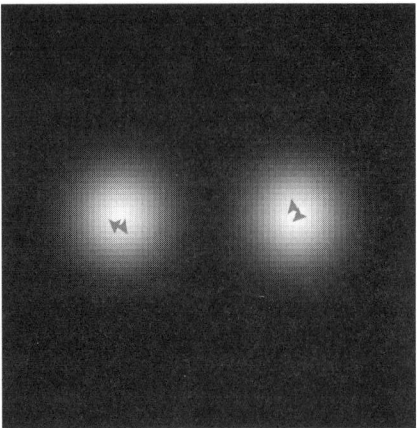

Figure 5.8. Screen shots of party positions in three-Hunter (left) and four-Hunter (right) benchmark runs with asymmetric voter populations: subpopulation centroids at −1.5 and +1.5 on the *x*-axis.

tention, the right panel of Figure 5.9 shows that all parties tend to stay close to one subpopulation centroid or the other, *almost never choosing policy positions at the center of the* x*-dimension*.

Party System Representativeness

It is quite remarkable that the two panels in Figure 5.9 characterize vote-seeking party competition in *precisely the same aggregate population*. In contrast to the perversely unrepresentative positions taken by two vote-seeking Hunters, when there are four or more Hunters, competition among parties *within each subpopulation* now results in party positions that are close to the bulk of voters' ideal points. Figure 5.10 plots representativeness of evolved configurations of party positions, by decision rule, number of parties, and polarization of voter ideal points. The left panel plots results for all-Aggregator party systems that we now know generate optimally representative configurations of party positions. This panel thus shows upper bounds on the representation of voter ideal points in the different environments we investigate. The right panel of Figure 5.10 is worth a thousand words. It shows that *representativeness of evolved Hunter policy positions goes through a sea change as the number of these vote-seeking parties hits four or more*. Hunter party policy positions tend to be *very* unrepresentative in asymmetric populations when there are fewer than four vote-seeking Hunters. The lower

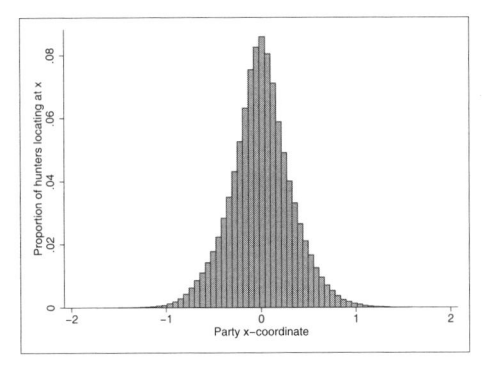

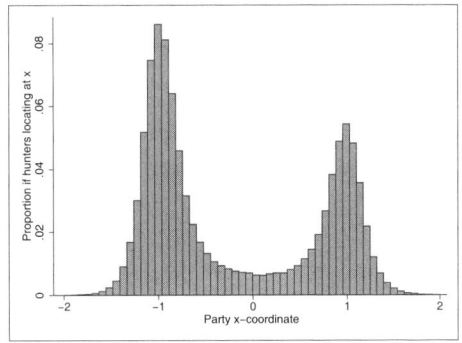

Figure 5.9. Histograms of party *x*-coordinates, for two- and four-Hunter benchmark runs in asymmetric population.

band shows that this pattern is especially strong when subpopulations are highly polarized.

As we have seen, two vote-seeking Hunters tend, perversely, to compete for votes in the almost unpopulated center ground. With four or more parties, competition between pairs of Hunters keeps them close to subpopulation centroids and generates a much more representative configuration of party positions. Indeed it is striking that, as the number of parties increases in asymmetric populations, there is increasingly little difference between the representativeness of all-Aggregator and all-Hunter party systems. This is in clear contrast to the situation in symmetric populations, in which all-Aggregator party systems are systematically more representative than all-Hunter systems. As a general rule, these results suggest that highly polarized voter populations may tend to be well represented by evolved configurations of party policy positions, except when the party system comprises just two or three vote-seeking Hunter parties.[12]

CONCLUSIONS

We set out in this chapter to use methods and procedures we specified in chapter 4 to get started on the analysis of the model of party competition we develop in the rest of this book. We also set out to move beyond the

---

[12] The relationship between the effective and absolute number of parties, shown in Figure E5.2 of the electronic appendix, was not affected by subpopulation polarization and was essentially the same as for symmetric populations.

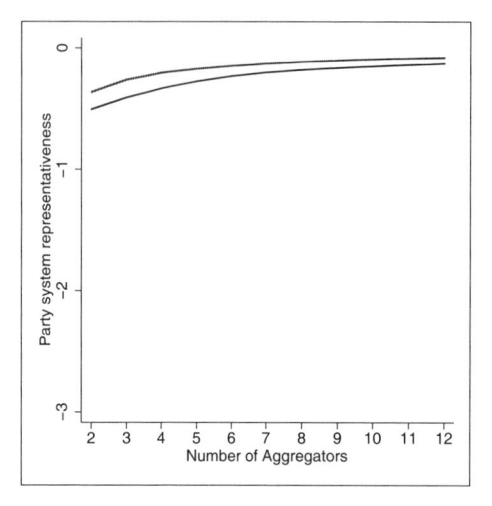

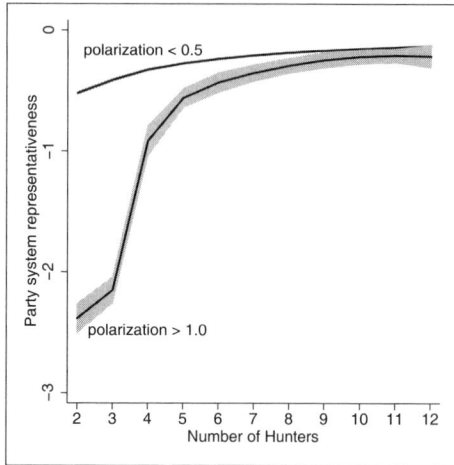

Figure 5.10. Party system representativeness, by decision rule, number of parties, and subpopulation polarization.

assumption of a symmetric bivariate normal distribution of voters' ideal points to investigate the more general ideal point distributions that arise in settings where the electorate comprises two distinct subpopulations of voters, for example representing ethnic, religious, or other social groups.

Our substantive headline results concern the *representativeness* of evolved configurations of party policy positions. In symmetric populations we find, paradoxically, that the ideal points of voters are *not* best represented by a set of (Hunter) parties who compete for their support by trying to find popular policy positions. Instead, voter preferences *are* better represented by a set of (Aggregator) parties that do not compete *with each other* on policy at all but instead seek to represent the policy preferences only of their current supporters. This happens because the dynamics of vote-seeking competition in this setting cause parties to set policy positions *closer* to the center of the policy space than would be needed for optimal representation—while at the same time avoiding the dead center of the space.

The situation is quite different in asymmetric voter populations. Vote-seeking competition between two Hunters now moves parties *away* from the centroids of subpopulation ideal points, resulting in typical configurations of party positions that are perversely unrepresentative. However, competition among four or more vote-seeking Hunters tends to result in party positions that are *close* to subpopulation centroids, making evolved configurations of party positions *much* more representative than in two- or three-Hunter systems. The shift from two- to four-Hunter competition generates a sea change in the representativeness of party positions in the vote-seeking party competition we model. In these circumstances, we see the emergence of what are to all intents and purposes two independent systems of party competition, one for each voter subpopulation. *Parties tend to "serve" one subpopulation or the other and to compete for votes with other parties serving the same subpopulation, rather than competing directly with parties serving other subpopulations.* We find this theoretically intriguing, as well as an empirically plausible account of real party competition in settings with polarized electorates.

CHAPTER SIX

Endogenous Parties, Interaction of Different Decision Rules

WE HAVE SO FAR MADE the preposterous assumption that political parties come to us as gifts from God or Nature. We did this to get started in our investigations of party competition, but we all know this is not true. We know that political parties are endogenous *outputs* of the process of party competition, not exogenous inputs to it. Any halfway realistic model of multiparty competition must treat the set of competing political parties as endogenous. This has of course not escaped the attention of scholars modeling party competition in the classical analytical tradition, but it has proved a hard nut for them to crack. As a consequence, the inevitable trade-off between rigor and realism has been pushed even further away from realism. "Party entry" and "citizen candidates" have been analyzed in extraordinarily sparse settings with one policy dimension, minuscule electorates, and at most two extant parties. One of the core aims of this chapter is to build on intuitions from this work and, liberated by our use of agent-based modeling rather than classical analysis, develop more realistic and interesting models in which the set of competing parties is a completely endogenous output of the process of party competition.

We also got things going in chapter 5 by making the very implausible assumption that party leaders are decision-making clones of each other, with every leader using precisely the same decision rule in the same intractable complex dynamic setting. We also know that this is not true. We know that different party leaders address themselves to the same setting using different decision-making styles. This is part of what is interesting about politics and is not something we should assume away. The second core aim of this chapter, therefore, is to model party competition when different party leaders use different decision rules in the same setting. We do this by building on an approach pioneered in a different context by Robert Axelrod (Axelrod 1980a, 1997, 1980b). This involves long-running computer "tournaments" that allow us to investigate the performance and "robustness" of decision rules in an environment where any politician using any rule may encounter an opponent using either the same decision rule or some quite different rule. We are interested in how each decision rule performs *against itself* and against opponents using the same rule and also in how each rule performs against opponents using *different* decision rules. We are *most* interested, however, in how a decision rule performs against anything the competitive environment might throw against it, including agents using decision rules that are difficult to anticipate and/or comprehend.

We define and investigate a large and eclectic set of decision rules for party leaders in the next chapter. In this chapter, our concern is to develop a scalable model of dynamic multiparty competition that describes interactions among politicians who choose from a set of different decision rules. We also take a big step toward a more realistic theoretical account of party competition by endogenizing the set of competing parties rather than setting this exogenously.

Modeling Competition among Agents Using Diverse Rules

Politics as a Tournament of Decision Rules

When a set of party leaders can choose any of a set of decision rules, the number of possible leader-rule combinations can be huge. It is given by the well-known formula for "combination with repetition."[1] With three decision rules currently specified and a number of parties that varies between 2 and 12, this gives 451 possible leader-rule combinations. This is not a gigantic number. We can specify exhaustive simulations of party competition under every possible rule combination. The problem is that this brute force method is not scalable. The number of possible leader-rule combinations increases explosively with both the number of decision rules and the number of party leaders. For example, Fowler and Laver investigated a system with typically 9 parties choosing from a set of 29 different rules (Fowler and Laver 2008). There are 124,403,620 different leader-rule combinations in this setting. Even with superfast modern computers, we run smack into a computational wall if we set out to investigate every one of these combinations in an exhaustive yet rigorous way. Clearly we must adapt our approach.

We do this by building on work by Fowler and Laver, which in turn built on a famous series of computer tournaments run by Robert Axelrod (Axelrod 1980a, 1997, 1980b; Fowler and Laver 2008). The Axelrod tournaments were designed to investigate strategies for playing the it-

---

[1] If r is the number of different decision rules and n is the number of parties who can choose these, then the number of different decision rule combinations (not paying attention to party names) is

$$\frac{(n + r - 1)!}{n!\,(r - 1)!}$$

erated two-person Prisoner's Dilemma (PD) game. Scholars were asked to submit decision rules for playing this game. These rules were pitted against each other in a series of computer simulations, which scored rules according to the payoffs they received. The first tournament (Axelrod 1980a) attracted fourteen entries. The winner was Tit-for-Tat: do to your opponent in round t whatever your opponent did to you in round $t-1$. There was then a second tournament; new entries could obviously take account of the published results of the first tournament (Axelrod 1980b). Tit-for-Tat won again, now beating sixty-two entries. In these tournaments, decision rules were predefined and immutable. In a more recent tournament, Axelrod explored the *evolution of new rules* for playing the iterated two-person PD game. He started with a set of random rules, as opposed to a set predefined by others, and applied the standard genetic operators of crossover and mutation to these over successive iterations, rewarding successful decision rules with higher fitness scores and hence higher reproduction probabilities (Axelrod 1997). Rules resembling Tit-for-Tat often emerged from this evolutionary process. Completely new types of successful rules also evolved, which beat Tit-for-Tat and involved strategies no game theorist had submitted to earlier tournaments.

Fowler and Laver (2008) adapted Axelrod's approach to the problem of assessing the performance of different decision rules pitted against each other in dynamic multiparty competition. They took the Laver (2005) ABM, programmed a version of this as a computational test bed, and published the test bed code. They invited scholars to submit new position-selection rules and offered a $1,000 prize for the rule most successful in winning votes in very long-running simulations. The four rules investigated by Laver (Hunter, Aggregator, Sticker, and Predator) were declared as pre-entered in the tournament but ineligible to win the prize. The Fowler-Laver tournament made three important substantive innovations. It specified a distinction between *interelectoral* and *electoral* periods of political competition It specified a *de facto threshold* that determined the continued survival of political parties. And it *forced the birth of new parties*, at random policy locations, using decision rules randomly chosen from the rule set under investigation. The latter is an artifact of the tournament method designed to "churn" rule combinations on a regular basis. We move beyond this below to a more realistic model of endogenous party birth. We see the first two innovations as substantively realistic features of any model of multiparty competition.

Distinguishing "Campaign" and "Election" Ticks

We have thus far assumed party competition to be a continuous process with no particular feature, such as an election, that distinguishes one day in politics from any other, one iteration of the model from the next. Elections do happen, however, so this is substantively unrealistic. Fowler and Laver (2008) made a distinction between

campaign ticks, during which politicians make decisions about party policy in response to published information, such as opinion poll feedback, about levels of party support;

election ticks, during which, in addition to decisions made during campaign ticks, voters make decisions about which party to vote for, rewards and punishments are administered, existing parties may die, new parties may be born.[2]

The distinction between campaign ticks and election ticks is substantively realistic. We thus modify our model to specify an exogenously fixed electoral cycle, with an election timing parameter, Ψ, specifying the frequency of election ticks relative to campaign ticks.[3] There is an election every Ψ ticks of the model. At the end of each of the Ψ-1 campaign ticks that happen between elections, party leaders choose policy positions and estimated levels of party support are revealed in published opinion polls. Politicians are not, however, subject to explicit rewards and punishments at the end of a campaign tick. In line with the wording of questions in real public opinion polls, published levels of party support at the end of campaign ticks reflect how people *would have voted if there had been an election that day*; they therefore offer crucial feedback to candidates. Campaign ticks allow parties to adapt and to evaluate their actions, but only at the end of an election tick do the chickens come home to roost. Only at elections do outcomes have real consequences for the success or failure of political parties.

Fowler and Laver specified an election every twenty model ticks. Since this value of Ψ was a published feature of model rules, the tournament was fair to all rule designers. Of course it was not "fair" to all conceivable decision rules, some of which could be at a relative disadvantage in an environment in which $\Psi = 20$.[4] This is why, while we replicate the Fowler-Laver tournament environment, we also treat election timing as a substantively interesting feature of the competitive environment. We thus treat Ψ as a free parameter in model runs, varying this within the range [10, 25].[5]

---

[2] For stylistic reasons, and using the same terminology as the NetLogo programming environment, we often use the word "tick" to refer to an iteration of the model.

[3] We thus do not model *endogenous* election timing. On this important matter see Smith (2004).

[4] A rule that explores the policy space for twenty ticks and then makes use of this information every twenty-first tick, for example, would be at an exquisite disadvantage when $\Psi = 20$.

[5] More precisely, we set Ψ at an integer value randomly chosen from a uniform distribution on the [10, 25] interval. We also investigated effects of sampling values of Ψ on the

Modeling Fitness, Survival, and Death

Any model of party competition that involves the "birth" of new parties with some positive probability axiomatically implies "death" of some existing parties. Otherwise the number of parties grows inexorably toward an absurd situation with an infinite number of parties. However it is clearly *not* the case in the real world that political parties die, or even become more likely to die, when they get old. Many political parties die young, while established parties often outlive their human founders. This led Laver and Schilperoord to model party "death" as a failure to maintain support above some critical "survival threshold," which is a key feature of each individual party system (Laver and Schilperoord 2007). We can see clearly that such thresholds do exist in the real world, since new parties are indeed born while the number of parties does not continue to grow inexorably. However, we find rather little in the political science literature, either on party death per se or on de facto party survival thresholds more generally.

We do of course know that there are typically thresholds embedded in the electoral formulas used for mapping votes cast into seats gained—for example the explicit 5 percent threshold in Germany. There are also implicit thresholds in all political systems that arise from interactions between electoral formulas, constituency size, and constituency-level concentrations of party support (Cox 1997). All of this, furthermore, is quite different from more general de facto survival thresholds for political parties, which refer to levels of voting support below which parties simply stop competing and go away. We know, for example, that de facto thresholds arise, among other things, from the candidate nomination process (how do you get yourself on the ballot?), the political financing process (who can give you how much money?), and the system of access to mass media (can you get your message across if you do not have any money?). We know informally that factors affecting party survival can arise from the cost and role of media advertising, public relations, private opinion polling, and all of the other things that can make running a really effective political campaign such an expensive proposition. The combination of these de facto survival thresholds clearly does have an impact. We know this axiomatically because party systems in different countries do experience the formation of new parties, while at the same time "sustaining" a long-run mean number of surviving parties that does not inexorably trend upward. And we know that de facto survival thresholds must differ among countries, since there are very different long-run

---

[5, 50] interval in exploratory work but found that there was no measureable effect once $\Psi > 25$. We found that setting $\Psi < 5$ could produce atypical results. Since the computational budget increases in linear proportion to Ψ, we confined subsequent experiments to sampling Ψ on the [10, 25] interval.

mean numbers of parties in different countries. We find two main parties in current U.S. politics at the federal level. There were ten parties in both the Dutch Tweede Kamer and the U.K. House of Commons after their respective general elections in 2010. This is despite superficially very similar electoral formulas in the United States and the United Kingdom and superficially very different formulas in the United Kingdom and the Netherlands.

Laver and Schilperoord (2007) modeled a diverse set of substantive effects by defining a single de facto survival threshold for political parties, specifying this in their simulations as 10 percent of the vote. This survival threshold, which we label τ, sets an axiomatic upper bound of $1/\tau$ on the number of surviving parties.[6] Hence, we treat τ in what follows as a substantively important party system parameter, specifying suites of simulations with Monte Carlo parameterizations in which the value of τ for each run is randomly picked from a uniform distribution on the [0.05, 0.30] interval. At the upper end of the values of τ we investigate, we expect to find something close to the two-party competition analyzed so intensively by many classical formal models. At the lower end of this range, the axiomatic upper bound on the number of parties is twenty, though this can arise only if all parties are of identical size. As we will see when we report computational results, the typical number of parties when the threshold is 0.05 is much fewer than this.

Rather than thinking of political parties as ceasing to exist the very second they fall below some survival threshold, it is natural in a dynamic setting to think of people as having prior beliefs about key features of party competition, such as the electoral support of different parties, and updating these beliefs when new information is revealed to them. We model this updating process by building on an approach used by Laver and Schilperoord (2007). We specify a recursive algorithm for how agents update information about the "fitness" of individual political parties, denominating fitness in terms of long-run vote share. Quite simply, a party's fitness after election e is its fitness at election e-1, updated by new information about its success at winning votes at election e.[7] The scale

---

[6] When the survival threshold is 0.10, for example, there cannot possibly be more than ten surviving parties; if there are eleven parties, simple arithmetic tells us that at least one of them must get less than one-tenth of the vote and thus be below the survival threshold.

[7] This recursive updating algorithm generates a measure of party fitness that is mathematically equivalent to the exponentially backward discounted sum of past party vote shares. In the context of party competition, our updating model is directly analogous to an updating model proposed by Erikson, MacKuen, and Stimson for *voter perceptions of party policy positions* (Erikson et al. 2002). Their notion is that a voter's prior perception of a party's policy position is updated in this way, but not completely replaced, by new information about party policy—for example a new party manifesto. They also use a memory parameter, a, to measure how much a voter's prior belief about a party position is updated by new information.

of this update is determined by a parameter, α_f ($0 \leq \alpha_f \leq 1$), that reflects the extent of agent "memories" of parties' past fitness.[8] More precisely, if v_{pe} is p's observed vote share at election e, and f_{pe} is party p's fitness after election e, then,

$$f_{pe} = \alpha_f \cdot f_{p(e-1)} + (1 - \alpha_f) \cdot v_{pe} \qquad (6.1)$$

Parties "die" when their updated fitness, f_{pe}, rather than their instantaneous vote share, v_{pe}, falls below the survival threshold τ. When α_f ("fitness-alpha") is zero there is a "goldfish memory" regime in which every day is the first day and agents remember nothing at all from the previous election, measuring current party fitness only in terms of current party performance. Under this regime, parties die the instant they fall below the survival threshold. This is the deeply implicit assumption of current static formal models of party competition. When $\alpha_f = 1$ there is a memory regime in which agents *never* update their estimates of party fitness from their original priors. Old parties never die under this regime. We expect values of α_f in the real world to be somewhere in between these extremes and use our computational experiments to investigate the effect of different values of α_f. Our Monte Carlo model parameterizations thus randomly picked a real value of α_f for each run from a uniform distribution on the [0.00, 0.90] interval.[9]

The simple two-parameter (α_f, τ) model of party fitness and survival that we specify here seems to us to be an elegant and realistic way to capture the evolving dynamics of party success and failure, and we build on it in subsequent chapters. From now on, all party systems we model have endogenously evolving sets of surviving parties. Since both party fitness and τ are denominated in vote shares we must keep in mind that,

---

[8] Note that we do not index α_f by i, assuming all agents in the system have the same memory model.

[9] We found in our methodological investigations that setting $\alpha_f > 0.9$ generated serious problems with both model burn-in and convergence on a stochastic steady state. In addition, we also confronted an operational problem that could generate peculiar interaction effects when running models with high survival thresholds and low memory parameters. These arose because it is possible for a new party to create a situation in which all parties are driven simultaneously below the survival threshold. For example, with three evenly balanced parties, and a survival threshold of 0.30, a new party entering at the "right" location can force the four resulting parties into a situation in which they each get about 0.25 of the vote and, if the memory parameter is low so updates are weighted heavily, all parties fall simultaneously below the survival threshold leaving no survivor. In a long-running simulation this is almost certain to happen. Since this seems absurd, we added a model assumption to address it. Parties whose fitness falls below the survival threshold die, provided the result is a system with two or more parties. In situations where simultaneous party deaths would result in either one or zero surviving parties, below threshold parties die in random order until only two parties survive, whereupon the two surviving parties are left in contention.

in common with almost all classical formal models of party competition, this gives a vote-seeking orientation to the competitive environment we model. We do not see this as unrealistic, while any evolutionary setting involves exogenously determined fitness criteria. Death, alas, is not a matter of opinion, while none of us can ultimately avoid death because we do not want to die. In the context of this book, however, this does mean that we should keep in mind that vote-seeking decision rules such as Hunter are programmed to increase their agents' vote shares; rules such as Sticker and Aggregator are not. This means, for example, that an Aggregator party that dies because it does not gather enough votes may not have failed *in its own terms*, which involve representing the wishes of current party supporters, however few these might be. If these supporters are not numerous enough, the party may die nonetheless.

Endogenous Party Birth

The birth of new parties is self-evidently an endogenous product of political competition. As we have seen, orthodox static spatial models of party competition have been extended to analyze the comparative statics of actual or anticipated "entry" by new parties into an existing party configuration. Key features of this work are reviewed by Shepsle; more recent writing, mostly by economists, is discussed by Dhillon and by Austen-Smith and Banks (Austen-Smith and Banks 2005; Dhillon 2005; Shepsle 1991). It is not our job to re-review this burgeoning literature, though we note that these models must be extraordinarily spare if they are to gain any sort of traction using classical formal analysis. Models of endogenous parties fall into three broad categories: those that describe new parties in terms of the *entry* of new agents from outside the system (Osborne 1993; Palfrey 1984), those that focus on *realignment* of existing coalitions of politicians into new party configurations (Ray and Vohra 1999; Levy 2004), and those that involve changes of state of political agents from "citizen" to "politician" (Osborne and Slivinski 1996; Besley and Coate 1997). Choice of modeling assumptions depends upon whether party competition is modeled in an electoral or a legislative setting. From the perspective of *electoral* competition, incentives to form new parties include the value of a party label in communicating policy positions to voters (Snyder and Ting 2002) and the desire of politicians to commit to positions other than their own ideal points when offering policy positions to voters (Levy 2004; Morelli 2004). If the focus is primarily on *legislative* politics, then parties may be seen as cartels formed to control aspects of legislative decision making (Cox and McCubbins 2005; Eguia 2007) or simply as emergent groups of like-minded legislators (Krehbiel 1993).

Our focus is this book is on *electoral* politics. Furthermore, we have already specified a "two-breed" model of political competition that distinguishes ordinary decent voters from the politicians who compete for their support. For reasons we take to be self-evident, we prefer to describe the emergence of new political parties in terms of *changes within* the political system as opposed to *entry or invasion by outside agents*.[10] We therefore exploit one of the key intuitions of the existing formal literature and model the "birth" of new political parties as a response by disgruntled voters to the existing configuration of party policy positions. Our model is thus an agent-based implementation of the core idea of "citizen candidate" models of new political parties (Osborne and Slivinski 1996; Besley and Coate 1997). We leave for future work the development of a more explicit model of *intraparty politics* that might form the basis of a dynamic model of continuously evolving coalitions of legislators according to which new parties may be formed as a result of splits or fusions of existing parties.

Voter Dissatisfaction

Our model of endogenous party birth assumes that new parties are formed by disgruntled voters. We must thus characterize the disgruntlement of voters with a configuration of party policy positions. In effect, we already did this in chapter 3, when specifying a metric for measuring "distances" between policy positions and a loss function for describing the effect of such policy distances on agent utility. We specified the distance between an agent's ideal point and some other policy position using a Euclidean metric and defined the utility of a policy position at j for a voter with an ideal point at i as the negative quadratic distance between the two policy positions.[11] We went on to define the satisfaction of a voter with the *overall configuration of policy positions* in terms of the quadratic distance between her ideal point and the policy position of the *closest party*.

As we noted when defining party fitness, it is substantively implausible in a dynamic setting to assume that voters respond only to the current instantaneous state of the system. It is much more plausible to assume they use their observations at tick t to update rather than completely determine their evaluations of the party system. Crudely speaking, if the past one hundred opinion polls reported the support of some party as being in the range of 20–30 percent, and some new poll reports that this support has fallen to 2 percent, we expect voters to discount this new information

---

[10] New politicians did enter the political fray from other counties in some postcommunist party systems, for example, but this is not in any way typical.
[11] $U(i, j) = -d(i, j)^2$, where $d(i, j)$ is the Euclidean distance between i and j.

to some extent and not to forget everything that has gone before. They may lower their estimate of current party support, but they will not immediately and completely update their estimate to that of the new poll. In what follows, therefore, we follow Laver and Schilperoord (2007) and model voter disgruntlement by specifying a simple updating model that is directly analogous to our updating model for party fitness. This defines d^*_{ce}, citizen c's updated dissatisfaction with the party system at election e, in the following recursive fashion:[12]

$$d^*_{ce} = \alpha_b \cdot d^*_{c(e-1)} + (1 - \alpha_b) \cdot d_{min}(i_c, j_e)^2 \qquad (6.2)$$

In this updating model, α_b ("birth-alpha") is a memory parameter describing how a voter updates her dissatisfaction with party policy positions and $d_{min}(i_c, j_e)$ is the distance between her ideal point and her closest party. If $\alpha_b = 0$ there is a "goldfish memory" regime. Voters treat every day as the first day and remember nothing from the past. A voter's updated dissatisfaction is simply the quadratic Euclidean distance between her ideal point and the current position of her closest party. If $\alpha_b = 1$, the voter never updates her dissatisfaction with the configuration of party positions, no matter what (crazy) positions any party adopts at election e. When $0 < \alpha_b < 1$, then the memory parameter α_b determines the extent to which each voter updates her dissatisfaction with the party system on the basis of her dissatisfaction with the current configuration of party positions. Laver and Schilperoord (2007) set $\alpha_b = 0.50$. This implies that a voter's updated dissatisfaction eight elections earlier contributes about 1 percent of the updated dissatisfaction in the current election. In exploratory work, we added α_b, and hence another dimension, to our parameter space and investigated the effects of different values of α_b. Since we found no statistically significant effect of α_b on model outputs of interest, we conserved our computational resources for more interesting problems and followed Laver and Schilperoord (2007) by setting $\alpha_b = 0.50$ for all runs.

A Model of Endogenous Party Birth

We are now in a position to specify a "citizen candidate" ABM of endogenous party birth. We assume every voter always has the implicit, albeit improbable, option of forming a new party by changing state from voter to party leader. The probability, p_{ce}, that citizen c changes state to party leader following election e increases in direct proportion to her updated dissatisfaction with the configuration of party positions. Thus $p_{ce} = \beta \cdot d^*_{ce}$,

---

[12] Note we assume voters get disgruntled only on the basis of party choices they have at election time. They do no get disgruntled on the basis of party positions between elections.

where β is the "birth" parameter, the sensitivity of each citizen's probability of becoming a politician to her updated dissatisfaction with the evolving configuration of party positions. The birth parameter β is scaled to the units in which policy distances, and thus d^*_{ce}, are measured. Because they are associated with an expected number of new party births per election, substantively realistic values of β are a function of how we calibrate the model to real time. Different values of β have the effect of controlling how *fast* the system evolves, rather than *how* it evolves in a substantive sense. For this reason, although we investigated the effect of different values of β in our exploratory work, we do not treat β as a free parameter in the simulations that follow. Rather, we fix it at a value that generates new party births at what we take to be a substantively plausible rate.[13]

Experiment and Run Design

Every computational experiment we report in the rest of this book involves interactions of party leaders who may use different decision rules, including rules with stochastic components. These interactions take place in evolutionary settings, also with stochastic components, in which some surviving parties may "die" and new parties may be "born." Our diagnostic work, described in chapter 4, unambiguously implies that the model runs in these experiments are stochastic processes for which a time average does *not* provide a representative estimate of μ.[14] We therefore execute several run repetitions until the process reaches steady state and calculate an ensemble average of each of the values of the output variables we collect from each of the repetitions. We find that one thousand repetitions, implying a run sample size of one thousand observations, are sufficient to pass all five of our diagnostic checks.

To determine burn-in for these processes, as we describe in chapter 4, we must use the graphical method on the most extreme run of this experiment. In fact, we have already examined this case in the empirical burn-in subsection of chapter 4. As we note there, the most extreme run is when

---

[13] To give an intuitive sense of our calibration of the party birth model, we use the following algorithm to determine the probability that a new party is born in any given election. One of 2,809 discrete voter locations within 3 SD units of the voter centroid is selected at random. This location "sprouts" a new party with a probability $\beta \cdot d^*_{ce}$. We set $\beta = 1$. The median value of d^*_{ce} for the 2,809 voter locations, for the evolved six-party system that tends to arise when $\tau = 0.10$, is of the order of 0.10–0.20. Therefore, this generates a new party roughly every five to ten elections, which we feel is not unrealistic.

[14] Specifically, the R-hat statistics calculated for our summary measures, mean eccentricity and ENP, never fell below 1.1 even after very long-run repetitions of fifty thousand elections.

the survival threshold is set at 0.05 and there are many surviving parties. As we see from Figure 4.5, the summary variables, mean eccentricity and ENP, appear to be in steady state after 200 elections. We err on the side of caution and consider that a run repetition has reached steady state after 250 elections.

To summarize our run design, we employ a mean estimation strategy for stochastic processes for which a time average does not provide a representative estimate of μ. For each run, we execute one thousand separate run repetitions for 251 iterations, each iteration being an election tick in the model.[15] For each run repetition, we collect the values of all output variables at election 251. Finally, we calculate an ensemble average over the one thousand repetitions to generate a mean estimate of μ for each of the output variables for each run. We use this run procedure for all subsequent simulations we report in this book.

Turning to experimental design, we continue to employ the Monte Carlo method with one thousand runs per experiment. Each experiment therefore involves one million run repetitions in all—one thousand runs per experiment multiplied by one thousand repetitions per run.[16] Each of the one thousand runs has a Monte Carlo parameterization in which parameter settings are randomly chosen from ranges we have argued are substantively meaningful:

- Ψ: the number of campaign ticks per election; run parameter settings are randomly chosen from a uniform distribution of integers on the [10, 25] interval;
- τ: the de facto survival threshold—run parameter settings are randomly chosen from a uniform distribution of floating point numbers on the [0.05, 0.30] interval;
- α_p, the memory parameter in the model agents used to update party fitness—run parameter settings are randomly chosen from a uniform distribution of floating point numbers on the [0.00, 0.90] interval.

Moving beyond the assumption that distributions of ideal points are perfectly symmetric about the voter centroid, our computational work in the rest of this book is based on the asymmetric ideal point distributions that are aggregations of two subpopulations, as described in chapter 3. This distribution of voter ideal points has two parameters:

---

[15] We therefore do not count the campaign ticks between elections as iterations.

[16] Our computational budget for this experiment, given that we reach steady state by iteration 251, is therefore 1,000 runs × 1,000 repetitions × 251 elections = 251 million elections. Since each election on average requires 17.5 campaign ticks, this budget implies approximately 4.4 billion simulated campaign ticks.

118 • Chapter 6

n_l / n_r, the relative size of subpopulations, is sampled from a uniform distribution of floating point numbers on the interval [2.00 1.00];

μ_r (= $-\mu_l$), the subpopulation ideal point means, are sampled from a uniform distribution of floating point numbers on the interval [0.00, 1.50].

Multiparty Competition with Diverse Decision Rules

From this point on we investigate competitive environments where the set of surviving parties is endogenous and different party leaders typically use different decision rules. Many of our more interesting results concern the relative performance of different rules. As well as aggregate party system outputs we specified and reported above, therefore, we also look at the typical number of party leaders using each decision rule, the average vote share won by the set of parties using particular rules, and the mean policy eccentricity of parties using particular rules.

Vote Shares of Parties Using Each Rule

Figure 6.1 summarizes the first set of results derived from the experiment specified above. As before, we summarize the nonlinear relationships contained in this huge amount of simulated data using fractional polynomial prediction plots. The gray bands show 95 percent confidence intervals around these plots for the sets of data points generated by the simulation, arising from one thousand repetitions of one thousand model runs, each run with a Monte Carlo parameterization. The narrowness of these confidence intervals shows us that these estimates are very precise, vindicating our run design and estimation procedures.

Measuring success in terms of aggregate vote shares of sets of parties using each decision rule, the vote-seeking Hunter rule is by far the most successful—a conclusion that does not depend in any way on the precise parameterization of the environment for party competition. Taking into account all parameterizations of the competitive environment that we investigated in this experiment, mean vote shares of sets of parties using each rule were Hunter, 0.70; Aggregator, 0.21; and Sticker, 0.09.[17] Although it is not very surprising to find that the vote-seeking rule does best at finding votes, our simulations do demonstrate quite clearly that Hunter's Pavlovian vote-seeking algorithm works well. Of the two rules not explicitly programmed to seek votes, Aggregators were much more successful than Stickers.

---

[17] Standard errors of these means were, respectively, 0.003, 0.003, and 0.001.

Interaction of Different Decision Rules • 119

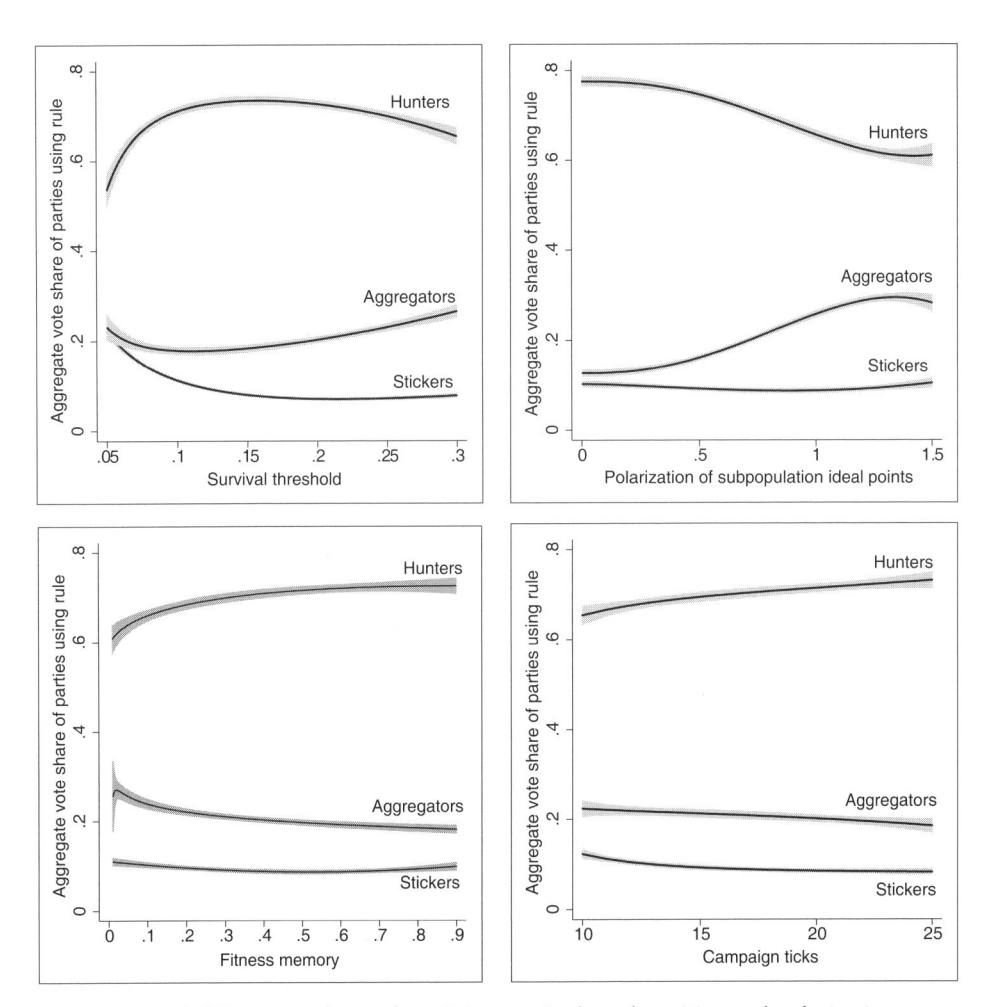

Figure 6.1. Mean vote share of surviving parties by rule, τ, Ψ, α_f and polarization of subpopulation ideal points. Each data point summarized in these plots represents the run mean estimate of the average vote share for each of the three decision rules for each of the one thousand runs of the experiment. Each run mean estimate is calculated by executing one thousand separate run repetitions for 251 elections, taking the results from the 251st election as the estimate of the steady-state decision rule vote shares for each repetition, and then taking the average of these one thousand repetition estimates.

Figure 6.1 also plots the relationships between the relative performance of decision rules and parameterized features of the competitive environment that we vary systematically in the computational experiment. The lower panels show that fitness memory, α_f, and election timing, ψ, have distinct if modest effects on the relative success of party decision rules.[18] Hunters fare better when party fitness updates more slowly (that is, for high values of α_f). This is because they make random exploratory moves when punished with lower support; these random moves carry no guarantee of success and may well, in the short run, result in *lower* levels of support. When $\alpha_f = 0$, a party's fitness is simply its current vote share; no account is taken of past success, and the party will be killed off the instant its vote share falls below the threshold. With higher values of α_f, the competitive environment is more "forgiving" of short-term dips in support, provided these are corrected. Parties are killed off only if their vote share stays below the threshold for a number of elections. The continuously adapting Hunter rule also tends to be less successful in environments with shorter election campaigns that allow parties less time to adapt, for example to the birth of a new political party close to them in the policy space.

The top two panels highlight the big news in these results, however. Party leaders using the Aggregator rule tend systematically to win more support, and those using Hunter to win less support, when survival thresholds are higher and when voter ideal points are more polarized. The relative success of the Aggregator rule is doubly enhanced when there are higher levels of polarization, if survival thresholds are also higher so that there are fewer parties. This is a classic interaction effect between polarization of the electorate and the number of parties that survive, given the survival threshold. Figure 6.2 plots this effect systematically. The gray bands summarize the performance of each decision rule when there are typically four parties or more. They show no significant relationship between rule performance and polarization in these settings. The black bands summarize the same relationship when there are three or fewer parties. Decision rule performance now responds sharply to electoral polarization. Aggregators now perform substantially better, and Hunters substantially worse, as electorates become more polarized. The black bands show that, with highly polarized subpopulations and few parties, Aggregators perform almost as well *at winning votes* as vote-seeking Hunters.

This happens because of the systematic emergence of the type of situation of shown in Figure 5.8. When survival thresholds are high, there tend to be only two or three parties, quite commonly three. In this event and with polarized electorates, one of the two subpopulations can axiomatically be "served" by just a single party. *If this party uses a vote-seeking rule such as Hunter*, then there is nothing in the dynamics of party competition to deter it from systematically moving away from "its" subpopulation and toward the other parties, in search of more votes. This is bad

---

[18] The relative size of the two voter subpopulations has no noticeable effect and is not shown here. This plot is shown in Figure E6.1 in the electronic appendix.

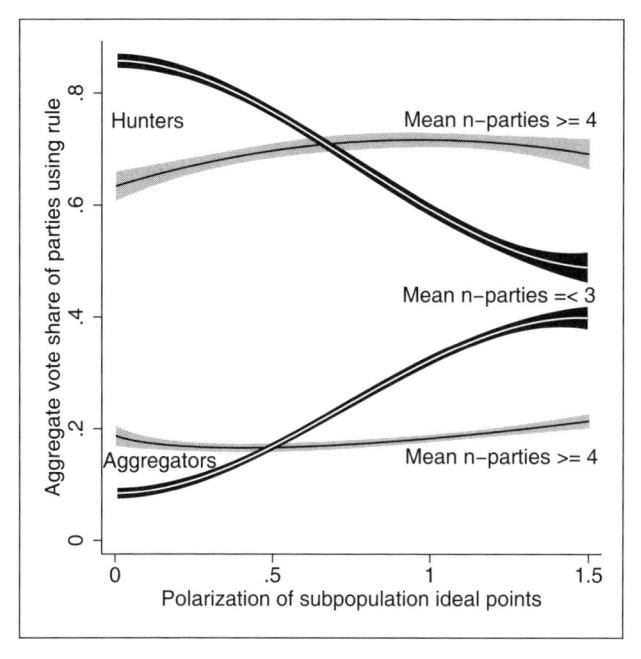

Figure 6.2. Aggregate vote share of parties using different decision rules, by ideal point polarization and number of surviving parties.

for representation of subpopulation ideal points, as we will soon see, but it is also bad for the party, which is now just one of three parties competing for vote share in the overall population.

In somewhat counterintuitive contrast, if the lone party serving one of the subpopulations uses an Aggregator rule, then it *tends to stay close to "its" subpopulation ideal point centroid and faces no incentive to move away from this*. The Aggregator party keeps well clear of the other two parties and the other subpopulation. Somewhat surprisingly, this is actually good for its vote share since it now monopolizes an entire subpopulation. This presages important and counterintuitive results that run throughout the rest of this book. We can systematically identify situations in which, if you are a party leader, insatiably seeking more votes *may be bad for your vote share*. The only way for this thought-provoking conclusion to emerge is to specify and analyze dynamic models of party competition in which different party leaders use different decision rules.

Numbers of Surviving Parties Using Each Decision Rule

Figure 6.3 plots the effect of the survival threshold, τ, on the number of surviving parties using each rule. Recall that $1/\tau$ sets an axiomatic up-

122 • Chapter 6

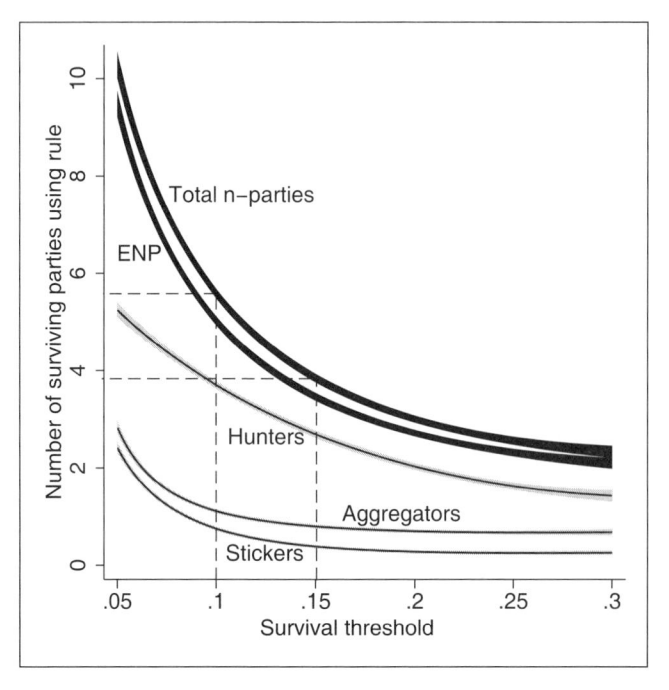

Figure 6.3. Mean number of surviving parties, by decision rule and survival threshold.

per bound on the total number of surviving parties. We thus expect a reciprocal relationship between τ and the total number of parties, and the upper black band of Figure 6.3 shows that this is what we find.[19] We see, however, that the number of surviving parties is typically much less than this axiomatic upper bound, which would be ten parties with a survival threshold of 0.10, for example. This is because the upper bound can be achieved only when all parties have identical and constant sizes, while the typical situation *in a dynamic party system* is that party sizes vary considerably over time.

Figure 6.3 gives us important substantive insights into dynamic party systems with endogenous parties. It shows, for example, that a survival threshold of 0.10 of the total vote tends to be associated over the long run with a five- or six-party system, and an effective number of parties (ENP) of about five. A threshold of 0.15 tends to be associated with a

---

[19] Plotting the number of parties or ENP against $1/\tau$, we get a straight line. See Figure E6.2 in the electronic appendix.

four-party system and an ENP of about 3.5; and so on. If we believe our model (and of course we do), this allows us, for any real party system that interests us, to "back out" the unobservable party survival threshold from the number of surviving parties we observe over the long run. If we tend to observe six surviving parties, this implies a de facto threshold of about 0.10; a four-party system implies a threshold of about 0.15; and so on.

The other striking pattern in Figure 6.3 is that, in an environment where parties "die" if their updated fitness falls below the survival threshold, far more surviving parties use Hunter than use any other rule. Lowering the de facto survival threshold radically increases the number of surviving parties using any rule, but until thresholds get very low and there are six or more surviving parties, it particularly increases the number of parties using relatively successful rules such as Hunter. This is the first sign of *evolutionary* dynamics in the party systems we model, dynamics that will color most of the rest of this book. These dynamics arise because relatively unfit parties die, relatively fit parties survive, so *the set of surviving parties is relatively fit*. We can access this type of conclusion, of course, only if we model continuously evolving dynamic systems with endogenous political parties.[20]

Life Expectancy of Political Parties

Closely related to party survival is party life expectancy—typical party ages at death in an evolving party system in which the surviving parties are those that stay above the survival threshold. Figure 6.4 plots the effects of the party survival threshold and the rate of fitness updating, on the median longevities of parties whose leaders use different decision rules.[21] Hunter parties tend to survive for *much* longer as the survival threshold decreases and as party fitnesses update more slowly (that is, as α_f increases). This effect is disproportionately greater for Hunter than for other rules.

Very tight confidence intervals in the left-hand plot show that the relationship between survival thresholds and party longevities is, as might be expected, extraordinarily crisp. While a more "forgiving" fitness regime, which updates more slowly, is less likely to kill off Hunters that have briefly fallen below the survival threshold in random searches for

---

[20] Figure E6.2 in the electronic appendix shows that, in line with results reported in Figure 6.1, the rate of updating of party fitness also has some effect on the number of parties using Hunter, while polarization of subpopulation ideal points or campaign length have no significant effect.

[21] We use the median rather than the mean as a summary of party life spans because, as with any survival process, the exponential distribution of party life spans is highly skewed.

124 • Chapter 6

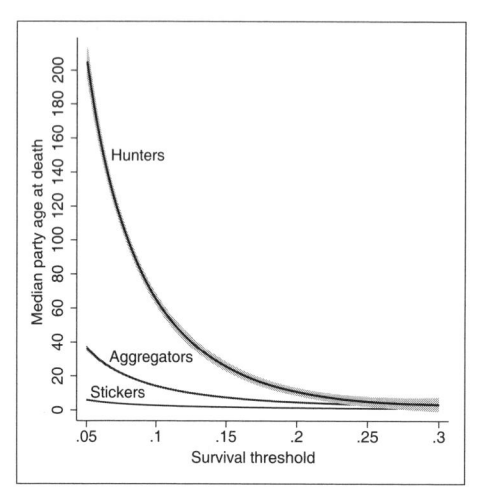

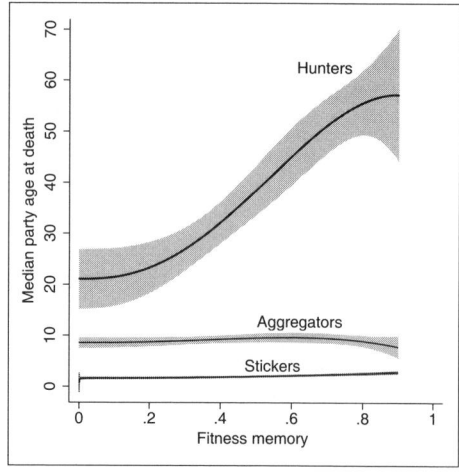

Figure 6.4. Median party age (elections survived) at death, by decision rule, survival threshold, and fitness memory.

higher voter shares, wider confidence bands around Hunter longevity in the right-hand plot reflect the very sharp effect of different party survival thresholds on Hunter longevity holding fitness memory constant. In short, there are more Hunter parties, as we saw in Figure 6.3, leading to a greater level of success for the Hunter rule, as we saw in Figure 6.1, because *Hunter parties are much more likely to survive than parties using other rules*, especially when survival thresholds are low.[22]

Since new parties choose decision rules at random in this environment,[23] and since parties using the Hunter rule are much more likely to survive than other parties, there is a preponderance of Hunters in the set of surviving parties. This is the key to the success of Hunter in the party systems we investigate here. It is not that surviving Hunter parties tend to win more votes—for the most part they are competing with other Hunter parties after all. The relative success of the Hunter rule arises because, quite simply, *there are more surviving Hunter parties* in this evolutionary setting.

---

[22] Figure E6.3 in the electronic appendix shows that polarization of subpopulation ideal points and the number of campaign ticks between elections have no substantial effect on party longevity.

[23] We turn in chapter 8 to a setting in which rule replication probabilities are endogenous.

Policy Positions of New and Surviving Parties

Analyzing typical party policy eccentricities in "one-rule" party systems, we found in chapter 5 that parties using the vote-seeking Hunter rule systematically pick more central policy positions than parties using other rules. The gray bands in the left panel of Figure 6.5 plot mean policy eccentricities of parties using different decision rules, now in an environment where the set of surviving parties and the set of decision rules they use are both endogenous. Hunter parties, now competing directly with parties using different decision rules, still systematically choose policy positions that are closer to the center than other parties, regardless of the parameterization of the competitive environment. The black band shows the typical policy positions of endogenous party births. Strikingly, we see that party births tend systematically to be at policy positions that are significantly more eccentric than those of surviving parties, whatever decision rule these parties use. Averaged across all random parameterizations of the competitive environment, mean policy eccentricities of *surviving* parties using various decision rules were Hunter, 0.61; Aggregator, 0.94; Sticker, 0.74. The mean policy eccentricity of new party births was 1.25.[24]

Although in no way designed to do this, our model generates dynamic party systems in which *new parties typically emerge at relatively eccentric locations in the policy space and typically adapt over time to take more central policy positions*. For Stickers, who never change position, this involves more eccentric Stickers tending to die and less eccentric Stickers tending to survive. For parties using other rules, in addition to the increased likelihood that more eccentric parties will die, the more central location of surviving parties arises because, following party birth, party leaders tend to adapt their policy positions centripetally. This seems to us to be substantively plausible, as well as being a clearcut empirical implication of our model. Previewing results we report in chapter 11, we do indeed find that typical policy positions of surviving parties in real party systems are systematically less eccentric than those of new party births.

The right panel of Figure 6.5 shows that party policy positions are *sharply sensitive to the centroids of subpopulation ideal points*. As voter subpopulations become more polarized, so do typical party policy positions. This is true regardless of the party decision rule, though Hunter parties still systematically choose policy positions closer to the center than other parties. The dashed diagonal line in Figure 6.5 shows what would happen if party policy eccentricities were precisely the same as

---

[24] Standard errors of each of these mean estimates were 0.01.

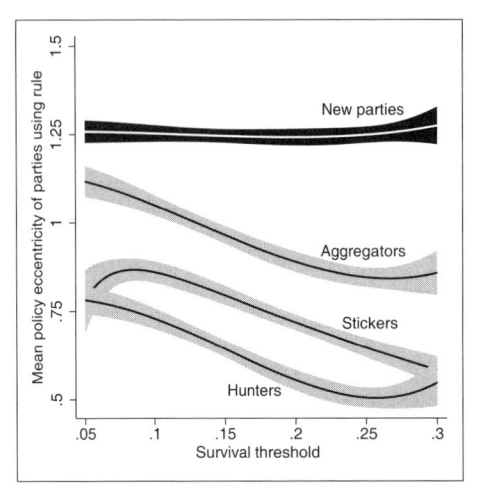

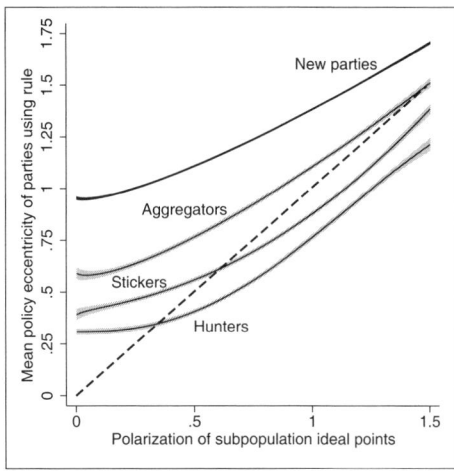

Figure 6.5. Mean policy eccentricity of surviving and new parties, by τ and the polarization of subpopulation ideal points.

those of subpopulation ideal point centroids. Reprising results reported in chapter 5, we find that when voter polarization is low and ideal point densities are therefore unimodal, typical party policy positions are more eccentric than the voter centroid. As voters become more polarized, surviving Aggregators tend to pick policy positions that approach subpopulation ideal point centroids. It is also clearly the case that Hunter parties, while always tending to be more central than Stickers and Aggregators, do also tend to pick policy positions that respond in a very precise way to the centroids of subpopulation ideal points.

The results plotted in the right panel of Figure 6.5 are substantively important. Ever since the original Hotelling-Black-Downs model of one-dimensional spatial party competition, substantive interest in modeling party competition has focused on the extent to which, both in models and in reality, political parties tend to converge on the ideological center ground. We saw in chapter 5 that, even without making any extra assumption to constrain party movement in some way, convergence on the center is *not* generic in dynamic multiparty competition in multidimensional policy spaces. We now see that, when voters are structured into relatively polarized subpopulations, adaptive parties tend to converge on *subpopulation* voter centroids when setting party policy positions in dynamic multiparty competition. Thinking of these distinct subpopulations as social or ethnic groups, for example, then Figure 6.5 suggests that these groups may tend to become *better* served by "their own" political parties as subpopulations become more polarized—in effect because party competition increasingly becomes an intragroup rather than an intergroup activity.

Representativeness of the Party System

A core substantive and normative concern of this book is the representativeness of configurations of party policy positions that typically emerge in different competitive environments. We know from chapter 5 that representativeness of the party system is sharply affected by both the number of parties and the polarization of the electorate. We have now made the number of parties an endogenously evolving feature of party competition, and we saw in Figure 6.3 that this is sharply affected by the survival threshold. Competitive environments with lower survival thresholds sustain more parties. The top panel of Figure 6.6 both plots and summarizes each of the one thousand data points generated by our experiment and shows the crystal clear pattern resulting from all of this.[25] Representativeness of the party system is sharply affected by the survival threshold; higher survival thresholds imply less representative party systems.

We also see a systematically increasing scatter of points as the survival threshold increases. This happens because, as we show below, higher thresholds imply fewer parties and, when there are fewer parties, polarization of the electorate also has a huge effect on representativeness, holding the threshold constant. When there are lower thresholds and consequently more parties, in contrast, ideal point polarization has almost no effect on the representatives of emergent configurations of party policy positions.[26]

The bottom-left panel in Figure 6.6 shows the impact on party system representativeness of the "sea change" we observed in Figure 5.10. In polarized electorates, when the number of parties drops below four, one of the two subpopulations must be "served" by at most one party. If this party is a Hunter, as Figure 6.3 shows us it is most likely to be, then it will not be punished when it searches for more votes by moving party policy away from the centroid of voter ideal points in the subpopulation it is currently serving. As we saw from the example in Figure 5.8, the short-run effect of this is an entire subpopulation of voters with no party representing their ideal points. Given our model of endogenous party birth, this situation is now likely to be remedied at some point by a party birth in the "deserted" subpopulation, but if survival thresholds

---

[25] Recall that each data point is estimated from one-thousand-run repetitions.
[26] This is one of the main examples of such heteroscedasticity in the data generated by our simulations.

128 • Chapter 6

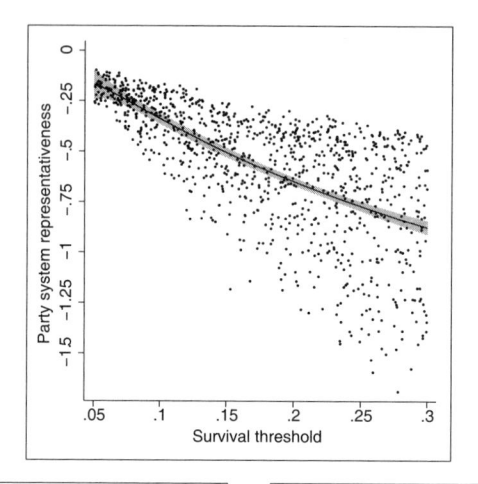

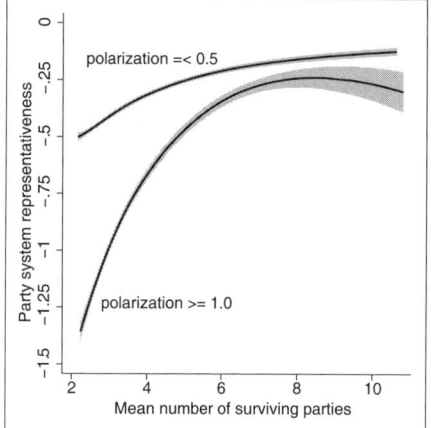

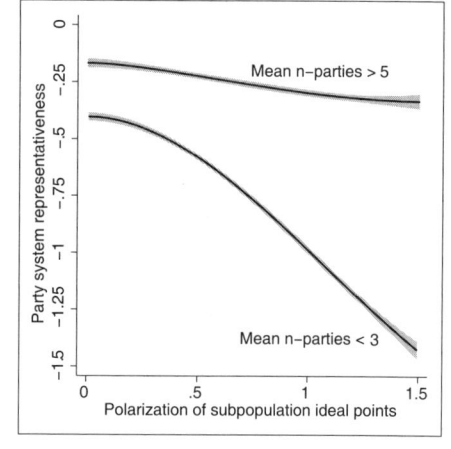

Figure 6.6. Mean party system representativeness by τ, mean number of surviving parties, and polarization of ideal point centroids.

are high the cycle of desertion will then repeat itself. With four or more parties in contention, there is typically more than one party serving each subpopulation. In this event, party system representativeness both is relatively high and shows little variation, being unaffected by other party system parameters.[27]

All of this can be seen clearly in the bottom-left panel of Figure 6.6, which plots the relationship between the typical number of surviving

---

[27] Figure E6.5 in the appendix plots the effects of other party system parameters on representativeness.

parties and party system representativeness, distinguishing electorates with high ($\mu_r \geq 1.0$) and low ($\mu_r \leq 0.5$) ideal point polarization. When polarization of the electorate is low, the aggregate distribution of voter ideal points is unimodal (if asymmetric), and we see that the number of surviving parties has a relatively small effect on representativeness of the evolved configuration of party policy positions. In contrast when polarization is high and the aggregate population distribution is bimodal, the steep slope of the lower band in this panel shows that the number of surviving parties has a sharp effect on party system representativeness.

This effect is further illustrated in the bottom-right panel of Figure 6.6, which plots representativeness against subpopulation polarization, distinguishing settings where the typical number of surviving parties was fewer than three from those where it was more than five. The lower band shows that, when there are typically fewer than three surviving parties, representativeness of the emergent set of party policy positions declines steeply as voter polarization increases. In contrast, when there are typically more than four surviving parties, party positions tend to represent voter ideal points well, no matter how polarized the voting population. As we have seen, this is because party competition tends to evolve into competition for votes within one or the other subpopulation, with effectively no competition among parties representing different subpopulations. A striking empirical example of this can be found in Northern Ireland, where elections are played out between a set of parties competing for the support of nationalist/Catholic voters and a quite different set competing for the support of unionist/Protestant voters.

CONCLUSIONS

We move far beyond our baseline model of party competition in this chapter, to model evolving dynamic multiparty systems in which the set of *surviving* political parties is an endogenous output of party competition, and where the leaders of different surviving parties may use different decision rules to set party policy positions. This takes us deeply into a theoretical realm in which rigorous and systematic investigations are feasible only using the new technology of computational agent-based modeling, as opposed to traditional pencil and paper formal methods.

This extension of our model has revealed interesting and important substantive conclusions. Some of these concern the endogenous set of surviving parties. Since the de facto survival threshold imposes an axiomatic upper bound on the number of surviving parties, we expect to find that higher survival thresholds imply fewer surviving parties (Figure 6.3) with shorter life expectancies (Figure 6.4). The set of surviving parties is conditioned but not determined by the survival threshold since, in a dynamic party system, (1) party support shares vary continuously and (2) the memory regime in the competitive environment affects the extent to which short-term dips in party support below the threshold are "forgiven" if these are subsequently reversed. Given all of this, the results summarized in Figure 6.3 allow us to back out the unobservable de facto survival threshold of any real party system from the observable number of surviving parties over the long run. We see that, if we typically observe four surviving parties over the long run, for example, this implies a de facto survival threshold of about 15 percent of the vote. Similarly, the two-party system we observe in the United States implies a survival threshold of about 30 percent of the vote.

Over and above the effect of survival thresholds on the set of surviving parties, our new conclusions in this chapter concern an interesting and substantively important interaction effect—between survival thresholds and the degree of ideal point polarization in the electorate. As we saw from Figure 6.1, Hunter parties remain very successful at winning votes when they compete with parties using other decision rules. But we also saw from Figure 6.2 that the *relative success of Hunter parties is strongly conditioned by an interaction between survival thresholds and electoral polarization*. Vote-seeking Hunters perform relatively worse at finding votes, and Aggregators are relatively better at doing this, when survival thresholds are high, so there are few parties, *and* the electorate is polarized. In these settings Aggregator parties, programmed only to please their *current* supporters, may win more votes over the long run because they do not, in search of more support in the short term, desert a subpopulation for which they are the sole party in contention.

This interaction between survival thresholds and polarization strongly conditions our results on representativeness of emergent configurations of party policy positions. Figure 6.5 shows that, whichever decision rule party leaders use, *party policy positions sharply track subpopulation ideal point centroids* as electorates become more polarized. This strongly affects representativeness, as we can see in Figure 6.6. The lower panels of Figure 6.6 show the interaction between survival thresholds and polarization of the electorate in two different ways. The key point is that, when survival thresholds are low and there are four or more parties in contention, the dynamics of competitive party position taking do *not* affect the representativeness of emergent configurations of party policy positions in any substantial way, even in highly polarized electorates. In such polarized settings, party competition tends to resolve into competition among parties within two subpopulations; there is little or no competition among parties in different subpopulations. For the same high level of electoral polarization, however, high survival thresholds that typically result in three or fewer parties can have disastrous effects on representativeness, as vote-seeking parties face incentives to "desert" any subpopulation within which they are currently the sole contender.

Putting on the uniform of social planners concerned above all to enhance the representativeness of emergent configurations of party policy positions, the interaction between the de facto survival threshold and voter polarization is very significant. It implies that engineering low survival thresholds—by changing the electoral system, laws on party financing, or rules dealing with access to mass media at election time, for example—*is of particular importance when the voting population is polarized*. In such polarized settings, Figure 6.6 shows us that high survival thresholds, and the resulting low number of surviving parties, have particularly severe effects on representativeness. In contrast, if voters are relatively unpolarized, then the number of surviving parties does not have a huge effect on representation. Our results thus provide strong support for arguments in favor of using proportional representation electoral systems in divided societies (Lijphart 1994, 1999; Lijphart and Waisman 1996).

Another way of thinking about this is to imagine electorates that become more, or less, polarized for reasons exogenous to our model. Think of a two-party system such as we find in the federal politics of the United States, for example, which self-evidently must have a high de facto survival threshold. If both parties are insatiable vote seekers, then the emergent configuration of party policy positions will become increasingly less representative if voters become more polarized. Conversely, if parties seek only to please their current support base, in effect using an Aggregator rule, polarization of the electorate will not have the same adverse effects on party system representativeness, as the parties' policy positions track the diverging ideal point centroids of their support base. Furthermore, if one party were to use a vote-seeking rule while the other was an Aggregator, the vote-seeking party would desert its own support base and "chase" the Aggregator well away from the center ground. Under our model of endogenous parties, however, a new party birth (or rebirth) would occur in the deserted subpopulation. But then the cycle would repeat itself again, and again

CHAPTER SEVEN

New Decision Rules, New Rule Features

WE WENT FAR BEYOND our baseline model of party multiparty competition in the previous chapter, and also beyond much of the existing work in this subject. We did this by modeling the set of competing parties as an endogenous output of, not an exogenous input to, the dynamic process of multiparty competition, and by modeling competition between party leaders using different decision rules in this complex environment. Those decision rules for setting party policy, however, were limited to the set of three baseline rules we specified in chapter 3: Sticker, Aggregator, and Hunter. We now go well beyond this to investigate implications of having a very large and diverse set of decision rules that any party leader might use.

We define two completely new vote-seeking rule "species." We also identify and specify a range of parameterized "features" of all decision rules, such as the "speed" at which party policy is changed, or the extent to which party leaders are "satisfied" with any given vote share. We specify and investigate a set of 111 different decision rules in what follows, although the approach we set out is entirely scalable.[1] More rule species, features, and parameterizations can easily be defined and added by anyone who might be interested. The model we specify below can comprehend a gigantic rule set. We confine ourselves here to investigating "only" 111 different decision rules, however, since we like parsimonious models that generate easily interpretable results. At the same time, these results give us good intuitions about dynamic multiparty competition when party leaders may choose from a large and diverse rule set.

SPECIFYING THE RULE SPACE

The last thing we want to do is to define a whole set of new decision rules for multiparty competition in an ad hoc way off the top of our heads. The result would be a model that is impossible to investigate using the carefully designed and rigorous computational experiments that are the

---

[1] More precisely, these are "rule parameterizations" or even "rule-leader parameterizations," but we often refer to them for stylistic reasons as decision rules in what follows.

sine qua non of this book. We therefore expand the rule set by identifying and specifying a well-parameterized *rule space* for party leaders—a space that in essence underlies the type of parameter grid we describe in chapter 4 and illustrate in Figures 4.1 and 4.2. We specify this rule space in two different ways.

First, we define two new "species" of vote-seeking rules for party leaders. One of these is a new version of the *Predator* rule identified by Laver (2005). This uses the policy position of the largest party as evidence of high voter densities. The second new rule species we investigate derives from seminal ABMs of multiparty competition put forward by Kollman, Miller, and Page (1992). We call this rule *Explorer*. It is a "hill-climbing" rule species that searches for votes by sampling policy positions in its local neighborhood and moves to locations yielding higher vote shares. We now have a rule space with five discrete species: Sticker, Aggregator, Hunter, Predator, and Explorer.

We expand this rule space by identifying and specifying some important general features of decision rules for multiparty competition. The most plausible and interesting of these, generating the most important results in this chapter, is *satisficing*. A satisficing politician does nothing at all if the current state of the world is generating utility at or above some internal "comfort threshold," which we label κ, but implements decision rule R, whatever R might be, whenever utility income falls below κ. The "insatiable" rules we investigated thus far are special cases of satisficing rules, with comfort thresholds set so high that party leaders are never satisfied and always want more. The most important result in this chapter is that satisficing rules for multiparty competition, despite often mandating inaction, can in *dynamic* settings systematically outperform insatiable rules that always seek higher vote shares.

In addition to satisficing, we identify and specify the rule feature of *speed*. Some people adapt to changing environments more quickly than others. While speed of adaptation obviously has no meaning in static models of party competition, the relative speed of any decision maker is critical in any *dynamic* model. As every gunslinger knows, it is no good finally finding the exquisitely perfect move if the game is over, you are dead, and everyone has gone home before you figure this out.[2]

---

[2] We investigated two additional rule features in our exploratory work. These were *jitter*, which involved random perturbations around any otherwise specified policy position, and *wobble*, which involved random perturbations around any otherwise specified direction of movement. An extensive series of exploratory experiments showed that the effects of these two rule features were not in the end very interesting. We found that the larger the random shocks involved in jittering and wobbling, and hence the more the party simply made random policy moves, the less successful was any decision rule. This is a non-negligible finding, but it is very predictable. Having confirmed it in exploratory runs, our finite com-

New Rule Species: Predator

A vote-seeking *Predator* rule was defined by Laver (2005). The rule mandates that you stand still if you are the largest party, else move directly toward the largest party. Laver's results showed that this rule generates pathological emergent behavior when more than one Predator is in contention. This is because all such Predators have the same "prey," the largest party; they all therefore move toward an identical point in the policy space. Having converged on this point, all Predators then move in lockstep forever after. Watching simulations in motion, we see that "predators" look much more like zombies than anything else. Notwithstanding this, *using the manifest success of other agents to inform your own decision making* is an important heuristic device. We therefore redefine the Predator rule to model decision rules that work by exploiting successful choices made by other agents.[3] Taking account of the fact that there may well be more than one Predator in contention, we redefine the Predator rule so that Predators prefer "prey" parties that are closer to them in the policy space. Attacking closer prey parties yields quicker results and means that Predators in different locations may well identify different prey parties.[4] Instead of always moving toward the party with most support, we program Predators to move toward the *closest party with more support than themselves*.[5] Thus reprogrammed, a set of Predators no longer have the emergent behavior of all attacking precisely the same prey. This gives us

---

puting resources were far better invested in computational work yielding the deeper and more intriguing results we report below. We also considered two other rule features: "secret handshakes," whereby rules are programmed to recognize and possibly coordinate with other agents using the same rule; and "anticannibal" programming, whereby rules are programmed not to attack other agents using the same rule. We rejected these because we find it very plausible substantively to assume different party leaders using the same decision rule indeed do indeed attack each other, and very implausible to assume party leaders secretly tell each other they are using the same decision rule. We would not want to balance a model of party competition on such assumptions.

[3] Akin to Predators but with a less glamorous public image, some rules submitted to the Fowler-Laver (2008) tournament can be seen as *parasites*. It is however more plausible in the context of party competition to think of predators rather than parasites. The behavior we have in mind involves attacking *different* prey parties in succession, rather than a parasitic agent insinuating itself in a *single host* and staying with this.

[4] This intuition modifies a similar "niche-predator" rule, submitted to the Fowler-Laver (2008) tournament by Jo Andrews, which identifies a set of "adjacent" prey parties.

[5] This aspect of the Predator rule is deterministic; we could make it stochastic by making the probability a Predator moves toward any given party, including itself, some function of the matrix of party support levels and positions on each policy dimension. As we already noted, however, we prefer simple decision rules.

Predator: If you are the largest party: stand still. Else: identify your "prey" as the closest of the set of parties with more support than you; set heading toward prey; move in the resulting direction.[6]

New Rule Species: Explorer

An important feature of the competitive environment we have specified is the distinction between *campaign* ticks, which yield information but not rewards or punishments, and *election* ticks, during which rewards and punishments are meted out in the form of fitness updates. The seminal paper on dynamic party competition by Kollman, Miller, and Page (hereafter KMP) makes a similar distinction. One of the main decision rules KMP investigate is what they call a "climbing adaptive" rule. This explores immediately adjacent positions between elections, moving at election time to the investigated position that yields the most votes (Kollman et al. 1992). We generalize this hill-climbing heuristic here, defining a new rule we call *Explorer*. This exploits the period between elections to explore a neighborhood of the policy space that is close to the current party policy position. "Close" is specified in a precise way, using a parameter η ("neighborhood-eta") that sets the Euclidean radius of the local neighborhood around the current party position. During campaign ticks, Explorer picks random positions in this neighborhood and tests these for levels of party support. Each election tick, Explorers move to the best-supported policy position found in their explorations since the previous election, provided this has more support than they won at the previous election. Thus,

Explorer: Each *campaign* tick, test a random policy position in the neighborhood radius η from your current position. Each *election* tick: move to the most popular position found during campaign exploration, if this generated more support than you received at the previous election; else stand still.

A hill-climbing agent investigates every one of its immediately adjacent locations on some grid, known as its "Moore neighborhood." Explorer is a generalization of this. It can be parameterized to come close to KMP's climbing adaptive party rule by setting a small local neighborhood, but differs by randomly sampling real points in this neighborhood rather than testing every location on some grid. The rule is thus scalable to allow Explorers to investigate policy neighborhoods of arbitrary size, up to the full policy space.

---

[6] We will shortly specify the size of the move that is made.

It is critical to keep in mind, however, that the entire party system is in motion during the process of exploration. A hill-climbing rule deployed in an environment with no other *moving* agent will find, and climb to the top of, the closest hill—in the context of party competition some local maximum in the voter density landscape. However, *when several agents are simultaneously engaged in competitive spatial location, there is no guarantee that local exploration will result in actual hill climbing*. This is because actions taken by other agents (for example if two or three other agents happen to move toward the *Explorer* at the same time) can result in a loss of support for the *Explorer* even when it is in fact climbing the steepest local gradient in the voter density function. It is quite possible that local exploration in this complex dynamic setting will not result in hill climbing. It is also quite possible, when the configuration of *other* parties' positions evolves during the process of local exploration, that such exploration indicates moving to a policy position that is not, *at the time of the election*, the best supported of those explored. Changes elsewhere in the party system *after* a given policy position was explored may result in some alternative in the set of explored positions now being better; but *Explorer* has no way to know this.

New Rule Feature: Satisficing

Having specified two new "species" of decision rule, we now specify two new rule "features" that may be part of any decision heuristic for choosing party policy positions during a process of dynamic multiparty competition. The first of these concerns the notion *satisficing*, which derives from the huge literature on "bounded rationality," the core ideas of which are synthesized elegantly by Rubinstein (1998). Satisficing decisions select elements from the set of available alternatives that are not necessarily optimal, but satisfy some "aspiration level."[7] Substantive justifications for assuming that agents use satisficing decision rules include the following.

- *Decision costs*: It is not worth my while walking up and down an entire subway train in search of the perfect vacant seat for a one-stop journey; if I did this you would fear for my sanity.
- *Perceptual limitations*: I personally cannot tell the difference between a $5,000 sound system and a $50,000 sound system even though, according to you and all independent lab tests, the more expensive system is better.
- *Cognitive limitations*: I am not as good as my local grandmaster at finding the best chess move from any position—my "personal best" chess move can easily be bettered by others.

[7] For a rigorous formal definition of satisficing, see Rubinstein (1998: 12).

- *Behavioral assumptions*: I am the sort of person who chooses actions that make me just plain happy, not necessarily as happy as I can imagine in my wildest dreams. To be otherwise would make me miserable in almost any situation I find myself.

All of the above justifications for assumptions about satisficing are essentially *static*. With the results we report below, we find a significant new rationale for satisficing in a *dynamic* context. This is that "insatiable" agents who always seek higher payoffs typically perform less well in a complex dynamic setting than agents who are satisfied with some finite level of payoff.

Whichever substantive justification we use, satisficing rules incorporate the key feature that they condition behavior on some *comfort threshold*, which we label κ (comfort-kappa). This is defined in terms of some output metric K, such that the agent is "sated" when outputs of K are at or above κ, but looks for better courses of action whenever outputs are below κ.[8] Satisficing is thus a generalization of any given baseline rule, such as Hunter. The "insatiable" rules that we have investigated thus far are special cases with κ set so high that agents are never satisfied. Any given rule R can now be generalized to a "κ-satisficing" version:

κ-*satisficing-R*: If the value of the output metric $K < \kappa$, do R; else do nothing.

Given the fitness metric we use in our model of endogenous party birth and death, we use a party's *current vote share* as our satisficing metric, K. The essence of satisficing as we specify it in our model is to sit back and do nothing when your fitness update (short-run vote share) is at or above κ. You do something designed to increase your vote share—thereby your updated fitness, thereby your survival prospects—when your fitness update is below κ. Thus a $\kappa = 0.20$ Hunter, for example, uses the Hunter rule if its party's vote share falls below 0.20; otherwise it does nothing. *Satisficing*, parameterized by κ, is an important new dimension of our rule space.

We could in theory define satisficing generalizations of any baseline decision rule. It makes no substantive sense, however, to define satisficing versions of Sticker or Aggregator. A satisficing Sticker would do nothing if its short-run vote share was at or above κ, else it would do nothing. In relation to Aggregator, satisficing has no substantively meaningful interpretation. The comfort metric is vote share, but Aggregator is not designed to increase party vote share. A satisficing Aggregator does nothing if its vote share is at or above κ, else it does something not designed to

---

[8] As opposed to a *comfort threshold* κ, the discussion of satisficing in Rubinstein (1998) refers to an output metric V and an *aspiration level* for this of v^*. Note that Rubinstein's approach is analytical rather than computational since, in contrast to multiparty competition in a multidimensional policy space, the underlying choice problems he models are analytically tractable.

increase vote share. This takes us back to the point, discussed in chapter 6, that the survival-of-the-fittest evolutionary environment we model involves an *exogenous* fitness regime for political parties. Ultimately, this means that "success" of a political party turns on its ability to win votes and survive over the long run. This is why we have now specified satisficing in terms of the same metric, short-run vote share, which is used for fitness updates in our survival regime. This means of course that Sticker and Aggregator parties are not engineered for long-run survival in this evolutionary environment. We will however continue to keep Sticker and Aggregator as part of the rule set available to party leaders, because it is crucial for us to measure how each decision rule performs when competing against a diverse array of alternatives. We will also see, furthermore, that Aggregator can perform surprisingly well at winning votes in certain settings, for reasons that are very instructive.

New Rule Feature: Speed

Astute readers have long since noticed that the Hunter rule, defined in chapter 3 and investigated in chapters 5 and 6, has an important implicit parameter. It makes a unit move in a rewarded direction or, when punished, makes a unit move in a different direction. But what is a "unit"? Our coordinate system for policy positions is based on standard deviations of the distribution of voter ideal points, and the unit move thus far specified for Hunter is 0.1 standard deviations. It thus takes a Hunter thirty unit moves in a straight line to get from the position of an extreme voter ideal point, three standard deviations from the centroid, to the voter centroid itself. We can thus think of 0.1 as a measure of the adaptive *speed* of a Hunter, which we label γ (speed-gamma). Hunters for which $\gamma = 0.2$ would move twice as fast as the Hunters we have investigated so far. *Speed* in this sense, parameterized by γ, *i*s an important new dimension of our rule space.

Three of the rules species we identify have an implicit speed setting. Of our other two rule species, Stickers never move, so speed does not arise, while the binding constraint on movement by Explorer parties is set by η, the size of their exploration neighborhood. Given our new definition of speed, we generalize the Hunter rule as follows:

> *Hunter:* if the last move increased support, move distance γ in the same direction; else, reverse heading and move γ on a heading chosen randomly from the arc ±90° from the direction now being faced.[9]

---

[9] It is easy to imagine more sophisticated "artificial intelligence" versions of Hunter in which γ is not a constant but a strictly increasing function of the level of reward (or punishment), or of some other metric derived from the history of the system. We postpone consideration of this for future work, however.

As we have currently specified the Aggregator rule, Aggregators may move as much as it takes to jump to the ideal point centroid of their current supporters. Watching simulations in motion, we see that this can result in moves much bigger than those made by other parties. Seeing this as unrealistic, we now respecify the Aggregator rule so that Aggregators move at speed γ *toward* the ideal point centroid of current supporters, not jumping straight to this.

> *Aggregator:* Identify the mean coordinate on each dimension of the ideal points of your current party supporters; move distance γ in this direction unless this causes you to overshoot,[10] in which case move to the mean of supporter ideal points.

Finally, we just specified a new Predator rule species in terms of unit moves. We now generalize this in the same way as for Hunters:

> *Predator:* If you are the largest party: stand still. Else: identify your "prey" as the closest of the set of parties with more support than you; set heading toward prey; move a distance γ in the resulting direction.

Parameterizations of the Rule Space

We have specified a four-dimensional space of decision rules for party leaders choosing policy positions in dynamic multiparty competition. The first "dimension" of this rule space is categorical and describes five different *rule species*: Sticker, Aggregator, Hunter, Predator, and Explorer.[11] The second dimension describes *satisficing* and is spanned by values of the comfort threshold, κ, on the satisficing metric, K. In our model we specify the satisficing metric as current party vote share. The third dimension describes *speed* of adaptation and is spanned by values of the speed parameter, γ, which we specify in standard deviations of the baseline distribution of voter ideal points. The fourth dimension describes parties' *exploration neighborhoods* and is spanned by values of η, the neighborhood radius parameter, which we also specify in standard deviations of the baseline voter ideal point distribution.

Note that some features are *redundant* for some rules. Thus we can give a Sticker settings for γ, η, and κ if we find this amusing, but these parameters are mere adornments to the Sticker rule and make no difference whatsoever to Sticker behavior. Agent behavior indicated by the

---

[10] We did not need the "overshoot" qualification when Aggregators were programmed to jump immediately to the precise ideal point centroid of current supporters.

[11] NetLogo code implementing these rules can be found in Table E7.1 of the electronic appendix.

TABLE 7.1
Parameterizations of the Rule Space

Rule species	Comfort threshold, κ (vote share)[a]	Speed, γ (SDs)	Neighborhood size, η (SDs)	No. of distinct parameter settings per rule
Sticker	n/a	n/a	n/a	1
Aggregator	n/a	0.025, 0.05, 0.10, 0.20, 0.40	n/a	5
Hunter	0.06, 0.11, 0.16, 0.21, 0.26, 0.31, 1.00	0.025, 0.05, 0.10, 0.20, 0.40	n/a	35
Predator	0.06, 0.11, 0.16, 0.21, 0.26, 0.31, 1.00	0.025, 0.05, 0.10, 0.20, 0.40	n/a	35
Explorer	0.06, 0.11, 0.16, 0.21, 0.26, 0.31, 1.00	n/a	0.2, 0.4, 0.6, 0.8, 1.0	35

Hunter rule species can be affected by parameterizations of κ and γ but not by η—and so on.

Next, moving from general rule features to their specific realization in our computational work, we do not randomly pick rule parameterizations but instead parameterize rule features using the discrete "grid" shown in Table 7.1. We do this because our analysis is structured in terms of a *finite set of decision rule parameterizations*, and we want to accumulate systematic information about interactions among agents choosing from these. Following exploratory runs that highlighted the considerable importance of satisficing, and faced as always with a finite computational budget, we defined a finer seven-setting grid in relation to κ, the comfort threshold, than we did for speed or the radius of the exploration neighborhood, for which we used a five-point grid.[12] Finally, as we also note in Table 7.1 given the redundancy of some parameters for some rule species, there are 35 distinct parameterizations each for Hunter, Predator, and Explorer, 5 for Aggregator, arising from different speed settings, and just 1 for Sticker, which has no nonredundant parameters. We thereby specify 111 distinct rule parameterizations for dynamic multiparty competition.

---

[12] Precise settings of κ anticipate decisions we make later in the book that will involve investigating a small number of discrete settings of the party survival threshold.

We have thus far been talking in terms of *decision rules* with particular parameterized realizations, but an alternative interpretation may be more compelling. We can think in terms of *party leaders using any given rule* as having personal parameters that specify their own distinctive comfort thresholds, speeds of adaptation, or exploration radii. We would then think of parameterized *agent-rule pairings* rather than parameterized rules. As it happens, it makes no difference to our model, or to our computational experiments, whether we think in terms of parameterized realizations of rule species or of parameterized agent-rule pairings. We ourselves prefer to think substantively in terms of different parameterized agent-rule pairings, but we often for stylistic reasons refer to different parameterized rules or even simply to different decision rules.

EXPERIMENTAL DESIGN

Expanding the set of possible agent-rule pairings generates an explosive increase in the number of possible *combinations* of these that can be in contention at any given time. Our experiment in chapter 6 involved three decision rules and typically about six party leaders. This generates 28 different rule combinations that might be in contention at any given time. In this chapter we define and investigate 111 different agent-rule pairings. The number of different combinations of these that could arise at any given time rises to 2,967,205,528. This generates an equivalent increase, of an order of about a hundred million, in the size of our model's state space. We have no hope of mapping out this state space in a feasible computational experiment so that that, as in chapter 6, we employ the run design we developed for stochastic processes for which a time average does *not* provide a representative estimate of μ.

The experiment we specify here has the same design as that described in chapter 6. It involves one thousand repetitions of one thousand runs. For each run, the three parameters of the competitive environment were given Monte Carlo parameterizations in precisely the same way as in chapter 6. These were polarization (μ_r) and relative sizes (n_l/n_r) of the two voter subpopulations and the de facto survival threshold, τ. As with the experiment specified in chapter 6, new parties were assigned parameterized decision rules at random. The key difference is that the leaders of new parties were given a rule-leader parameterization that was a random draw from the 111-point grid described in Table 7.1. Run design, estimation strategy, and therefore computational budget were otherwise precisely the same as for the experiment we report in chapter 6.

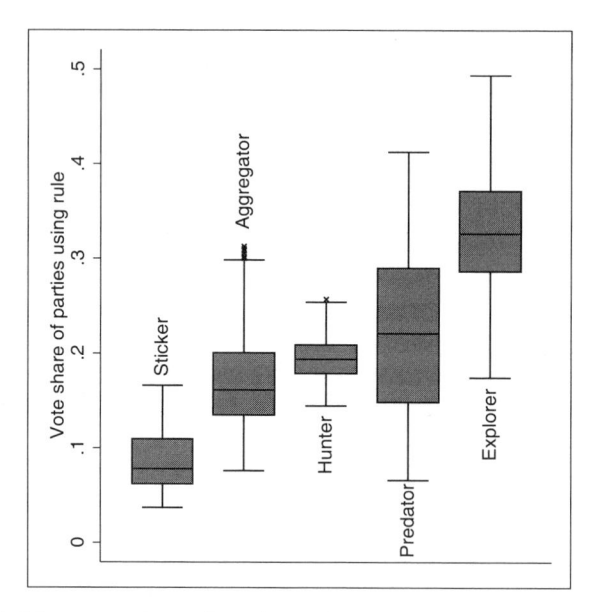

Figure 7.1. Mean vote shares, by rule species.

Party Competition with a Diverse Set of Decision Rules

Behavior of New Vote-Seeking Rule Species

We begin by assessing the relative performance of the three different species of vote-seeking decision rule we have now defined: Hunter, Predator, and Explorer. Figure 7.1 shows box and whisker plots of estimated vote shares won by sets of parties using each of the five rule species, over the entire set of model parameterizations we investigate.[13] The news is that Hunter is now the *least* successful of the three vote-seeking rule species in contention. The relative success of Hunter in the three-rule party system we investigated in chapter 6 clearly happened because it was the only vote-seeking rule; it looks less impressive in competition with other vote-seeking rules. Averaged over all parameterizations of party competition we investigate, the newly specified Explorer rule, with on average 32 percent of the vote, significantly outperforms the reprogrammed Predator (22 percent), while both of the new vote-seeking rule species outperform Hunter (19 percent). Aggregator has now been redefined to move at speed γ toward the centroid of its supporters' ideal points, rather than jumping straight to this. It is striking that the typical vote share for the

---

[13] The central line is the median estimate, the boxes show the interquartile range around this, and the whiskers show the 5th and 95th percentile observations.

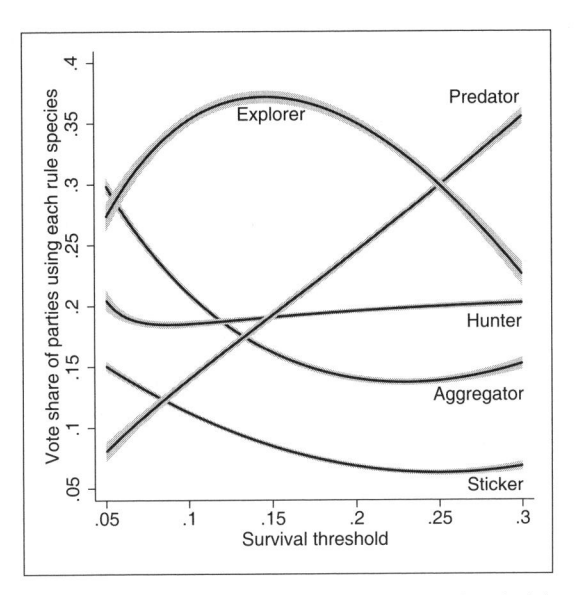

Figure 7.2. Party vote shares, by rule species and survival threshold.

set of Aggregator parties, at around 17 percent, is only slightly lower than that in the three-rule system we investigate in chapter 6.[14]

The big picture is that parties using vote-seeking decision rules win similar vote shares in the 3-rule system we investigate in chapter 6 (about 72 percent) and the 111-rule system we investigate here (about 74 percent). Summarizing results across the entire range of party systems we investigate, the vote share won by vote-seeking parties is now split between the three vote-seeking rule species, with Explorer significantly the most effective of these. The decline in Hunter performance and the robustness of Aggregator performance, when other rule species are added to the mix, highlight an important general point that *the performance of different types of decision rule depends critically on the precise set of rules with which they must compete.*

Figure 7.1 masks substantively important patterns of party competition, however. As Figure 7.2 shows in a crystal clear fashion, the most striking of these is that the *relative performance of different vote-seeking decision rules depends sharply on the survival threshold* and hence on the number of surviving parties. In particular we see that, when survival thresholds are low and the number of surviving parties high, Predator is

---

[14] Standard errors for Explorer, Predator, Hunter, Aggregator, and Sticker vote shares are 0.003, 0.004, 0.001, 0.002, 0.001. See Table E7.2 in the electronic appendix for more detailed information.

the *least* successful of all rule species at its programmed objective of winning votes. In stark contrast, Predator is the *most* successful rule when survival thresholds are high and the number of surviving parties low.

Watching simulations in motion, we see why this happens. Predators, programmed to move toward other parties with higher vote shares, are *prone to attack each other* if they become successful. Predators need prey, and the overall success of the species is limited when they prey on other Predators. This means that Predators are most likely to be successful at winning votes when there is only a single Predator in the system, which is much more likely to happen when the number of parties is low. Predator is therefore an especially good example of a decision rule that *performs well in competition with other rule species, but performs badly in competition with itself.*

Precisely the opposite pattern can be seen for Aggregator rules, which perform much *better* when there are lower survival thresholds and more surviving parties. Relative performances of Aggregator and Predator rules, indeed, are inversely related to each other. This is because Aggregators are vulnerable to all vote-seeking rules but particularly vulnerable to Predators, for reasons that are illustrated in the example shown in Figure 7.3, which shows the Voronoi dynamics of position taking by Aggregator parties. Aggregators tend to "run away" from vote-seeking parties that approach them and are in effect "chased" into regions of the policy space with lower votes.

Figure 7.3 shows three parties, a Predator, an Aggregator, and a third party whose position we hold constant—for example a Sticker—with initial policy positions of P1, A1, and S. Voronoi boundaries between these positions are shown by the thinner solid lines. The Voronoi region of the Aggregator is shown by the combined shaded areas, both light and dark gray. Given the Aggregator rule, A1 is at the centroid of the set of voter ideal points in this region. If the Aggregator has more votes than the Predator, the Predator moves toward the Aggregator, changing its position, say, from P1 to P2. The move pushes the Voronoi boundary between the Predator and the Aggregator, shown by the dashed line, toward A1. The inevitable result, holding all else constant, is that *A1 is no longer at the centroid of its new Voronoi region.* The Aggregator therefore adapts toward the centroid of its new region, A3. This will inevitably involve a move away from P2 and generates yet another new set of Voronoi boundaries, shown by the thicker solid lines. When it reaches the centroid of its new Voronoi region, shaded dark gray, the Aggregator will have moved away from the Predator and lost the support of all voters in the lighter shaded area.[15]

---

[15] There is also a very small exchange of territory with the Sticker.

New Decision Rules, New Rule Features • 145

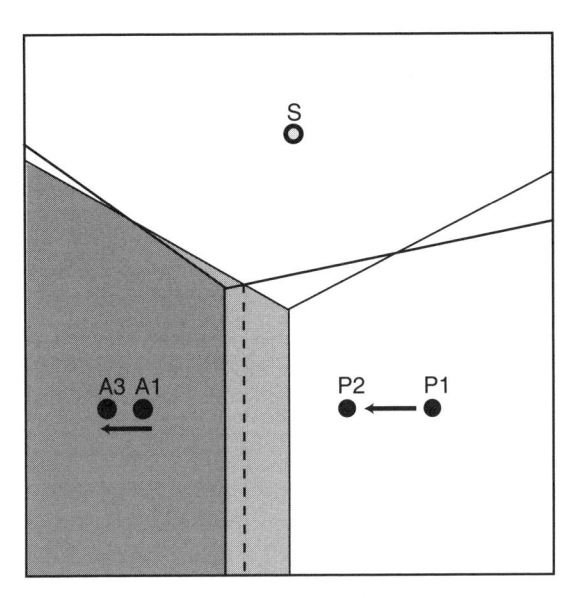

Figure 7.3. Voronoi dynamics of position taking by Aggregators.

We can think of an empirical story about this that might arise when a party loses an election and then for some reason decides to set party policy to satisfy its existing "base" rather than attract new voters. This results in a change to the party decision rule, to what amounts to Aggregator. Part of the reason for doing this may be concerned with turnout, which we do not consider here. Turnout notwithstanding, a consequence is that the new Aggregator may be doubly vulnerable. A vote-seeking rival not only can "take" votes by moving toward the Aggregator (from P1 to P2 in effect, pushing the boundary between parties to the dotted line in Figure 7.3), but the Aggregator then also "cedes" votes by adapting its policy position to the ideal points of its shrinking support base (moving from A1 to A3, allowing the boundary to move to the heavy solid line in Figure 7.3). If nothing else happens—though in reality something else typically does happen—this could result in a spiral of decline.

Given all of this, it is important to understand why typical Aggregator vote shares remain relatively robust, despite the fact that these parties are now competing with rivals using a range of different vote-seeking rules. We find the answer in Figure 7.4, which plots typical party policy eccentricities. The gray band shows 95 percent confidence intervals around typical policy eccentricities of Aggregator parties. Consistent with the "avoidance" behavior illustrated in Figure 7.3, Aggregators tend systematically to set policy positions in more eccentric regions of the space than

146 • Chapter 7

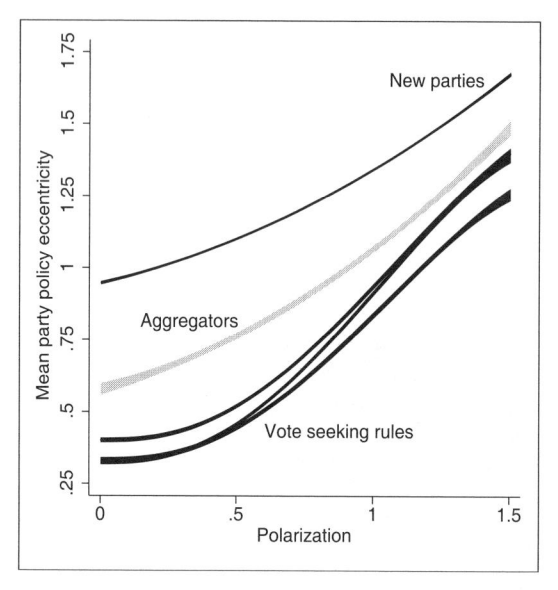

Figure 7.4. Typical party policy eccentricities, by rule species and ideal point polarization.

the typical positions of vote-seeking parties. Watching simulations in motion, we do indeed see that Aggregator parties that find themselves in more central locations (perhaps because they have just been born there) tend to get "chased" away from these positions by vote-seeking rivals.[16]

In contrast, close bunching of the three black bands shows it is hard to distinguish policy positions chosen by parties using one of the three vote-seeking rule species now in contention. Aggregators therefore tend not to be in direct policy competition with vote seekers, while vote seekers using different decision rules tend to slug it out with each other in the same regions of the policy space.[17]

---

[16] Plots of mean party policy eccentricity against other party system parameters can be found in Figure E7.3 in the electronic appendix.

[17] Confirming results reported in the previous chapter, Figure 7.5 also shows that all party policy positions respond sharply to voter polarization, whatever rule species is used, and that typical policy positions of new political parties are systematically more eccentric than the positions of surviving parties. The party policy eccentricities plotted in Figure 7.4 clearly have a bearing on the representativeness of the emergent configuration of party policy positions, shown in Figure E7.4 in the electronic appendix. The key relationship between representativeness and the survival threshold is essentially the same as that reported in chapter 6, though the 111-rule systems we investigate here are systematically somewhat more representative in equivalent settings that the 3-rule systems we investigate in chapter 6.

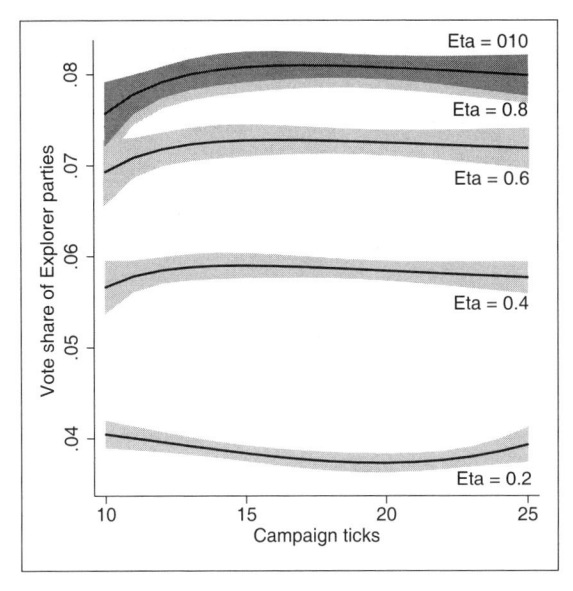

Figure 7.5. Typical vote share of Explorer parties, by Ψ and η.

Exploration Neighborhoods

The big news about the new rule species we have defined, highlighted in Figure 7.1, is the success of Explorer at winning votes in competition with the other vote-seeking rule species. Explorer is a generalized version of the hill climbing rule originally proposed by Kollman, Miller, and Page (1992). The KMP rule explores a party's immediately adjacent (Moore) neighborhood; our generalization explores random locations in a policy neighborhood of radius η from the current party position. Figure 7.5 plots simulation results that help us understand the success of Explorer, showing the relationship between vote share, size of exploration neighborhood, and length of election campaign.[18] One striking pattern is that all of the confidence intervals, plotted in gray, are effectively flat. *Increasing the length of election campaigns does not systematically improve the performance of Explorer rules.* We rarely present negative results in this book, but this negative result is important because it runs counter to naïve intuition.

---

[18] Note that the vote shares from all of the settings of eta plotted in this figure need to be combined to give the Aggregator vote share won by Explorer parties.

It might seem that longer election campaigns should help Explorers, offering more campaign ticks with which to test random policy positions in the neighborhood and thereby offering a higher probability of finding better supported party policy positions. "Obvious" as this might seem, it is implicitly grounded in a *static* notion of exploration. Each party's vote share depends not only on its own policy position but also on the positions of all adjacent parties with which it shares Voronoi boundaries. In the dynamic system of multiparty competition we model here, *each of these adjacent parties may well be moving*. We already saw in Figure 5.3 that small policy moves by adjacent parties in multidimensional policy spaces can generate magnified "scissor-like" shifts in the Voronoi boundary between them, and thus have relatively large effects on party vote shares. This is important for hill-climbing rule species such as Explorer. Because *payoffs arising from any given point in the policy space are continually changing*, possibly by large amounts, longer election campaigns do not necessarily help hill climbers explore that space. In this environment, information collected about party vote shares at the beginning of a long election campaign can become out of date and potentially misleading by the end of the campaign. Longer campaigns generate more information, but also *more potentially misleading informatio*n in a dynamic setting. Our negative finding on the relationship between campaign length and Explorer vote shares confirms this expectation that longer campaigns do not systematically enhance the vote shares of Explorer parties; neither, it seems, do they harm these.

The second big pattern in Figure 7.5 is that the size of the exploration neighborhood does make a difference. This confirms the simple intuition that Explorers who can explore larger regions of the policy space have a better chance of finding a position that increases their vote share. The detailed findings reported in Figure 7.5 are not quite as simple as this, however. Parties exploring the smaller neighborhoods we test do tend to perform less well. Looking at the bands from the top to the bottom of the figure, the smaller the value of η, the smaller the typical party vote share. We also see from the top of the figure, however, that this effect is severely attenuated as size of the exploration neighborhood increases. Indeed, plotted confidence intervals for $\eta = 0.8$ and $\eta = 1.0$ overlap, showing no significant increase in vote share for parties with the larger of these two exploration neighborhoods. Our conjecture is that, as the size of exploration neighborhoods increases, an effect akin to having longer election campaigns begins to emerge. Larger exploration neighborhoods, which other things equal generate more information, also increase the chance that a point explored is close to some other moving party. This in turn increases the probability that scissor like shifts in Voronoi boundaries, taking place after the time of exploration, will render information collected about party vote shares out of date and potentially misleading.

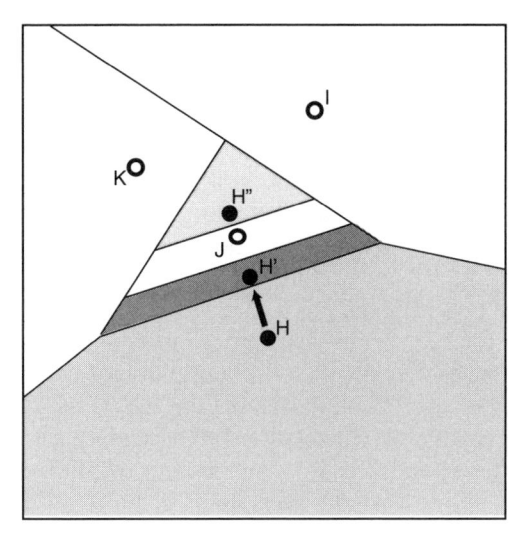

Figure 7.6. "Overshooting" by a Hunter party.

Speed of Adaptation

Turning from Explorer to the other vote-seeking rule species, Hunter and Predator, the speed with which parties adapt their policy position is analogous, as a constraint on policy movement between elections, to the size of the local exploration neighborhood. Watching simulations in motion, we see that parties can adapt their policy positions "too fast," in effect overreacting to feedback from party competition. Figure 7.6 gives a sense of one way in which this can happen to a Hunter party. It shows a Hunter with a policy position at H and three other parties with policy positions at I, J, and K. The Hunter has been rewarded with a higher vote share for its move to H and will make another move in the same direction, shown by the arrow.

The Hunter's current Voronoi neighborhood is the lightly shaded area in the bottom half of the space. Making a move from H to H' pushes the Hunter's Voronoi boundary toward J and adds, to its existing large support base, the support of all voters with ideal points in the darker shaded area around H'. The Hunter's vote share increases. If, however, it makes a policy move twice the size of the move from H to H', the result is a move to H". This overshoots J and may have a disastrous effect on the Hunter's vote share. The party, now at H", loses all existing support in the lower part of the space and now has a much smaller new Voronoi region, the shaded area around H". If we assume for the moment a uniform voter density region, then the new Voronoi region contains fewer voter ideal points than the party's original Voronoi region, generated by H. The Hunter's vote share falls. It is worth noting that the dramatic changes in Voronoi regions produced by the type of overshooting shown in Figure 7.6, combined with the scissor-like leverage of Voronoi boundaries arising from small policy moves by adjacent parties shown in Figure 5.3, are two of the reasons why the dynamics of competitive location in multidimensional policy spaces are so intractable analytically.

Hunters do not know the policy positions of any other party. They simply respond in a Pavlovian manner to rewards and punishments, so they cannot be programmed not to overshoot some other party position. The trade-off for Hunters is that larger policy moves may yield better outcomes as long as they do not overshoot, but larger moves also increase the probability of overshooting. We see the effects of such overshooting in Figure 7.7, which plots the relationship between the survival threshold and typical Hunter and Predator vote shares, for different settings of γ. The left panel shows that the vote share of Hunter parties is strongly affected by speed of adaptation for all parameterizations of party competition. The light gray confidence bands show that typical vote shares increase as γ increases from 0.025 to 0.05 to 0.10 but then tend to *decrease* as γ increases further to 0.2 and 0.4. It is the *medium* speed Hunters in our simulations that perform most effectively at finding votes in competition with other vote-seeking rules. Looking at simulations in motion we see that when Hunters adapt "too fast" they do tend to overshoot in the manner we just discussed.

Moreover, the darker gray confidence bands in both panels of Figure 7.7 show that faster moving (γ = 0.2 and 0.4) vote-seeking rules systemically perform better when survival thresholds are high and the number of surviving parties is low. This adds support to the interpretation that faster moving Hunter rules are more likely to overshoot, since the probability of such overshooting is clearly lower when there are fewer parties.

Figure 7.7 also shows us one reason why Hunter performs systematically less well in the simulations we report here than in those we report in previous chapters. The specification of Hunter in chapters 5 and 6, as well as in the original Laver (2005) simulations, sets γ = 0.1 by default. It turns out that this default setting, picked in a more or less arbitrary manner, optimizes Hunter performance as far as speed of adaptation is concerned. Given the five-point parameter grid for γ that we use in this chapter and random rule parameterization, only one-fifth of Hunters now have this optimum speed setting, lowering the overall performance of Hunter rules.

While the Pavlovian Hunter rule works best when it responds neither too much nor too little to feedback from the party system, the right panel of Figure 7.7 shows that *all* Predators, regardless of speed of adaptation,

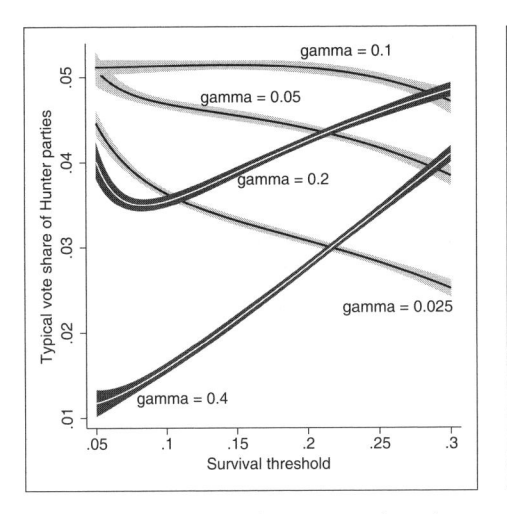

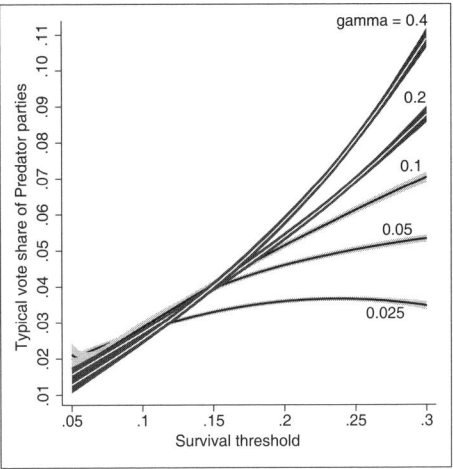

Figure 7.7. Typical Hunter and Predator vote shares, by γ and τ.

perform poorly when survival thresholds are lower and there are more parties. As survival thresholds increase and the typical number of parties decreases, all Predators perform better, but our simulation results show that the fastest moving Predators benefit most. Recalling that Predators are programmed not to overshoot their prey's location we see that, in settings where Predators do well, faster moving Predators do better.

Satisficing and Vote Seeking

We turn now to the most striking and substantively interesting general result emerging from the simulations we report in this chapter. This concerns the surprisingly effective performance of satisficing rules at winning votes, even when these are in direct competition with insatiable vote maximizers. Figure 7.8 plots typical party vote shares by the party leader comfort threshold, κ, and the party survival threshold, τ. Convergence of the plotted confidence intervals on the left-hand side of the plot shows that with very low survival thresholds, a party's comfort threshold makes no significant difference to its ability to win votes. Competitive environments with low survival thresholds tend to have more parties, and typical party vote shares thus tend to be lower. This in turn means that party leaders will typically not win vote shares above their comfort threshold, so they will not be satisfied and will use their vote-seeking rule. There should be no observable difference in the behavior of $\kappa = 0.16$ and $\kappa = 0.21$ party leaders, for example, if the survival threshold is so low and

152 • Chapter 7

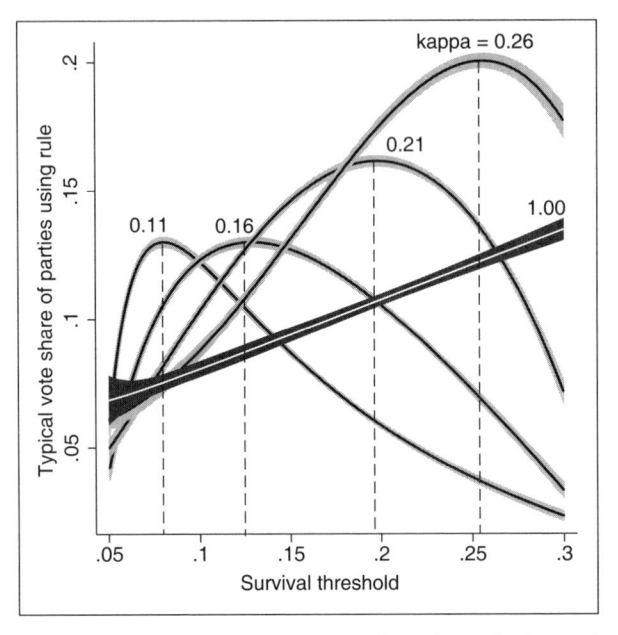

Figure 7.8. Typical party vote shares, by τ and κ. Plots of relationships between other model parameters and τ can be found in Figures E7.4 and E7.5 of the electronic appendix.

the number of surviving parties so high that typical party vote shares are well below 0.16, so that both leaders are typically dissatisfied with their vote shares.

Clearly, we expect satisficing party leaders to perform poorly when their comfort threshold is "too low," in the sense that the *comfort threshold is below the survival threshold*. In that case, the party falls below the survival threshold and dies before its vote-seeking algorithm is activated. Figure 7.8 confirms expectations of a rapid drop-off in vote share whenever $\kappa < \tau$, seen on the right-hand side of the plotted gray bands for each setting of κ short of 1.0. To take the example of the band plotting the performance of $\kappa = 0.21$ rules, the right-hand side declines precipitously when $\tau > 0.21$.

The big news in Figure 7.8 concerns the upward slopes on the *left*-hand side of each plotted band. *Satisficing party leaders systematically perform less well when their comfort threshold is "too high,"* that is when κ is much greater than τ. Thus $\kappa = 0.26$ leaders, for example, typically perform very well when the survival threshold is high. They systematically underperform $\kappa = 0.11$ leaders,[19] however, when the survival threshold drops below about 0.12. On the face of things, this seems quite puzzling. When two party leaders each have about 20 percent of the vote, a more easily satisfied $\kappa = 0.11$ leader does nothing and a harder to satisfy $\kappa = 0.26$ leader keeps looking for more votes. Somehow, however, this systematically tends to harm the hard to satisfy leader who keeps looking for votes. The most dramatic example of this is shown by the dark gray band in Figure 7.8. *Insatiable ($\kappa = 1.0$) party leaders who are always looking for votes systematically underperform satiable leaders for whom $\kappa > \tau$.*

This becomes easier to understand by thinking through an example. If, for instance, the survival threshold is 0.15 then, from our earlier simulations, we expect to find four surviving parties.[20] Each of the four parties, none of which differs from any other in any material respect, has a long-run expectation of one quarter of the vote. Consider a short-run situation in which the leader of the largest party has a comfort threshold of 0.26 and this party wins 0.30 of the vote, while the remaining three parties split 0.70 of the vote among them, each getting a vote share above the comfort threshold of their leader. In this case, no leader will change position. The system will remain in a short-run stationary state in which all party leaders harvest their respective vote shares election after election—a state that can be perturbed only by the birth of a new party. The largest party continues to receive a short-run vote share above its long-run expectation. The fact that its leader is satisfied means that the party system remains in a state that allows her to continue to exploit this situation. Furthermore, the leader's comfort threshold of 0.26 means that no short-run state can remain in place for which her party's vote share is below her long-run expectation of 0.25. In effect the leader of the largest party is exploiting the fact that some of the other party leaders must either have lower comfort thresholds or be using non-vote-seeking rules since, if κ equaled 0.26 for all four leaders, the system would obviously never have reached the stationary state.

If, in contrast, the leader of the largest party is insatiable, she will *never* be satisfied with a vote share of 0.30 and will *always* make a move in search of more votes. There will be no short-run stationary state. In the short term such moves may, if successful, increase vote share. But since the competitive environment is analytically intractable it is impossible to predict the long-run consequences of perturbing a short-run station-

---

[19] The $\kappa = 0.26$ confidence band drops below the $\kappa = 0.11$ confidence band.
[20] Figure E7.2 in the electronic appendix gives precise estimates for the simulations we report here.

ary state yielding vote shares above long-run expectations. Perturbing the short-run state will eventually provoke other vote-seeking party leaders into moving and will, for want of better information and thus other things equal, lead to proportionate vote shares that are below the above average vote shares the party received from the previous short-run stationary state that was destroyed. Also note that this account of satisficing depends upon there being a heterogeneous rule set, with some party leaders using decision rules, such as Sticker or Aggregator, that are not programmed to increase vote share and/or other vote-seeking leaders with comfort thresholds that leave them satisfied with a less than proportionate vote shares.

The dynamic environment we model therefore favors satisficing party leaders with comfort thresholds that are above long-run ceteris paribus expectations, but not so high as to indicate a move more or less regardless of feasibly attainable vote shares. This allows the satisficing leaders to *exploit short-run situations yielding vote shares above long-run expectations*. At the same time a party leader with a comfort threshold that is above long-run expectations will perturb any short-run situation yielding a vote share below these expectations. In stark contrast an *insatiable vote-seeking party leader never leaves in place a short-run state that yields a vote share above long-run expectations*. The insatiable leader's "greed" for ever more votes in such a situation in effect causes her to kill the goose that lays the golden egg.

Analyses of simulation results generated by our dynamic agent-based model have thus revealed an intriguing "best is the enemy of the good" account of satisficing in a long-run dynamic environment. This reflects a version of the classic exploration-exploitation trade-off in reinforcement learning. *Satiable agents can outperform insatiable agents in complex dynamic settings that are analytically intractable.* They use what amounts to an "ain't broke, don't fix it" rule of thumb to exploit high-paying short-run situations rather than perturbing these in an insatiable search for even higher payoffs. We find this the most striking result in this chapter and one of the most striking in the entire book.

CONCLUSIONS

Our core aim in this chapter was to apply our model to a world in which party leaders choose from a wide variety of possible decision rules when addressing the intractable problem of choosing party policies in the multiparty settings that interest us. We defined two new "species" of vote-seeking decision rule, Predator and Explorer, each characterized by a distinctive decision heuristic. We identified systematic features of decision rules for setting party policy: speed of adaption and satisficing. Having done this, we specified a grid of parameter settings for the rule features that we investigate in our simulations. The net result was a rule set of 111 parameterized realizations of five distinct rule species, in contrast to the three realized rules we investigated in chapter 6.

One set of findings in this chapter illustrates the important general principle that the performance of any decision rule can *depend critically on the other rules with which it must compete*. Simulation results we analyze in chapter 6 show that Hunter was effective at finding high vote shares in competition with Sticker and Aggregator. Figure 7.1 shows that other vote-seeking rule species, Predator and Explorer, now systematically outperform Hunter. This is at least in part because, as we saw in Figure 7.7, the parameterization of Hunter we used as a default in chapter 6 turns out to have specified an optimal setting for speed of adaption. It is also because Hunter simply performs less well when its opponents may be using Predator or Explorer rules. Robust decision rules perform well against anything the competitive environment might throw at them, and the Hunter rule investigated in chapter 6 proves to be less robust than we might have thought. In contrast, we found that the (albeit lower) vote shares of parties whose leaders use the non-vote-seeking Aggregator rules are robust to the addition of new vote-seeking rules.

The most successful of the vote-seeking rule species we now investigate is Explorer, a generalized hill-climbing rule that explores local policy neighborhoods between elections in search of higher vote shares. Digging deeper into the sources of this success, we find that, contrary to naïve intuition, having longer election campaigns with which to explore the local policy neighborhood does not enhance Explorer performance. Our conjecture on this is based on a significant potential problem for hill-climbing rules in competitive settings where rival agents may be moving at the same time. When rivals are also moving, information gleaned from exploration early in the election campaign may well be out of date and misleading. It may well not be a good idea to base decisions about party competition on information gathered during the early stages of a long campaign.

Figure 7.2 shows another important lesson to emerge from simulation results generated by our dynamic ABM of party competition. The relative success of different vote-seeking rule species depends sharply on the parameterization of the competitive environment. Predators, to take the most striking example, perform significantly better when survival thresholds are high and there are relatively few parties, and perform significantly worse when survival thresholds are low and there are more parties. This is because successful Predators tend systematically to attack each other. *There is no rule for setting party policy that is "best" for all parameterizations of the competitive environment we describe in our model.*

An important feature of the rule space we have defined concerns how fast leaders adapt party policy positions. Figure 7.7 shows that very small policy moves between elections are associated with lower long-run vote shares. We also find, however, that the highest speeds of adaptation also tend to be associated with lower vote shares. Our conjecture on this is that adaption must be large enough to benefit from party system feedback, but not so large that there is overshooting of short-run optimal policy positions. *In extremis*, for example, if Hunters react to rewards and punishments by continuously leaping from one side of the policy space to the other, we do not expect this to be good for their vote share. Adapting is good, overreacting is bad.

For us, the most important finding in this chapter is reported in Figure 7.8 and concerns satisficing. *Insatiable* vote-seeking party leaders continually adapt party policy in a restless search for more votes, regardless of their party's current vote share. *They are systematically outperformed by satiable leaders*, who adapt party policy only when the party vote share is below some specified comfort threshold, and otherwise do nothing at all. This is conditional, of course, on the comfort threshold that triggers action by the party leader being above the party survival threshold. Our conjecture on this refers to the exploration-exploitation trade-off we encounter in many adaptive behaviors. Insatiable leaders engage in dynamic multiparty competition, *always explore* for more votes, and *never exploit* favorable short-run situations that may arise for whatever reason in intractable settings. In effect, insatiable leaders look gift horses in the mouth. Even when they are doing very well indeed, they want to do even better. In contrast, satiable party leaders *always exploit favorable short-run situations*, never perturbing these in search of even more votes. Satiable party leaders accept gift horses with open arms. This striking result is revealed by our dynamic ABM of multiparty competition but would be inaccessible using static models analyzed with traditional techniques.

PART THREE

Extensions and Empirics

CHAPTER EIGHT

The Evolutionary Dynamics of Decision Rule Selection

OUR MODEL OF ENDOGENOUS party birth and death in a dynamic party system uses updated vote share as a measure of party fitness. As we have seen, this creates a "survival-of-the-fittest" evolutionary environment in which fitter parties tend to survive and less fit parties tend to die. As a result, parties using more effective decision rules tend systematically to live longer. In this chapter, we develop our evolutionary model of dynamic party competition by moving beyond the substantively unrealistic assumption that leaders of new political parties pick their decision rules at random. We now assume they *are more likely to pick decision rules that have a history of past success*.

In making this assumption, we model an evolutionary environment where rule replication probabilities are not static for all time and equal for all rules, as we have assumed up to now, but evolve endogenously as a function of each rule's history. This adds *positive feedback to rule replication probabilities* and thereby implements a version of what has become known as evolutionary, or replicator, dynamics (Weibull 1995; Taylor and Jonker 1978).[1] We expect this feedback, which makes more successful rules more likely to be chosen and thereby further enhances their success, to sharpen performance differentials between successful and unsuccessful rules. Potentially—though this remains an open question to be investigated—it may create an evolutionary environment in which one successful decision rule "drives out" all others and tends to be used by all party leaders.

We find below that positive feedback does indeed sharpen performance differentials between different decision rules. We also find, however, that the presence of evolutionary shocks, introducing "mutations" whereby the choice of decision rules by party leaders has a random component, means that no decision rule parameterization ever dominates over the very long run. While some particular rule may come to be used by all party leaders over some era in our simulations, there is ultimately always

---

[1] Page and Nowak provide a good synthesis of the main ideas (Page and Nowak 2002). For introductions to economic applications of evolutionary dynamics see Friedman (1998), Mailath (1998), and Borgers and Sarin (1997).

160 • Chapter 8

a sequence of shocks that leads to a new era in which an alternative rule tends to dominate. We also find, furthermore, that different decision rules may coexist over extended periods of time.

The Replicator-Mutator Dynamics of Decision Rule Selection

Replication and Imitation

The new feature of this chapter is the evolving probability p_{re} that the leader of a party born immediately after election e chooses decision rule r from a finite rule set **R**. One common approach to this problem, typically referred to as *replicator dynamics*, sets this probability equal to the *proportion of agents currently using rule r*. The substantive interpretation of this is quintessentially biological; all surviving agents are assumed to have an equal probability of "giving birth" to new agents and thereby of passing on their decision rules to their offspring. This implies that the probability that any new agent uses r is simply the proportion of surviving agents who use r. Evolution occurs because fitter agents are more likely to survive and give birth than less fit agents. These evolutionary dynamics are driven by a competitive environment that determines relative agent fitnesses and a death regime that kills off less-fit types of agent at a faster rate. Agent fitnesses affect the set of rules used by new agents *indirectly*, by driving the rule mix in the set of *surviving* agents—any of whom may give birth to offspring who then use the same decision rule as their parent.[2] The dynamics arise because more successful agents are more likely to survive and pass on their decision rules to agents in the next generation.

In the context of party competition, however, it is hard to imagine political parties having babies. Hence, we find it more plausible to think of an evolutionary process in which replication probabilities are driven by *imitation* (Macy and Willer 2002), whereby leaders of new parties choose decision rules from an available rule set, taking account of the relative success of previous party leaders who have used each rule. The net effect is the same: more successful decision rules for multiparty competition are

---

[2] This is before we take into consideration the genetic operators of mutation and crossover. The former applies to all replication, the latter applies only to replication arising from "sexual" interaction between two agents with different rules. In the case of sexual reproduction, it may well be that nonrandom selection of sexual partners means that fitter agents are more likely to reproduce than others. However, since we can think of no plausible analogy for sexual intercourse between political parties, we do not pursue this matter.

more likely to replicate than less successful rules. This is the core modification we make to our model in this chapter.

An Updating Regime for Rule *Fitness*

We specify a very simple evolutionary environment. The selection of decision rules by the leaders of new parties is a function of each rule's previous performance. We model the updated fitness of *decision rules* by defining an updating regime that is directly analogous to the regime for updating the fitness of *political parties*, though this is parameterized in a different way. We first set all *rule* fitnesses equal at the start of each model run.[3] In line with our existing model of party fitness, we then model the updated rule fitness, f_{re}, of rule r after election e as rule r's fitness after election e-1, updated by, v^*_{re}, the total vote share of the *set of parties using rule r* at election e. Thus,

$$f_{re} = \alpha_r \cdot f_{r(e-1)} + (1 - \alpha_r) \cdot v^*_{re} \quad (8.1)$$

The memory parameter α_r (rule-fitness-alpha) is similar in function to α_f (party-fitness-alpha). It determines the relative weight of past success when updating the relative fitness of *decision rules*. If $\alpha_r = 0$ we have a regime in which updated rule fitness depends only on the success of agents using the rule in the current period. When $\alpha_r = 1$ we have a regime in which rule fitness never updates. Having specified rule fitness, we now assume that the probability the leader a new party forming after election e chooses rule r, p_{re}, is equal to f_{re}, the updated fitness of rule r:

$$p_{re} = f_{re} \quad (8.2)$$

Our substantive interpretation of this is that, when choosing a rule for themselves, the leaders of new parties take into account not only the number of parties using a rule, but also the updated past success of parties using the rule. This updates evolving rule replication probabilities on the basis of the number of agents using each rule (as in pure replicator dynamics) but weights these agents by their updated success at winning votes.

Note that, as well as using updated party vote share as our metric for *party fitness* in the survival regime that governs the endogenous birth and death of political parties, we now also use updated vote share as our metric for *rule fitness* in the endogenous choice of decision rules by the leaders of new political parties. Since the replicator equations 8.1 and 8.2

---

[3] $f_{r0} = 1/|R| \ \forall \ r \ \varepsilon \ R.$

specify a recursive system with positive feedback for higher vote shares, we expect the replicator dynamics we specify to further privilege the vote-seeking decision rule species, Hunter, Predator, and Explorer, relative to the Aggregator and Sticker rule species, which are not designed to increase party vote shares in a systematic way.

Replication Errors and Mutation

We ignore two vital matters if we assume that rule replication probabilities are always perfectly determined by evolved rule fitness. The first concerns whether rule replication is error free—whether, once a rule has been selected for replication, it will in fact be perfectly replicated. As we discuss more fully below, we can think in terms of rule "mutation" when a rule is not perfectly replicated. The second matter has to do with "evolutionary stability" of the system for rule replication or imitation (Taylor and Jonker 1978; Page and Nowak 2002; Weibull 1995). A dynamic system is in an "evolutionarily stable state" (ESS), if it achieves a state that is robust to perturbations, shocks, or "mutations."

A possible ESS will arise in our system of replicator dynamics if a single successful rule "drives out" all others, so that all agents then use the same rule.[4] Imagine, as seems likely, that the simple three-rule system of party competition we specify in chapter 6 evolved, under our implementation of replicator dynamics, so that Hunter drove out the other two decision rules. This would almost certainly happen.[5] Hunter was more successful than the other rule species; this would now cause its replication probability to increase, causing Hunter to be used by more parties, causing it to be even more successful. This feedback loop would iterate until the replication probability approached unity, driving down the replication probabilities of other rules to a level arbitrarily close to zero. As a result of positive feedback in replication probabilities for Hunter, other rules would become effectively extinct. Before we conclude that the all-Hunter party system thereby evolving is *evolutionarily stable*; however, we need to know that, even if shocked, or "invaded" by parties using other decision rules, evolutionary dynamics will drive the party system back to one with only Hunter parties.

---

[4] Another example of a possible ESS is a cycle of coevolving fitnesses, such as we find in a wolf-sheep-grass system where wolves eat sheep, sheep eat grass, and there is more grass when there are fewer sheep to eat it. There may be no stationary state in the populations of grass, sheep, and wolves, but instead stable cycles of these. Such cycles are nicely illustrated by running the wolf-sheep predation model in the NetLogo models library, turning grass growth on, and lowering grass-regrowth time to twenty.

[5] It has indeed happened in every simulation we have run of this.

As it happens, modeling the possibility of random errors in decision rule replication also allows us to test the evolutionary stability of the rule mix in an evolved party system. Random rule replication errors are the shocks with which we test the evolutionary stability of the decision rule mix. We do this by assuming the possibility of *mutation*, at the point of rule replication when the leader of a new party chooses a decision rule. The standard way to do this is to define a *mutation matrix* Q, with elements q_{rs}. Each element gives the probability that rule r, if selected for replication, is actually replicated as rule s (Page and Nowak 2002).[6] The diagonal elements in Q, the q_{rr}, give the probability there is *no* mutation of rule r on replication; if selected for replication, rule r replicates as rule r. Pure replicator dynamics is thus a special case of a more general evolutionary system involving replication errors, with all of the q_{rr} elements set equal to 1. The value of $1 - q_{rr}$ gives the probability there is a mutation—that, if selected for replication, rule r is not in fact replicated as rule r but as some other rule. The mutation matrix can easily be defined to comprehend the possibility that rule r, if subject to mutation, may be replicated with higher probability as some non-r rules rather than as others—that different parameterizations of Hunter, for example, are more likely to mutate into each other than into an Aggregator.[7] Absent any strong alternative theory about party rule replication, however, we begin here by assuming that rule r, if subject to mutation, is equally likely to mutate into any other rule in the rule set.

Following Fowler and Laver (2008) we specify a probability p that there is an evolutionary shock to the rule replication system. With probability $(1 - p)$ there is no shock; the decision rule for any new party is chosen with a probability proportional to current evolved rule fitness, as defined above. With probability p there is a shock; the new party's decision rule is chosen by setting probabilities equal for all rules in $\mathbf{R}$.[8] We thereby specify a rule replication system with "replicator-mutator" dynamics, under which new parties choose rules from $\mathbf{R}$ with probabilities proportional to the past success of each rule, but with the possibility of random errors in the imitation process. Our evolutionary model for party competition in effect uses a very simple mutation matrix that derives from the shock probability, π, which is an important new param-

---

[6] The rows of Q thus sum to unity.

[7] Thus we expect a five-fingered human, subject to mutation on replication, to be much more likely replicated as a six-fingered human than as a kangaroo.

[8] We find it more intuitive to reverse Fowler and Laver's definition of p and $(1 - p)$; thus π is a *shock* probability, not a *nonshock* probability.

eter in our model of evolving dynamic multiparty competition.[9] The rule that is drawn from the rule set with probability, p_{re}, specified by our replicator equations at 8.1 and 8.2, is then subjected to the following mutator equations:

$$q_{rr} = (1 - \pi) + \pi/|R| \quad \forall \ r \in R. \quad (8.3)$$
$$q_{rs} = \pi/|R| \quad \forall \ r \neq s \in R \quad (8.4)$$

When $\pi = 1$ there is no replicator dynamics. There is always invasion, and rule replication probabilities are equal for each rule—as with the model we investigated in chapter 7, which is now a special case of the replicator-mutator model we specify here. When $\pi = 0$ there are no replication errors. This has the striking implication that, if any decision rule ever becomes "extinct" (has effectively zero probability of replication), then it remains extinct forever and can never be reincarnated. This is because decision rules with zero evolved fitness can only ever be chosen as a result of replication errors.

This has special substantive significance for dynamic multiparty competition. There are *many possible party decision rules* but, in dramatic contrast to most evolutionary settings, there are *only a few surviving parties* at any given time. (It is very hard to imagine how the animal kingdom would have evolved if there could only be between five and ten actual animals alive at any given time.) Take the specific example of a party system with a survival threshold of 0.10, and thus with typically about six surviving political parties at any given time. Considering the 111 available possibilities in the rule set we investigate in chapter 7, it is axiomatically true with six surviving parties that at least 105 of these rules cannot be used by any surviving party at any given time. The fitness update for all currently unused rules is zero, so the resulting updated fitness of all unused rules must decline, since α_r must be less than unity if fitnesses are ever to update.

This directs our attention back to the memory regime for rule fitness. If there is a goldfish memory regime in which $\alpha_r = 0$, then rule fitness is no more and no less than the total current vote share of the parties using the rule. This in turn means that, when $\pi = 0$ and there is no possibility of an evolutionary shock, a decision rule becomes immediately and forever extinct whenever it is not used in an election by at least one party leader. The rule's current updated fitness is zero, it has zero chance of being

---

[9] Note that under our implementation of a replicator-mutator regime, where a shock means that rule replication is random, such a shock may still with some probability result in the selection of the originally chosen rule.

selected by the leader of a new party, and thus it has zero chance of ever winning any support in the future and having a positive fitness update.

This seems grossly unrealistic in the context of party competition.[10] Unlike biological organisms that pass on their genetic material to offspring, it seems plausible to model an environment in which decision rules that were once used by the leaders of defunct political parties but that have languished unused for some time, will still be known, and could be selected with some probability by the leader of a new political party. This is the reason why we include a nonzero probability of mutation, π, and set α_r close to 1 in our model. If α_r is relatively close to 1 (i.e., the rule fitness regime has a long memory), then the past fitness of currently unused rules still contributes to the rule's current updated fitness, and thus to its current chances of being selected by a newborn party. Thus it seems plausible to assume, given a setting in which there is a relatively large number of possible decision rules and a relatively small number of surviving parties at any given time, that the rule fitness regime must have a long memory, and that rule fitnesses evolve relatively slowly, so that the past success of decision rules has a significant bearing on their current probability of replication.

Taking all of this into account, and on the basis of exploratory runs that showed us that the precise value of α_r made little difference to results as long as this was above 0.80 and below 0.95,[11] we fix α_r at 0.85, and we investigate three values of π: 0.05, 0.10, and 0.15.

Retaining a Large but Finite Rule Set

When we extended the rule set of our model from three rules to 111, we did this in part by identifying and parameterizing a set of decision rule "features," such as speed and satisficing. Each parameter could in theory be specified as a real number. However, we chose in chapter 7 to specify a coarse grid of parameter values, rather than a real space of these, because we did not want to generate a potentially infinite number of possible decision rules, which is what would happen if we simply drew rule parameters from a real space. The use of a finite grid of rule parameterizations is even more critical for the replicator-mutator system we now specify. If we

---

[10] Of course this is part and parcel of biological evolution. If there is a day on which no human being at all is alive, and there are no evolutionary shocks, then there will be no human being the next day, since there is no human to give birth to future humans. This is how species do indeed become extinct. The difference in the setting of multiparty competition is that we do not like to think of political parties as having babies and passing on their decision rules in this way but rather of new parties imitating decision rules used by previously successful parties, including those rules that exist only on the historical record.

[11] Severe problems of model burn-in arise when α_r is above this level.

had millions of surviving parties at any given time, each choosing from a small set of decision rules, then the average number of party leaders using each rule would be high. We would derive valuable information if a replicator-mutator system evolved so that some rules were rarely used by any agent. If in contrast we have millions of possible decision rules and very few surviving agents at any given time, then only a tiny proportion of the rules can be used at any one moment. The vast *majority of rules are axiomatically constrained to be unused*; the fact that some rule is not used by any surviving agent thus conveys much less information about its effectiveness.

All of this means that what we model in this chapter is an evolutionary process with a finite set of rules. What evolves, as a result of the replicator-mutator dynamics we define above, is a *vector of rule replication probabilities*. Our evolutionary model will never, as a result of random rule mutation for example, generate a hitherto unheard of decision rule that was previously undefined.[12] The evolution we model takes place within a finite set of possible decision rules, most of these constrained not to be realized at any given time since the number of possible rules is far larger than the number of surviving parties. Our fundamental interest concerns whether, within this somewhat unusual evolutionary setting, there are rule species, or rule parameterizations, that tend systematically to emerge as more successful than others.

Experimental Design

To a large extent, experimental design issues for computational implementations of our replicator-mutator model are the same as those for other stochastic processes for which a time average does not provide a representative estimate of μ, which we specified in chapter 4 and implemented in chapters 6 and 7. We have, however, introduced a very important complication with a replicator system that adds positive feedback to evolving rule selection probabilities. This can be seen most clearly if we set $\pi = 0$, so that there is never a rule replication error. In this extreme case, the positive feedback arising from what would be a pure replicator dynamics system would mean that our model not only would be path dependent but also would be what Scott Page calls "early path" dependent (Page 2006). Being picked at random early on would make a big difference to the success of any rule. The first rule picked would have a big boost in its replication probability, while other rules would have a

---

[12] This is without doubt an exciting and challenging modeling prospect. We eagerly await the work of others who might master it.

big drop in their replication probabilities. This would make the first rule picked much more likely to be picked again, thereby increasing its fitness, reducing the fitness of other rules, and so on. With no replication errors, positive feedback in rule replication probabilities means that, once one rule dominates, it will stay dominant; and *which* rule dominates may well depend on the early stochastic path of the system.

The possibility of replication errors when $\pi > 0$—which we analyze below—means that any evolved stationary state dominance of a single rule will be "tested" by a series of evolutionary shocks. This means we know axiomatically that the evolutionary system is not path dependent, but ergodic: there exists some path generated by some sequence of shocks, however improbable, from any state to any other state. An all-Hunter system may be in place for ten thousand elections, for example, but could still be shocked into an all-Sticker system by a long series of random draws, at the point of new party birth, that specified an invasion and, given an invasion, specified that the leader of the new party chooses the Sticker rule. This might be very improbable indeed, but it will nonetheless certainly happen during an infinite model run. If $\pi = 0$ there are no shocks and this can never happen. While the evolution of our modeled party system is formally not path dependent when $\pi > 0$, we do find that one rule can easily become dominant for a long period, before being displaced by the "right" sequence of evolutionary shocks. This does not matter in an infinite run but means that observed output from any finite run is not characteristic of the model's stochastic steady state for a given parameterization. In essence, the positive feedback introduced by replicator-mutator dynamics means that we now face a much more intense version of the problem that any feasible finite model run is a small unrepresentative sample of the ergodic process.

We specified an experimental design solution to this problem in chapter 4, using the ensemble means of outputs from multiple burnt-in repetitions of the same run, each repetition with the same parameterization but a different random seed. A new and important problem arises, however, concerning burn-in of the replicator-mutator system. The "classic" burn-in period that we have already specified is still necessary because we do not want the random start of any simulation to have an impact on rule replication probabilities under replicator-mutator dynamics. We want to "turn on" the replicator system only once the model has burnt in from a random start. Having turned it on, we then need to give the replicator-mutator system itself time to take effect, as the relative success of decision rules over a sequence of elections feeds back into the vector of rule replication probabilities. The whole point of the computational experiment we specify in this chapter is to observe the party system *after* this positive feedback has taken effect and the system has reached a new stochastic steady state, associated with the new Markov transition probability matrix that incorporates the positive feedback and random errors in rule replication probabilities. The new methodological question concerns how many model iterations are "enough" for us to observe this new stochastic steady state in a reliable way.

Returning to our methodological discussions in chapter 4, we see that this problem can be addressed by specifying an appropriate state space summary variable, plotting this, and observing when it appears to have entered a stochastic steady state. The output variable of special interest to us in this chapter is the effective number of rules (ENR). This is because our theoretical expectation is that, once the replicator-mutator system is turned on, ENR will tend to decrease systematically as the more successful rules become more likely to be selected by the leaders of new parties and the less successful rules become less likely to be selected. Furthermore, when one single rule has driven out all others for a finite period, and as we shortly see this is a situation we do indeed observe, then ENR = 1 for this period—until the system is shocked into some other state. We are thus interested in observing when the ENR measure output by our model has entered a stochastic steady state that includes finite periods during which ENR = 1.

The top panel of Figure 8.1 plots ENR over a sequence of four thousand elections for a typical replication of a single run of the model we specify in this chapter, in which the replicator-mutator system was turned on after a long burn-in of five hundred elections. The "classic" burn-in phase can clearly be seen in the rapidly rising line on the left-hand side of the plot. This is followed by burn-in of the replicator-mutator system, which shows the expected rapid decline in ENR. Flatlining of ENR at a value of 1.0 first occurs after about fourteen hundred elections—this is the first time that one rule has driven out all others. Following this, there are alternating periods of flatlining model output with ENR=1.0, followed by collapses of this short-run steady state following successful random invasions. The bottom panel of Figure 8.1 plots the same run extended to twenty thousand elections and shows that model-generated ENR does seem characteristic, in a stochastic steady state, after about fourteen hundred elections. Conversely, the model-generated ENR does not appear characteristic until it first flatlines at about fourteen hundred elections.

On the basis of a series of plots like that in Figure 8.1 for the most extreme parameterizations of party competition, we found that it can take a long time for the replicator-mutator system to burn in and achieve a characteristic distribution of states. The upshot is that we specify the experiments in this chapter with a 250-election conventional burn-in, followed by a further 2,500-election period during which the replicator system is burnt in. System outputs are recorded for election 2,751, and the

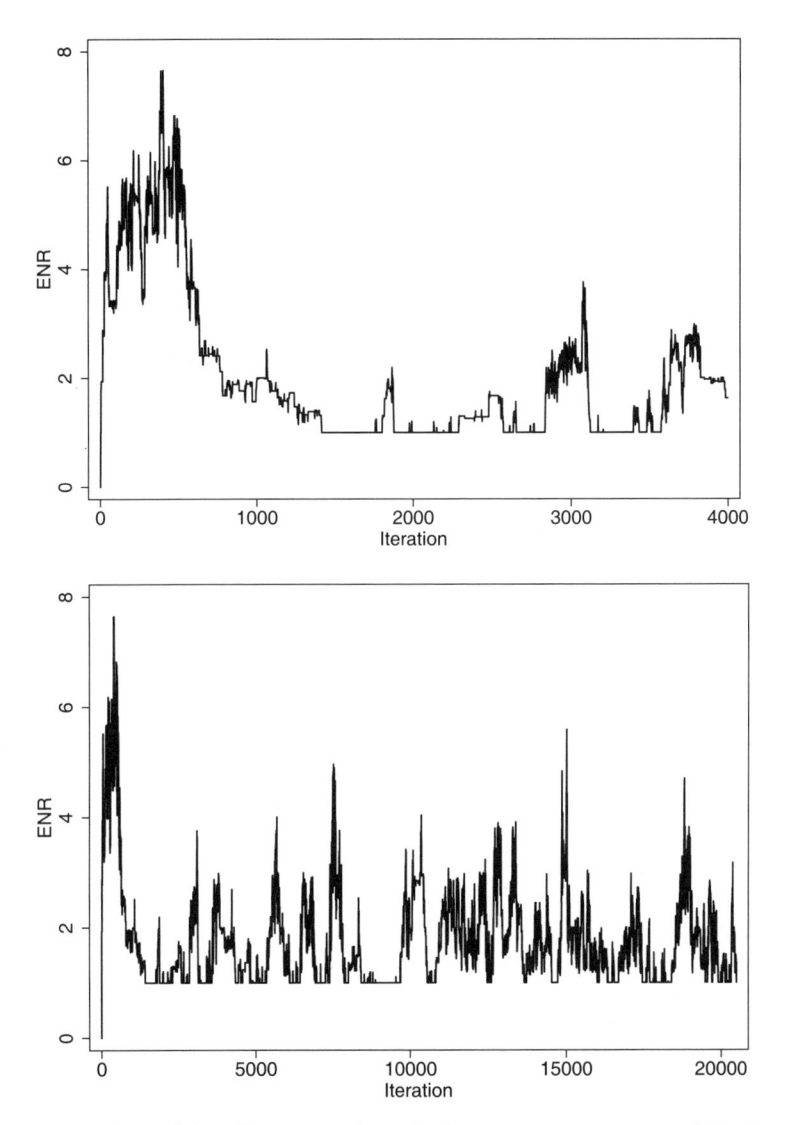

Figure 8.1. Plots of the effective number of rules (ENR) over a series of elections, with a replicator-mutator system turned on after a five-hundred-election burn-in.

repetition is stopped immediately after this. This implies a much heavier computational budget per repetition than for the simulations we report in chapter 7. Each repetition requires running the model for 2,751 rather than 251 elections.

Since our main substantive concern in this chapter is the replicator-mutator system we have introduced into the model, and since we investigated the effects of other model parameters in chapter 7, we now move away from Monte Carlo parameterization of our model to a stripped-down grid parameterization that captures the main features of the parameter space that we identified in previous chapters as being salient. As already noted we fix a_r at 0.85 and investigate three values of π (0.05, 0.10, and 0.15). We investigate six values of the survival threshold τ (0.05, 0.10, 0.15, 0.20, 0.25, 0.30) and four of the population polarization parameter μ_r (0.0, 0.5, 1.0, 1.5). We fix other environmental parameters (a_f at 0.75, ψ at 15, and n_1/n_2 at 1.5) as we have seen these have less striking effects on outcomes of interest. Our model parameterization, including our grid parameterization of rule features, is otherwise identical to that for the simulations we report in chapter 7. The net result is that rather than the 1,000 Monte Carlo model parameterizations we used in chapter 7, we now have a 72-point grid of environmental parameters.[13] The results we report below thus summarize output from 1,000 repetitions of each of 72 model runs with a grid parameterization, each repetition involving a 250-election model burn-in and a 2,500-election burn-in of the replicator system.[14] We want to compare simulation results for the replicator-mutator system specified in this chapter to those generated by the model with random rule selection we specified in chapters 6 and 7. We therefore generated a benchmark for the results we report below by rerunning the computational experiment we designed in chapter 7 but using the stripped-down grid parameterization we now specify.

Multiparty Competition with Replicator-Mutator Dynamics

The Effective Number of Surviving Decision Rules

The big change we have made to our model is to add positive feedback to the probability that leaders of new political parties pick a particular decision rule from the available rule set. A pure rule replicator system

---

[13] Six values of τ, four of μ' and three of π.

[14] The computational budget for the experiment reported in this chapter is thus 1,000 x 72 x 2,751 = 198,072,000 elections, which is of the same order of magnitude as the 251,000,000 elections for the experiment reported in the previous chapter.

Evolutionary Dynamics • 171

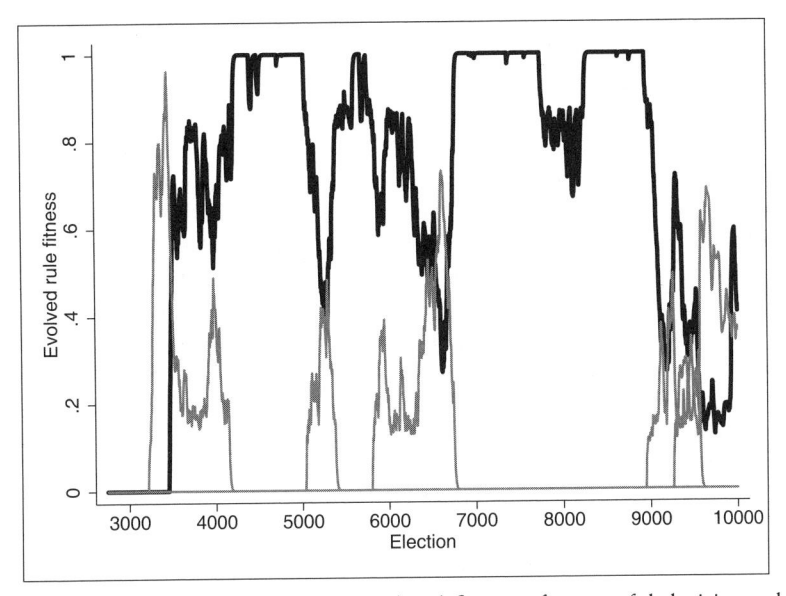

Figure 8.2. Time series plots of the updated fitness of successful decision rules over a single repetition of a single model run under replicator-mutator dynamics.

would be "early path dependent," since rules with lucky random draws early in the process would be systematically advantaged and this early advantage would feed back into the system. This is why we specified a mutation probability $\pi > 0$, so that the party systems we model generate ergodic outputs and are "evolutionarily stable" in the sense that typical outcomes are robust to evolutionary shocks. The evolutionary shocks in our model can be seen substantively as either rule replication errors—one rule choice is specified but another random rule is actually chosen—or as random "invasions" of parties using decision rules not specified by the replicator system. This leaves open the possibility that a single decision rule for party competition drives out all others for some long era of elections, before a particular sequence of shocks perturbs this short-run stationary state. Figure 8.2 gives an example of model output under these conditions. It plots the performance of several different decision rules over a single repetition of a single run of our model.[15]

---

[15] This simulation ran for 10,000 elections, of which the first 2,750 were treated as burn-in. It was conducted for the purpose of generating this figure and is not part of the general results we report. Run parameters were $\tau = 0.10$, $\psi = 15$, $\pi = 0.10$, $\alpha_f = 0.75$, $\alpha_r = 0.90$, $\mu_l = -\mu_r = 1.0$.

The most successful rule parameterization by far in this particular repetition has an updated fitness, denominated in vote share, plotted by the black line. This was an Explorer rule for which $\kappa = 0.16$ and $\eta = 1.0$. Parties with leaders using this rule won about 70 percent of the vote over the entire burnt-in era of this run repetition. Four other rule parameterizations (two Hunter rules,[16] two Explorer rules[17]) accounted for more than 2 percent of the vote over this run repetition and are plotted in gray.

The patterns shown in Figure 8.2 are both instructive and typical. First, note that the most successful rule dominates completely, with an evolved fitness at or arbitrarily close to unity, about one-third of the time.[18] Also note, however, that it took over four thousand elections before this pattern emerged. Other decision rules are in contention for the remaining two-thirds of elections. Second, note that some of these other rules were fittest for certain, albeit shorter, eras of party competition. Third, note that even very long periods of apparent rule hegemony, when the most successful rule seems finally to have driven out all others, can still be destroyed by random invasions. The most successful rule in Figure 8.2, for example, might have appeared to have driven out all others once we had entered the 2,145-election era between elections 6,800 and 8,945, even resisting an invasion in the middle of this. However, we now know with the benefit of hindsight that successful invasions by other rules after election 8,945 completely changed this picture. In short, though of course we cannot be certain about this, there is nothing in Figure 8.2 that leads us to conclude that after 10,000 elections the decision rule represented by the solid black line will eventually come to dominate party competition forever. Notwithstanding this, we can also draw the *statistical* inference from the available data that this rule parameterization is systematically the most successful in the competitive environment under investigation.

Figure 8.3 shows one of the main results we report in this chapter. It plots, over the full range of competitive environments we investigate, the effective numbers of parties (ENP) and decision rules (ENR) under both random rule selection (left panel) and replicator-mutator dynamics (right panel). The comparison is both striking and consistent with theoretical expectations. *The typical ENR in use by surviving parties is much lower under replicator-mutator dynamics.*

---

[16] With, respectively, (κ, γ) parameterizations of (0.11, 0.25) and (0.31, 0.25).

[17] With, respectively, (κ, η) parameterizations of (0.26, 0.60) and (0.31, 0.40).

[18] More precisely, its evolved fitness is greater than 0.99 for 32.7 percent of elections 2,751–10,000.

Evolutionary Dynamics • 173

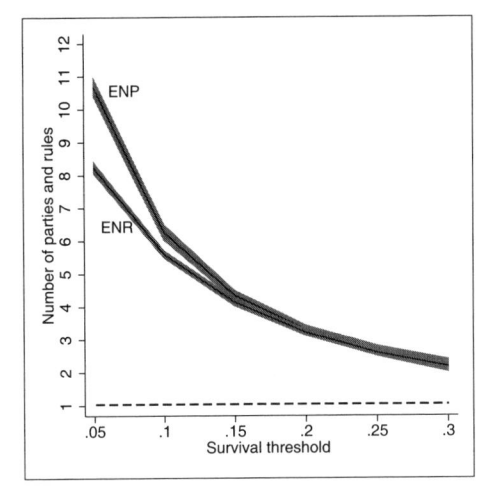

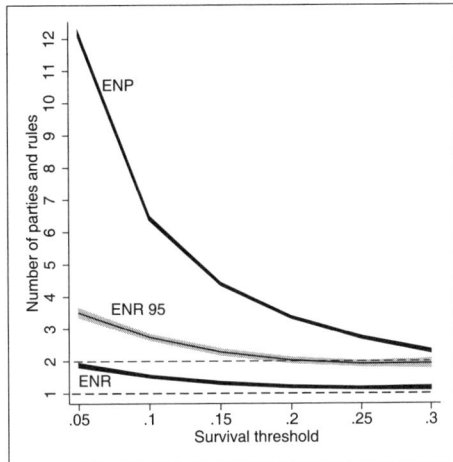

Figure 8.3. Mean effective numbers of parties and decision rules by τ; random rule selection (left), replicator-mutator dynamics (right).

With random-rule selection, when a small number of party leaders *randomly* choose decision rules from a large set of possibilities, we expect that each party leader would typically choose a different rule. The number of different rule-leader pairings should typically be the same as the number of surviving parties, implying $ENR \approx ENP$. The left panel of Figure 8.3 shows that this is indeed the case. ENP and ENR are statistically indistinguishable when survival thresholds are high ($\tau > 0.13$) and there are consequently fewer than four parties. ENR and ENP diverge, though they remain close, as survival thresholds drop and there are more surviving parties. In settings with more parties, it is sometimes the case that two or more party leaders use the same decision rule. But it never comes close to being the case that all party leaders use the same rule. ENR is always well above unity.

The right panel of Figure 8.3 shows that introducing positive feedback into rule replication probabilities makes it *much* more common for all party leaders to use the same parameterization of the same rule. As a result, ENR is typically much lower than ENP. Indeed we see that $ENR \approx 1$ for some parameterizations of party competition, in particular those with relatively high survival thresholds and consequently few parties. This means that it is typically the case in such environments that, at any given time, a single decision rule parameterization dominates party competition—though as we have seen which particular rule this is may

[Figure: plot of Effective number of rules vs Survival threshold, showing ENR95 and ENR curves]

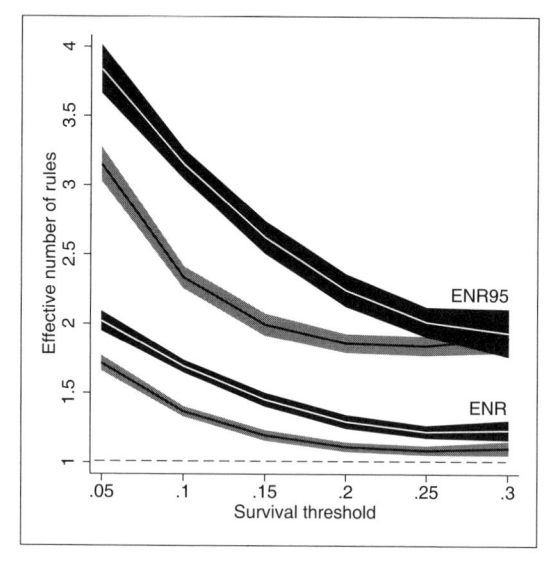

Figure 8.4. Effective number of rules (ENR) by invasion probability and survival threshold. Black confidence bands plot ENR for $\pi = 0.15$, gray bands for $\pi = 0.05$.

be perturbed by random shocks. We also see, however, that mean *ENR* is typically not equal to unity and is always statistically distinguishable from this,[19] recalling that *ENR* = 1 at any given time if and only if a successful decision rule has driven out all others. A good indication of this is given by the "*ENR95*" band in the right panel of Figure 8.3, showing the 95th percentile of observed *ENR* for each run; thus 5 percent of observations generate *ENR* values above the gray band. We see that typical 95th percentile *ENR* converges on *ENR* = 2, not *ENR* = 1. *Even with the positive feedback introduced by replicator-mutator dynamics, it is not uncommon to find at least two different decision rules in serious contention at any given time.*

While the positive feedback introduced by replicator dynamics systematically drives down the typical number of decision rules in use by surviving parties, we expect that the higher the mutation probability, the less pronounced this effect. Figure 8.4 shows that this is indeed the case. It plots the combined effects of survival threshold and the mutation probability on both mean and 95th percentile *ENR*. Higher values of π, plotted by the black confidence bands, generate competitive environments in which all party systems, including those dominated at some

---

[19] The 95 percent confidence bands around plotted ENR never intersect the ENR = 1 line.

Evolutionary Dynamics • 175

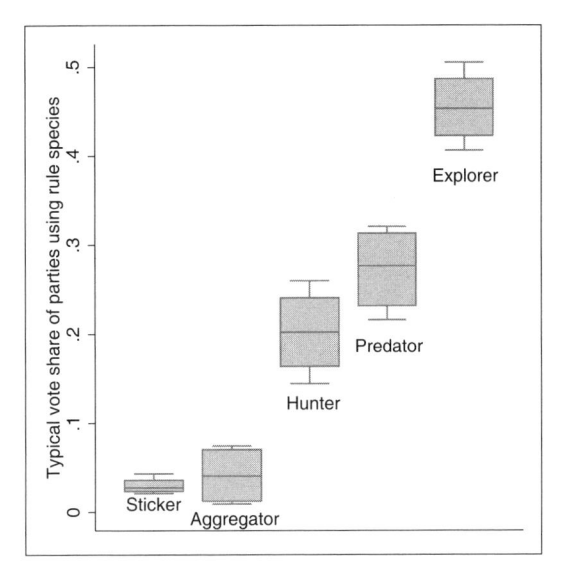

Figure 8.5. Typical vote shares of sets of parties using different rule species, in competitive environments where $\tau = 0.30$ and $\pi = 0.05$

point in time by a single decision rule, are more likely to be shocked. We expect, and indeed find, that more decision rules are typically in contention, and thus *ENR* is systematically higher, in such settings.[20] Two quite different substantive processes are combined here. First, when mutation probabilities are higher, there are likely to be more different rules in contention simply because there are more replication errors resulting in random rule selection. Second, if the dynamic party system has "locked in" to a short-run stationary state in which all leaders use the same decision rule, exemplified by the flatlining shown in Figure 8.2, higher mutation probabilities speed up the process of shocking the party system out of this state.

The results plotted in Figure 8.4 show that, at least for the values of π we investigate, rule diversity, whether measured by mean or 95th percentile *ENR*, remains significantly above unity. There is no competitive environment in which a single rule parameterization typically drives out all others over the long run. Figure 8.5 shows this in more substantive terms. For the competitive environment that generates the *least* rule diversity, with the highest survival threshold and the lowest invasion probability, it plots typical vote shares, by rule species.

---

[20] Black and gray confidence bands for plotted mean ENR never overlap.

176 • Chapter 8

Even though mean *ENR* (at 1.09) is as close to unity as we observe in any of the competitive environments we investigate, Figure 8.5 shows clearly *that no one rule species dominates the party system*. The normal state of affairs, over time, is that there is diversity in the set of decision rules in use by surviving party leaders. While the low vote shares won by parties using Aggregator and Sticker rules in this environment could arise simply as a result of random invasions, the relatively high vote shares won by parties using any of the three vote-seeking rules, combined with the low mean *ENR* of 1.09 in this setting, show that any one of these three rules might be dominant at any given time.

Under the replicator-mutator system we specify, rules with a past history of success are more likely to be chosen. A key feature of the simulation results we report here is that this positive feedback in rule replication probabilities can indeed cause the party system to "lock in" to short-run states in which all party leaders use the same decision rule. However, given the possibility of random mutation, in the form of rule replication errors or invasions by parties using randomly selected rules, our simulations suggest that *party systems never evolve to steady states in which a single "best" decision rule ultimately drives out all others forever*. The typical evolutionary pattern we find is like the example we plot in Figure 8.2. It involves eras of elections, which can be quite long, during which particular decision rules dominate, alternating with eras in which a small number different decision rules are in contention at the same time.

Sharpened Performance Differentials between Decision Rules

We just saw that modifying our model of multiparty competition to make rule replication probabilities a function of past success reduces the number of decision rules in use at any given time. While one rule never drives about all others, eras of dominance by some rule are followed by eras of dominance by others. Nonetheless, as we now see, all rule parameterizations are not equal. On the contrary and as expected, the introduction of replicator-mutator dynamics into our *model sharpens performance differentials between successful and unsuccessful rules*. In a nutshell this is because, when $\pi = 1.0$ (there are always invasions) as in chapter 7 and there is no positive feedback in the model, relatively unsuccessful rules have a higher chance of being chosen at random. Party leaders who choose unsuccessful rules do tend to die young in the survival-of-the-fittest evolutionary setting we model in chapter 7, but their parties gather some votes before they die. In the setting we model here, party leaders systematically tend not to choose unsuccessful rules.

Figure 8.6 plots typical vote shares won by parties using different rule species, both for benchmark party systems with random rule selection

Evolutionary Dynamics • 177

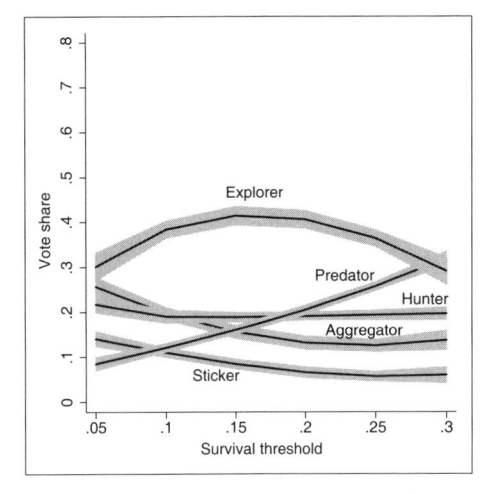

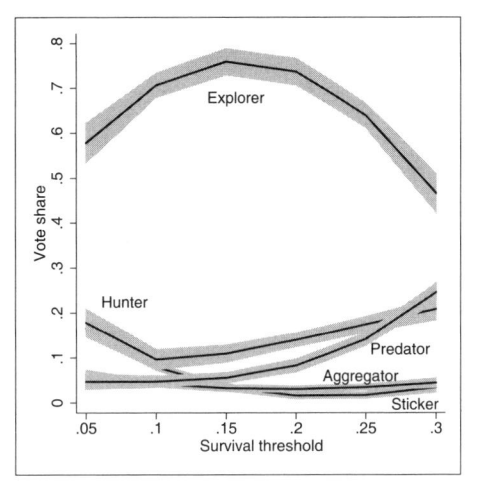

Figure 8.6. Typical vote shares of parties using different rule species, by τ; equivalent parameterizations of random rule selection (left), replicator-mutator dynamics (right). Confidence bands are notably wider than those in the analogous Figure 7.2 because, as we noted when discussing experimental design, the greatly increased computational load arising from the need to burn in the replicator-mutator system for an additional 2,500 elections before recording any observations forced us to use a seventy-two-point grid parameterization for the competitive environment rather than the one-thousand-point Monte Carlo parameterization we used for the work we report in chapter 7.

(left panel) and for party systems with positive feedback in rule replication probabilities (right panel).[21] This gives us the first sight of the second big result in this chapter. In line with our expectations, *if decision rules perform relatively well under random rule selection, they perform even better under the positive feedback introduced by replicator-mutator dynamics*. The shapes of the main effects in the two plots are the same, notably the sensitivity of decision rules to the survival threshold, but these effects are magnified by positive feedback. In results we do not show here, the main parameter of our replicator-mutator system, the mutation probability π, has no significant effect on relative rule performance.[22] It is positive feedback in replication probabilities per se that affects the rela-

---

[21] The benchmark results reported here give a slightly higher long-run vote share to Explorers, and a lower vote share to Predators, than those reported in chapter 7. This arises from our grid parameterization, which fixes α_f at 0.75. The top-left panel of Figure E7.1 in the electronic appendix shows that this tends to favor Explorers relative to Predators.

[22] See Figure E8.1 in the electronic appendix.

tive performance of different decision rules, not the precise parameterization of this feedback. The net substantive result we see in Figure 8.6 is a dramatic improvement in the performance of Explorer rules and a significant decline in the performance of Aggregators.[23]

The key to these findings is that the metric for the positive feedback we have now introduced to rule replication probabilities is *updated party vote shares*. While the survival-of-the-fittest environment specified in chapter 7 uses updated vote share as the *survival* metric, party vote share now enters our model a second time, as the *rule replication* metric in our replicator-mutator system. The effect of this, measuring success in terms of vote share, is to lower the success rate of the non-vote-seeking rule species, Aggregator and Sticker, from a combined share of about 25 percent of the vote under random rule selection to about 10 percent when rule replication probabilities are a function of the past vote shares won by parties using each rule.[24] In contrast, the most successful vote-seeking rule, Explorer, has about twice the vote share of the other vote-seeking rules under our benchmark system, therefore a much higher chance of being selected by the leaders of new parties—and this endlessly feeds back into the recursive rule replication system we have specified.

Figure 8.7 illustrates the workings of our replicator-mutator system in relation to the two rule species most affected by it, Explorer and Aggregator, plotting the number of parties using each rule species at any given time. The party survival threshold is the main feature of the competitive environment that drives the number of surviving parties. Comparing the two panels of Figure 8.7 we see that, for any given survival threshold, there are significantly more party leaders using Explorer rules, and significantly fewer parties using Aggregator, when there is positive feedback in the rule replication system (right panel). A non-vote-seeking rule such as Aggregator may be able to survive and garner a moderate vote share (as we have seen, typically by avoiding other parties) *if it is chosen by a party leader*. And it is just as likely to be chosen as any other rule when party leaders pick decision rules at random. When party leaders pick decision rules on the basis of these rules' past success at winning votes, however, the non-vote-seeking Aggregator rule is simply much less likely to be chosen than successful vote-seeking rules such as Explorer.

Focusing on the successful Explorer rule, the main rule parameter we specify is the size, η, of the party leader's exploration neighborhood. Comparing the left and right panels of Figure 8.8, we see once again that

---

[23] This decline is not affected at all by the precise parameterization of Aggregator in terms of γ.

[24] Numerical estimates for both vote share and life expectancy in other settings are given in Table E8.1 in the electronic appendix.

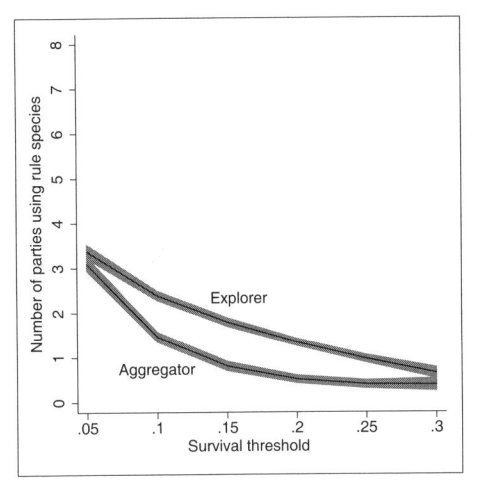

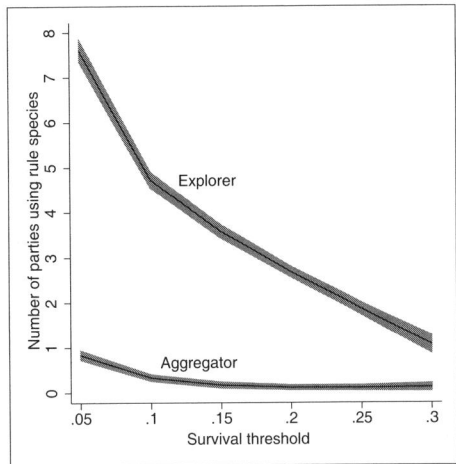

Figure 8.7. Typical number of parties using Explorer and Aggregator rules, by τ; equivalent parameterizations of random rule selection (left), replicator-mutator dynamics (right).

the effects we estimated under random rule selection are magnified when positive feedback is added to rule replication probabilities. We found in chapter 7 that smaller exploration neighborhoods tend to be associated with lower voter shares for Explorer parties but that the largest neighborhoods were not necessarily associated with the highest vote shares. Figure 8.8 shows us that this pattern is magnified when we add positive feedback to rule replication probabilities. Figure 8.9 plots similar results for the analogous relationship between speed of adaptation and the typical vote shares of Hunter parties, whereby the highest vote shares won by Hunters are won by those that adapt neither "too fast" nor "too slowly." In results we do not show here,[25] we also find that satisficing parties whose comfort threshold, κ, is slightly above the party survival threshold perform relatively better under replicator-mutator dynamics than they do under random rule selection.

The relationships between the various parameters of our model of party competition and the mean policy eccentricity of parties using different decision rules are essentially the same as those we report in chapter 7.[26] Typical party policy positions remain strongly affected by the polarization of voter ideal points, as well as by the party decision rule, but *party policy positions are not affected in any significant way by the positive*

---

[25] These results are shown in Figure E8.2 in the electronic appendix.
[26] These results are shown in Figure E8.3 in the electronic appendix.

180 • Chapter 8

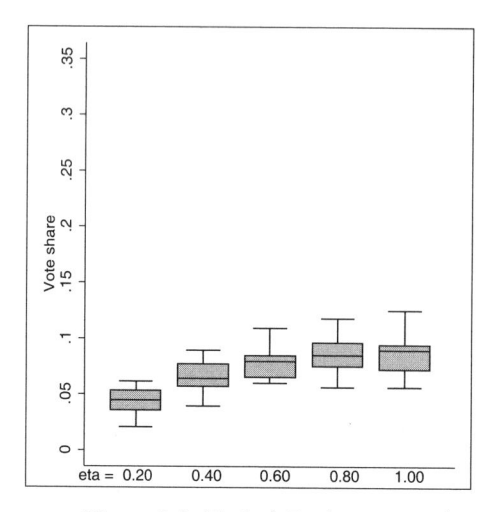

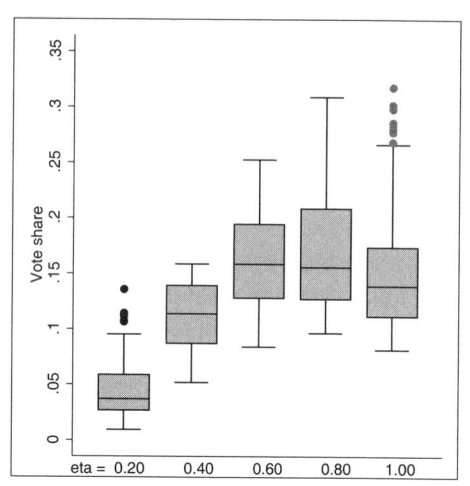

Figure 8.8. Typical Explorer vote shares by η; equivalent parameterizations of random rule selection (left), replicator-mutator dynamics (right).

feedback introduced under replicator-mutator dynamics. An important consequence of this is that there is effectively no difference between the representativeness of evolved configurations of party policy positions under random rule selection and those arising under replicator-mutator dynamics.[27] If the leaders of new parties select decision rules on the basis of their past success at winning votes, this does not result in any change in party policy eccentricity nor in either more or less representative configurations of party policy positions. We feel these negative results are of considerable substantive interest.

Conclusions

We specified a major addition to our model of multiparty competition in this chapter, now assuming that the leaders of new political parties are more likely to pick decision rules that have been more successful at winning votes in the past. This sharpens our focus on *vote-seeking* decision rules. Not only are updated party vote shares the *survival metric* in our model of endogenous party birth and death, they are now the *replication metric* in our new model of endogenous choice of party decision rules. Crudely, the success of decision rules at winning votes is now "doubly endogenized" in our model. In this chapter, we set aside for the time being

---

[27] These results are shown in Figure E8.4 in the electronic appendix.

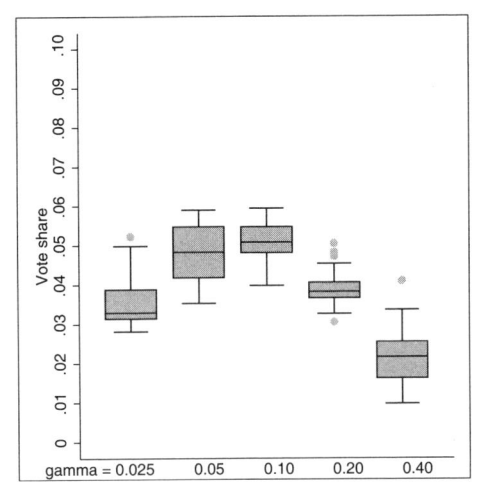

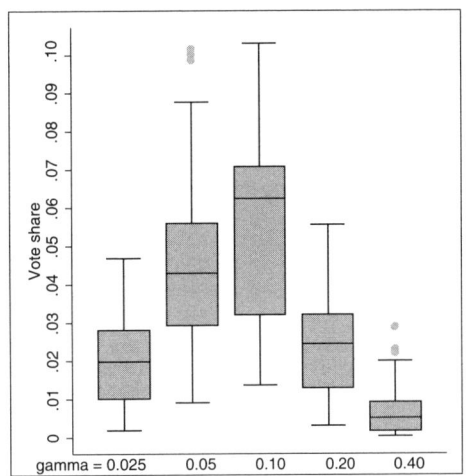

Figure 8.9. Typical Hunter vote shares by γ; equivalent parameterizations of random rule selection (left), replicator-mutator dynamics (right).

the possibility that new party leaders might be uninterested in winning votes, a possibility we return to in chapter 10, when we consider party leaders who also care about their own private policy preferences.

The positive feedback we introduced into our model of multiparty competition gave us two clear theoretical expectations. First, we expect positive feedback to be associated with sharper differences in the relative performance of different decision rules and stronger effects of party system parameters. Figures 8.6–8.9 show clearly that we do indeed find this. They also show that the Aggregator rule species is a particular "casualty," and Explorer a particular "winner," of having positive feedback in rule replication probabilities. This arises directly from the fact that the rule replication metric is vote share. Aggregators are not programmed to seek votes, while Explorer is the most successful vote-seeking rule. The systematically differential success at winning votes that arises feeds back into rule replication probabilities, driving down the number of Aggregators and driving up the number of Explorers. This feedback is iterated many times over the course of a long series of elections, further driving down the probability that new party leaders choose Aggregator. By the time this process has taken full effect, non-vote-seeking rules such as Aggregator and Sticker tend to be chosen only as a result of random mutations or "invasions."

Our second expectation is that the number of different decision rules being used by party leaders at any given time, measured by ENR, will be significantly lower in party systems evolving under replicator dynamics.

We left open the question of whether the positive feedback might typically result in outcomes in which one rule parameterization drives out all others. Figures 8.3–8.5 show that rule diversity is systematically much lower under replicator dynamics, while the sample run plotted in Figure 8.2 illustrates how one single rule parameterization may dominate for long eras of electoral competition. However, given the probability of rule replication errors that is also a core feature of our replicator-mutator system, we typically find both an alternation of rules that dominate for finite eras of elections and an alternation of eras of single-rule dominance with eras in which several decision rules are in contention. The net result is that, not only is there no single decision rule that dominates all others in all settings, there appears to be no single rule that dominates any given setting over the very long run.

CHAPTER NINE

Nonpolicy Factors in Party Competition

SPATIAL MODELS OF PARTY COMPETITION, of their essence, deal with how politicians compete with each other by setting rival policy positions. They are, as we have seen, models of competitive spatial location, where the spaces under consideration are *policy* spaces that describe how voters feel about different potential outcomes of the policy process. Clearly, *nonpolicy factors* may also have an impact on political competition. Indeed local commentators often stress nonpolicy factors when interpreting the current state of politics in any given setting. These include, but are by no means confined to, the intangible but nonetheless potent charisma of certain candidates; damaging gaffes and scandals; individual reputations for competence, reliability, trustworthiness; and access to the financial and media resources needed to turn potential support into votes actually cast on the day of the election. Scholars have devoted a lot of attention to spatial models of party competition that also take account of nonpolicy factors such as these. We do the same in this chapter, modifying our dynamic model of multiparty competition to comprehend a world in which voters support particular candidates for reasons that go beyond the set of rival policy positions on offer.

The attributes of particular candidates that may appeal to voters, over and above their policy positions, are commonly described in terms of electoral *valence*. Unfortunately, different authors interpret the notion of "valence" in somewhat different ways, and we must resolve this ambiguity before moving on. Contemporary discussions of valence can be traced to a seminal critique of the Downsian spatial model by Donald Stokes, who distinguished between "position" issues, which can be described in terms of points on some policy dimension, and "valence" issues, which, he argues, cannot (Stokes 1963).

> I will call "*position*-issues" those that involve advocacy of government actions from a set of alternatives over which a distribution of voter preferences is defined. . . . I will call "*valence*-issues" those that merely involve the linking of the parties with some condition that is positively or negatively valued by the electorate. . . . It will not do simply to exclude valence issues from the discussion of party competition. The people's choice too often depends upon them. (Stokes 1963: 373)

Valence issues, according to Stokes, are those on which there is "overwhelming consensus as to the goal of government action" (Stokes 1963: 374); they are also issues that, for *exogenous* reasons, help or harm particular candidates in a disproportionate way. All voters agree, for example, that crime is bad. No rational politician campaigns for more crime. In the account of valence first put forward by Stokes there also tends, for reasons outside the model, to be a popular consensus about which candidate is best equipped to lower crime rates. Crucially, this consensus on who can best tackle crime is assumed in valence models to be an exogenous input to the process of party competition, not an endogenous consequence of the policy positions on crime put forward by rival politicians. This is an essentially empirical claim, not only about popular consensus on some "valence" issue such as crime but also about popular consensus on the relative abilities of different candidates to deal with this issue. For Stokes, *valence is about policy*, but valence issues are a particular type of policy issue, distinctive in the way we have just described. This view is shared by Ansolabehere and Snyder (2000: 327–28) in a widely cited article on "valence issues . . . that is, issues on which all voters have the same position."

Notwithstanding ritual citation of Stokes, other scholars modeling the impact of candidate valence on electoral competition also use valence to describe *nonpolicy* effects. According to Groseclose, for example, ". . . [O]ften one of the candidates has an advantage due to a *nonpolicy* factor, such as incumbency, greater campaign funds, better name recognition, superior charisma, superior intelligence, and so on. Stokes has dubbed such factors valence factors, and he has noted their importance in U.S. elections" (Groseclose 2001: 862).[1] He adds the significant rider that "[m]any, and perhaps most, valence factors are associated with benefits that incumbency confers" (Groseclose 2001: 862n1). For Schofield, who has devoted considerable attention to the topic, "[v]alence refers to voters' judgements about positively or negatively evaluated aspects of candidates, or party leaders, which *cannot be ascribed to the policy choice of the party*. One may conceive of the valence that a voter ascribes to a party leader as a judgement of the leader's *quality or competence*" (Schofield 2006: 184).[2] Aragones and Palfrey, on the other hand, distinguish conceptually between nonpolicy effects and valence issues before effectively bundling these together for analysis:

> The implications of our model are actually more general than simply an investigation of the effects of charisma, or other "exogenous" can-

[1] Emphasis added.
[2] Emphasis added.

didate characteristics. The results apply for any particular nonpolicy advantage one candidate has over another, which is valued by all voters. Thus, endogenous political phenomena such as office-holding experience, incumbent performance, constituency service, and advertising (campaign expenditures) can also generate similar effects. . . . In addition to the candidate-specific image dimension, there are also broader "valence" issues . . . such as economic performance . . . and military success, that are irreversibly linked to a candidate. (Aragones and Palfrey 2002: 132)

On the face of things, there is thus a surprising divergence among authors who are all writing about the "same" key concept of valence. On Stokes's view, valence concerns *policy issues on which there is widespread consensus*, about both desirable outcomes and candidates' abilities to deliver these. On the Schofield/Groseclose view, valence concerns *nonpolicy attributes* of candidates for election. On closer inspection, however, scholars who add an exogenous valence component to a spatial model invariably do this by adding a *systematic candidate effect that is independent of the candidate's position in the policy space under investigation*. Formal *models* of valence are all similar in this regard, even if their *substantive motivation* tends to differ between authors. The main exception to this is an extended "activist" valence model by Schofield (2006, 2008), which adds *endogenous* valence generated by activists to exogenous candidate valence, with activist valence being a function of the distance between candidates' policy positions and activists' ideal points.

Putting all of this together, what critically distinguishes valence issues from other types of issues is not popular consensus on the best policy position, providing incentives for all candidates to take similar positions, but popular consensus on the relative ability of candidates to deliver the favored policy positions. It is this *consensus on candidate quality* that gives favored candidates their valence advantage. This advantage does not derive from policy positions per se, which by assumption or deduction are shared on all such issues by all vote-seeking candidates. It derives from popular consensus on candidates' *perceived ability to deliver* these positions. Notwithstanding talk of valence "issues," valence *effects* are essentially nonpolicy effects. They reflect a systematic electoral advantage that can accrue to high-valence candidates, over and above their policy positions. Clearly, when there is no consensus on desired outcomes, for position issues in Stokes's sense, there will be no consensus on how good it is for some candidate to be able to deliver a controversial outcome. If we hate the policies you propose, we see it as no advantage whatsoever that you will be very good at delivering these policies if elected. Rather, we would prefer you to be an incompetent moron.

Modeling "Nonpolicy" Valence

Notwithstanding significant variation in how different authors motivate and interpret the notion of candidate valence, there is widespread practical consensus on how such valence should be *modeled*. Valence is essentially about the preferences of voters and is modeled by adding a new term to the voter utility function. Higher valence candidates are assumed to deliver more utility to any given voter than lower valence candidates *with the same policy position*. The key implication is that utility gained from higher valence may outweigh utility lost from greater policy distance. A voter may in this way get more utility from a higher valence candidate further away from her ideal point than from a lower valence candidate closer to her. Moreover, since valence effects arise from *consensus among voters* about candidate quality, these effects are modeled by adding a *party-specific* valence constant to the utility function of each voter. We have used the common assumption of quadratic loss when defining the utility U_{ij} for a voter with an ideal point at i for party J with a policy position at j, with $d(i, j)$ being the Euclidean distance between i and j. We now add a "valence" term, V_J, to the voter utility function:

$$U_{ij} = \lambda \cdot V_J - (1 - \lambda) \cdot d(i, j)^2 \qquad (9.1)$$

The valence parameter λ ($0 \leq \lambda \leq 1$) measures the relative importance to the voter of a party's valence and its policy position.[3] We can specify the "pure policy" model we have investigated up until now by setting $\lambda = 0$. In this case the utility function for each voter is exactly as before: $U_{ij} = -d(i, j)^2$. A "pure valence" model assumes $\lambda = 1$, so that party policy positions are completely irrelevant. All that voters then care about are party valences: $U_{ij} = V_J$. This latter assumption is analogous to assumptions made by "issue ownership" or "saliency" models of party competition.[4] The more general model of party competition we investigate in this chap-

---

[3] There is an analogous mixing parameter in most published valence models, which Schofield (2006: 187) calls a "spatial parameter" and implements what amounts to $U_{ij} = V_J - \beta \times d(i, j)^2$. However, we prefer the λ, $(1 - \lambda)$ specification we use in this book since it gives a clearer intuition about the relative contribution of the two distinct sources of voter utility, maintains a scale for U_{ij} that is independent of the mixing parameter, and is such that different settings of λ generate "valence only" or "policy only" models of party competition. This assumes we measure valence and policy loss on the same metric, but since units for measuring valence are arbitrary, this involves no loss of generality.

[4] In "issue ownership" models of party competition, as well as the "saliency theory" motivating the work of the Comparative Manifestos Project, the implicit $\lambda_v = 1$ assumption arises because all voters are in effect assumed to have the same preferences on key issues, choosing between candidates on the basis of common assessments of which candidate they see as "better" on, or "owning," each key issue. See, for example, Budge et al. (2001).

ter assumes voters care about both party policy positions *and* nonpolicy attributes and competences of different parties, so that $0 < \lambda < 1$.

Because any particular candidate's valence attributes are, by definition, both common knowledge and valued equally by all voters, they can all be described using the candidate's valence term in the voter utility function.[5] This means that the valence term V_J in the voter utility function is *indexed by party but not voter*. Party *J* has the same valence for all voters. It might seem tempting to think of a more general model in which valence is indexed by both party and voter, thereby assuming that each voter has an idiosyncratic perception of candidate quality. Note, however, that all scholars writing about valence assume this to be constant for a given candidate across all voters; this consensus, indeed, is what is distinctive about valence. Following Adams, Merrill, and Grofman (Adams et al. 2005), it is helpful to think of *party-specific* nonpolicy effects that vary between voters in a systematic way as something else—as *partisanship* or *demographic* effects, for example—rather than electoral valence.

We build valence into policy-based models of party competition because it is *substantively* realistic to see different candidates as having different levels of voter appeal, over and above their distinctive policy positions. A compelling analytical result that arises from this is that all parties do *not* converge on the regions of the policy space with the highest voter densities. Instead, higher valence parties tend to locate in regions with higher voter densities, while lower valence parties are forced into regions with lower voter densities (Schofield 2008). The key substantive intuition is that vote-seeking lower valence parties must stay away from higher valence parties because, when both occupy policy positions very close to each other, the higher valence party wins almost all votes in the policy neighborhood of the two parties. Since lower valence parties for this reason tend to distinguish themselves in policy terms from higher valence parties, this makes high-valence parties the five-hundred-pound gorillas of the policy space. They are able to sit wherever they feel like sitting, leaving others to sort themselves out around this. And high-valence parties will want to sit in the regions of the policy space with high voter densities. The striking implication of all this is that "nonpolicy" valence affects all party policy positions. Note that it is not party valence per se

---

[5] To emphasize a point we have made already, this assumption leaves moot the matter of whether or not the valence term reflects policy issues on which there is voter consensus, on both the best position and the best party to deliver this position, and thus on which all voters in effect have the same ideal position. The crucial aspect of the valence term is that it does *not* reflect party position on issues for which there is no consensus, which are captured in varying party positions and voter ideal points and thus in the policy loss term in voter utility functions. On these issues, different parties offer different utilities to voters with different ideal points.

that has this effect, but *valence differentials* among parties. These differentials serve to separate the typical policy positions of high- and low-valence parties. As we now see before going on to specify and analyze our computational model, we gain considerable leverage on this substantively important effect by setting nonpolicy valence in the context of the Voronoi geometry of competitive spatial location.

THE GEOMETRY OF VALENCE

We saw in chapter 3 that the spatial model of party competition is a special case of the much more general geometric problem of competitive spatial location. This gives us useful insight into valence effects as well as access to directly relevant results from Voronoi geometry. We model electoral valence by adding a party-specific valence, or "weight," term that gives the quadratic voter utility function shown in expression 9.1. This expression is identical to what is known to mathematicians as the *additively weighted power distance*,[6] which generates a particular type of weighted Voronoi diagram, known as a *power diagram* (Okabe et al. 2000).

A striking and substantively relevant geometric result for power diagrams is that a generating point (party position) may be outside its own (valence) weighted Voronoi region (of party supporters' ideal points). Indeed it is easy to find examples where generating points with lower weights are located in the power weighted Voronoi regions of generating points with higher valences. In the substantive context of party competition, this means lower valence parties can easily find themselves in the Voronoi regions (among the supporters) of higher valence parties. A very striking feature of using quadratic voter utilities with additive valence terms, therefore, is that the *leaders of lower valence parties might well not vote for themselves* if they were voters and their policy positions were their ideal points; they would instead vote for a nearby higher valence party. This intriguing result is easily overlooked by authors who focus on the algebra, as opposed to the geometry, of valence.

Figure 9.1 gives the core intuition behind this striking potential effect of nonpolicy valence. There are six parties, with policy positions at A, B, C, D, E, and F. All of these have equal valence, except party F, which has relatively low valence. The Voronoi boundaries between parties are shown by the lines in Figure 9.1. With classical Downsian proximity voting, as we have seen, a party's Voronoi region is given by the set of voter ideal points that are closer to the party's policy position than to the posi-

---

[6] Once we invert all signs to turn the utility function into a distance measure.

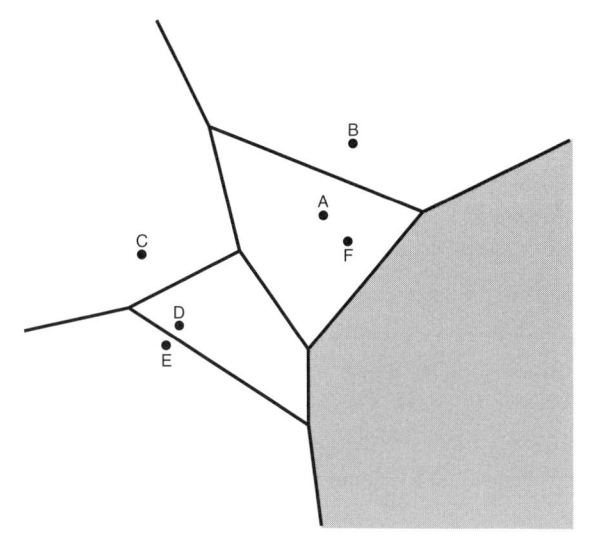

Figure 9.1. Additively weighted power diagram generated by six party positions, including that of a low-valence party F.

tion of any other party.[7] In the valence model we now specify with expression 9.1, a party's Voronoi region is given by the set of ideal points for which the party policy position maximizes expression 9.1. That is, it is the set of voter ideal points for which each voter, *taking the different party valences into account*, derives more utility from that party than from any other party.

In the specific example shown in Figure 9.1, this means that low-valence party F is actually in the Voronoi region of high-valence party A, while the (shaded) Voronoi region of party F actually has no party position in it. Voters with an ideal point at or close to F are "closer" in policy terms to F than to A, but A's valence advantage over F swamps this difference. The result is that voters with an ideal point at or close to F actually prefer party A. Because the effects of policy distance in expression 9.1 are quadratic, however, increasing policy distances are disproportionally important. This means that, for a voter with an ideal point in the shaded area, the valence advantage that A has over F is not enough to overcome the difference in the *quadratic* distances between the voter's ideal point and the policy positions of the (closer) party F and the (more distant) party A. Party F does have supporters. Given valence differentials among

---

[7] To recall, the Voronoi boundary between two points is given by the perpendicular bisector of the line joining these points.

190 • Chapter 9

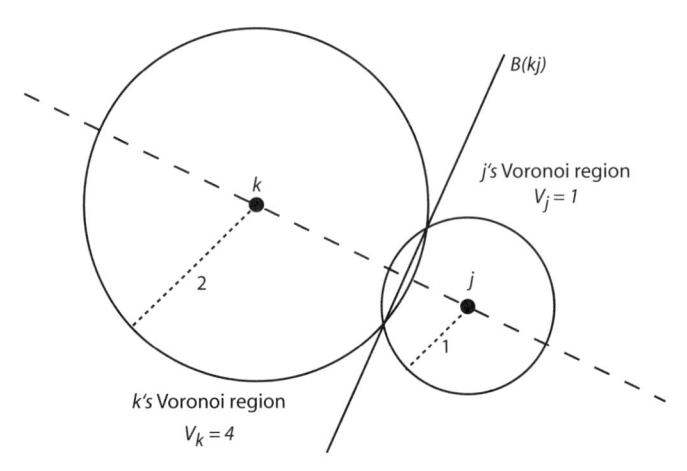

Figure 9.2. Power balls and Voronoi regions for parties J and K.

parties, however, these have ideal points in a region that does not "surround" party F's policy position. Voronoi geometry shows us that this somewhat counterintuitive result is always possible, though by no means inevitable, when we specify a valence model using a voter utility function that adds a party-specific valence term to a quadratic term for policy loss.

A more general geometric interpretation of the power distances and related power diagrams that arise from valence models of voting is shown in Figure 9.2. A party J, with valence V_J added to the quadratic Euclidean policy loss function in expression 9.1, is associated geometrically with a "ball" (a circle in the two-dimensional Euclidean space shown in Figure 9.2) of radius $\sqrt{V_J}$. Take two parties with positions at j and k and valences (powers) V_J and V_K. There is a line jk between these positions. There are "power balls" (circles) centered on j and k with radii $\sqrt{V_J}$ and $\sqrt{V_K}$, respectively. It has been shown (Okabe et al. 2000) that the boundary $B(kj)$ between the Voronoi regions of K and J is a perpendicular hyperplane (line in Figure 9.2) bisecting the line kj and running through the intersections of the power balls of parties J and K. Clearly, the larger party K's power (valence), the larger its power ball and thus, holding J's valence constant, the larger its Voronoi region (area of potential voter support). The size of this region increases as a function of $\sqrt{V_K}$.

The implications of this are considerable and have a bearing on how, substantively, we assess the assumption of quadratic as opposed to linear Euclidean policy loss in voter utility functions. The assumption of *linear* policy loss gives rise to an "additively weighted" Voronoi diagram, as opposed to a power diagram, and it is mathematically impossible for generating points to be located outside their Voronoi regions. With linear loss, increasing the power (valence) of *K* in Figure 9.2, relative to *J*, expands *K*'s Voronoi region by pushing the Voronoi boundary between *K* and *J* toward but never beyond *J* (Okabe at al. 2000). Crudely speaking, if we think that it is substantively implausible for a party's policy position to be located outside the region occupied by its own supporters' ideal points, yet we think it is substantively plausible to add a nonpolicy valence term to voter utility functions, then the geometry of Voronoi diagrams axiomatically implies we should not use quadratic loss terms with Euclidean distances. Conversely, we might think it perfectly plausible that a party leader would indeed not vote for herself *if she were a voter*, given the close policy proximity of some other higher valence party. These are substantively intriguing and largely unappreciated issues that we do not adjudicate here. Rather, to maintain consistency with models in previous chapters, and in line with many though not all authors of valence models, we keep the assumption of quadratic policy loss in the voter utility function and thus specify a model of competitive spatial location that is in effect a dynamic power diagram.

All of this does go to show, however, that what may seem like arcane technical modeling decisions can have major substantive implications. It might seem a simple theoretical move to take account of the nonpolicy appeals of different candidates by adding a candidate-specific valence term to the voter utility function. As we have seen, however, this changes the geometric implications of the underlying model of competitive spatial location in nonobvious ways. Above all, of course, it shows that we do actually need a well-specified model to be able to get a sense of what party competition is like when voters trade off the policy positions of the various political parties against the various nonpolicy attractions of these same parties.

PARTY VALENCE DIFFERENTIALS AND PARTY DECISION RULES

The valence model we define above has different implications for parties using different decision rules. A *low-valence Predator*, for example, is poorly suited to a competitive environment in which parties have different valences. Predators are programmed to move toward the closest larger party, but a larger party is likely, other things equal, to have higher valence than a low-valence Predator. As it gets ever closer to its higher valence rival, a low-valence Predator will at some point start rapidly losing votes and move into the Voronoi region of the other party, as with the example of party F in Figure 9.1. Nothing in the Predator rule stops a low-valence Predator from moving toward a larger high-valence "prey." Watching simulations in motion, we see that low-valence Predators look like kamikaze pilots programmed to find and attack larger, higher valence, opponents and doomed to destruction when they do so. When a Predator party has the highest valence level, it is still programmed to attack larger, likely high-valence, parties; but it will be at no relative disadvantage when it does so. The only situation in which party valence differentials are good for the Predator rule is when the Predator's prey is a larger but lower valence party. Since lower valence parties tend to be smaller, however, these situations are much less typical than those in which the Predator's prey has higher valence. One way to address this pathology is to modify the Predator rule so that the prey is defined as the closest larger party *that does not have higher valence*.[8] The other option is to let evolution take its course, in which case we expect only high-valence Predators to survive. In the spirit of the evolutionary environment we analyze in this book, we consider it more appropriate to let evolution take its course and cull low-valence Predators. We therefore expect *lower valence Predators to perform particularly poorly in an environment with valence differentials among parties*.

Low-valence Aggregators are affected in quite a different way when there are valence differentials among parties. When Aggregator parties are approached by some other party, we saw in Figure 7.3 that they are in effect programmed to move away from this. The Voronoi boundary between the two parties moves toward the Aggregator, causing the ideal point centroid of the Aggregator's current supporters to move away from the "attacker." Readapting to this new ideal point centroid, the Aggregator's indicated policy position also moves away.[9] This becomes a positive advantage in an environment with valence differentials among parties. Since Aggregators systematically move away from other parties that approach them, they systematically move away from higher valence parties. In contrast to our expectation for Predators, therefore, we expect parties using the Aggregator rule not to be systematically disadvantaged by a competitive environment with valence differentials among parties.

---

[8] We could thus modify the NetLogo code as follows:

   set prey min-one-of other parties with [mysize > me and valence <= [valence] of myself] [distance myself]

[9] Note that we did not modify the Aggregator rule to take account of a competitive environment with valence differentials among parties. Aggregators still go to the centroid of the set of voter ideal points that are closer to the party policy position than to that of any other party. They do not take account of valence differentials among parties, though it would of course be possible to modify the Aggregator rule to do this.

The essence of the Pavlovian *Hunter* rule is that it responds to feedback on its vote share. This feedback turns negative when the Hunter approaches, or is approached by, a party with higher valence. The Hunter rule is thus well suited to an environment in which parties have different valences. It is in effect programmed to stay away from higher valence parties and, conversely to move toward lower valence parties, all other things equal. *We thus expect the Hunter rule to perform better in an environment with valence differentials among parties.*

We are uncertain about the relative effectiveness of the Explorer rule in an environment where parties have valence differentials. On one hand, Explorer, like Hunter, takes account of valence differentials when polling support during campaign ticks. On the other hand, Explorer is even more vulnerable in a dynamic environment to what we can think of as "late-breaking campaign developments." If a higher valence party moves toward an Explorer late in the campaign, it may now make sense to move to a position explored earlier in the campaign which, because the higher valence party was then further away, seemed less attractive than staying put. But the Explorer would have dismissed this move as suboptimal. We thus have no firm expectation about whether the Explorer rule will perform better or worse when there are valence differentials among parties.

The key point of the discussion in this section is that the decision rules we have thus far specified, and investigated in chapters 5–8, were conceived in relation to $\lambda = 0$ environments in which valence did not matter, or environments in which all parties have the same valence. *Once we assume parties may have valence differentials, we expect the relative performances of different decision rule species to change in systematic ways.*

AN ABM OF MULTIPARTY COMPETITION WITH VALENCE DIFFERENTIALS AMONG PARTIES

Specifying Valence Effects

As noted above, we add nonspatial valence effects to a spatial model of party competition by modifying the voter utility function to give expression 9.1. Earlier models in this book implicitly set $\lambda = 0$ and can now be seen as special cases of the valence model. We now extend our ABM so that a voter with an ideal point at i supports the party maximizing the combined valence-policy utility Ui_j, given each party's valence V_J and policy position j. That is, voter i strictly prefers a higher valence party K to a lower valence party J, despite the fact that J is closer to i, iff: $Ui_K > Ui_J$, or equivalently substituting into 9.1, iff:

$$\lambda \cdot V_K - (1-\lambda) \cdot d(i, k)^2 > \lambda \cdot V_J - (1-\lambda) \cdot d(i, j)^2$$

Rearranging the above, we see that voter i prefers party k iff:

$$\lambda \cdot (V_K - V_J) > (1-\lambda) \cdot (d(i,k)^2 - d(i,j)^2) \qquad (9.2)$$

That is, voter i prefers higher valence but more distant party K if the *valence differential* (weighted by λ) between the parties exceeds the difference in their quadratic distances from voter i's ideal point (weighted by $1 - \lambda$).

Rather than allowing values of party valence, V_J, to be any real number within some range, our computational implementation uses the type of "grid" parameterization of valence that we used for party decision rules, specifying five possible valence levels for party leaders. We do this in part for the *methodological* reason that we want to update and cumulate information on the evolving fitness of parties having leaders with different valences and need to "bin" valence levels for this purpose. More important, however, is the *substantive* argument that, despite all that has been written about valence and despite its regular appearance as a real-valued parameter in analytical models, little is known in *empirical* terms about real voters' perceptions of valence. We ourselves suspect that public perceptions of party leader valences are coarse grained and crude, and we therefore feel it appropriate to specify valences in terms of a small number of possible levels rather than as a real number within a prespecified range. More precisely, we specify that party J may have one of five possible settings of V_J: (0.25, 0.50, 0.75, 1.00, 1.25). These settings are denominated in precisely the same units as the policy distances in our model, that is, in standard deviations of the distribution of voter ideal points. The valence differential between the highest and lowest valence parties is thus equivalent to one standard deviation of the distribution of voter ideal points.[10]

Specifying Other Model Parameters

An important design issue concerns whether the valence model of party competition we now specify should assume that new parties select rules at random, as in chapter 7, or should assume that rule replication probabilities are a function of evolving rule fitnesses, as in chapter 8. The update to rule fitnesses in the replicator-mutator system we specified in chapter 8 derives from the vote shares of parties using each rule. These vote shares, and hence rule fitness updates, are now affected by parties'

---

[10] An implicit assumption in *any* valence model is that valence differentials between candidates can be rescaled to policy distances. Valence in such models is always implicitly denominated in policy distance.

valences as well as by their policy positions and the effectiveness of their decision rule. For this reason, we specify our valence model by building on the model we specified in chapter 7 rather than that in chapter 8. Substantively we do this because we want to factor out the effects of differential candidate valences on party competition in general, and on the relative performance of different rule species in particular. In line with previous accounts of valence, we see valence as exogenous to party competition. We do not want implicitly to endogenize valence effects by building these into an updating regime for rule fitness.[11]

Judging that we have by now gleaned most of the intuition we are likely to get about the effects of speed of adaptation γ and size of exploration neighborhood η on different decision rules, and once more in the interest of parsimony, we set these rule parameters at the central values used in our simulations in chapter 7, $\gamma = 0.1$ and $\eta = 0.6$, but retain the existing seven-point grid parameterization of κ for the three vote-seeking rule species.[12] This gives 5 valence levels and 7 settings of κ, generating a grid with 35 leader parameterizations of the three voter seeking rule species. To this we add 5 valence settings each for leaders using Aggregator and Sticker, making 115 different agent-rule pairings generated by rule-κ-V combinations. When a new party is born it is randomly assigned a rule species as well as settings of κ and V.

Experimental Design

The stochastic processes generated by the valence model we specify here are the same as those generated by the model we specify in chapter 7. No new methodological issue arises, over and above the issues resolved when we designed the experiments specified in chapter 7. Our research design therefore involves suites of 1,000 runs with Monte Carlo parameterizations, each run with 1,000 repetitions with different random seeds, each repetition burnt in for 250 elections.[13] Observations were made for the first election after this burn-in period. Parameters of the

---

[11] More prosaically, but in practice crucially, the replicator-mutator system we specified in chapter 8 took a very long time to burn in. Full burn-in took 2,750 elections, rather than the 250 elections for the model we investigate in chapter 7. This forced us to use a very spare grid parameterization of the political environment. We have now added the new valence parameter, λ, to our model in this chapter. The much quicker burn-in of the model with random rule replication that we specify in chapter 7 frees up computational resources to allow us to investigate the effects of this parameter in a much more comprehensive way.

[12] We expected that satisficing might have striking interactions with valence effects, but we did not in the end observe these. Nonetheless, the model we investigate here is set in the more general context in which different party leaders have different comfort thresholds.

[13] The computational budget for this experiment, as in chapter 7, is thus 251,000,000 elections since there are 1,000 repetitions of 1,000 runs of 251 elections.

competitive environment, and their sampled ranges, are precisely the same as in the experiments we specified in chapter 7. We also now investigate the new parameter arising from the valence model, λ. We sample this from a uniform distribution of floating point numbers on the interval [0.0, 0.5].

COMPETITION AMONG PARTIES WITH DIFFERENT VALENCES

We just argued that the model of multiparty competition that we have now specified, taking account of valence differentials among parties, has different implications for parties using different decision rules. Before turning to simulation results on this matter, we must take account of a striking effect of valence differentials on typical party vote shares and survival prospects.

Valence Effects on Party Vote Shares and Survival

The left panel of Figure 9.3 shows typical vote shares of parties with different valence levels, plotting this against λ, the relative importance of valence in voters' utility functions.[14] When $\lambda = 0$, so that party valences have no effect at all on voter utilities, there will be no systematic difference in the vote shares won by parties with different valences. Valence is irrelevant, and typical vote shares of the sets of parties with each of the five different valence levels should be 0.20. The effects of valence differentials among parties should increase as λ increases and nonpolicy valence becomes more important to voters. We see this clearly in the simulation results summarized in Figure 9.3. The plotted bands diverge as λ increases. More precisely, the upper plotted band diverges from the others, showing that the effects of valence differentials in our simulations arise entirely as a result of an increasing vote share won by the set of highest valence parties. While there is a sharp increase in the typical vote share won by the highest valence parties, as λ increases the vote share won by all other parties decreases. It is not just that valence effects become more pronounced as λ increases, what happens is that the *dominance of the highest valence parties becomes progressively greater*.

One explanation for the disproportionate advantage of high-valence parties arises from the survival-of-the-fittest evolutionary system in our dynamic model of multiparty competition. Lower valence parties systematically win lower vote shares *because* they have lower valence. They are

---

[14] Mean (*SE*) vote shares for parties with each valence level, from lowest to highest, are as follows: 0.02 (0.001), 0.03 (0.001), 0.06 (0.001), 0.18 (0.002), 0.71 (0.005).

Nonpolicy Factors in Party Competition • 197

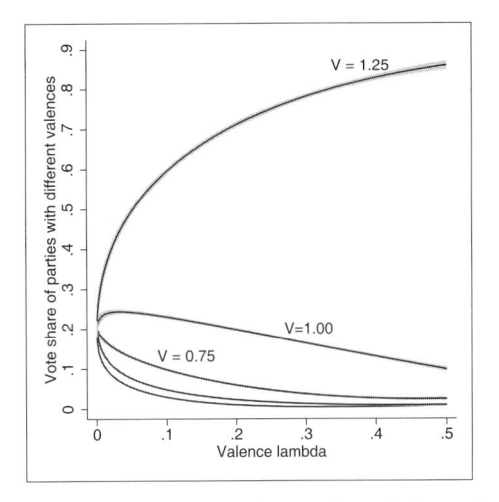

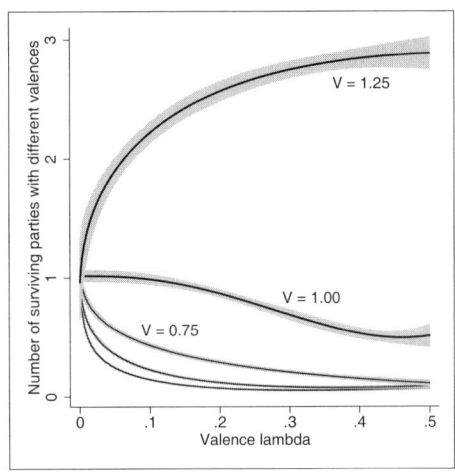

Figure 9.3. Typical vote share (left), and number of surviving parties (right), by party leader valence, λ.

therefore systematically more likely to fall below the survival threshold and die. Conversely, higher valence parties are more likely to survive. This leads to a relative proliferation of *surviving* higher valence parties, and this effect increases as valence becomes more important to voters. We see this clearly in the results we summarize in the right panel of Figure 9.3. The relative proliferation of higher valence parties means that any surviving lower valence party typically finds that its neighbors in the policy space, the set of parties with which it shares Voronoi boundaries, have higher valence. These valence differentials mean that competition for votes with these neighbors will systematically tend to be won by higher valence parties. This feeds back to increase the vote shares, and thereby the survival prospects, of higher valence parties, at the same time reducing vote shares and survival prospects of lower valence parties. All but the highest valence parties are in this position. The net result of this continuously iterated differential feedback on the survival prospects of parties with different valence levels will be an increasing dominance of the highest valence parties. As lower valence parties tend to die and higher valence parties tend to survive, the net effect is the *evolution of narrower valence differentials within the set of surviving parties*. A key consequence of this is to *reduce the scale of valence effects in the evolved party system*.

In a nutshell, we do not expect to see valence effects as large in our dynamic evolutionary model as those we might find in an otherwise analogous static model. Our evolutionary model does not endogenize the

198 • Chapter 9

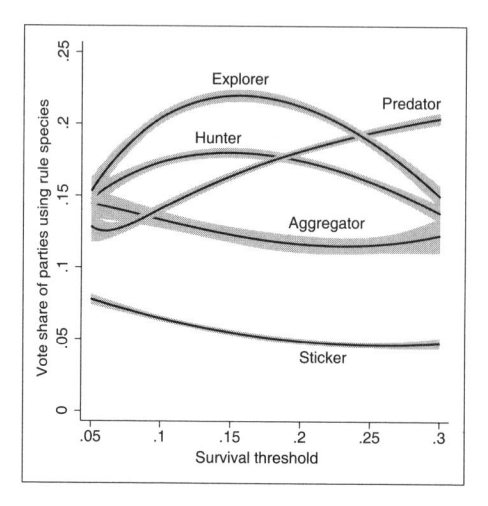

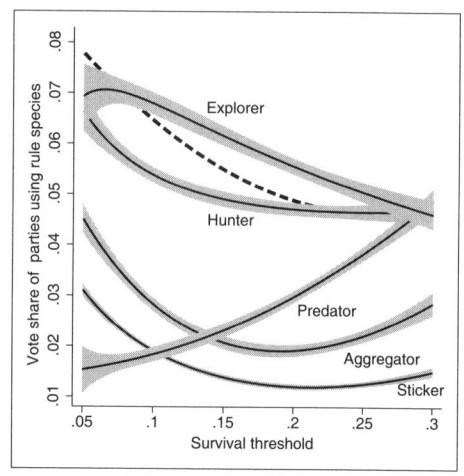

Figure 9.4. Typical party vote shares, by rule species and survival threshold. Left panel: $V_j = 1.25$; right panel: $V_j = 1.00$.

valence of any given party leader; this is exogenously determined, as in static models. Our dynamic ABM does however *endogenize valence differentials in the set of surviving parties*, and it is these differentials that drive valence effects. This complex dynamic process cannot be seen by using static valence models. Indeed, the *evolutionary stability of valence differentials* among parties is a very important matter that can be modeled by our dynamic ABM of multiparty competition, but not by static models of party competition with valence differentials.

Effects of Valence Differentials on Decision Rule Performance

Comparing the left and right panels of Figure 9.4 gives us considerable insight into the effects of differential party valences implied by our dynamic model of multiparty competition. The left panel is analogous to Figure 7.2 and plots the relationship between vote shares and party survival thresholds, for parties with the highest valence leaders ($V_J = 1.25$). The right panel shows analogous results for party leaders with the next highest valence level ($V_J = 1.00$). Equivalent plots for leaders with other valence levels show the same patterns as those in the right panel of Figure 9.4.[15]

---

[15] These plots are shown in Figure E9.1 of the electronic appendix.

Comparing the scales of the vertical axes of these two plots, we see that valence effects are big, reinforcing the conclusions we drew from Figure 9.3. The dashed black line in the background of the right panel helps us compare the two plots. It shows, in the plot for $V_J = 1.00$ party leaders, typical vote shares in equivalent settings won by the $V_J = 1.25$ parties using the least successful rule, which was Sticker. We see that valence effects largely dominate decision rule effects. Whatever decision rule they use, the most successful $V_J = 1.00$ party leaders rarely beat the least successful $V_J = 1.25$ party leaders. Put another way, in multiparty competition as we model it, having systematically high valence is typically better for a party's vote share than having a better decision rule.

We saw from the right panel of Figure 9.3 that, especially when λ is higher so that voters tend to attach more value to nonpolicy valence when deciding which party to support, party competition tends to evolve into a situation in which most contestants are high-valence parties. As a consequence, surviving lower valence parties are very likely to find themselves competing for votes with higher valence neighbors. We noted above that the Predator rule is poorly equipped for vote seeking in this type of setting because lower valence Predators systematically tend to "attack" higher valence neighbors, with typically disastrous effects. This shows up very clearly in our simulation results. Plotted effects in the left panel of Figure 9.4 are confined to the highest valence parties; they are essentially the same as those in Figure 7.2 for a setting with no valence differentials. Plotted effects in the right-hand panel are for parties with a valence level one notch below the highest and are quite different. *Predators are systematically the least successful of the vote-seeking parties with $V_J = 1.00$ party leaders.* This is also true for Predators with lower valence levels.[16] As expected, therefore, lower valence Predators systematically underperform in settings where there are valence differentials among parties, an effect magnified by the fact that most surviving parties tend to have higher valence. Crudely put, if you are going to be a Predator, you had better have the highest valence in town.

Comparing Figures 9.4 and 7.2, the net beneficiaries of declining Predator performance appear to be vote-seeking parties using a Hunter rule. We did expect Hunter's Pavlovian avoidance of higher valence parties to help it in competitive environments with valence differentials among parties. This effect is modest, however, possibly because it was specifically the lower valence Hunters that we expected to benefit from such settings but, as we saw in Figure 9.3, there tend to be relatively few *surviving* lower valence parties of any stripe. The systematic evolution of narrower valence differentials among parties attenuates any relative benefits to

---

[16] See Figure E9.1 in the electronic appendix.

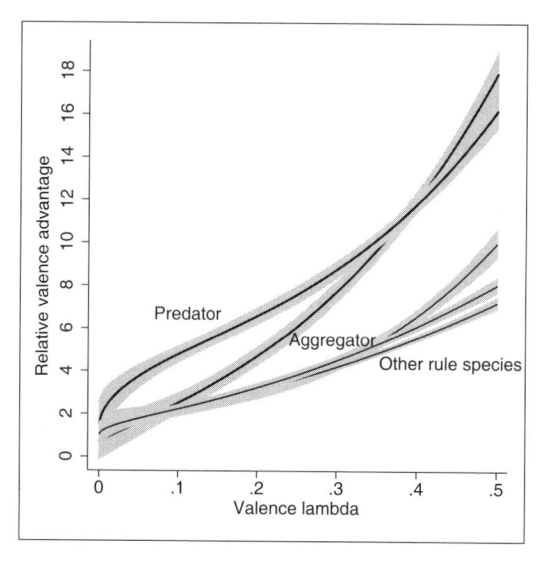

Figure 9.5. Relative valence effects on party vote shares, by rule species and λ.

lower valence Hunters. In simple terms, most of the votes are summarized in the left panel of Figure 9.4 because most of the surviving parties are high-valence parties. This attenuates the relative benefits for lower valence parties of using decision rules such as Hunter.

Figure 9.5 describes valence effects in more detail. It shows, for different settings of λ, the "relative valence advantage" of parties using different decision rules. This simple but intuitive measure is the ratio of vote shares won by $V_j = 1.25$ parties relative to those won by $V_j = 1.00$ parties using the same decision rule in the same competitive environment.

If $\lambda = 0$ then voters do not care at all about nonpolicy valence and there is no relative valence effect. Plots for all rule species converge on the origin. As λ increases and party valences become more important to voters, we see the increasing effects of valence differentials on party vote shares. At the highest levels of λ we investigate, the highest valence parties typically win between eight and eighteen times as many votes, in the same settings, as parties with a valence level one notch down. This in turn tells us that, *with levels of λ at the high end of the range we investigate, pretty much all of the action in party competition is driven by relative party valences.*

Figure 9.5 also confirms that Predator is significantly more affected by relative valences than the other vote-seeking rule species. The relative advantage for the highest valence Predators increasingly diverges from that for the other vote-seeking rules, Hunter and Explorer. We also see strong relative valence effects for parties using Aggregator rules, which as we have seen tend to adapt their policy positions away from those of any approaching party. Figure 9.5 shows that high-valence Aggregators do strikingly better than other Aggregators. Watching simulations in motion, our conjecture on this matter is that, when high-valence Aggregators face lower valence rivals, they are less likely to be "chased away" from regions of the policy space with high voter densities, in the manner we describe in Figure 7.3. This is because, in contrast to a situation where all parties have equal valences, a lower valence party approaching a higher valence Aggregator will tend to lose vote share because of the valence differential among parties, and therefore be punished for this move.

Valence Effects on Party Eccentricities and Party System Representativeness

As we have seen, a key prediction emerging from traditional static valence models is that higher valence parties should tend to occupy more central policy positions, forcing lower valence parties into more peripheral locations (Ansolabehere and Snyder 2000; Aragones and Palfrey 2004; Groseclose 2001; Schofield 2008). We now investigate this prediction using our dynamic ABM of multiparty competition. Recall from chapter 3 that, given the asymmetric and often bimodal distributions of voter ideal points we consider here, lower density regions may tend to be in the "center" of the policy space. In what follows, therefore, we look at what we call each party's "net" policy eccentricity. We measure this by subtracting the eccentricity of the nearest subpopulation ideal point centroid from observed party policy eccentricities. A positive net eccentricity means the party policy position is more peripheral than the subpopulation ideal point centroids, and vice versa.[17]

Comparing the left and right panels of Figure 9.6 we see that valence effects on typical party policy positions are much sharper when voter ideal points are polarized. The left panel plots typical net party policy eccentricities, for parties with different valence levels, in populations with an ideal point polarization greater than 1.0. The lighter gray confidence bands show that, in polarized populations, lower valence parties

---

[17] For example, if ideal point centroids are at ±1.0 on the *x*-axis and 0 on the *y*-axis, and party policy is 0.5 from the origin, then net eccentricity is 0.5 - 1.0 = −0.5 since the party is *closer* to the center than the ideal point centroids. If party policy is 1.5 from the origin in this setting, its net eccentricity will be +0.5, since party policy is 0.5 units *more* eccentric than ideal point centroids.

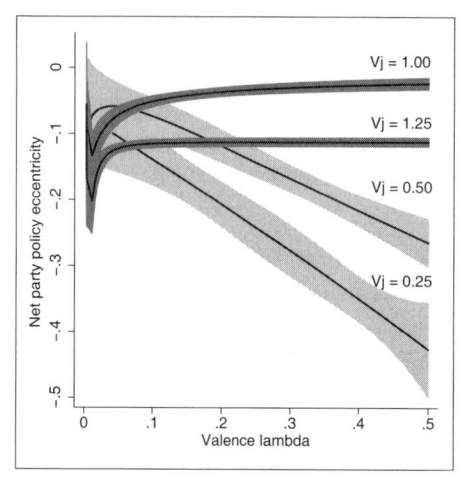

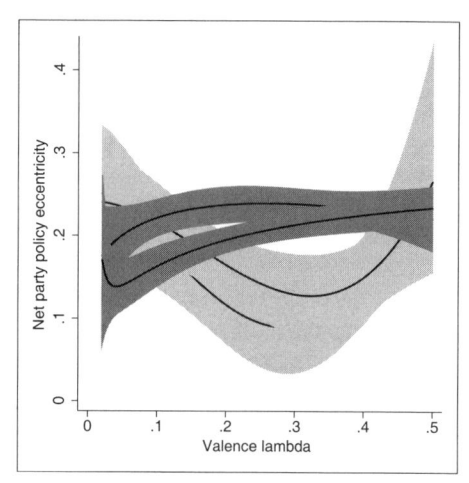

Figure 9.6. Net party policy eccentricity, by leader valence and λ. Ideal point polarization > 1.0 (left panel); and < 0.5 (right panel).

(V_j = 0.25 or 0.5) typically locate in lower density *less eccentric* regions of policy spaces, and do this more as the importance of valence to voters increases.[18] Arising from exactly the same process, the horizontal darker plotted bands show that typical policy positions of higher valence parties (V_j = 1.00 or 1.25) are unaffected by λ. Adapting the results of static valence models for polarized electorates, as valence becomes more important to voters, lower valence parties tend to locate further from higher density regions of the space, though these regions tend to be in the center of polarized electorates. Conversely, the policy positions of higher valence parties are unaffected as valence becomes more important. Figure 9.6 shows us that *valence effects on party policy positions arise entirely from the displacement of lower valence parties*, and not from higher valence parties locating in different policy positions than when there are no valence effects.

The right panel of Figure 9.6 shows that these effects are much less clear-cut when subpopulations are less polarized and the distribution of ideal point densities is unimodal. The overlapping confidence bands imply that it is difficult to distinguish typical policy positions of parties with different valence levels in less polarized settings. We do nonetheless see from the darker plotted bands that typical policy positions of high-valence parties in these settings are less affected than the positions of low-valence parties as the importance of valence increases.

[18] The light gray plotted bands slope steeply downward.

Nonpolicy Factors in Party Competition • 203

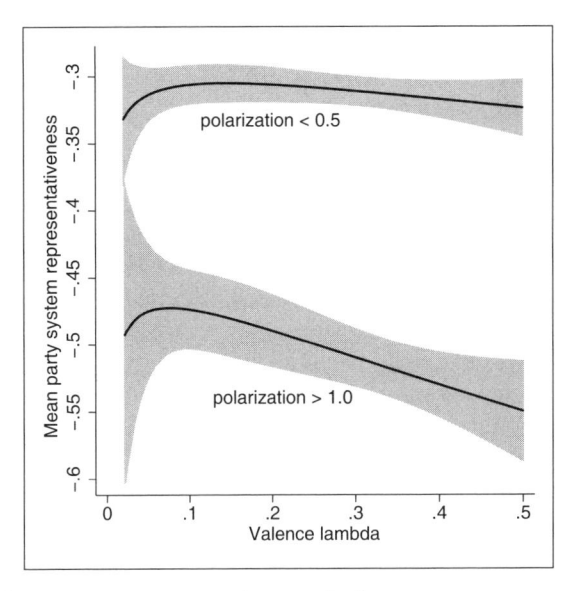

Figure 9.7. Party system representativeness, by λ.

Differential valences thus have systematic effects on typical party policy positions, an effect that we see from the left panel of Figure 9.6 is particularly pronounced in polarized electorates. We expect this to have a knock-on effect of the representativeness of the evolved configuration of party policy positions. Figure 9.7 plots the relationship between party system representativeness and the importance to voters of party leader valence, distinguishing between more and less polarized electorates.

We expect higher levels of λ, which specify a lower importance of party policy positions for voters, to be associated with less representative party systems. When voters are motivated less by policy and more by other matters, voters' ideal points should have a smaller effect on the emergent configuration of party policy positions, thereby lowering representativeness. The downward slopes of the gray confidence bands in Figure 9.7 show that this is indeed what we observe, though the effect of differential party valences is sharper when electorates are polarized (lower band). This arises from the systematic pattern whereby lower valence parties are driven into more central regions of the policy space where, in polarized populations, there are fewer voter ideal points. Party system representativeness is indeed reduced when voters care more about party leader valences although, given the typical evolution of party systems whereby most surviving parties have high valences, these effects are not huge.

Summary and Conclusions

As Adams, Merrill, and Grofman point out, adding differential "nonpolicy" valences to spatial models of party competition allows us to "nest" a Downsian model within more a general model that takes account of a range of party-specific nonpolicy effects by adding a valence term to the voter utility function (Adams et al. 2005). In our own terms, spatial models of party competition that ignore differential party valences are special cases of a more general spatial model.

The most important result in this chapter reflects the fact that valence effects are more complex in the model of evolving dynamic multiparty competition we develop in this book than in conventional static valence models. Higher valence parties are more likely to survive in an evolutionary environment, while lower valence parties are more likely to die. The net effect of these differential survival prospects is that *valence differentials among surviving parties narrow endogenously* as the party system evolves, an effect completely beyond the scope of static valence models. Our main substantive task when using dynamic valence models is thus to understand why low-valence parties survive at all and high-valence parties do not dominate absolutely. This problem is sidestepped by static models that analyze a cross-section of an evolving dynamic system, a cross-section that may not be dynamically stable.

One implication of multiparty competition in analytically intractable settings with valence differentials among parties is that we must reevaluate the relative effectiveness of the different types of vote-seeking decision rule that might be used by party leaders. These rules may well be affected by valence differentials. We see this clearly in Figure 9.4. This plots the systematic underperformance of low-valence Predators, which relentlessly attack higher valence larger rivals, with typically disastrous consequences. We find that typical beneficiaries of this are parties using Hunter rules, whose Pavlovian response to punishments makes them tend systematically to move away from higher valence rivals. And we also find that high-valence Aggregators, at least when they face lower valence rivals, are less likely to be "chased" away from higher density regions of the policy space.

The "classic" result from traditional static analytical valence models is that lower valence parties are typically forced into regions of the policy space with lower densities of voter ideal points. Given assumptions about voter densities in these models, these are often peripheral regions, though they may also be relatively central low-density locations in highly polarized electorates. Figure 9.6 shows that we also find this effect in the dynamic settings we model, though it is more pronounced in more polarized populations. In these settings, as in static valence models, lower valence parties tend systematically to be forced away from high-density regions around subpopulation ideal point centroids. We deepen this result by showing that policy divergence between high- and low-valence parties is entirely generated by the displacement of lower valence parties, with the policy positions of higher valence parties unaffected by the weight of party leader valence in voters' utility functions. In a nutshell, valence differentials among parties mean that leaders of higher valence parties do more or less what they would have done anyway. In contrast, lower valence parties, at least those that survive, are forced into policy positions well away from those of higher valence parties.

CHAPTER TEN

Party Leaders with Policy Preferences

UP UNTIL NOW we have been modeling a political world where *voters* care about policy but *party leaders* completely ignore their own personal policy preferences when they adapt party policy to evolving patterns of voter support. This is also the world described by classical Downsian spatial models of party competition. In this chapter, we adapt our dynamic model of multiparty competition to take into account the possibility that *party leaders take their own preferences into account when they set party policy*. If they do this, they must make trade-offs between satisfying their private policy preferences and some other objective, whether this is maximizing party vote share or pleasing current party supporters. Models that specify such trade-offs have often been found intractable using traditional analytical techniques. As we show, however, they are straightforward to specify and analyze using computational agent-based modeling, though this does require a rethinking of the types of decision rules that party leaders might use. Our main substantive finding is an analogue of our earlier finding that insatiable party leaders may win fewer votes than satiable leaders. The most striking feature of the results we report here is that *leaders who care only about their party's vote share may win fewer votes over the long haul than leaders who also care about their own policy preferences.*

POLICY-SEEKING POLITICIANS

There is a substantial literature on spatial models of party competition that assume politicians have policy preferences, most of this referring to early work by Donald Wittman (Roemer 2001; Wittman 1973, 1977, 1983; Smirnov and Fowler 2007; Duggan and Fey 2005; Chappell and Keech 1986). The type of model that is specified typically applies only to two-party systems with winner-take-all elections, often with only one dimension of policy, though sometimes with more (Duggan and Fey 2005). Politicians are typically assumed to be motivated *only* by policy and to be bound to implement their campaign promises instantly and completely if they win the election.[1] These models insert a policy loss term into politi-

---

[1] Duggan and Fey (2005) do extend their model to include an element in the politician's utility function for straight-down-the-line office payoffs.

cians' utility functions and give each politician the task of finding a policy position. Politicians pick policy positions that maximize their utility, given the election result implied by the equilibrium configuration of policy positions and taking account of the fact that all their rivals are doing the same thing. This quintessentially implies that candidates "may face a tradeoff between desirable and successful policy platforms" (Duggan and Fey 2005: 494). Many authors describe this underlying "Wittman" model as analytically intractable, though some suggest it is amenable to computational solutions (Roemer 2001; Smirnov and Fowler 2007). In the spirit of this latter suggestion, we now set out to go beyond intractable analytical work to a dynamic agent-based computational model of multidimensional, multiparty competition in which party leaders have policy preferences.

For reasons we set out earlier in this book, we model elections but not subsequent government formation, policy making, and policy implementation. Complex strategic calculations may arise during government formation in multiparty systems in which some party leaders care intrinsically about policy. The set of politicians who go into government, the joint policy program they agree on, and the policies they eventually implement cannot simply be read off from the election result, as in "Wittman models." These vital matters depend in complicated ways on bargaining among party leaders. This book is not about government formation and the subsequent implementation of policy by coalition cabinets in evolving multiparty systems. Accordingly, we make the following assumption about government formation and downstream policy implementation in the complex dynamic settings we model: politicians use a rule of thumb that, *other things equal, winning more votes typically raises the probability of getting into government and realizing desired policy outcomes*. This is not always true in every case, but we assume that real politicians typically adopt this rule of thumb when the competitive environment they face is analytically intractable. This implies that politicians who care only about policy also have an *instrumental* interest, other things equal, in their party's vote share.

Turning to the crucial matter of *which particular policies party leaders care about*, we assume that a party leader cares about the distance between her ideal point, i_p, and the party policy position she promotes, j_p. The assumption made by theorists in the Wittman tradition is that the winning party or coalition instantly, automatically, and perfectly implements its published policy position (Chappell and Keech 1986). We too are silent on the politics of downstream policy making and implementation in the multiparty systems we model. We therefore assume that party leaders use the rule of thumb in the analytically intractable environment they face that, if they get into office, it will be costly for them to renege on the policy promises they made to voters at election time. Why reneging is costly is exogenous to our model. Perhaps party leaders are concerned with the *credibility of future promises* they may want to make at future elections. Perhaps they are concerned with the *damage to their public image and electoral valence* they may suffer if they are attacked in the media for reneging on their promises. We could build these ideas into future more complicated models but here, as always, we keep things simple. For now, our assumption is that party leaders use the rule of thumb, other things equal, that *it is costly to promise one thing at election time and then do something completely different once elected to office*. In other words, if politicians care about policies that are actually *implemented* after the election, they also care about policy *promises* made at election time.

We could further justify this by using a much more controversial premise—that *politicians are honest*, feeling pain if they promote policy positions they have no intention of implementing. We are free as theorists to assume whatever we please. We note with interest, however, that the "honest politician" assumption is not common in political science. Political scientists typically assume that politicians tell the truth only when this is *instrumentally* useful, deriving no *intrinsic* satisfaction from honesty. Fascinated as we are by the possibility of modeling party competition between honest politicians, we do not base the model we specify in this chapter on such a controversial premise. We rely instead on the conventional assumption of instrumental party leaders who expect to face downstream costs if they do get into office and then do not implement policy positions they promoted at election time. Combined with the assumption that politicians care at least somewhat about their own policy preferences, this implies that party leaders prefer, other things equal, to promote *electoral* policy positions that are closer rather than further away from their own ideal points.

We anticipated trade-offs between private policy preferences and party vote share when we defined a general utility function for party leaders in expression 3.2.[2] Recall that v_p and j_p are the vote share and policy position of party p. If i_p is the leader's ideal point and k_p is the ideal point centroid of p's current supporters, then party leader utility is

$$U(v_p, i_p, j_p, k_p) = (1 - \varphi_1 - \varphi_2) \cdot v_p - \varphi_1 \cdot d(i_p, j_p)^2 - \varphi_2 \cdot d(j_p, k_p)^2$$

where $\varphi_1 + \varphi_2 <= 1$. There are two trade-off parameters, which specify different ways in which party leaders may balance their own personal policy

---

[2] We have in effect assumed $\varphi_1 = 1$ for all *voters*, that is, that voters care only about the policy position, and not at all about the vote share, of the party they support. Since this book is essentially about party leaders rather than voters we maintain this assumption here, noting that it is clearly something that could be generalized and investigated in future work, to take in the possibility that there are voters who intrinsically like to support larger rather than smaller parties.

preferences against other objectives. The trade-off between the leader's personal policy preferences and party vote share is specified by φ_1, the trade-off between the leader's policy preferences and those of current party supporters is specified by φ_2.

Note that a pure vote-seeking ($\varphi_1 = \varphi_2 = 0$) party leader generates a potential tension in our "citizen candidate" model of endogenous party birth. According to this model, new parties form at the ideal points of disgruntled voters but, in a dynamic setting, the leader of a new party may go on to ignore the party's "founding" ideal point when setting party policy in subsequent elections. A cynical reading of this is that the temptations of practical politics do indeed corrupt lofty ideals, so that citizen candidates morph into a new species of agent, "party leader," with a different utility function. Even politicians who were once idealistic may leave their ideals far behind them once they "smell the leather" in the corridors of power, justifying this to themselves in the middle of the night on the ground that they need a firm grip on power before they can do good for others.

Just as we need not go as far as assuming that all politicians are honest, however, we need not assume that all fledging politicians become corrupted the moment they run for election. It is pleasingly consistent to assume that citizen candidates who become party leaders remain the same people they always were. Looking more closely at the party leader's function we see that, given certain uncontroversial assumptions, this does indeed reduce to the *voter* utility function we specified above. Comparing voters to party leaders, voters have no party to lead, so there is no party vote share for them to care about. Voters also have no supporters, so there are no supporters' ideal points for them to care about. Setting the first and third terms of the party leader utility function to zero for these reasons, we are left with

$$U(\cdot) = -\varphi_1 \cdot d(i_p, j_p)^2$$

This is the utility function we already specified for voters. For any $\varphi_1 > 0$, implying that personal policy preferences are at least somewhat important, voters maximize utility by supporting the party with the policy position, j_p, closest to their ideal point i_p.

We could motivate our model by assuming that citizen candidates, when they make the transition from citizen to candidate, are transformed overnight from idealists into vote-seeking psychopaths.[3] But we do not need to do this. We simply need to assume that a citizen faces new trade-offs if she becomes a candidate. These are trade-offs between three things:

---

[3] As always, since we have no model of intraparty politics in complex dynamic settings, candidates and party leaders are analogous in our model.

her ideal point, her stated party policy position, and the ideal points of her current supporters. The latter two were not relevant when she was just a voter. Becoming a politician need not transform her into a vote-hungry psychopath, but it does confront her with new temptations.

"Types" of Politicians

The utility function we specify for party leaders is very general. Real party leaders may care somewhat about the views of their supporters, somewhat about their own policy preferences, and somewhat about increasing their party's vote share. In what follows, however, and in the interest of parsimonious modeling, we constrain φ_1 and φ_2 in particular ways to define particular types of party leader.

We already made implicit assumptions about party leaders' utility in the decision rules we assumed them to use. Whenever $\varphi_1 = 1$, for example, the utility function we specify reduces to $U_p(\cdot) = -d(i, j_p)^2$. Such politicians are, like voters, best pleased when the party they lead has a policy position at their own ideal point. Once party policy is at her ideal point, a leader for whom $\varphi_1 = 1$ will never change this, whatever decision rule she nominally uses. She can be modeled *as if* she is using a Sticker rule. We implicitly assumed that party leaders who use an Aggregator rule do so because they care only about the policy preferences of their current party supporters and not at all about their own preferences. In terms of the utility function we specify, these are leaders for whom $\varphi_2 = 1$, so that $U_p(\cdot) = -d(j_p, k_p)^2$. Finally, we assumed that some party leaders care only about their own party's vote share, so that $\varphi_1 = \varphi_2 = 0$ and the leader's utility function reduces to $U_p(\cdot) = v_p$. These are the party leaders modeled by traditional Downsian vote-seeking spatial models of party competition. We assumed such party leaders use one of three vote-seeking decision rule species: Hunter, Predator, or Explorer. Moving beyond these stark ideal types, we now constrain our party leader utility function to specify more general classes of politicians who make different types of trade-offs among their preferred policy position, their stated party policy, and the ideal points of their current party supporters.

Party Leaders Trading Off Private Policy Preferences against Party Vote Share

We first constrain utility functions of party leaders to take account of a received wisdom that real politicians do care about both policy and votes (Müller and Strøm 1999). Rather than setting $\varphi_1 = \varphi_2 = 0$ for leaders using vote-seeking decision rules, we keep $\varphi_2 = 0$, leaving party leaders attaching no *intrinsic* value to the policy preferences of current supporters, but allow the policy-votes trade-off to vary such that $1 > \varphi_1 > 0$.[4] One class of leader we investigate thus trades personal policy preferences against party vote shares at a rate specified by φ_1. The leader's utility function is a version of expression 3.2, constrained by setting $\varphi_2 = 0$ to give

$$U_p(\cdot) = (1 - \varphi_1) \cdot v_p - \varphi_1 \cdot d(i_p, j_p)^2. \tag{10.1}$$

As before, v_p represents the vote share of party p and $d(i_p, j_p)^2$ represents the squared Euclidean distance between the party leader's ideal point, i_p, and some party policy position, j_p. Note that φ_1 is a party leader parameter. The way a party leader mixes office and policy in her utility function is idiosyncratic to her.[5] Two party leaders with precisely the same ideal point evaluate precisely the same policy position in different ways if they trade off policy and votes at different rates. This is the essence of any model that assumes party leaders trade off vote shares against personal policy preferences.

The substantive meaning of constraining φ_2 at zero is that the type of politician we specify here is inherently *selfish*. These party leaders care only about their own vote share and their own policy preferences. They please their supporters only as an unintended byproduct of satisfying their own private desires. This is the type of politician typically encountered in both Downsian and Wittman-style models of party competition, both of which are special cases of our more general specification, generated by different settings of φ_1. Set $\varphi_1 = 0$ for a Downsian model; set $\varphi_1 = 1$ for a Wittman model.

Both the ideal points of party leaders and their idiosyncratic settings of the policy-votes trade-off parameter φ_1 are clearly critical. We treat φ_1 as an important party leader parameter in our model and design computational experiments to investigate the systematic effects of varying this. In relation to actual locations of party leaders' ideal points, we return to the intuitions of our "citizen candidate" model of endogenous party birth, illuminated by the conclusion that both citizens and candidates can have the same utility function as long as $\varphi_1 > 0$. This gives us a "founding" party policy position, the policy position at which the party endogenously came into existence, which was also the ideal point of some disgruntled voter. If the new party leader is a citizen candidate, as in our model, it is natural to assume *that the party's founding policy position is the ideal point of*

---

[4] As we have just seen, since $\varphi_1 > 0$, this also includes a citizen candidate who attaches no intrinsic value to the ideal points of current party supporters.

[5] We keep the notation simple by not indexing φ_1, as indeed we did not index γ, κ, or η, by p.

the new party leader. We now run this assumption backward, so that *the ideal point of the party leader is her party's founding ideal point*. In doing this, we set on one side the intraparty politics that might explain why some decisive coalition within some political party subsequently picks a different leader with a different ideal point from that of the founder. The intraparty politics of leadership selection is an intriguing and important matter, but it is not our concern in this book. We sidestep this with the assumption that the founding party leader is still in the saddle at the moment we examine our model or, if not, that she has been replaced by someone with similar policy preferences.

Party Leaders Trading Private Policy Preferences against Those of Current Supporters

Another class of party leader we investigate is fundamentally policy oriented and uninterested in party vote share. We characterize such leaders by setting $\varphi_1 + \varphi_2 = 1$ in the leader utility function, which has the effect of attaching no value at all to party vote share. Thus far we assumed that party leaders choose Aggregator rules because they are *altruists* for whom $\varphi_2 = 1$; they care only about their supporters and not at all about themselves. We now generalize this by making less extreme assumptions about party leaders who use Aggregator rules, while maintaining the assumption that they are purely policy oriented and get no *intrinsic* utility from their party's vote share. The φ_2 parameter can be thought of substantively in this context as characterizing how altruistic the party leader is. Higher values of φ_2 imply more concern for the views of party supporters and less concern with personal policy preferences. This type of party leader is not one we typically find in theoretical models of party competition. In the real world, however, we do encounter parties, some Social Democratic and Green parties for example, that bind themselves in their formal decision making procedures to take account of the views of current party members, and even supporters, when setting party policy.

We model this type of party leader by constraining the leader utility function, allowing φ_2 to take different values but constraining $\varphi_1 + \varphi_2 = 1$, so that $\varphi_2 = 1 - \varphi_1$. Rearranging the leader utility function, this gives us

$$U_p(\cdot) = -\varphi_1 \cdot d(i_p, j_p)^2 - (1 - \varphi_1) \cdot d(j_p, k_p)^2 \qquad (10.2)$$

This makes use of the constraint that $\varphi_1 + \varphi_2 = 1$ and allows us to state expressions 10.1 and 10.2 in a way that makes φ_1 a common parameter with a clear intuitive meaning. It is the relative weight given by the party leader to her personal policy preferences, whether weighed against vote share, as in 10.1, or against supporters' ideals points, as in 10.2. Subject to the constraints we have specified, we can think in terms of a single party leader parameter φ. This specifies how policy oriented the party leader is, with "high-phi" party leaders giving more weight to their own ideal points than low-phi leaders.

Decision Rules for Party Leaders Who Care about Policy

The more general party leader utility functions set out in expressions 10.1 and 10.2 force us to reconsider each of the decision rule species, other than Sticker, that we specified and investigated in previous chapters. The vote-seeking Hunter and Explorer rules have straightforward redefinitions in terms of our more general parameterization of utility functions for party leaders who may care about policy and are based on the utility function set out in 10.1:[6]

Hunter: If the previous policy move increased your *utility*, move γ on the same heading; else, reverse heading and move γ on a heading chosen randomly from the arc ±90° from the direction now being faced.

Explorer: Each campaign tick, test a random policy position in the neighborhood radius η from your current position. Each election tick: move to the position found during campaign exploration that generated the most *utility*, if this generated more *utility* than you received at the previous election; else stand still.

Predators, unlike Hunters or Explorers, do not use party leaders' utility functions but instead use the vote shares of larger *other* parties to pick a direction of movement that is expected to increase their own vote share. For party leaders who have the type of utility function set out in 10.1, a possible extension of Predator is thus to modify the "target" policy position for the party leader, from the position of the closest larger party to some trade-off, parameterized by φ, between the ideal point of the party leader and the position of the *largest* party—the latter seen as an indication of a position that will increase vote share.[7] This generates a modified Predator algorithm:

---

[6] Table E10.1 in the electronic appendix gives NetLogo code for the redefined algorithms that we specify in this chapter.

[7] Recall that we modified the target position of the Predator rule specified by Laver (2005) from the position of the largest party, to that of the closest larger party, because the original specification generated pathological behavior arising from the fact that all Predators had identical target positions. This does not arise with the Predator rule we now define since party leaders using Predator rules have idiosyncratic ideal points, and hence idiosyncratic target positions.

> ***Predator:*** Identify your target position t_d on each policy dimension d with reference to your own ideal point i_d and the policy position, j_d, of the largest party on this dimension, such that $t_d = \varphi \cdot i_d + (1 - \varphi) \cdot j_d$. Move γ toward t_d unless you will overshoot this, in which case move to t_d.

Up until now, party leaders using Aggregator rules have been assumed to be perfect altruists for whom $\varphi_2 = 1$. We now relax this constraint and use expression 10.2 as the utility function for this type of party leader. Party leaders using an Aggregator rule may care about both their own personal ideal policy positions and the policy preferences of current party supporters. Using a similar logic to that we used to modify the Predator rule generates a modified Aggregator algorithm:

> ***Aggregator:*** Identify your target position t_d on each policy dimension d with reference to your ideal point i_d and the mean policy position, k_d, of current party supporters on this dimension, such that $t_d = \varphi \cdot i_d + (1 - \varphi) \cdot k_d$; move γ toward t_d unless you will overshoot this, in which case move to t_d.

An important consequence of the way we have just modified decision rules for party leaders is that the model we now specify is a generalization of our dynamic model of multiparty competition. If we set $\varphi = 0$ for all party leaders, then we generate the type of model we investigated in previous chapters, in which party leaders pay no attention at all to their own ideal points when setting party policy. This can now be seen as a special case of a more general class of models for which $0 \leq \varphi \leq 1$, which describe multiparty competition in settings where party leaders may well take their personal policy preferences into account when deciding what to do, trading off these policy preferences against other objectives at a rate specified by φ.

PARTY COMPETITION WHEN PARTY LEADERS CARE ABOUT POLICY

Party Survival

The model of party competition we investigate in this chapter specifies trade-offs in party leaders' utility functions that generate costs when party policy diverges from party leaders' ideal points, at a rate specified by φ. We therefore expect leaders to set party policy closer to their ideal points, the higher their settings of φ. For the same reason, we expect the vote shares of parties whose leaders use vote-seeking rules to decline, other things equal, as φ increases and the leader is more inclined to give up vote share to fulfill personal policy objectives. We saw in striking terms, when investigating party-specific nonpolicy valence in chapter 9, that similar trade-offs in the voter utility function have complex effects in a dynamic party system with a survival-of-the-fittest evolutionary regime in which the survival metric is vote share. In the present context, other things equal, the more policy-oriented leaders should tend to get lower vote shares than more vote-oriented leaders. We thus expect that policy-oriented (high-phi) leaders may tend to find it harder to keep their parties above the survival threshold. Conversely, as with higher valence parties, more vote-oriented (low-phi) leaders may find it easier to keep their parties over this threshold, which is denominated in vote share.

On the face of things, this might seem to imply the evolution of party systems with more vote-seeking than policy-oriented party leaders. More policy-oriented leaders could face evolutionary pressures directly analogous to those facing leaders with lower party valence. Things are more complicated than this, however. While party valences are completely exogenous to our dynamic model of multiparty competition, *party leader ideal points are endogenous*. Our citizen candidate model of endogenous party birth does *not* randomly select new party leaders whose ideal points might be at any point at all in the policy space. New parties have founding policy positions, thus their leaders have ideal points, at *points in the policy space for which there is manifest demand from voters*. More policy-oriented leaders do give less weight to vote share when setting party policy positions, but at the same time they give more weight to their own ideal policies. In a complex competitive environment where leaders' ideal points are endogenous to party competition, setting party policy in light of these is not necessarily bad for their party's vote share. We do not have clear theoretical expectations about how the effects of these complex interactions will emerge in our dynamic model of multiparty competition and leave this important matter to be illuminated by out computational results.

Party Policy Volatility

In the party systems we model in previous chapters, some parties are in continual motion. This is especially true for parties with insatiable leaders who never stop looking for more votes. Whether the extent of this continual motion is substantively unrealistic is a moot point, absent any calibration of policy distances in the model to policy distances in real party systems. Now that we assume party leaders may also be motivated to keep party policy close to their own ideal points, one important implication is that, other things equal, there should be less policy movement by political parties between elections. There is no cost for roaming all over the policy space in search of more votes if the party leader is motivated solely by vote maximization ($\varphi = 0$). A party leader motivated solely by personal policy preferences ($\varphi = 1$) has no incentive to set a position other than her ideal point, therefore no incentive ever to change party policy. More generally, *the higher the value of φ for the party leader, the less policy movement we expect from the party*.

In light of these new theoretical expectations, we specify two new output metrics for our dynamic model of multiparty competition. The first measures "policy loss" for each party leader. This is the quadratic loss term, $-d(i_p, j_p)^2$, in the party leader utility functions specified in expressions 10.1 and 10.2, and is thus identical to the policy loss for a voter who votes for a party with a policy position that is not her ideal point. The second new measure is the "policy shift" of party p, Δ_p, from one election to the next. We specify this as the Euclidean distance between a party's position at election e and its position at election $e-1$. Both new measures can be aggregated in various ways: across all surviving parties, for example, or all surviving parties with given decision rules or settings of φ. We expect a *positive* relationship between φ and $-d(i_p, j_p)^2$. The more party leaders care about their own ideal points, the closer typical party policy to these ideal points. We expect a *negative* relationship between φ and Δ_p. The more party leaders care about their own ideal points, the less the typical movement in party policy from one election to the next.

EXPERIMENTAL DESIGN

We could specify and investigate our model of multiparty competition when party leaders care about their own policy preferences as an extension of a model in which new parties chose decision rules according to replicator-mutator dynamics and/or in which different party leaders have different nonpolicy valences. There is nothing at all in the model we develop in this chapter that precludes this. As always, however, we strongly believe that more parsimonious models give better intuitions because their results are easier to interpret. They also allow for the cleaner design of experimental work. Our key substantive focus in this chapter is the trade-off, parameterized by φ, between the party leader's ideal point and some other attractive policy position. Our key analytical focus, therefore, is to investigate the effects of manipulating φ. We therefore specify the *computational implementation* of the theoretical model we develop in this chapter as a modification of the model we investigated in chapter 7.[8]

---

[8] In other words, rule replication probabilities are specified as uniform-random.

We first simplify the analysis of this model as we did in chapter 9, setting speed of adaptation and exploration neighborhoods of party leaders at central values.[9] We have already gleaned our main intuitions about satisficing, and our core substantive focus is now on whether even insatiable party leaders who care more about their own policy preferences will tend to change party policy less. We therefore specify all party leaders as insatiable ($\kappa = 1$). This simplification allows us to "make room" in the computational experiments we specify in this chapter for the crucial new trade-off parameter, φ, which is idiosyncratic to party leaders. Just as we investigated a discrete set of leader valence levels in chapter 9, we now investigate a discrete set of party leader settings for φ. We specify six values of this parameter, spanning its entire valid range, for leaders using Aggregator, Hunter, Predator, or Explorer rules: $\varphi = (0.0, 0.2, 0.4, 0.6, 0.8, 1.0)$. Adding the Sticker rule, this gives a total of twenty-five distinctive rule-leader pairings. Monte Carlo parameterizations for the competitive environment are exactly the same as in chapter 7.[10]

Party Competition When Leaders Trade Off Policy Preferences against Vote Share

Our core concern in this chapter is competition among parties whose leaders take account of their own personal policy preferences. We developed our model in a way that allows us to capture key effects of this by varying a single trade-off parameter, φ. High-phi party leaders are more interested in their own personal policy preferences, while low-phi leaders are more interested in some other objective, whether this is increasing the party vote share or satisfying the preferences of party supporters. We return below to consider leaders of Aggregator parties for whom the other objective may be satisfying party supporters. For now, we focus on vote-seeking party leaders who use one of the three decision rules designed to increase party vote shares, but who may also take account of their own policy preferences when deciding what to do.

---

[9] To recall, these are $\gamma = 0.1$, $\eta = 0.6$. All party valences are assumed equal and normalized to zero.

[10] That is, α_f is sampled from [0.00, 0.90]; τ is sampled from [0.05, 0.30]; ψ is sampled from [10, 25]; μ_1 is sampled from [0.00, 1.50]; n_1/n_2 is sampled from [1.00, 2.00]. It is as always important to bear in mind that there could be different computational investigations of our model that would be generated by different decisions about which parameter to fix, which to vary, and how to vary them.

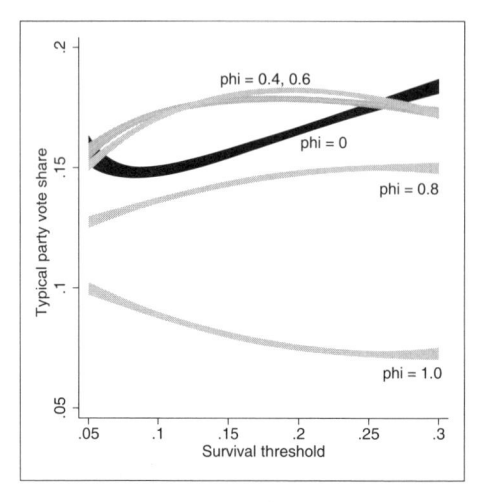

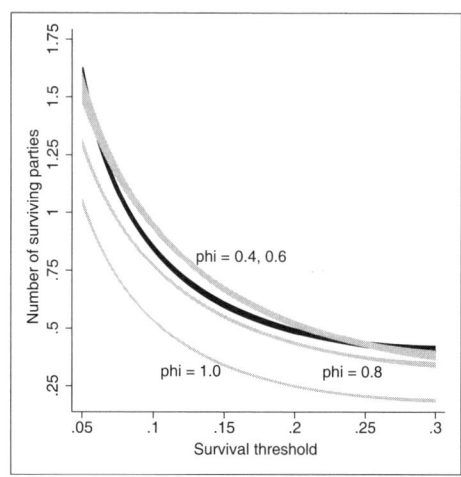

Figure 10.1. Typical vote shares (left) and numbers (right) of surviving parties, by survival threshold and party leader φ.

Survival and Vote Shares of Policy-Oriented Parties

When party leaders have different levels of valence, we found that a survival-of-the-fittest evolutionary regime implies that lower valence parties tend to die. Since the survival metric in our evolutionary regime is party vote share, the question we now ask is whether there is a similar implication for parties with high-phi leaders who are more concerned with their personal policy preferences than with their party's vote share. As we noted above, however, this implication does not necessarily follow in a complex system where, in contrast to exogenous leader valences, leaders' ideal points are *endogenous* to party competition. Figure 10.1 plots typical vote shares (left panel) and numbers (right panel) of surviving parties, by party leader φ.[11] The results are clear-cut. The evolutionary regime that killed off low-valence party leaders does *not* create an environment in which nearly all surviving parties have leaders who care mainly about party vote share.

The lowest gray ($\varphi = 1$) confidence band in the right panel shows that we are indeed less likely to encounter surviving party leaders who pay no attention whatsoever to party vote share. Even for these parties, however, survival prospects are not disastrous when survival thresholds are lower and there are more parties. They in no way look like the low-valence par-

---

[11] Confidence bands for $\varphi = 0.2$ party leaders have been suppressed to clarify presentation; these bands are close to those for $\varphi = 0$ leaders.

ties in chapter 9. The bunching of the other confidence bands in the right panel of Figure 10.1, however, shows that we are pretty much equally likely to encounter party leaders with any of the other settings of φ. In other words, *our dynamic model of multiparty competition in this setting sustains parties with leaders who do not just focus on party vote share, but also take account of their own personal policy preferences.* This key result colors the rest of the findings we report in this chapter.

The left panel of Figure 10.1 plots effects of survival thresholds on vote shares of parties whose leaders have different levels of φ. The positive slope of the black confidence band for $\varphi = 0$ leaders shows that competitive environments with higher survival thresholds and fewer parties tend to favor party leaders who are exclusively concerned with vote share. The low level of the confidence band for $\varphi = 1$ leaders shows that parties whose leaders care only about their own personal policy preferences tend systematically to win lower votes shares.

The big result in the left panel of Figure 10.1, however, is that the gray confidence bands for "medium-phi" ($\varphi = 0.4$ or 0.6) leaders show that *parties whose leaders trade off vote share against their personal policy preferences typically win higher vote shares than parties whose leaders care only about vote share.*[12] This striking result, the most important in this chapter, answers our open question about the interaction between our model of endogenous party birth and our survival-of-the-fittest evolutionary regime, with its survival metric of vote share.

As we noted, our model of endogenous party birth means that the ideal points of agents who become party leaders are endogenous to party competition and tend to be located at positions in the policy space where there is manifest "demand" for a new party from disgruntled voters. The more disgruntled voters in the neighborhood of some policy position, the greater the probability of a new party birth with a founding policy position at that location. We now see from our simulations—the results of which we have found to be very robust—that "medium-phi" leaders, who take account of these endogenous founding policy positions even at the expense of short-run vote gains, can enhance their party's vote share over the long run. We see two different reasons why this might happen.

First, since parties tend not to emerge endogenously at unpopular policy positions, they always tend to have a "policy constituency" in the voting population that generated the original demand for the party's birth. Voter ideal points never move in our model, so this constituency

---

[12] Mean vote shares for the set of parties with $\varphi = 0.4$ or 0.6 leaders are 0.175 in each case, whereas the mean vote share for parties with $\varphi = 0$ vote-seeking leaders is 0.163. Standard errors of these means are 0.0004 when $\varphi = 0.4$ or 0.6 and 0.0007 when $\varphi = 0$.

of voters will always be a source of support for any party staying close to its founding policy position over the long run, whatever short-run fluctuations of support may arise as a result of movements by other parties.

The second reason has to do with indirect "deterrence" of the entry of new party rivals. We do not model *strategic* party positioning with the explicit intention of deterring new party entry. Such models quickly become very difficult, even in very simple settings (Austen-Smith and Banks 2005; Dhillon 2005; Shepsle 1991). Furthermore, intractability of the multidimensional Voronoi Game that we discussed in chapter 2 tells us very precisely that models of strategic entry deterrence in multidimensional multiparty systems are intractable. We do know, however, that every party in our endogenous party system was a once a new entrant. Each party has a founding policy position; its leader had an ideal point, which does not change, at a position in the policy space where there were incentives for citizen candidates. Maintaining this policy position and thereby satisfying voter demand in this policy neighborhood *reduces incentives for subsequent entry* in the same locale of the space. Moving away from this position, other things equal, increases the incentives for, and hence the probability of, a new entry in the local neighborhood. If the entrant is a new policy "neighbor" of the existing party,[13] the undeterred entry will axiomatically reduce the size of the existing party's Voronoi region and hence vote share. Our conjecture is therefore that parties whose leaders take account of their own policy preferences when setting party policy in an endogenous party system, even at a cost in terms of short-run vote share, tend to locate at policy positions that have the *indirect* effect of "deterring" the entry of new local rivals and thereby enhancing long-run vote share, even though this is in no way an explicit calculation.

Policy Loss and Policy Movement

If party leaders take their own ideal points into account when setting party policy and if, as we assume, these ideal points do not change, then party policy positions are to a certain extent "anchored" by the party leader's ideal point. The extent of this anchoring depends on the leader's policy-votes trade-off parameter, φ. We therefore expect parties to change their policies less when their leaders care more about their own private policy preferences. As we measure these things, we expect Δ_p to decrease as party leader φ increases. For the same reason, we expect the "policy losses" suffered by party leaders to increase systematically as φ decreases

---

[13] That is, the existing party shares a Voronoi boundary with the new entrant.

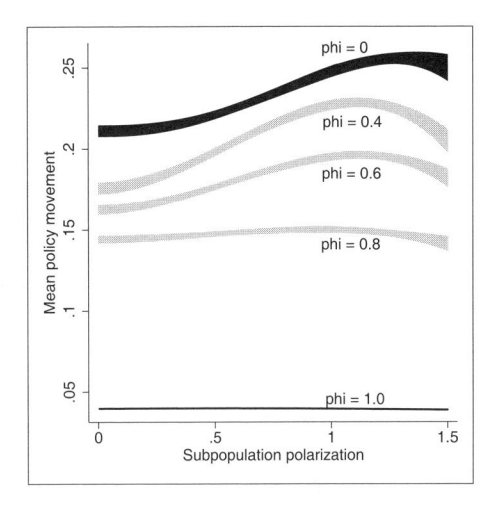

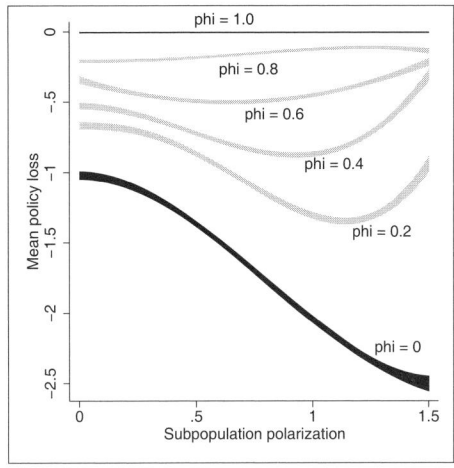

Figure 10.2. Mean policy movement (left) and policy loss (right), by leader φ.

and party leaders care less about policy. Figure 10.2 plots the relationships between subpopulation polarization, the main driver of party policy positions, party leader φ, and party policy movement between elections (left panel) as well as between polarization and policy losses by the party leader (right panel).

The right panel shows that effectively zero policy losses are suffered by $\varphi = 1$ party leaders, who typically set policy at or very close to their ideal points. The lower confidence bands show that party leader policy "losses" mount steadily as φ decreases, though this happens of course because leaders care less about their own policy preferences and more about winning votes, so they do not necessarily suffer a net *utility* loss. The left panel shows that, as expected, party policy movement between elections systematically increases as φ decreases and party leaders care less about their own policy preferences. The sequence of confidence bands shows that volatility of party positions increases from constant and very low levels when $\varphi = 1.0$ to significantly higher levels when φ is lower.[14] This suggests that some of the volatility of party policy positions in the competitive environments we model in previous chapters is a product of the assumption that party leaders pay no attention to their own ideal points when setting party policy. In short, *interelectoral party policy movement*

---

[14] The residual movement for $\varphi = 1.0$ leaders arises entirely from stochastic "jittering" by Hunters, who relentlessly make random moves in search of a more utility-maximizing policy position than the leader's ideal point, but of course never find one.

is *"dampened" when party leaders take their own policy preferences into account*; it is dampened more, the more they take these preferences into account.

Figure 10.2 also shows us that differences between party leaders with different levels of φ widen considerably as subpopulation polarization increases. The trade-off between vote seeking and policy seeking is much starker, so that *vote seeking results in significantly more policy movement when voting populations are highly polarized*. In highly polarized settings, as suggested by the black band in the right panel of Figure 10.2 and as can be seen by watching simulations in motion, parties with $\varphi = 0$ vote-seeking party leaders can come into existence in one voter subpopulation but then move freely from one subpopulation to another in search of votes. This generates at lot of policy movement between elections. The higher φ, and thus the higher the contribution of policy loss to the party leader's utility, the less likely a party is to "desert" the subpopulation that was the cause of its original foundation, since some ideal point in this distribution is also the ideal point of the party leader.

Performance of Vote-Seeking Rule Species

The relative performance of the three different vote-seeing rule species in the experiments we report in Figure 7.2 means that, when party leaders care about only vote share and voters care about only policy, parties using Explorer rules are the most successful overall. We have seen in this chapter that, when party leaders also care at least somewhat about policy, it is parties with "medium-phi" leaders, who trade off vote share against personal policy preferences, who in the long run tend to win the most votes. These two effects interact. We see this in Figure 10.3, which plots typical party vote shares, by vote-seeking rule species, survival threshold, and party leader φ.

Strictly speaking, we should compare the performance only of Hunter and Explorer rules, plotted with gray confidence bands. This is because we modified these rules in the same way, from vote-seeking to utility-seeking rules, in which leaders may also take account of their personal policy preferences, so that $0 \geq \varphi \geq 1$. We modified Predator in a quite different way, using φ to weight the direction of movement chosen, between the leader's ideal point and the policy position of the largest party. Regardless of rule species, however, and especially for Hunters and Explorers, typical party vote shares are lower for $\varphi = 0$ vote-seeking party leaders than for $\varphi = 0.6$ leaders who trade off vote share against personal policy preferences. This pattern is most striking for Explorer rules, which remain significantly the most effective rule species across the board. The

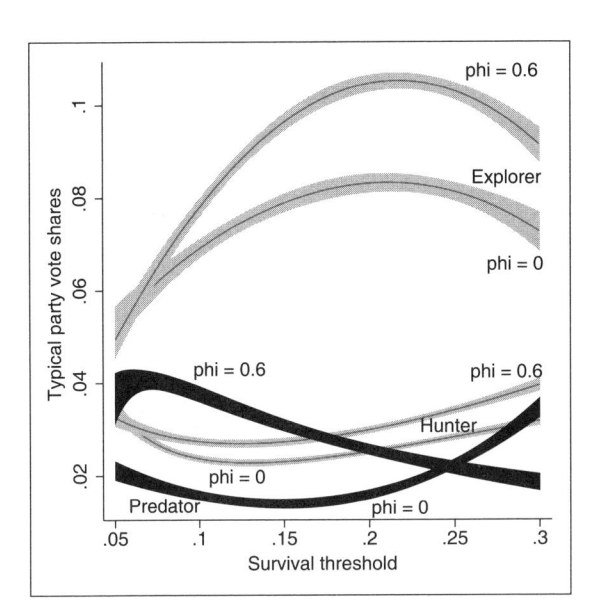

Figure 10.3. Typical party vote shares, by rule species, survival threshold, and leader φ. Predator rules plotted in black, Hunter and Explorer rules plotted in gray.

"medium-phi effect" is not specific to a particular vote-seeking rule species and is greatest for the most successful rule species.

Leaders Trading Off Personal against Supporters' Preferences

Thus far we have focused on party leaders who trade off their party's short-run vote share against their own personal policy preferences when setting party policy. We now turn our attention to party leaders who trade off their own personal policy preferences against those of current party supporters. Recall from expression 10.2 that lower values of φ for such leaders mean they put more weight on the preferences of current party supporters and less on their own. All Aggregators we investigated in previous chapters had $\varphi = 0$ party leaders who take no account at all of their own policy preferences.

Figure 10.4 plots typical vote shares and policy volatilities of parties with leaders who use Aggregator rules, with different plots for leaders who trade off their own preferences against those of their supporters at different rates. The left panel shows that lower phi Aggregator party lead-

224 • Chapter 10

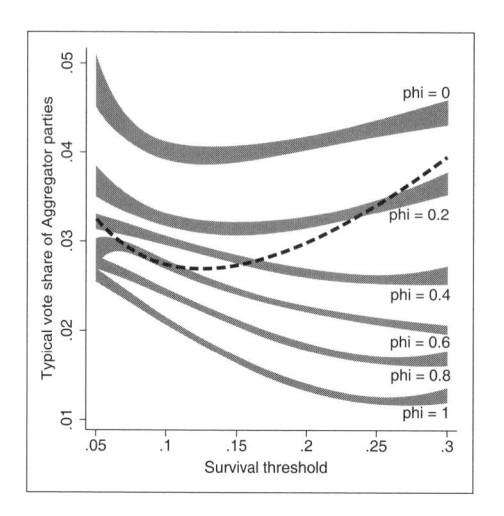

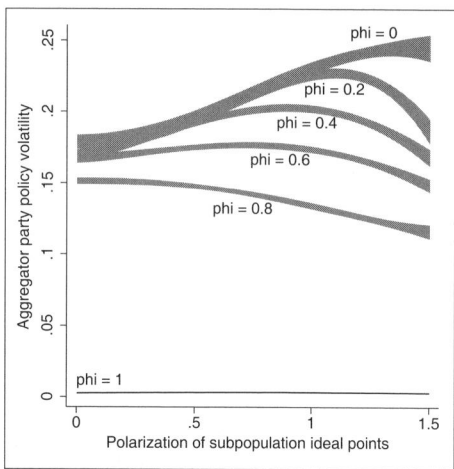

Figure 10.4. Typical vote shares (left) and policy volatility (right) of parties with leaders using Aggregator rules, by φ. Dashed line is $\varphi = 0.6$ Hunter.

ers, *who care least about their own policy preferences and most about those of their supporters, systematically win higher vote shares.* There is no "medium-phi" effect for Aggregators. While Aggregator is in no sense a vote-seeking rule, we see that being *more* of an Aggregator, in other words increasing the relative weight you attach to the preferences of your current supporters as opposed to your own, is good for your vote share. As a consequence, some Aggregators now perform as well at winning votes as leaders using the vote-seeking Hunter and Predator rules. To highlight this, the left panel of Figure 10.4 also plots, as the dashed black line, typical vote shares of the most successful leaders using Hunter rules, which were those for which $\varphi = 0.6$. Low-phi Aggregators who care exclusively or almost exclusively about their supporters' ideal points are better at winning votes than these Hunters. Even if you never look for new supporters, there is clearly a degree of *implicit* vote-seeking that arises from keeping your current supporters happy rather than just pursuing your own private desires.

The right panel of Figure 10.4 shows the effects of party leader φ on the policy volatility of parties led by leaders using Aggregator rules. As expected—and as with party leaders using any of the vote-seeking rule species we investigate—it is $\varphi = 0$ Aggregators, who attach no weight to their own ideal points, who are associated with the greatest policy volatility. When party leaders attach more weight to their own ideal points,

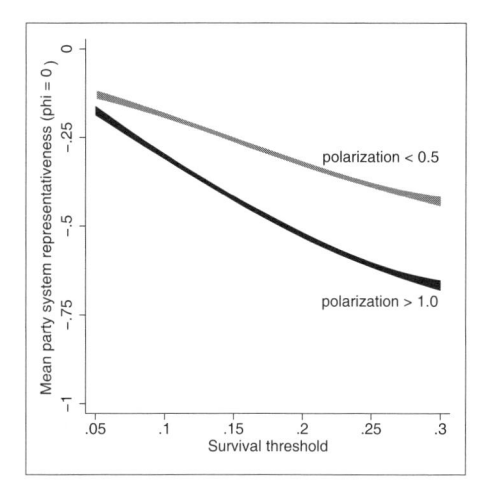

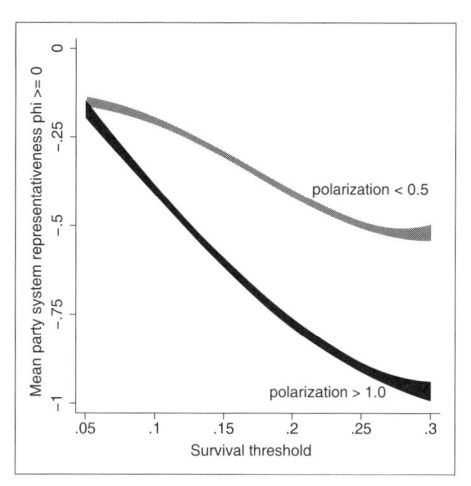

Figure 10.5. Representativeness of party policy positions, by survival threshold and polarization of voter ideal points. Left panel: $\varphi = 0$ for all leaders; right panel: $0 \leq \varphi \leq 1$.

this anchors party policy so that the policy volatility of their party is significantly lower.

Representativeness When Party Leaders Care about Policy

Party leaders who care at least somewhat about their own policy preferences are less likely to set party policy in a way that appeals to as many voters as possible (if they are voter seekers), or to their current supporters (if they are Aggregators). It is therefore natural to ask whether party policy positions are typically less representative when leaders trade off party vote shares against personal policy preferences. Figure 10.5 plots representativeness of the evolved configuration of party policy positions against its main driver, the survival threshold.[15] The left panel plots results taken from the simulations we report in chapter 7, for party systems in which $\varphi = 0$ for all leaders. The right panel plots results for the party systems we model in this chapter, where $0 \leq \varphi \leq 1$.

We noted in chapter 6 that, when survival thresholds are high and there are few surviving parties, the representativeness of evolved party

---

[15] Figure E10.1 in the electronic appendix plots party policy eccentricity by voter polarization and leader φ.

policy positions is particularly compromised in polarized electorates.[16] We therefore show separate plots for the relationship between representativeness and survival thresholds in polarized and unpolarized electorates.[17] As always, representativeness is sharply affected by the survival threshold, with high survival thresholds implying fewer parties and less representative configurations of party policy positions.[18] Over and above this effect, and especially in polarized electorates (black bands), representativeness of the evolved configuration of party positions is systematically lower when party leaders also care about their own policy preferences (right panel) than when they do not (left panel). As expected, therefore, voters do tend to be less well represented by the emergent configuration of party policy positions when party leaders care somewhat about their own policy preferences. This effect is strongest, consistent with our findings in chapter 6, when there are few parties and voter opinion is polarized.

CONCLUSIONS

The assumption we made in previous chapters, that party leaders have no concern whatsoever for their own preferences when setting party policy, is common in the theoretical literature but clearly overstated in relation to real-world politics. Formal models in the "Wittman" tradition do assume that politicians act on personal policy preferences, but these models are tractable only in massively simplified settings. Here, we modify our assumptions about the utility functions of party leaders to take account of the possibility that they trade off, in some well-specified way, the utility arising from setting party policy close to their ideal point against the utility arising from some other objective—which may be increasing party vote share or satisfying current party supporters. We achieved this by activating, but nonetheless constraining, the two trade-off parameters in the general utility function we specified in chapter 3. Modifying party leaders' utility functions in this way requires a respecification of the various decision rule species we investigate. We do this in different ways for Hunter and Explorer rules, on the one hand, and for Aggregator and Predator rules, on the other. Hunter and Explorer rules have natural extensions in this new setting. Instead of Hunting or Exploring for more *votes*, they Hunt or Explore for more *party leader utility*, defining utility

---

[16] See Figure 6.6.
[17] $\mu_r > 1.0$ and $\mu_r < 0.5$, respectively.
[18] Both confidence bands in both panels slope down and are very narrow.

in the more general way we have now specified. For Predator and Aggregator rules, we modify the *target* party position that these rules indicate.

One systematic consequence of assuming that party leaders take their own preferences into account when setting party policy is that party policy *movement* between elections is anchored to some extent by the leader's ideal point, and thereby dampened. Assuming policy-motivated party leaders also has implications for the representativeness of the evolved configuration of party policy positions. As expected, party system representativeness tends to be lower when party leaders take account of their own policy preferences, in addition to trying to appeal to as many voters as possible, when setting party policy positions. This effect is sharpest with high survival thresholds and highly polarized electorates.

The most striking results in this chapter, however, are plotted in Figures 10.1 and 10.2. For leaders using one of the modified utility-seeking rule species, it is those with *intermediate* levels of φ who typically enjoy the highest vote shares. These leaders derive utility from a mix of keeping party policy relatively close to their own ideal points and increasing short-run party vote share. The apparent but robust paradox is that *leaders who focus exclusively on increasing their party's vote share do not maximize this vote share over the long run*. Our interpretation of this arises from the fact that, absent a dynamic model of leadership change inside political parties, the leader's ideal point is the same as the founding party policy position. Given a citizen candidate account of endogenous party birth, founding party policy positions, and hence leaders' ideal points, not only are *endogenous to party competition* but also are *more likely to arise at points in the policy space where there is manifest voter demand*. The net effect is that taking account of the leader's ideal point is good for long-run party vote share because leaders who tend to keep policy close to these founding positions tend (1) to keep policy at positions for which there is manifest voter demand and (2) to preempt voter disgruntlement and the birth of new parties in the region of these same positions. This striking phenomenon is an excellent example of how, once the outputs of party competition today recursively feed back as inputs to party competition tomorrow, as they do by endogenizing the ideal points of party leaders in our dynamic ABM of multiparty competition, the complex system thereby generated can throw up counterintuitive and intriguing results.

CHAPTER ELEVEN

Using Theoretical Models to Analyze Real Party Systems

WE BUILD THEORETICAL MODELS to help us understand the world. We call our own model a model of "party competition," our agents "party leaders" and "voters," because we believe these artificial constructs do in some meaningful way resemble party competition, party leaders, and voters in real political settings. The real political settings that interest us involve party competition in modern democracies, more precisely, in a list of specific postwar democracies about which we have some systematic knowledge.[1] In this chapter, we use our model to analyze recent party competition in these postwar democracies in order to satisfy ourselves that empirical implications of our theoretical model can indeed be systematically observed in real party competition. This is easy to say but hard to do in a rigorous way. Fundamental difficulties arise from two distinct sources. The first concerns *calibration* of key parameters of our theoretical model to the real political environments we use it to analyze. The second concerns *data*, specifically the need for reliable empirical observations of the real world that can be compared with theoretical implications of our model. We discuss these two methodological problems before moving on to compare empirical implications generated by our model, calibrated to real party systems, with empirical observations of these same party systems.

---

[1] The party systems we model are those for which the longstanding Eurobarometer series of public opinion surveys has generated reasonably rich time series observations of party support shares: Britain, Denmark, France, Germany, Greece, Ireland, Luxembourg, the Netherlands, Spain. We excluded Belgium because constitutional changes dealing with the representation of language groups in the cabinet generated major changes in the party system, with the main Belgian parties all splitting on a linguistic basis into two independent if related parties. We excluded Italy because of the complete transformation of the Italian party system following corruption scandals, resulting in almost no continuity among parties competing in 1989 and 2002. We excluded Portugal because severe calibration problems suggested that our two dimensional representation of the Portuguese party space was missing key features of party competition in Portugal. Other EU members for which there are Eurobarometer data do not have observations running back to 1989, the year for which we have "starting" expert survey estimates of party positions.

CALIBRATING OUR MODEL TO REAL POLITICAL SYSTEMS

We devoted much attention in previous chapters to developing and implementing computational methods that allow us to characterize substantively important implications of our model for a given vector of parameter settings. Each parameter vector specifies a particular configuration of the competitive environment. Each configuration can be seen as representing a particular real party system at a particular point in time. We estimate effects of individual model parameters, in a way similar to the comparative statics used by analytical theorists, by systematically varying parameter settings, then computing and analyzing associated model outputs. Whether we use a predefined "grid" to vary model parameters in a systematic way or randomly sample parameter settings, we can investigate only a discrete set of model parameterizations, having previously specified some predefined distribution of "interesting" values for each parameter. We specify these distributions of investigated parameter settings in ways that we take, informally, to be empirically realistic.

Thus far we have used our models to make statements about competition in a *general class* of democratic multiparty systems. While these are all democratic multiparty systems, they differ considerably from one another in terms of specific parameters of their competitive environments. The theoretical exercise is, precisely, to model *different* multiparty systems, developing models that account for observable implications of these differences. For this reason, we investigated effects of model parameters when these parameters are distributed over fairly broad ranges—ranges we nonetheless believe to be substantively realistic. In relation to the de facto party survival threshold, for example, we investigated values in the range $0.05 \leq \tau \leq 0.30$. We did not pick this range out of a hat but because we knew from previously published work that, given this range for τ, our model is likely to generate party systems that tend to have between two and ten political parties over the long run (Laver and Schilperoord 2007). This range of party system sizes matches the range we observe in the general class of democratic multiparty systems that interest us. In picking the range $0.05 \leq \tau \leq 0.30$, we thereby *calibrate* model parameter τ to the general class of party systems we want to model. Our model calibration up to this point has been to a general class of democratic multiparty systems that nonetheless differ in the details of their competitive environments because we wanted to use our model to derive general propositions about, and hence empirical implications for, multiparty competition *in general*.

Our task is now quite different. We now seek to compare implications of our model with systematic observations of *particular real party sys-*

tems at particular times. We must therefore generate empirical implications of our model in specific competitive environments, represented by specific model parameterizations. For example, if we are interested in party competition in Germany during the 1990s, then we want our model to generate empirical implications when its parameters are calibrated to Germany in the 1990s, not to some general class of democratic multiparty systems. One reason that empirical implications generated by our model may not match empirical observations of German politics in the 1990s is not that the model is "wrong" in some sense but that it is *badly calibrated*. The solution in this event is better model calibration, not a better model.

Our life would be much easier if there were a big book somewhere listing all key parameter values for Germany in the 1990s, and in every other place and time that interests us. Alas, this big book does not and can never exist. Many key parameter settings for our model are fundamentally unobservable in real Germany. This is a general problem for models in the social and indeed other sciences, though it is rarely dragged out into plain view by the authors of published work.[2] Logically, this leaves us with two possible courses of action.

The first possible way forward is to calibrate our model's parameter settings to, say, Germany in the 1990s using a set of assumptions or inferences we feel are empirically plausible. We could then use our model, calibrated by assumption, to generate empirical implications for recent German party competition and compare these to independent empirical observations. The problem is that we can often generate empirical implications that match reality by making the "right" plausible calibration assumptions. The grave danger is that, absent any independent information about how to calibrate key model parameters, we find particular calibration assumptions to be "plausible" precisely because they make our model generate empirical observations that fit our data. What looks superficially like "testing" model implications using independent data becomes an implicit exercise in fitting the model to the data.

Suspecting that this happens more often in the social sciences than many would like to admit, we recognize this problem and in effect turn it on its head. We do this by assuming our model to be valid, at least as a first recourse, then using the model to search for parameter settings that are associated with the best possible predictions about, say, recent German party competition. We *explicitly* fit the model to the data, "auto-

---

[2] A favorite hiding place for the informal calibration assumptions of theoretical models, when these are explicit at all, is in little-read and widely scattered footnotes, whose cumulative effect is rarely considered.

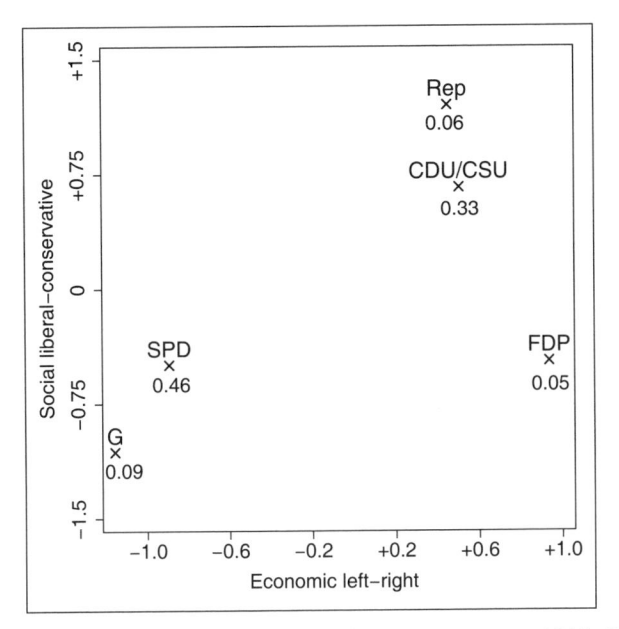

Figure 11.1. Party policy positions and vote shares in Germany, 1988–89.

calibrating" model parameters to empirical data generated by real party systems of interest.

For example, if we assume that real voters do tend to support their closest party—an assumption at the heart of our model—then observed sizes and policy positions of political parties give us substantial information about possible distributions of voter ideal points. Figure 11.1 plots German party policy positions on two salient policy dimensions for the period circa 1988–89, estimated using an expert survey (Laver and Hunt 1992) as well as party vote shares estimated using Eurobarometer opinion surveys for the same period. We assume these policy dimensions are what motivate German voters and that social interaction among German voters is structured as if they all belong to one of two subpopulations. We then seek parameterizations of relative subpopulation sizes, ideal point centroids and standard deviations that, given this configuration of party policy positions, generate the party vote shares we observe. There are actually very few parameterizations that do this.

One is as follows: the "rightmost" of the two subpopulations on the left-right dimension is 1.67 times larger than the leftmost; ideal point centroids of right and left subpopulations are at (0.05, 0.57) and (−1.35, −0.35) respectively; and the standard deviations of the ideal point distributions of both subpopulations are 0.55. Call this parameter vector G_1. Proximity voting by a German electorate with a G_1 parameterization, given the policy positions shown in Figure 11.1, implies vote shares for the three largest German parties that differ on average by only 0.4 percent from those observed in real Germany.[3] Random parameterizations of the distribution of voter ideal points in Germany typically imply vote shares that differ by very much more than this from the vote shares we actually observe. Hence, we can take G_1 as a potentially realistic parameterization of the German electorate, calibrated to the observed party vote shares in 1989. If we prespecify some level of precision for matching predicted to observed votes shares, then we can search for potentially realistic parameterizations and run simulations for all of those that we find. In fact, once we start searching for population parameterizations that calibrate party sizes and policy positions to observed party vote shares in Germany, we find several possibilities, and these are not all similar to G_1.[4] What we are doing in this process of autocalibration is not finding the "one true model calibration" but excluding model calibrations that are manifestly wrong. This leaves us with a set of calibrations (we search until we have found one thousand of these in the empirical work we report below) that are potentially valid. As we discuss below, we then characterize model outputs for the best 5 percent of these calibrations.

Having calibrated *population* parameters of our model in this way, we can conduct a similar exercise designed to calibrate other features of our model to recent party competition in Germany, including the decision rules used by German party leaders and precise parameterizations of these rules. We do this, in ways we specify in more detail below, by finding settings of party leader/decision rule parameters that enable our model to best predict *changes* in the German party system between two time points for which we have reliable empirical observations, 1989 and 2002.

We have to be brutally honest and face the fact that the autocalibrated empirical analyses we report in this chapter do not in any meaningful sense constitute a formal "test" of our model. We are not using our model to generate empirical implications and then testing the model by comparing these implications with independent empirical data. Rather, we are finding calibrations of fundamentally unobservable model parameters that generate empirical implications matching the data we have. We

---

[3] These values were found using an "autocalibrating" version of our model, described in more detail below.

[4] Trivially, one of these would divide the electorate into as many subpopulations as there are political parties, with subpopulation sizes proportional to party vote shares, subpopulation ideal point centroids identical to party policy positions, and subpopulation ideal point standard deviations set to zero.

could of course have engaged in an autocalibration exercise, implicit or explicit, behind closed doors. We could then have ostensibly "assumed" some (eminently plausible) calibrations for which the model generates empirical implications that fit the data very nicely. We could then claim to have "tested" the model, reporting some splendid predictive successes. Most readers would have been none the wiser, but, as scientists, we were not for one second tempted to do this. Given the fundamental calibration problems we face, our claim in this chapter is more modest. It is indeed possible to find calibrations of our model, calibrations that do furthermore seem plausible to us on the face of things, which allow our model to generate empirical implications that match what we actually observe in specific real party systems. If you are already somewhat convinced by our model, this will give you further comfort.

MEASURING THE DYNAMICS OF "REAL" PARTY COMPETITION

Even if by some miracle we had perfect calibrations of unobservable model parameters to specific real party systems, our *empirical observations* of any real party system would always be flawed and unreliable. Since our substantive interest is in national political processes of democratic multiparty competition over the postwar period, we are pretty much stuck with the data that have already been laid down on the historical record and must make the best use we can of these. This problem is greatly exacerbated by the fact we are interested in evaluating *dynamic* spatial models of policy-based party competition. Quintessentially, these models generate dense times series of party policy positions. While these do exist in the real world, in some hypothetical sense, the *evidence available for measuring* dense time series of party policy positions is problematic to say the least. This is in contrast to the other quintessential outputs of dynamic models of multiparty competition. These are dense time series of support levels for different political parties, for which there is decent opinion poll evidence in each of the countries that interest us. We first discuss our time series data on party support shares, before returning to the problem of measuring changes in party policy positions.

Eurobarometer Data on Changing Party Support Shares

It is not hard to find reliable series of public opinion surveys that measure observed levels of party support at reasonably frequent intervals. These surveys measure party support with error but, if they are based on properly conducted sampling methodology, their error processes are well understood and can be taken into account. In particular, we can rely on the highly regarded Eurobarometer series of opinion surveys, which have been carried out twice yearly since 1974 in European Union (EU) member states. As well as asking questions about matters directly related to the EU, these surveys collected information on voters' attachments to political parties. While there has been some criticism that translated question wordings differ in significant ways among states and over time (Sinnott 1998), the general professional consensus is that, especially if direct comparisons between countries are not required, Eurobarometer surveys have generated a reliable time series of party support levels in EU member states.[5] Accordingly, our core data source on party support levels is the set of Eurobarometer surveys running from 1974 to 2002. These generate a maximum of fifty-five observations of party support levels, in the nine countries that were EU members when the Eurobarometer started in 1974,[6] with the time series beginning later in other countries, as these joined the EU.[7] For reason we explain shortly, however, we use these data only for the period 1989–2002.[8]

Problems with Time Series Data on Party Policy Positions

As we noted above, the main data limitation we face concerns time series of party policy positions, one of the quintessential outputs of our model. This is a matter of ongoing concern and discussion within the profession, particularly in the context of a time series of party positions that is often used, the expert-coded content analysis of party positions generated by the Comparative Manifestos Project (CMP) (Budge et al. 2001; Budge et al. 1987; Klingemann et al. 2006; Laver and Budge 1992). The CMP data cover thousands of policy programs, issued by 288 parties in twenty-five countries over the course of 364 elections during the period 1945–98. Notwithstanding the fact that these data are reported as error-free point estimates, they surely contain measurement error. Benoit, Laver, and Mikhaylov, for example, calculate bootstrapped standard errors for CMP estimates of party policy positions that simulate just one of the error processes involved in generating these data. They find that only about 38 percent of estimated "movements" of party policy positions between adjacent time points in the CMP's widely used left-right scale are

---

[5] For a full description of these, see www.ec.europa.eu/public_opinion/index_en.htm.

[6] Belgium, Britain, Denmark, France, Germany, Ireland, Italy, Luxembourg, and the Netherlands.

[7] This gives forty-three polls for Greece, thirty-three for Portugal and Spain, sixteen for Finland, and thirteen for Sweden and Austria.

[8] Eurobarometer estimates of party support shares in 1989 and 2002 are given in Table E11.1 in the electronic appendix.

statistically significant (Benoit et al. 2009). Setting aside measurement error, three other serious issues arise from the need to estimate dense times series of party policy positions.

The first is that the election manifestos used to generate the CMP data do not lay down a *dense* time series of party positions. We already noted in chapter 2 that 213 elections were held over the 50-year period from 1950 to 2000 in fifteen Western European democracies, an average of 14.2 elections in each country, or one every 3.5 years. Neither election results nor election manifestos generate many time series observations for any real political system, even over a 50-year period. While we can use frequent public opinion surveys to measure evolving patterns of party support, no such reliable data exist for measuring evolving configurations of party policy positions.[9]

The second problem is that analyses of party manifestos issued at successive elections may not, strictly speaking, constitute a *time series*. This is because positions are estimated on scales *that may not have a constant meaning over a fifty-year period*. The substantive meanings of "left" and "right" are clearly very different today, following the demise of the former Soviet Union, the end of the cold war, and the transformation of Maoist China, than they were in the 1950s. Formal models, whether analytic or computational, either are static or assume a constant metric for measuring dynamics. Theoretical time series of positions on policy dimensions are assumed to have a constant meaning over time. It is almost certain, however, that equivalent policy dimensions in the real world *evolve over time*. This makes it difficult to factor out aspects of observed policy "movement" that reflect actual choices made by politicians and those that reflect changes in the substantive meaning of the scale on which such positions are measured. The latter cause policy positions measured on the same scale to *appear* to change even if their authors did not intend this.

The third problem is that, while there is some acceptance within the profession of a *one-dimensional* representation of party policy positions based on the CMP's left-right scale derived from coded party manifestos, generating the *multidimensional time series of policy positions* we require here has proved deeply problematic. Addressing this problem, we ourselves made determined efforts to generate reliable and valid two-dimensional time series of party policy positions from CMP data. It would have been very convenient for us had we been successful. We simply did not feel, however, that the multidimensional policy estimates we

---

[9] It is not inconceivable that such a source might emerge as a result of the development of automated text analysis algorithms, though the real issue is the assembly of authoritative text *corpora*, not the analysis of these.

generated were in any way close to being reliable and valid. No scholar we are aware of, furthermore, has succeeded where we failed.

This leaves us with expert surveys as our source of data on party policy positions at different points in time. Expert surveys do no more and no less than summarize, in a systematic way, the received wisdom of experts on party politics in each of the countries concerned. They are accepted as valid for this reason and have also proved to be reliable. The problem now is that expert surveys are rare, generating their reliable and valid observations at very few time points. Reluctantly, therefore, we are forced to confine ourselves to predicting party movements between two time points on which we do have very good information, using expert survey data collected in 1989 and in 2002 (Laver and Hunt 1992; Benoit and Laver 2006). While there are somewhat earlier expert surveys than those reported for 1989 by Laver and Hunt, these still do not take us back to the start of the Eurobarometer time series *and* deal only with a single left-right ideological dimension (Castles and Mair 1984). While there are no time series expert survey estimates of party policy positions, the Laver-Hunt survey was replicated in 2002 (Benoit and Laver 2006). This allows us at least to estimate party movements between 1989 and 2002, and thus to evaluate model-generated predictions about such movements, a matter to which we shortly return. We thus restrict the time period we investigate to 1989–2002, a period for which we do feel confident in our estimates of both party vote shares from the Eurobarometer and party policy positions from expert surveys.

Given our coordinate system for describing party policy positions, we measure party positions *relative to the centroid of voter ideal points*. To find this centroid we adapt a method suggested by Kim and Fording for measuring the position of the *median* voter on a given policy dimension (Kim and Fording 1998). On each dimension, we find the mean of all party policy positions, as estimated from the relevant expert survey, weighting each party position by the party's vote share, estimated from the relevant Eurobarometer survey.[10] Each policy position is now expressed in our coordinate system, not as a raw expert survey score but as a *deviation* from the vote-share-weighted mean position on the dimension concerned for the country and year in question. Negative scores are for parties to the left of this weighted mean, positive scores are for parties to the right.[11]

---

[10] In making this calculation we, as always, assume Downsian proximity voting, as do Kim and Fording.

[11] Estimated policy scores for parties in 1989 and 2003, transformed into the NetLogo coordinate system, are reported in Table E11.1 in the electronic appendix.

Macro-Evidence on Party Birth Locations

Before moving on to report our own detailed empirical findings, we pause to draw attention to a piece of additional evidence that lends support to a key empirical implication of our citizen-candidate model of endogenous party birth and death. This arises from comparing results from the Laver-Hunt and Benoit-Laver expert surveys (Benoit and Laver 2006; Laver and Hunt 1992). We can compare the 1989 policy positions of thirty-nine parties that existed in 1989 but not in 2002 (party deaths), the 2002 positions of twenty-nine parties that existed in 2002 but not in 1989 (party births), and the 2002 positions of seventy-nine parties existing in both 1989 and 2003 (party survivors). Using a two-dimensional representation of the policy space in each country that described party positions on economic policy and social liberalism, Laver and Benoit found that *the policy positions of party births and deaths were significantly more eccentric than the policy positions of party survivors* (Laver and Benoit 2007).[12] These findings are consistent with the empirical implications of our model of endogenous party birth, reported in Figures 6.5 and 7.4. These figures show very clearly that the locations of model-generated party births are systematically more eccentric than the locations of party survivors. In relation to endogenous party births, therefore, there is at least one piece of systematic and completely independent empirical evidence that is consistence with the empirical implications of our model.

Using Our Model to Analyze the Dynamics of Real Party Systems

We base our empirical analyses in this chapter on a version of the model we set out in chapter 9, which specifies a diverse set of rule species and parameterizations and also comprehends different party leaders who have different levels of nonpolicy valence. We do not implement the replicator-mutator system we specify in chapter 8, for the prosaic but crucial reason that the run of data that we have for each country is not long enough for the evolutionary process modeled by such a system to take effect. Also for lack of the necessary data, we do not model the possibility that party leaders have different levels of concern for their own private policy preferences, which depends on making a crucial empirical distinction between the ideal points of party leaders and the policy positions they implement. While we can observe *the actions of party leaders*,

---

[12] See Tables 7 and 8 of Laver and Benoit (2007). Differences in policy eccentricities were statistically significant at better than the .01 level.

we have no data that give us *independent estimates of the ideal points* of these same leaders. If we depend on making such a distinction, we are clearly not justified in assuming that the ideal points of all party leaders happen to be at their stated party policy positions in 1989, a year that marks the start of our investigations but has no substantive political significance. We therefore "switch off" the possibility that party leaders trade off higher voter shares against a concern for their own personal policy preferences, setting $\varphi = 0$ in the model runs we specify below.

Calibrating Distributions of Voter Ideal Points

As we noted above, we can calibrate population parameters of our model to politics in a particular country by finding settings of these that,[13] given observed party policy positions and the assumption of proximity voting, imply support shares for the top three parties that are close to those we observe.[14] We therefore programmed a voter-calibration routine that randomly picks parameters for two subpopulations, thereby using the same assumptions about voter ideal points that we made in our theoretical work. Given the distribution of voter ideal points generated by these random parameters and observed party policy positions, the program calculates the party vote shares implied by proximity voting. The program then iterates this process, searching for random parameterizations of the distribution of voter ideal points such that proximity voting implies vote shares for the three largest parties that deviate on average less than a predefined tolerance level of .01 from the observed vote shares of these same parties.

For each country we investigated, we searched for 1,000 "tolerated" parameterizations of the distribution of voter ideal points, calibrated to observed party positions and vote shares during 1989. This would be effectively impossible to do by hand, since we typically discarded about 5,400 possibilities for every tolerated population calibration. This rejection rate is striking and substantively interesting in itself. Very few parameterizations of a two-dimensional distribution of voter ideal points

---

[13] These parameters are subpopulation size, plus the mean and standard deviation of normally distributed subpopulation ideal points.

[14] We chose to calibrate our model to the vote shares of the top *three* parties—as opposed to two, four, or six parties—for two main reasons. First and most important, we know axiomatically that three party positions can always be represented in a two-dimensional space. We are using what we assume to be the "best" two-dimensional representation of the policy space in each country, which we interpret to mean we have a "good" representation of the three main parties. It is quite possible that we would need additional policy dimensions to represent the positions of the fourth largest and even smaller parties. Focusing on the top three parties for calibration thus lowers the probability that, with more parties, positions of smaller parties are not well captured in the two-dimensional policy spaces we investigate. Second, using the top three parties for our calibrations also means that we can use the same calibration standard for every party system, even those with relatively few parties.

are consistent with observed voting patterns in any given country in any given year. Our method does not tell us that the tolerated calibrations we find are in some sense "right." It does tell us, however, that they are "not demonstrably wrong," that they are not among the vast number of possible calibrations of the voting population in each country that do *not* fit observed vote shares to observed party positions.

We found it easiest to calibrate voter ideals points in Britain, France, Germany, Greece, and Luxembourg to a two-dimensional policy space with two subpopulations, with the x- and y-dimensions being left-right economic policy and social liberalism *versus* conservatism, respectively. In each of these countries, the mean error in the predicted vote shares of the top three parties was .005. The least precise calibrations were in Spain and Denmark, where it proved impossible to achieve a calibration tolerance of .01 and we had to use more relaxed tolerances. Possibly, voters in these countries are not behaving like voters in other countries. More plausibly, the two-dimensional policy maps we are using may fit real politics in these countries less well. We expect our model to work less well in these countries, since it is not so well calibrated to them.

Having achieved one thousand "tolerated" calibrations of the distribution of voter ideal points in each country in the way we just described, we selected for further analysis only those calibrations that were in the top fifth percentile, in terms of ability to predict vote shares in 1989 from party positions in 1989. That is, we used the fifty most accurate calibrations of voter ideal points that we found. The mean prediction errors of the calibrations thereby selected are summarized in Table 11.1.[15]

Calibrating Other Parameters of the Competitive Environment

One of the most striking calibrations we need to perform, before we can apply our model to the dynamics of real party systems and indeed before we can perform other model calibration, is to calibrate model ticks to real time. One thing that we do know very well is how many elections were held in each of the party systems under investigation between our two expert survey estimates of party policy positions, in 1989 and 2002. The mean and median numbers of elections in the target party systems over this period are both four.[16] Given this, each run of our model was specified as applying to run for four elections from the starting configuration

---

[15] The relevant calibration data are reported in Table E11.1 in the electronic appendix. This gives two-dimensional party positions estimated for 1989 using the Laver-Hunt (1992) expert surveys and party vote shares estimated for the same period as mean vote shares for each party in Eurobarometers 29–32.

[16] Precise numbers of elections between 1989 and 2002 are as follows: Britain 3, Denmark 4, France 3, Germany 4, ,Greece 5, Ireland 4, Italy 4, Luxembourg 3, the Netherlands 4, and Spain 4.

TABLE 11.1
Mean Prediction Errors in the Fifty Best 1989 Population Calibrations

	Mean	Min	Max
Britain	0.002	0.000	0.002
Denmark	0.067	0.063	0.069
France	0.003	0.002	0.004
Germany	0.005	0.001	0.007
Greece	0.003	0.001	0.004
Ireland	0.012	0.008	0.014
Luxembourg	0.003	0.001	0.003
Netherlands	0.010	0.004	0.012
Portugal	0.035	0.028	0.037
Spain	0.021	0.011	0.025

observed in 1989. This leaves open the calibration of the unobservable parameter ψ, the number of campaign ticks per election, which is an almost metaphysical undertaking. Since we have no empirical information that might throw light on this, we follow our strategy in chapter 8 of assuming a "central" value for ψ of 15. This assumption has implications for our calibration of other parameters below, notably "speed," γ, and η, the size of an exploration neighborhood, which both concern the extent of possible movement of party positions between elections.

A crucial parameter of the valence model we specify in chapter 9 concerns the extent to which voters, when deciding which party they prefer, trade off policy proximity against each party leader's nonpolicy valence. We have assumed that all voters do this in the same way, so that the key trade-off parameter, λ, is in effect a parameter of the competitive environment. In the model runs that follow we span the valid range of this parameter by randomly assigning one of five values (0.0, 0.2, 0.4, 0.6, 0.8) for the policy-valence trade-off parameter λ.[17]

We have noted at several points in this book that the de facto party survival threshold τ has a strong effect on the absolute and effective numbers of surviving parties, numbers we can easily observe in any real party system. To take the example of Britain, party support shares, as observed in the Eurobarometer time series, generate ENP measures in the range (2.31,

---

[17] We do not investigate the possibility that $\lambda = 1.0$ since this implies voter choice is driven entirely by leader valence, with no account taken of party policy, while ours is still at heart a policy-based model of multiparty competition.

3.98). We can use results of simulations reported in chapter 7 to estimate the range of values of τ, for this example (0.13, 0.30), that are consistent with the range of observed ENP measures.[18] While this may seem on the face of things a promising way to calibrate τ, we also know from the Eurobarometer survey series that very small political parties often survive over sustained periods of time in each of the party systems we investigate. In Britain, for example, there were parties that survived for substantial periods of time despite typical vote shares, of about 2 percent of the national vote, much lower than the "survival" threshold we might infer from observed ENP. We find similar situations in each country we investigate.

Given the very limited time series data at our disposal, we simply do not have the ability to determine precisely how this situation arises. It could be, for example, that the party fitness regime in each country has a long "memory," characterized in our terms by a value of α_f that is close to unity. The implication of this is that the small parties we observe would not survive over the very long run but do survive with vote shares below the survival threshold over the timescale for which we have opinion data. We might in contrast conclude that the survival threshold is much lower than implied by the number of surviving parties and that the mix of surviving small and large parties we observe is explained by enduring valence differentials among parties. As we noted in chapter 9 it is difficult, however, in a survival-of-the-fittest evolutionary setting, to explain long-term survival of low-valence parties, unless in some sense different fitness regimes apply to different types of party. In the end, while this is not a very satisfying solution, we leave open the question of how to explain the survival of very small parties over substantial periods of time. Our model is not good at explaining this, although no other model of multiparty competition of which we are aware has a convincing answer to this question; indeed, most models ignore it. Given this, we feel that the best solution is to accept that we do not have an empirically compelling account of party "death" in the very short-run empirical contexts for which we have data, while we also do not have many real party "deaths" to predict. For this reason we set the party survival threshold at zero. To do otherwise would be to force our model to kill off all small parties immediately, when we know for a fact that many of these parties did indeed survive over the short period under investigation. Since we do not implement a party survival threshold, we do not have a memory parameter α_f for the party survival regime.[19]

---

[18] We report analogous estimates for each country we investigate in Table E11.2 in the electronic appendix.

[19] As in all other chapters in this book, for our citizen candidate model of party birth we set α_m at 0.50 and the birth parameter β at 1.00.

Calibrating Leader-Rule Parameters

The dynamic model of multiparty competition we use in this chapter takes into account five different vote-seeking decision rule species and four rule-leader parameters: speed of policy change, γ; size of exploration neighborhood, η; the party leader's comfort threshold κ; and the party leader's nonpolicy valence, V. Our assignment of rule species to parties was not random. We assumed that any party winning the support of fewer than 5 percent of voters in 1989 was either a Sticker or an Aggregator. For each model run, therefore, we randomly assigned one of these rules to each of these parties. The somewhat crude rationale for this assumption is that each of these real party systems had been running for a long time by 1989, so that the low vote shares of these parties are ipso facto evidence that they are not using pure vote-seeking decision rules. For parties winning more than 5 percent of the vote in 1989, each model run we randomly assigned one of the five rule species under investigation.[20]

Our next set of calibration decisions concerns (fundamentally unobservable) parameters of decision rules used by real party leaders. The first of these we consider is κ, the comfort threshold for party leaders. The two largest parties in each country we investigate have typical vote shares above the largest comfort threshold we specify and would thus be predicted not to change their policy positions. Empirically, however, they do typically change these positions. Given this, the only way we can calibrate the rule feature of satisficing is to set $\kappa = 1$, implying insatiable party leaders.

For the other unobservable leader-rule parameters, we use a strategy similar to that for calibrating distributions of voter ideal points. We use our model to search for calibrations that generate realistic predictions of the dynamics of party competition in each country under investigation. Our dynamic model, of its essence, sets out to explain *changes* in party policy positions and vote shares. We therefore take the best calibrations for each country to be those that best fit model predictions to *changes* in observed party vote shares and policy positions between 1989 and 2002. We start each model run for a given country with the observed party positions in 1989 plus one of our "top fifty" population calibrations and run the model forward for four elections, recording predicted party positions and vote shares in 2002. We perform a large number of runs for each country, each run with random rule species assignment to party leaders, as described above, and a different Monte Carlo parameterization

---

[20] The specific rule species assumptions we made about each party in each country that we investigated are explicitly set out in Table E11.3 in the electronic appendix.

of leader-rule parameters.[21] We observe which of these parameterizations generates a good fit between predicted and observed policy positions and support shares for the three largest parties in 2002.[22]

We specify an unambiguous and intuitively compelling benchmark for what constitutes a "good" fit between model predictions and empirical observations of party sizes and policy positions in 2002. Our dynamic model should be better at predicting party positions in 2002 than a static model that predicts that no party changes position between 1989 and 2002. We therefore take 1989 party positions and vote shares as the default predictions for 2002 and, for the three largest parties, calculate the mean error in each of the three following quantities: party vote share, party positions on the economic policy dimension, and party position on the social policy dimension. This gives us three baseline "tolerance" levels for predictions made by our dynamic model, summarized for each country in Table 11.2.

This table alerts us to the important issue that some countries pose much sterner tests than others, if our criterion is that our dynamic model must out-predict a static model that nothing changes between 1989 and 2002. Table 11.2 shows that there were large changes between these years in Britain, for example, especially in party vote shares. In France, Germany, Ireland, and Luxembourg, by contrast, changes between 1989 and 2002 were much less striking, giving any dynamic model a much smaller "target" since the null prediction that nothing changed is much closer to the truth. This forces us to confront another observational equivalence that makes it difficult to "test" our dynamic model on real party systems. If the task is to improve over a static model in which nothing changes over time, we have to take account of the fact that, as we saw in previous chapters, our dynamic model can settle into short-run stationary states, before being flipped out of these by some random event such as a new party birth. Though this may sound like special pleading, the observation that no party changes policy position in some setting does not necessary mean that our model is "wrong," since this also frequently happens in our own simulation runs.

---

[21] The resulting grid parameterization of leader-rule features is shown in Table E11.4 in the electronic appendix.

[22] Our focus on the three largest parties is driven by two considerations. First, we can use the same standard for every country we investigate, since each has at least three parties. Second, our two-dimensional representation of the policy space is at least potentially capable of representing the positions of three parties. When there are more parties, each of which may emphasize different policy dimensions in the positions they promote to voters, we may need more than two dimensions to represent these positions.

TABLE 11.2
Baseline Error Tolerances in Predictions of Vote Shares and
Party Position in 2002

Country	Vote share	Economic policy[a]	Social policy
Britain	0.147	3.504	3.445
Denmark	0.053	2.028	1.395
France	0.037	1.232	0.912
Germany	0.037	4.325	1.612
Greece	0.047	4.286	1.847
Ireland	0.033	2.386	1.025
Luxembourg	0.033	2.884	2.248
Netherlands	0.107	2.356	4.085
Portugal	0.057	0.581	1.979
Spain	0.147	4.172	5.802

[a]Positions are given in NetLogo coordinates; divide by 10 for position denominated in standard deviations of the distribution of vote ideal points.

Experimental Design

Our experimental design involves a suite of "prediction runs" for each country, each run designed to predict vote shares and party positions in 2002, given party positions in 1989 and the calibration strategy outlined in the previous section. The first stage of this strategy was to calibrate distributions of voter ideal points. Using a specially programmed version of our model in the manner described above, we found one thousand potential calibrations of population parameters for each country. The second stage of this strategy was to calibrate leader-rule parameters for each real party system under investigation. For this we focused on the "most accurate" fifty population calibrations we found in the first stage.[23] For each of these fifty vectors of calibrated population parameters, we then generated fifty prediction runs as follows. First, we randomly assigned rule species and leader-rule parameterizations to each party in existence in 1989, in the manner described in the previous section. Second, we ran the model, thus parameterized, for four elections and observed party positions and vote shares. If the mean deviations for the top three parties

---

[23] Results of doing this are summarized in Figure E11.1 and Table E11.5 in the electronic appendix.

between predicted and observed vote shares and party positions on the economic and social policy dimensions were greater than the baseline error tolerances for each country specified in Table 11.2, then we executed a new run with a new Monte Carlo rule-leader parameterization. If the mean deviations for all three quantities were equal to or less than the relevant error tolerances, then we recorded all parameters associated with this "tolerated" prediction. We then repeated this procedure with a new Monte Carlo rule-leader parameterization, continuing until we had recorded fifty tolerated predictions. At the end of the prediction experiment for each of the nine real party systems under investigation we thus had a set of twenty-five hundred tolerated predictions, fifty predictions for each of the best fifty vectors of calibrated population parameters.

RESULTS

It is important to note that the results we report below characterize the values of model parameters that generate "tolerated" predictions runs, that is prediction runs with output party vote shares and positions in 2002 that were at or under the baseline error tolerances set out in Table 11.2. It is not informative to report predicted policy positions and vote shares in 2002 of parties that existed in 1989, since this information has been used as part of the process of specifying the error thresholds for tolerated prediction runs. We could (dishonestly) have claimed credit for making marvelous predictions of these matters, but these good predictions arise simply because we tolerated only those runs that made good predictions and discarded those that did not. In short, we do have *great* predictions of party positions and vote shares, but only because we discarded model runs that did not make great predictions.

We have not, however, as part of the process of generating tolerated prediction runs, used several key leader-rule parameters: rule species; speed of adaptation, γ; size of exploration neighborhood, η; and party leader valence, Vp. In what follows, therefore, we discuss the predictions that our model makes about these parameters for each of the party systems under investigation. While for reasons we discussed above we specified the model in a way that generated no party "deaths" over a four-election period, we left open the possibility of new party births. We are thus also able to characterize model predictions about the policy positions of new party births and to compare these with the observed positions of new party births during the period under investigation.

We used our model to investigate multiparty competition in nine different European countries. Here, we focus on four representative analyses, for Britain, France, Germany, and Spain. We report the results for

Denmark, Greece, Ireland, Luxembourg, and the Netherlands in the electronic appendix to this book.

Britain

Our analysis of party competition in Britain is confined to the three main political parties: Labour, Conservatives, and Liberal Democrats. Several other small parties are represented in the British legislature, but these are regional parties. They contest only areas such as Scotland, Wales, and Northern Ireland and distinguish themselves with policies tailored to these areas, a complication we do not address in our model. We used our dynamic model in the way we have described to make 2,500 tolerated predictions for Britain in 2002, resulting in 50 predictions for each of the 50 best population calibrations we found. We discarded 309 of these because, while they were within the error tolerances we specify in Table 11.2, none of the top three parties was predicted to change position between 1989 and 2002.[24] This left 2,191 predictions that were better than a static model *and* had at least one of the three main parties moving. Results are summarized in Table 11.3.

The first thing to note from the top panel of Table 11.3 is that virtually all tolerated predictions are associated with the Labour Party leader using a vote-seeking rule. Not one of the 2,191 tolerated predictions, furthermore, involves the Labour leader using an Aggregator rule. If we believe our model, this implies unambiguously that *Labour during this period was not adapting its policies to suit the preferences of current supporters, but was instead actively seeking new supporters*. This comports with received wisdoms about British party politics during this period, according to which the Labour Party was transformed into a vote-seeking party after Tony Blair took over as leader in 1994. The other two parties, Conservatives and Liberal Democrats, tend strongly to be characterized as Stickers in our tolerated predictions.[25] The only British party that, according to our model, might possibly be using an Aggregator rule is the Conservative Party. Finally on decision rule species, our results strongly suggest that the Liberal Democrats are either Stickers or vote seekers of some stripe.

Turning to the nonpolicy valence of the various British party leaders during this period, the bottom panel of Table 11.3 shows substantively

---

[24] These predictions were tolerated because of predicted new party births that resulted in tolerated predictions for the three large parties.

[25] Note that, when a party is the largest in the system, as was the British Conservative Party in 1989, Sticker and Predator rules are observationally equivalent since Predators do not move if they are the largest party.

TABLE 11.3
Prediction Run Results for Britain 1989–2002

| Party | Proportion (SE) of parties using rule species |||||
	Sticker	Aggregator	Hunter	Predator	Explorer
Conservative	0.409	0.210	0.071	0.164	0.145
	(0.011)	(0.009)	(0.005)	(0.008)	(0.008)
Labour	0.097	0	0.300	0.257	0.346
	(0.006)		(0.010)	(0.009)	(0.010)
Liberal Democrat	0.575	0.012	0.104	0.103	0.206
	(0.011)	(0.002)	(0.007)	(0.006)	(0.009)

| Party | Mean (SE) value of leader-rule parameter |||
	Valence, V_p	Speed, γ	Neighborhood size, η
Conservative	0.748	0.587	3.56
	(0.007)	(0.009)	(0.092)
Labour	0.785	0.640	4.39
	(0.008)	(0.008)	(0.057)
Liberal Democrat	0.722	0.468	2.73
	(0.008)	(0.012)	(0.058)

important patterns in our tolerated predictions. Recall that the mean randomly assigned party leader nonpolicy valence in our simulations was 0.75 and that it is valence *differentials* among parties that are important. Our striking finding on valence is that *the British Labour leader's valence was very significantly above average* in tolerated predictions. The Liberal Democrat leader was significantly below average, with the Conservative leader's valence not significantly different from the mean randomly assigned value of 0.75. This result is in line with the interpretation that Tony Blair was a high-valence and charismatic leader of the British Labour Party during this period, who contributed significantly to his party's electoral success in 2001. Our model thus gives us a way to estimate valence differentials between party leaders, and our results on this are very much in line with received wisdoms about party leader valences in Britain during the 1990s.[26]

---

[26] Other leader-rule parameters that we can characterize for tolerated predictions include speed of adaptation, γ, for Aggregator, Hunter, and Predator rules, and the size of the exploration neighborhood, η, for Explorer rules. The bottom panel of Table 11.3 suggests

248 • Chapter 11

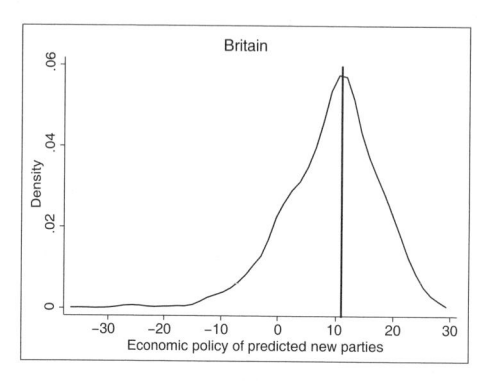

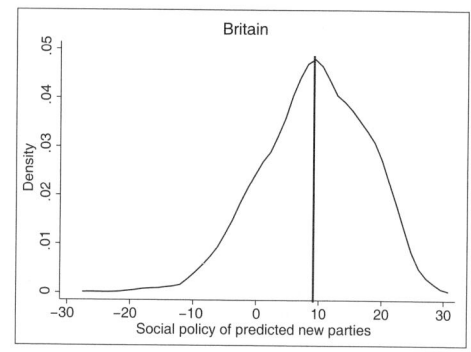

Figure 11.2. Model-predicted locations of new party births in Britain, 1989–2002.

No new national party was born in Britain between 1989 and 2002; the British first-past-the-post electoral system, not a feature of our model, is notoriously unfriendly to new parties. Our simulation results, summarized in Figure 11.2, do however show where our model suggests that latent demand for a new party in Britain might have been arising. This was at the center-right of both economic and social policy dimensions and somewhat to the left of the Conservative Party position in 2002.[27] In essence our model suggests that, given the Conservative Party's lack of policy movement on the right, in contrast to Labour's vote-seeking convergence on the center, the main potential for a new party in Britain during this period was on the center-right.

A crude summary of our empirical results for Britain between 1989 and 2002, therefore, suggests that the Labour Party was almost certainly seeking votes from new supporters rather than seeking to please current supporters, with no evidence that the other main parties, the Conservatives and Liberal Democrats, were systematic vote seekers during this period. Our results also imply that the Labour leader, Tony Blair, had significantly higher valence than other party leaders. As a consequence of policy positioning by a vote-seeking high-valence Labour Party, if pent up demand for a new party existed in Britain during this period, our model suggests that it would have been on the center-right. Reiterating that all

---

that the Labour Party was significantly faster moving than the other parties during the period investigated and had a larger exploration neighborhood if it was using an Explorer rule.

[27] The Conservative position in 2002 was (11.4, 13.2) in NetLogo coordinates (see Table E11.1), as opposed to the predicted values of about (10, 10) for new parties.

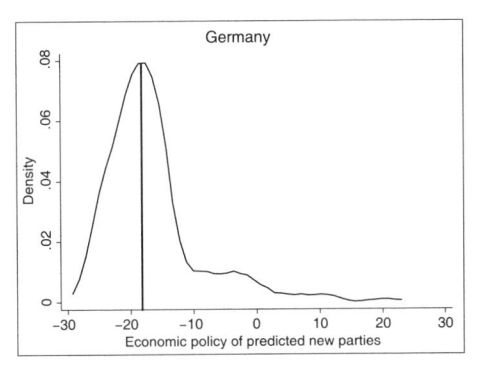

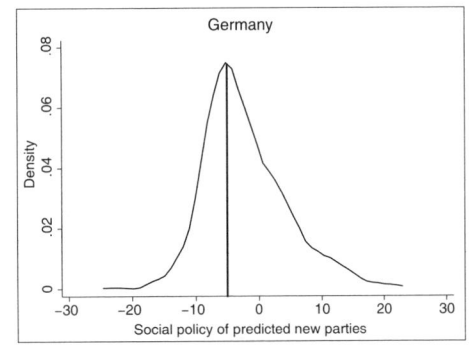

Figure 11.3. Model-predicted locations of new party births in Germany, 1989–2002.

of this does not constitute a rigorous test of our model, what we can say is that the model has generated an account of British party politics during the period under investigation that has good face validity.

Germany

A striking feature of German politics during the period under investigation is the emergence of a substantively significant "new" political party following the unification of the former East and West Germany. This was the PDS, usually described as deriving from the former East German Communist Party. Figure 11.3 plots the policy positions at which our model predicted the formation of a new party in Germany.

Our model, calibrated to Germany, tends systematically to predict the formation of a new political party at a policy position that is solidly on the left of the economic policy dimension and somewhat on the liberal side of the liberal-conservative dimension. Particularly in relation to the economic policy dimension, this corresponds closely to the policy position of the PDS in 2002, as estimated by the Benoit-Laver expert survey.[28]

The top panel of Table 11.4 shows that very few tolerated predictions are associated with German party leaders, even of the Green Party, using an Aggregator rule. Indeed, most tolerated predictions are associated with the leaders of Greens, as well as of the Free Democrats (FDP) and the far-right NDP, using a Sticker rule. Of the two largest parties, the

---

[28] Median predicted locations, on the NetLogo metric, are (−18, −3); observed locations, transformed to the same metric, are (−15.9, −10.1).

250 • Chapter 11

TABLE 11.4
Prediction Run Results for Germany 1989–2002

	Proportion (SE) of parties using rule species				
Party	*Sticker*	*Aggregator*	*Hunter*	*Predator*	*Explorer*
SDP	0.094 (0.011)	0	0.047 (0.008)	0.502 (0.020)	0.357 (0.019)
CDU/CSU	0.506 (0.020)	0.005 (0.003)	0.167 (0.015)	0	0.322 (0.018)
Greens	0.818 (0.015)	0.012 (0.004)	0.122 (0.013)	0	0.049 (0.008)
NPD/Rep	0.939 (0.009)	0.061 (0.009)	0	0	0
FDP	0.989 (0.004)	0.011 (0.004)	0	0	0

	Mean (SE) value of leader-rule parameter		
Party	Valence, V_p	Speed, γ	Neighborhood size, η
SDP	0.744 (0.014)	0.582 (0.015)	3.48 (0.102)
CDU/CSU	0.764 (0.014)	0.546 (0.027)	2.87 (0.096)
Greens	0.750 (0.014)	0.466 (0.027)	2.56 (0.205)
NPD/Rep	0.762 (0.014)		
FDP	0.758 (0.014)		

Social Democrats (SDP) were strongly associated in tolerated predictions with leaders using vote-seeking rules. In contrast, the Christian Democrats (CDU/CSU) were associated with Sticker rules for about half of all tolerated predictions.

Our model therefore implies that the only German party with a leader during the period we are investigating who was unequivocally a vote seeker was the SDP. The SDP leader in the second half of this period was Gerhard Schroeder, who led the SDP to electoral victory and was German prime minister between 1988 and 2005. Consistent with this, the bottom panel of Table 11.4 suggests that, when the German parties used vote-seeking rules, the SDP adapted faster and explored larger policy neighborhoods than the CDU. However, the bottom panel of Table 11.4 also shows that, in striking contrast to the situation in Britain, tolerated predictions in Germany were *not* systematically associated with any particular party leader having a significant valence advantage.[29] In a nutshell, our model suggests that it was effective vote-seeking policy shifts by the SDP during this period that allowed the SDP to win elections, as opposed to any personal charisma and/or nonpolicy valence associated with the SDP leader.

France

The most striking pattern that emerges from our analysis of party competition in France between 1989 and 2002 concerns the decision rules that our model implies were used by the various party leaders. Table 11.5 shows our model to suggest that the RPR, a center-right party in the Gaullist tradition led by Jacques Chirac, who succeeded in becoming president in 1995, was unequivocally a vote-seeking party. Only 18 percent of tolerated predictions imply that the leader of the RPR was using anything other than a vote-seeking rule. Furthermore, of the three possible vote-seeking rule species considered, the hill-climbing Explorer is identified unambiguously as the most likely.

The other large party in France during this period was a center-left party, the Parti Socialiste (PS). Led in 1989 by François Mitterrand, who was at that time president of the Republic, the party lost the presidency to Chirac in 1995 and again in 2002. We see from the middle panel of Table 11.5 that Mitterrand is estimated by our model to have had a higher valence than any other French party leader at the time, though his valence advantage is not huge. Given that the PS was a large party and a traditional party of government, it is striking that one-third of our tolerated predictions are associated with its party leader using a Sticker rule. This is consistent with an ongoing debate inside many European socialist parties, including the PS, between a faction that favors ideological purity and a faction that favors making policy compromises in order to get into power. The PS did not significantly change its policy positions during the period after it lost the presidency, according to the expert survey data,[30] and did not regain power. The French Communist Party (PCF) was led for much of the period under investigation by Robert Hue. After the fall of the Soviet Union, The PCF introduced a policy of *mutation* (change) that was designed in large part to make the party more electable. As we see from the top panel of Table 11.5, our simulations suggest that, during this period, the leader of the PCF was most likely using a vote-seeking Explorer rule with a relatively large exploration neighborhood.

---

[29] All estimated party leader valences in Germany are statistically indistinguishable from the mean randomly assigned valence level of 0.75.
[30] See Table E11.1 in the electronic appendix.

TABLE 11.5
Prediction Run Results for France 1989–2002

	Proportion (SE) of parties using rule species				
Party	Sticker	Aggregator	Hunter	Predator	Explorer
PS	0.339 (0.014)	0	0.079 (0.008)	0.323 (0.014)	0.259 (0.013)
RPR	0.175 (0.011)	0	0.194 (0.012)	0.038 (0.006)	0.593 (0.014)
UDF	0.728 (0.013)	0.006 (0.002)	0.082 (0.008)	0.003 (0.002)	0.182 (0.011)
Verts	0.705 (0.013)	0	0.053 (0.007)	0.123 (0.010)	0.119 (0.010)
PCF	0.253 (0.013)	0.008 (0.003)	0.074 (0.008)	0.054 (0.007)	0.611 (0.014)
FN	0.500 (0.015)	0.500 (0.015)			

	Mean (SE) value of leader-rule parameter		
Party	Valence, V_p	Speed, γ	Neighborhood size, η
PS	0.775 (0.011)	0.616 (0.013)	4.03 (0.094)
RPR	0.769 (0.011)	0.570 (0.018)	3.34 (0.062)
UDF	0.738 (0.010)	0.430 (0.023)	3.01 (0.103)
Verts	0.713 (0.010)	0.595 (0.020)	3.11 (0.133)
PCF	0.730 (0.010)	0.566 (0.022)	3.91 (0.057)
FN	0.749 (0.011)	0.639 (0.12)	n/a

No significant new party was formed in France during this period and, in contrast to the results for Britain and Germany, Figure 11.4 shows that our simulations are more ambiguous as to where the latent demand for a new French party might be. If anything this demand is on the center-right, but this is much less intensely concentrated than in Britain and Germany.

Spain

The most striking feature of the set of tolerated prediction runs for Spain concerns party leader valence. Our model implies, as we see from the bottom panel of Table 11.6, that the Spanish party with the highest valence leader, by some considerable margin, was the Spanish Socialist Party

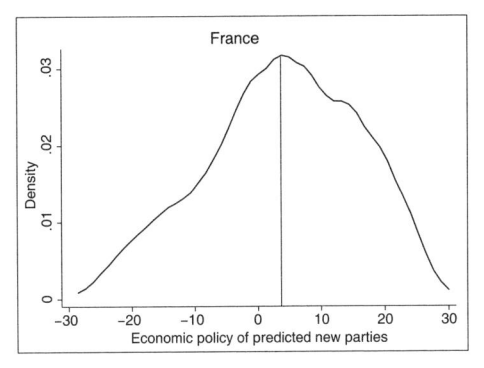

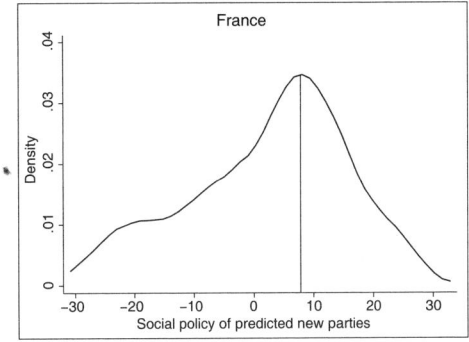

Figure 11.4. Model-predicted locations of new party births in France, 1989–2002.

(PSOE). Felipe Gonzalez, who led the PSOE for most of the period under investigation, was a charismatic and popular politician who won the prime ministership four times between 1982, five years after the end of the Franco dictatorship, and 1996. Our model suggests that his valence advantage over other Spanish party leaders was even greater than that of Tony Blair in Britain. Our model does not suggest a huge difference between the main Spanish parties,[31] in terms of the decision rules apparently being used by their leaders. If anything, the conservative PP seems less likely than other parties to have been using vote-seeking rules during this period and, when it did use vote-seeking rules, to have changed policy positions more slowly.

We do not observe any significant new party formation in Spain during this period, but Figure 11.5 shows that, if anything, the latent demand for a new party was somewhere in the center of the policy space.

Relative Prevalence of Different Rule Species

There is much that cannot be compared across the nine countries for which we were able to complete our empirical investigations. Table 11.7, however, does report one useful and interesting summary of our results. It shows the relative prevalence of different rule species in the tolerated prediction runs across all nine countries.[32] Calibrating our model to each

---

[31] As with Britain, a number of regional Spanish parties are omitted from this analysis since our model does not take account of regional party competition.

[32] The table summarizes results for the set of parties that we assumed in our model calibrations to be using any one of the five possible rules species—see Table E11.3 in the electronic appendix. There were thirty-five parties in the nine countries we investigated for which this was the case. Each of these thirty-five parties was estimated in our predic-

254 • Chapter 11

TABLE 11.6
Prediction Run Results for Spain 1989–2002

	Proportion (SE) of parties using rule species				
Party	*Sticker*	*Aggregator*	*Hunter*	*Predator*	*Explorer*
PSOE	0.211 (0.008)	0.034 (0.004)	0.202 (0.009)	0.278 (0.009)	0.275 (0.009)
PP	0.210 (0.008)	0.219 (0.008)	0.170 (0.008)	0.120 (0.007)	0.282 (0.009)
CDS	0.215 (0.008)	0.005 (0.001)	0.072 (0.005)	0.629 (0.010)	0.079 (0.005)
IU	0.131 (0.007)	0.190 (0.008)	0.201 (0.008)	0.236 (0.008)	0.244 (0.009)

	Mean (SE) value of leader-rule parameter		
Party	*Valence, V_p*	*Speed, γ*	*Neighborhood size, η*
PSOE	0.874 (0.007)	0.610 (0.008)	4.24 (0.060)
PP	0.767 (0.007)	0.480 (0.008)	4.14 (0.062)
CDS	0.605 (0.006)	0.619 (0.007)	3.08 (0.106)
IU	0.772 (0.007)	0.616 (0.007)	4.34 (0.064)

party system in 1989 and then finding tolerated model predictions of key party system outputs in 2002, we see three main patterns. First, the vast majority of parties are either Stickers or using vote-seeking rules. About one-third of the parties in our tolerated model predictions are not adapting their positions at all; about 60 percent appear to be using a vote-seeking rule. Second, almost none of the parties are using an Aggregator rule. Third, of the vote-seeking rules, Explorer is by a wide margin the most common rule species associated with our tolerated model predictions. Our results suggest that vote-seeking parties appear to be much more likely to use the hill-climbing Explorer rule than the Hunter or Predator rules.

Of course, we cannot conclude that real party leaders are actually using different species of decision rules in the proportions set out in Table

---

tion runs to be using each rule species with some relative frequency. Table 11.7 reports the means and standard deviations of these relative frequencies across all thirty-five parties. "Standard errors" also refer to these thirty-five mean estimates.

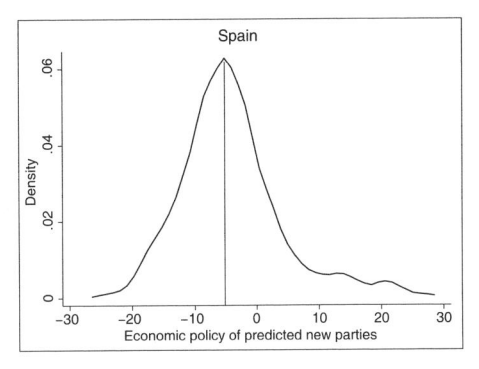

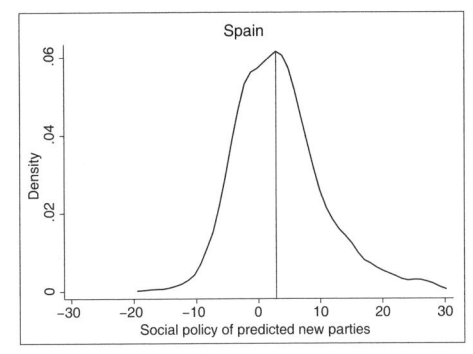

Figure 11.5. Model-predicted locations of new party births in Spain, 1989–2002.

11.7. It is quite possible, for example, that there are other decision rule species in widespread use by party leaders that we have yet to specify and investigate. What we can say, however, is that the proportions reported in Table 11.7 are consistent with a calibration of our model to real election results, suggesting that it is rare for party leaders to use the Aggregator rules that are associated with optimal representation, that it is quite common for party leaders to state a policy position and stick to it, and that hill-climbing Explorer-type rules are the most popular among party leaders seeking to increase their parties' vote shares.

CONCLUSIONS

We have shown it is possible to use our model to interpret multiparty competition in particular real settings, in ways we feel are interesting and informative. No aspect of the exhaustive calibration of our model to the politics of ten countries during the period 1989–2002, and of our subsequent interpretations of these, constitutes a formal "test" of our model. Nonetheless it is far better in our view to do what we have done than to do nothing—faced with fundamental problems of calibrating unobservable model parameters to party competition in particular real settings, compounded by a lack of reliable time series data with which to compare empirical implications of our model. We use tolerated predictions generated by our "autocalibrated" model to describe certain features of party politics in different countries, and these descriptions are on the face of things plausible. At the very least, our model predictions sit easily with uncontroversial accounts of reality, and this, given the paucity of dynamic data on party policy positions and the problems of

TABLE 11.7
Relative Frequency of Different Rule Species in Nine Countries

	Proportion of parties using rule		
Rule species	Mean	SD	SE
Sticker	0.33	0.23	0.039
Aggregator	0.06	0.08	0.013
Hunter	0.14	0.06	0.011
Predator	0.18	0.18	0.031
Explorer	0.29	0.16	0.028

calibrating unobservable model parameters, is as much as we can reasonably hope for.

For example, the description of the British Labour Party as a vote-seeking party with a high-valence leader in Tony Blair, who was more inclined than the leaders of the other main parties to change his party's policy positions, fits well with received wisdoms about British politics during this period. Our model identifies another high-valence party leader, of the PSOE in Spain. This fits well with the fact that the PSOE leader and Spanish prime minister for much of this period was Felipe Gonzalez, a high-profile and charismatic politician associated with Spain's transition to democracy. In contrast, our model did not identify party leaders with significantly higher valence in France and Germany, where our more interesting results concerned the decision rules apparently being used by different parties. In France, for example, our model strongly suggests that the most aggressively vote-seeking party was the Gaullist RPR under Jacques Chirac, while the other large party, the left-wing PS, was probably using a Sticker rule during this period. This comports with a reality in which the RPR took power from the PS. Similarly, tolerated predictions generated by our model characterize the German party system during this period as one in which most party leaders were using Sticker rules and not changing party policy to any great degree, with the notable exception of the SDP, which, toward the end of the period under investigation, took power under the leadership of Gerhard Schroeder. There was also a significant new party in Germany during the period under investigation, the PDS, and our model does well at "predicting" the policy location at which a new German party should have emerged.

In drawing these positive conclusions, we should not lose sight of the fact that dynamic models such as ours typically have more parameters, other things equal, than analogous static models. Some of these parameters, furthermore, are fundamentally unobservable in independent and reliable data sources. This generates *severe calibration problems* when we try to apply our theoretical models to real party systems. Problems of model calibration, while ever-present, have not tended to preoccupy political scientists conducting empirical work on static models, reports of which tend to be peppered with footnotes documenting brute force assumptions, often ad hoc, that are made in order to apply general theoretical models to specific real political systems. With more unobservable model parameters, our calibration problems are more severe, and we do not think it is helpful to solve these with a portfolio of brute force assumptions.

Ours is not a conventional approach to empirical research, but we feel in this context it is more helpful to move forward by autocalibrating our model to the real party systems we investigate. In effect we assume the model to be true and search for parameter settings that allow the model to make good predictions about real party systems. We thereby abandon the search for a "test" of the model in the classical sense. We instead rely on a more informal interpretative strategy, based on evaluations of whether parameter calibrations associated with "tolerated" model predictions at least comport with received wisdoms, and ideally with independent data, about the party systems under investigation. Crudely, we show we *can* fit the model to reality with appropriate parameter settings and that these parameter settings seem reasonable. We believe this is the best that can be achieved given the dynamic models and the data-poor universe with which we are dealing and that our approach has the potential to be useful in other taxing empirical settings.

CHAPTER TWELVE

In Conclusion

WE HAVE COME A LONG WAY TOGETHER since the beginning of this book. We started with the twin premises that understanding multiparty competition is a core concern for everyone interested in representative democracy and that we must understand multiparty competition as an evolving dynamic system, not a stationary state. Given these premises, we investigated the dynamics of multiparty competition using computational agent-based modeling, a new technology that, rigorously deployed, is ideally suited to providing systematic answers to the types of question we want to ask. This allows us to model decision making by party leaders, in what is clearly an analytically intractable setting, in terms of the informal rules of thumb that might be used by real human beings, rather than the formally provable best response strategies used by traditional formal theorists. We feel strongly that this is a highly plausible substantive assumption about human behavior, not just a convenient analytical device. So where did all this get us?

Parsimonious Models Are Still Best

There are many different and potentially interesting ways to extend the model of party competition we set out in this book. All of these make the model more complicated in one way or another. This draws our attention to something that is in many ways the great vice of agent-based modeling, and of computer simulations more generally. It is very easy—too easy—to add ever more features to an agent-based model, all of these features added as part of a well-intentioned search for enhanced realism. Very often, when we have presented our work to academic colleagues, they have asked us, "Why don't you do this? Add that? Try the other?" Our standard answer is always the same: "We could *very* easily enhance our model with the new feature you have helpfully suggested. But it would make the model more complicated. We believe strongly in parsimonious models, because parsimonious models are easy to understand. We dislike complicated models because it is hard to see how each moving part has a well-identified effect and, if we don't understand how a complicated model works, it gives us no intuition. If it gives us no intuition, it is pointless."

Computational methods undoubtedly facilitate the building of ever more complicated models. In contrast, parsimony is often self-policing when using traditional analytical models that can be hard enough to resolve even when they are very spare. However, there is nothing whatsoever about the distinction between computational and analytical models that takes away from the plain fact that, as a general rule, parsimonious models are better because they are easier to understand. All modelers, therefore, face the same stark trade-off between realism and parsimony. It is all too tempting to overcomplicate computational models in what may seem a noble quest for realism. But we hope readers will resolutely resist such temptations if, more optimistically *when*, they set out to build their own agent-based models to improve greatly on the work we present here.

Representativeness of Representative Democracy

Defining the *representativeness* of an evolved configuration of party policy positions as the closeness of these positions to the ideal points of voters, we know axiomatically that an *optimal representation* arises when all party leaders use the Aggregator rule, which sets party policy at the centroid of the ideal points of current supporters. When all party leaders do *not* use the Aggregator rule, we are likely to get less representative configurations of party policy positions. This highlights an apparent "paradox." *Vote-seeking parties make voters miserable.* Vote-seeking decision rules typically cause party leaders to set policy positions such that the configuration of all party positions taken together is not an optimal representation of voters' ideal points.

This emergent result must be refined for populations in which the distribution of voter ideal points is highly polarized. If only two or three parties are competing in such settings, and if party leaders use vote-seeking decision rules, then evolved configurations of party policy positions may be almost perversely unrepresentative. Vote-seeking parties may well converge on lightly populated regions of the policy space far way from subpopulation ideal point centroids. However, in stark and intriguing contrast, when there are four or more vote-seeking parties in contention, evolved party policy positions tend to converge on subpopulation ideal point centroids, enhancing representativeness of the configuration of party policy positions to a level close to that which can be achieved with an optimal representation. What this means is that, in the typical competitive environment with asymmetric distributions of voter ideal points, representativeness of the party system goes through a sea change as the number of competing parties goes from two or three to four or more.

What we tend to find when there are four or more parties is that the different voter subpopulations are in effect represented by "their own" political parties. When there are just two or three parties, vote-seeking parties tend to be tempted away, in their search for more support, from any subpopulation they are currently representing. When there are four or more parties, competition between parties representing different voter subpopulations is the exception rather than the rule, because parties tend to be punished with lower vote shares for moving away from some subpopulation they are currently representing. As a result, the most intense competition is among parties vying for support within the same subpopulation of voters.

Putting all of this together implies, perhaps counterintuitively, that more polarized electorates may be better represented by vote-seeking political parties, provided that party survival thresholds are low enough to enable the survival of four or more parties. Conversely, the paradox of representation we identify is exacerbated for polarized voter populations when only two or three vote-seeking parties are in contention, since the leaders of these parties now almost perversely ignore the distribution of voter ideal points when setting party policy positions.

Endogenous Birth and Death of Political Parties

Though this is marvelously convenient for analysts, it is self-evidently unrealistic to model party competition as a contest among a fixed set of political parties that are gifts from God or Nature. Real party systems evolve. New parties are born. Existing parties die. Real party competition always takes place among the set of *surviving* parties. Our model of endogenous party birth is inspired by "citizen candidate" models of party competition. New parties form probabilistically at the ideal points of disgruntled voters, measuring voter disgruntlement in terms of the distance between the voter ideal point and the closest surviving party. Wherever there is birth there is death, or else an inexorably rising population. Our model of party death assumes some de facto survival threshold as part of the political environment, denominated in vote share. Parties falling below this are no longer "on the radar" of party competition.[1] The party systems we model are therefore fully endogenous. The set of surviving

---

[1] While there may be many tiny parties in any real party system, and the Official Monster Raving Looney Party (OMRLP) in Britain is an excellent longstanding example, we ignore these on the assumption that they have no measurable impact on other parties or voters. Even this is not strictly true. On the rare occasions when a mainstream party candidate was beaten by a candidate from the OMRLP, it was very bad publicity indeed for the mainstream party.

parties at any given time is a product of evolutionary processes in the model; it is not exogenously imposed by the analyst.

Our results show that the number of surviving parties in contention is sharply related to the party system's de facto survival threshold. We also find that absolute and effective numbers of parties evolve to long-run limiting distributions with stationary means and variances. We feel this is a plausible characterization of real party systems. *It also allows us to infer the de facto survival threshold in any real party system from observations of the mean absolute or effective number of surviving parties.* If for example we observe that the long-run mean number of surviving parties in a given party system is about seven, this implies a de facto survival threshold for that system of about 10 percent. When survival thresholds are high and there are consequently few surviving parties, endogenizing the set of surviving parties adds force to the paradox of representation identified above. Leaders using Aggregator rules, which enhance representativeness, find it harder to survive in such settings. Leaders using vote-seeking rules, which tend to diminish representativeness when survival thresholds are high and there are relatively few parties, find it easier to survive.

New Decision Rules for Party Leaders

A central plank of our argument for using agent-based modeling is that real people making real decisions may deploy any of an eclectic portfolio of rules of thumb for deciding what to do. We address this by moving from three baseline decision rules, which model "ideological," "democratic," and "vote-seeking" party leaders, to a much larger set of 111 parameterized rules, drawn from five "rule species" and including two new vote-seeking species, Predator and Explorer. We could in principle have defined a much larger rule set than this, but given finite computing resources and the need for estimates to converge in a reliable way, we confine our analysis to about 100 different decision rules. In contrast to traditional analytical models, this still gives us huge variation in the types of decision rules that agents may deploy.

One substantively important feature of our results is that *the particular vote-seeking decision rule that is most effective at winning votes depends sharply on parameters of the competitive environment.* Specifically, Predator rules perform very effectively when survival thresholds are high and there are few surviving parties. They perform relatively badly, opening the door for Explorer rules, when there are lower thresholds and more parties. This is because Predators tend to attack each other in this setting, nicely illustrating the much more general point that the *relative success of any decision rule depends in part on how it performs when pitted against different rules, and in part on how it performs when pitted against itself.*

Turning to the specific ways in which we expanded the rule set for party leaders, the headline news in our results concerns the way in which, in a dynamic setting, satiable vote-seeking party leaders with comfort thresholds tuned to their competitive environment consistently win higher vote shares than insatiable leaders. Our conjecture on this has much more general implications. *Insatiable decision rules may fall foul of an exploration-exploitation trade-off.* Exploring for ever-higher payoffs, insatiable rules may perturb, and hence fail to exploit, short-run situations in which they are receiving flows of utility that are above their long-run expectations. Crudely speaking, a vote-seeking party in a seven-party system has no realistic expectation of winning 100 percent of the vote. A decision rule that is always looking for 100 percent of the vote, and always perturbs situations yielding nonetheless very high vote shares, may well be suboptimal. In this sense, satisficing may not involve "bounded" rationality at all in a dynamic setting. This is the type of conclusion we can draw only on the basis of a *dynamic* model of multiparty party competition; there is no way we could have derived it from a traditional static model.

Replicator-Mutator Dynamics

Our model of endogenous party birth and death introduces a survival-of-the-fittest evolutionary environment in which parties using successful decision rules survive, while parties using unsuccessful rules die. We refined this evolutionary environment in chapter 8, specifying a replicator-mutator system according to which, subject to random mutations, more successful decision rules are more likely to be chosen by new parties, thereby introducing positive feedback into our model. The main substantive effect of doing this is not to change any of the key results we report, but to sharpen these. Decision rules now perform better in settings where they had performed relatively well without positive feedback and worse in settings where they had performed relatively badly. Our crucial substantive finding from applying replicator-mutator dynamics to our model of multiparty competition is that, while positive feedback in rule replication probabilities drastically reduces the effective number of different decision rules deployed at any given time, and may lead to eras of party competition during which one rule parameterization tends to dominate, *we never find a competitive environment in which some particular rule parameterization always drives out all others.* We find no universally "best" rule parameterization in this sense.

Nonpolicy Valence of Party Leaders

Modeling the possibility that voters care about perceived nonpolicy attributes of political candidates, about candidates' "valences" as well as their policy positions, we replicated results from static analytical valence models and extended these in two important ways. First, we found that high-valence parties that use satisficing rules may well be satisfied with relatively eccentric policy positions and maintain these, contrary to the standard analytical result that high-valence parties tend to move toward the center. Second, and in our view far more important, we found that, while situations in which parties have very different valences are modeled as equilibriums at isolated time points by static models, these situations are almost *impossible to sustain as dynamic equilibriums in an evolutionary setting*. Quite simply, this is because lower valence parties tend to die at a much greater rate, all other things equal, than higher valence parties. This raises the possibility that current valence results are artifacts of using static valence models and suggests that the current analytical approach to modeling nonpolicy valence should be reconsidered.

Party Leaders with Policy Preferences

Most of this book is about politicians who set aside their own personal policy preferences in the interest of furthering other political ambitions, achieved by winning more votes or better representing the preferences of current supporters. We also use our computational model to take on another problem that is generally seen as intractable, the behavior of party leaders who trade off their own personal policy preferences against other objectives in a multiparty multidimensional setting. Echoing our findings on satisficing, we find that *party leaders who focus exclusively on short-run vote share do not necessarily maximize their vote share over the long run*, when competing with other party leaders who trade off short-run vote share against their own policy preferences. Our conjecture on this concerns the fact that the ideal points of surviving party leaders, which we assume to be the founding policy positions of their parties, are in no sense exogenous. All surviving parties in an evolved party system are the result of new party births at some previous stage, and these births were more likely to take place at policy positions where there was manifest demand from voters. Parties that stay close to these founding positions, therefore, stay close to the policy constituency that gave birth to them in the first place, which can be good for long-run vote share in a dynamic party system. It is also possible that staying close to founding party positions, where axiomatically there was at one time manifest demand for a new party, has the effect—though not the explicit intention—of forestalling new party births at similar locations.

REAL PARTY SYSTEMS

Our model of multiparty competition is called a model of multiparty competition because we do feel that it has important insights to give us about competition between real political parties in real countries. As with all theoretical models, whether traditional formal analytical models or the computational ABMs we develop in this book, the typical substantive insights we benefit from are intuitive. Despite widespread agreement about the rigorous and scientific methods that should be at the heart of any modeling exercise, the ultimate intuitions derived from even the very best work are ultimately personal. The most brilliantly rigorous work is futile if it gives us no useful intuition. More controversially, even flawed work can give us good intuitions. Ultimately, therefore, our readers are the ultimate judges of whether we have given *them* any useful intuition on any of the aspects of multiparty competition we have noted above.

Over and above ethereal notions of intuition, scientists also seek empirical confirmation that theoretical models have empirical implications consistent with what we observe in the real world. It is very common for political scientists to say this; it is surprisingly hard to do it in a way that is uncompromisingly honest. In our own case, we are unequivocally committed to a political "science," but found systematic and rigorous empirical evaluation of our model to be much more difficult than might be expected. This is because two problems that beset the rigorous empirical evaluation of even static formal models of political competition are greatly magnified when we consider dynamic models. The first is that reliable empirical data on the *dynamics* of party competition are hard to come by. This severely restricts the empirical implications of theoretical models that we can actually evaluate. The second is that dynamic models inevitably have more parameters, other things equal, than static models. Some of these parameters are fundamentally unobservable and thus hard to calibrate to real party systems, using independent and reliable data sources. Knowing what we happen to know about which model calibrations generate good predictions, we could easily have made a string of plausible "assumptions" about parameter settings and generated some impressive-looking empirical results. We feel it is better to drag this problem out into plain sight, however, and deal with it as best we can.

We do this by "autocalibrating" our model to the real party systems we investigate. This involves assuming the model to be true and searching for parameter settings that enable the model to make good predictions about real party systems. We do this for real party systems on which we have at least some decent dynamic data and find that we can indeed calibrate the model to generate good empirical predictions using parameter settings that we do feel to be plausible—though our justifications of plausibility depend on informal anecdotes, not formal datasets. While in an ideal world we would surely build formal datasets to enable more rigorous model calibration and evaluation, these anecdotes give us some small comfort that our model is not completely unrealistic.

THE WAY FORWARD

We started this book with a pious but sincere aspiration. We hope that a few readers will take the ideas and suggestions we put forward and improve these beyond all recognition. To make this as easy as possible, we implemented our models in NetLogo, a freely downloadable package we think is the most accessible and easy-to-use software environment for agent-based modeling. All of the programs that generate all of the results in this book are freely available on our website. Given the ease with which NetLogo can be programmed by anybody with a modicum of programming skill, our hope is that readers will download our programs, run them, modify them, and make new discoveries. Hopefully, this is but the start of a long and fruitful journey. Where do we think this journey should be headed? If we could answer that question, we would already be galloping down the road in the right direction. We can, however, start to answer it by listing some of the questions we would have liked to address in this book but did not alas address—for lack of time, space, or good ideas.

This book is fundamentally about decisions made by party leaders. *Voters* do figure in our models, of course, but we for the most part assume that voters support the closest party and devote little attention to different decision rules that real voters might actually use when deciding which party to support. We also take the ideal points of voters as given and do not model the evolution of voters' preferences as part of the process of party competition. It is thus easy to imagine a complementary book, which we have not written but could have written, that is fundamentally about decisions made by *voters*. We already have some programmed model sketches, presented briefly in the appendix to chapter 3, about how social interactions among voters may lead from any arbitrary starting point to the types of voter ideal point distributions that we assume in this book. We took inspiration from this intuition when we modeled asymmetric populations of voters, specifying these as aggregations of normally distributed subpopulations, in a setting where voters tend strongly to interact *within but not between* subpopulations.

This is just one way to endogenize voter ideal points. Another mainstream approach to analyzing party competition is the psychological model of party identification associated with the "Michigan School," which in effect runs our model backward. This assumes that the model primitives are party policy positions and that voters take their attitudes from the positions of parties with which they identify. We also have programmed model sketches of this process of endogenous preference formation, but decided not to superimpose these on the models we present in this book because everything then would have become much too complicated for clear interpretation. However, for those whose main substantive interest is the evolution of voter preferences, the baseline model of multiparty competition that we present here can be taken as the foundation for a number of different ABMs that could be developed from the existing extensive literature on this topic.

This book is also fundamentally about vote shares at *legislative elections*. As we have noted at several points, we do not get into the various downstream political processes that follow any election in a representative democracy. For parliamentary government systems, these processes include, but are not limited to,

- an *electoral system*, proportional or otherwise, which turns a profile of votes cast into a profile of seats won by parties;
- a *government formation process*, which turns a profile of seats won by legislators into a (coalition) cabinet;
- a *policy making process*, which turns a (coalition) cabinet into a set of appropriately authorized policies;
- a *policy implementation process*, which turns appropriately authorized policies into actual policy outputs on the ground.

Each of these particular political processes, integral to party competition in parliamentary systems, is self-evidently interesting. It is quite feasible, furthermore, to graft models of these processes onto versions of our model. It would be easy, for example, to model plurality elections, according to which the party with more votes than any other wins the election outright. Similarly, we could model elections as we do in this book and hang a model of government formation and/or policy implementation on the election result. There is no end to the possibilities.

Whether people use our dynamic model of multiparty competition or some better model of this vital but complex political process, there is no doubt in our minds that the computational approach that we deploy in this book offers vast potential to ask and answer interesting and important questions. We are confident above all that, in the years to come, at least some of this potential will be realized and our understanding of politics will thereby be greatly enhanced.

References

Adams, James. 2001. "A theory of spatial competition with biased voters: Party policies viewed temporally and comparatively." *British Journal of Political Science* 31:121–58.

Adams, James F., Samuel Merrill, and Bernard Grofman. 2005. *A Unified Theory of Party Competition: A Cross-National Analysis Integrating Spatial and Behavioral Factors*. Cambridge: Cambridge University Press.

Amorin Neto, Octavio, and Kaare Ström. 2006. "Breaking the parliamentary chain of delegation: Presidents and non-partisan cabinet members in European democracies." *British Journal of Political Science* 36 (4): 619–43.

Ansolabehere, Stephen, and James M. Snyder. 2000. "Valence politics and equilibrium in spatial election models." *Public Choice* 103:327–36.

Aragones, Enriquetta, and Thomas Palfrey. 2002. "Mixed equilibrium in a Downsian model with a favored candidate." *Journal of Economic Theory* 103:131–61.

———. 2004. "The effect of candidate quality on electoral equilibrium: An experimental study." *American Political Science Review* 98 (1): 77–90.

Attneave, Fred. 1950. "Dimensions of similarity." *American Journal of Psychology* 63:546–54.

Aurenhammer, Franz. 1991. "Voronoi diagrams: A survey of a fundamental geometric data structure." *ACM Computing Surveys* 23 (3): 345–405.

Austen-Smith, David, and Jeffrey S. Banks. 2000. *Positive Political Theory I: Collective Preference*. Ann Arbor: University of Michigan Press.

———. 2005. *Positive Political Theory II: Strategy and Structure*. Ann Arbor: University of Michigan Press.

Axelrod, Robert. 1980a. "Effective choice in the prisoner's dilemma." *Journal of Conflict Resolution* 24:3–25.

———. 1980b. "More effective choice in the prisoner's dilemma." *Journal of Conflict Resolution* 24:379–403.

———. 1997. "The evolution of strategies in the iterated prisoner's dilemma." In *The Complexity of Cooperation: Agent-Based Models of Competition and Collaboration*, ed. R. Axelrod. Princeton: Princeton University Press.

Baylis, Thomas A. 1996. "Presidents versus prime ministers: Shaping executive authority in Eastern Europe." *World Politics* 46:297–323.

Benoit, Kenneth, and Michael Laver. 2006. *Party Policy in Modern Democracies*. London: Routledge.

Benoit, Kenneth, Michael Laver, and Slava Mikhaylov. 2009. "Treating words as data with error: Uncertainty in text statements of policy positions." *American Journal of Political Science* 53 (2): 495–513.

Besley, Timothy, and Stephen Coate. 1997. "An economic model of representative democracy." *Quarterly Journal of Economics* 112 (1): 85–106.

Black, Duncan. 1948. "On the rationale of group decision-making." *Journal of Political Economy* 56 (1): 23–34.

———. 1958. *The Theory of Committees and Elections.* Cambridge: Cambridge University Press.

Borgers, Tilman, and Rajiv Sarin. 1997. "Learning through reinforcement and replicator dynamics." *Journal of Economic Theory* 77:1–14.

Brennan, Geoffrey, and Alan Hamlin. 2000. *Democratic Devices and Desires.* Cambridge: Cambridge University Press.

Brennan, Geoffrey, and Loren Lomasky. 1993. *Democracy and Decision: The Pure Theory of Electoral Preference.* Cambridge: Cambridge University Press.

Brooks, Stephen P., and Andrew Gelman. 1998. "General methods for monitoring convergence of iterative simulations." *Journal of Computational and Graphical Statistics* 7 (4): 434–55.

Budge, Ian, Hans-Dieter Klingemann, Andrea Volkens, Judith Bara, Eric Tannenbaum, Richard Fording, Derek Hearl, Hee Min Kim, Michael McDonald, and Silvia Mendes. 2001. *Mapping Policy Preferences: Estimates for Parties, Electors and Governments 1945–1998.* Oxford: Oxford University Press.

Budge, Ian, David Robertson, and Derek Hearl. 1987. *Ideology, Strategy and Party Change: Spatial Analyses of Post-War Election Programmes in 19 Democracies.* Cambridge: Cambridge University Press.

Castles, Francis, and Peter Mair. 1984. "Left-right political scales: Some 'expert' judgements." *European Journal of Political Science* 12:73–88.

Chappell, Henry W., and William R. Keech. 1986. "Policy motivation and party differences in a dynamic spatial model of party competition." *American Political Science Review* 80 (3): 881–99.

Converse, Phillip E. 1964. "The nature of belief systems in mass publics." In *Ideology and Discontent*, ed. D. E. Apter. London: Free Press of Glencoe.

Cox, Gary W. 1997. *Making Votes Count: Strategic Coordination in the World's Electoral Systems.* Cambridge: Cambridge University Press.

———. 2001. "Introduction to the special issue." *Political Analysis* 9 (3): 189–91.

Cox, Gary, and Mathew McCubbins. 2005. *Setting the Agenda: Responsible Party Government in the US House of Representatives.* Cambridge: Cambridge University Press.

De Groote, Philippe, ed. 1995. *The Curry-Howard Isomorphism.* Louvain: Academia-Bruylant.

de Marchi, Scott. 1999. "Adaptive models and electoral instability." *Journal of Theoretical Politics* 11 (July): 393–419.

———, Scott. 2003. "A computational model of voter sophistication, ideology and candidate position-taking." In *Computational Models in Political Economy*, ed. K. Kollman, J. H. Miller, and S. E. Page. Cambridge, Mass.: MIT Press.

Dhillon, Amrita. 2005. "Political parties and coalition formation." In *Group Formation in Economics: Networks, Clubs, and Coalitions*, ed. Gabrielle Demange and Myrna Wooders. Cambridge: Cambridge University Press.

Downs, Anthony. 1957. *An Economic Theory of Democracy.* New York: Harper.

Dry, Matthew, Michael D. Lee, Douglas Vickers, and Peter Hughes. 2006. "Human performance on visually presented traveling salesperson problems with varying numbers of nodes." *Journal of Problem Solving* 1 (1): 20–31.
Du, Qiang, Vance Faber, and Max Gunzburger. 1999. "Centroidal Voronoi tessellations: Applications and algorithms." *Society for Industrial and Applied Mathematics Review* 41 (4): 637–76.
Duggan, John, and Mark Fey. 2005. "Electoral competition with policy-motivated candidates." *Games and Economic Behavior* 51:490–522.
Eguia, Jon X. 2007. "Voting blocs, coalitions and parties." New York: Department of Politics, New York University.
———. 2009. "Utility representations of risk neutral preferences in multiple dimensions." *Quarterly Journal of Political Science* 4 (4): 379–85.
Eisenhardt, Kathleen M. 1989. "Agency theory: An assessment and review." *Academy of Management Review* 14 (1): 57–74.
Erikson, Robert S., Michael MacKuen, and James A. Stimson. 2002. *The Macro Polity*. New York: Cambridge University Press.
Fowler, James H., and Michael Laver. 2008. "A tournament of party decision rules." *Journal of Conflict Resolution* 52 (1): 68–92.
Friedman, Daniel. 1998. "On economic applications of evolutionary game theory." *Journal of Evolutionary Economics* 8:15–43.
Gärdenfors, Peter. 2000. *Conceptual Spaces: The Geometry of Thought*. Cambridge, Mass.: MIT Press.
Gelman, Andrew, John B. Carlin, Hal S. Stern, and Donald B. Rubin. 2004. *Bayesian Data Analysis*. 2nd ed. Boca Raton, Fla.: Chapman & Hall/CRC.
Gelman, Andrew, and Donald B. Rubin. 1992. "Inference from iterative simulation using multiple sequences (with discussion)." *Statistical Science* 7:457–511.
Gigerenzer, Gerd, and Reinhard Selten. 2001. *Bounded Rationality: The Adaptive Toolbox*. Cambridge, Mass.: MIT Press.
Golder, Matt, and Jacek Stramski. 2010. "Ideological congruence and electoral institutions: Conceptualization and measurement." *American Journal of Political Science* 54:90–106.
Groseclose, Tim. 2001. "A model of candidate location when one candidate has a valence advantage." *American Journal of Political Science* 45 (3): 862–86.
Hahsler, Michael, and Kurt Hornik. 2007. "TSP: Infrastructure for the traveling salesperson problem." *Journal of Statistical Software* 23 (2): 1–21.
Hamilton, James D. 1994. *Time Series Analysis*. Princeton: Princeton University Press.
Hinich, Melvin J., and Michael C. Munger. 1994. *Ideology and the Theory of Political Choice*. Ann Arbor: University of Michigan Press.
Hotelling, Harold. 1929. "Stability in competition." *Economic Journal* 39 (153): 41–57.
Humphreys, Macartan, and Michael Laver. 2010. "Spatial models, cognitive metrics, and majority voting equilibria." *British Journal of Political Science* 40:11–30.
Izquierdo, Luis R., Segismundo S. Izquierdo, José Manuel Galán, and José Ignacio Santos. 2009. "Techniques to understand computer simulations:

Markov Chain analysis." *Journal of Artificial Societies and Social Simulation* 12 (1): 6. http://jasss.soc.surrey.ac.uk/12/1/6.html.

Jackson, John E. 2003. "A computational theory of electoral competition." In *Computational Models in Political Economy*, ed. K. Kollman, J. H. Miller, and S. E. Page. Cambridge, Mass.: MIT Press.

Kedar, Orit. 2009. *Voting for Policy, Not Parties: How Voters Compensate for Power Sharing*. New York: Cambridge University Press.

Kim, Heemin, and Richard C. Fording. 1998. "Voter ideology in western democracies, 1946–1989." *European Journal of Political Research* 33 (1): 73–97.

Klingemann, Hans-Dieter, Andrea Volkens, Judith Bara, Ian Budge, and Michael McDonald. 2006. *Mapping Policy Preferences II: Estimates for Parties, Electors, and Governments in Eastern Europe, European Union and OECD 1990–2003*. Oxford: Oxford University Press.

Kollman, Ken, John Miller, and Scott Page. 1992. "Adaptive parties in spatial elections." *American Political Science Review* 86 (December): 929–37.

———. 1998. "Political parties and electoral landscapes." *British Journal of Political Science* 28 (January): 139–58.

———. 2003. "Political institutions and sorting in a Tiebout model." In *Computational models in political economy*, ed. Ken Kollman, John H. Miller and Scott E. Page. Cambridge, Mass.: MIT Press.

Krehbiel, Keith. 1993. "Where's the party?" *British Journal of Political Science* 23 (1): 235–66.

Laakso, Markku, and Rein Taagepera. 1979. "'Effective' number of parties: A measure with application to Western Europe." *Comparative Political Studies* 12 (February): 3–27.

Laver, Michael. 2005. "Policy and the dynamics of political competition." *American Political Science Review* 99 (2): 263–81.

Laver, Michael, and Kenneth Benoit. 2007. "Le changement des systèmes partisans et la transformation des espaces politiques." *Revue Internationale de Politique Comparée* 14 (2): 303–24.

Laver, Michael, and Ian Budge. 1992. *Party Policy and Government Coalitions*. New York: St. Martin's Press.

Laver, Michael, and W. Ben Hunt. 1992. *Policy and Party Competition*. New York: Routledge.

Laver, Michael, and Michel Schilperoord. 2007. "Spatial models of political competition with endogenous political parties." *Philosophical Transactions of the Royal Society B: Biology* 362:1711–21.

Laver, Michael, and Norman Schofield. 1998. *Multiparty Government: The Politics of Coalition in Europe*. Paperback ed. Ann Arbor: University of Michigan Press.

Laver, Michael, Ernest Sergenti, and Michel Schilperoord. 2011. "Endogenous birth and death of political parties in dynamic party competition." In *Modelling Natural Action Selection*, ed. A. Seth, T. Prescott, and J. Bryson. Cambridge: Cambridge University Press.

Laver, Michael, and Kenneth A. Shepsle. 1996. *Making and Breaking Governments: Cabinets and Legislatures in Parliamentary Democracies*. New York: Cambridge University Press.

Law, Averill M., and W. David Kelton. 2000. *Simulation Modeling and Analysis*. 3rd ed. Boston: McGraw-Hill.

Levy, Gilat. 2004. "A model of political parties." *Journal of Economic Theory* 115:250–77.

Lijphart, Arend. 1994. *Electoral Systems and Party Systems: A Study of 27 Democracies 1945–1990*. Oxford: Oxford University Press.

———. 1999. *Patterns of Democracy: Government Forms and Performance in Thirty-Six Countries*. New Haven: Yale University Press.

Lijphart, Arend, and Carlos H. Waisman. 1996. *Institutional Design in New Democracies: Eastern Europe and Latin America*. Boulder, Colo.: Westview.

Ljungqvist, Lars, and Thomas J. Sargent. 2004. *Recursive Macroeconomic Theory*. 2nd ed. Cambridge, Mass.: MIT Press.

Lloyd, Stuart P. 1982. "Least squares quantization in PCM." *IEEE Transactions on Information Theory* 28 (2): 129–37.

MacGregor, James N., Edward P. Chronicle, and Thomas C. Ormerod. 2006. "A comparison of heuristic and human performance on open versions of the traveling salesperson problem." *Journal of Problem Solving* 1 (1): 33–43.

Macy, Michael W., and Robert Willer. 2002. "From factors to actors: Computational sociology and agent-based modeling." *Annual Review of Sociology* 28:143–66.

Mailath, George. 1998. "Do people play Nash equilibrium? Lessons from evolutionary game theory." *Journal of Economic Literature* 36:1347–74.

McKelvey, Richard D., and Norman Schofield. 1986. "Structural instability of the core." *Journal of Mathematical Economics* 15:179–98.

———. 1987. "Generalized symmetry conditions at a core point." *Econometrica* 55:923–33.

Morelli, Massimo. 2004. "Party formation and policy outcomes under different electoral systems." *Review of Economic Studies* 71:829–53.

Müller, Wolfgang C., and Kaare Strøm. 1999. *Policy, Office, or Votes? How Political Parties in Western Europe Make Hard Decisions*. Cambridge: Cambridge University Press.

Nowak, Martin, and Karl Sigmund. 1993. "A strategy of win-stay, lose-shift that outperforms tit-for-tat in the Prisoners' Dilemma game." *Nature* 364: 56–58.

Okabe, Atsuyuki, Barry Boots, Kokichi Sugihara, and Sung Nok Chiu. 2000. *Spatial Tessellations: Concepts and Applications of Voronoi Diagrams*. 2nd ed. New York: John Wiley.

Osborne, Martin J. 1993. "Candidate positioning and entry in a political competition." *Games and Economic Behavior* 5:133–51.

Osborne, Martin J., and Al Slivinski. 1996. "A model of competition with citizen candidates." *Quarterly Journal of Economics* 111 (1): 65–96.

Page, Karen, and Martin Nowak. 2002. "Unifying evolutionary dynamics." *Journal of Theoretical Biology* 219:93–98.

Page, Scott. 2006. "Path dependence." *Quarterly Journal of Political Science* 1:87–115.

Palfrey, Thomas R. 1984. "Spatial equilibrium with entry." *Review of Economic Studies* 51 (1): 139–56.

Ray, Debraj, and Rajiv Vohra. 1999. "A theory of endogenous coalition structures." *Games and Economic Behavior* 26:286–336.

Roemer, John E. 2001. *Political Competition: Theory and Applications.* Cambridge, Mass.: Harvard University Press.

Rubinstein, Ariel. 1998. *Modeling Bounded Rationality.* Cambridge, Mass.: MIT Press.

Schelling, Thomas C. 1978. *Micromotives and Macrobehavior.* 1st ed. New York: Norton.

Schofield, Norman. 1983. "Generic instability of majority rule." *Review of Economic Studies* 50 (4): 695–705.

———. 2006. "Equilibria in the spatial stochastic model of voting with party activists." *Review of Economic Design* 10:183–203.

———. 2008. *The Spatial Model of Politics.* London: Routledge.

Schofield, Norman, and Itai Sened. 2006. *Multiparty Democracy: Elections and Legislative Politics.* New York: Cambridge University Press.

Schuessler, Alexander A. 2000. *A Logic of Expressive Choice.* Princeton: Princeton University Press.

Shepard, Roger N. 1991. "Integrality versus separability of stimulus dimensions: From an early convergence of evidence to a proposed theoretical basis." In *The Perception of Structure: Essays in Honor of Wendell R. Garner*, ed. J. R. Pomerantz and G. L. Lockhead. Washington, D.C.: American Psychological Association.

Shepsle, Kenneth A. 1991. *Models of Multiparty Electoral Competition.* New York: Harwood.

Simon, Herbert A. 1957. *Models of Man: Social and Rational: Mathematical Essays on Rational Human Behavior in a Social Setting.* New York: John Wiley.

Sinnott, Richard. 1998. "Party attachment in Europe: Methodological critique and substantive implications." *British Journal of Political Science* 28:627–50.

Smirnov, Oleg, and James H. Fowler. 2007. "Policy motivated parties in dynamic political competition." *Journal of Theoretical Politics* 19 (1): 9–31.

Smith, Alastair. 2004. *Election Timing.* Cambridge: Cambridge University Press.

Snyder, James M., and Michael M. Ting. 2002. "An informational rationale for political parties." *American Journal of Political Science* 46:90–110.

Stokes, Donald E. 1963. "Spatial models of party competition." *American Political Science Review* 57 (2): 368–77.

Sutton, Richard S., and Andrew G. Barto. 1998. *Reinforcement Learning: An Introduction.* Cambridge, Mass.: MIT Press.

Taylor, Howard M., and Samuel Karlin. 1998. *An Introduction to Stochastic Modeling.* 3rd ed. San Diego: Academic Press.

Taylor, Peter D., and Leo B. Jonker. 1978. "Evolutionary stable strategies and game dynamics." *Mathematical Biosciences* 40:145–56.

Teramoto, Sachio, Erik Demaine, and Ryuhei Uehara. 2006. "Voronoi game on graphs and its complexity." Paper read at the 2nd IEEE Symposium on Computational Intelligence and Games, Reno, Nev.

Weibull, Jörgen W. 1995. *Evolutionary Game Theory.* Cambridge, Mass.: MIT Press.

Wittman, Donald. 1973. "Parties as utility maximizers." *American Political Science Review* 67 (2): 490–98.
———. 1977. "Platforms with policy preferences: A dynamic model." *Journal of Economic Theory* 14:180–89.
———. 1983. "Candidate motivation: A synthesis of alternative theories." *American Political Science Review* 77 (1): 142–57.

Index

Adams, James, 39, 187, 204
adaptive learning, 5, 45
Aggregator rule, 9, 11, 28–29, 42–44, 49, 87–88, 90–92, 96–104, 113, 118–26, 130–33, 137–46, 175–79, 192, 198–201, 210–14, 223–27, 246–56, 259, 261; and Lloyds algorithm, 49, 90, 98; relative frequency of, 254–56
Ansolabehere, Stephen, 184
Aragones, Enriquetta, 185–85
aspiration level, 136. *See also* comfort threshold; satisficing
attractor, 51–52
autocalibration, of models, 14, 232–33, 255, 257, 264–65
average: ensemble, 66–72, 76–77, 80, 87–88, 116–17; time, 10, 66–81, 89–90, 116–17, 141, 166
Axelrod, Robert, 106–8

Benoit, Kenneth, 17–18, 234–37, 249
Black, Duncan, 16
Blair, Tony, 246, 253, 256
bounded rationality, 5, 136–38, 262
Britain, party competition in, 246–49
Brooks, Stephen, 70
burn-in, 65–76, 87–89, 116, 167–70, 195

calibration, of models, 14, 58, 116, 228–33, 238–46, 255, 257, 264–65
centroidal Voronoi tessellation (CVT), 10–11, 20, 48–49, 87, 90, 98–99, 259
charisma, 13, 183–84, 247, 251, 253, 256
Chirac, Jacques, 251, 256
Christian Democrats, German (CDU/CSU), 249–50
citizen candidate models, 106, 114–15, 209, 211, 215, 220, 227, 237, 260
city block metric, 37–38
coalitions, 40–41, 113–14
comfort threshold, 133, 137–41, 151–56, 179, 242, 262. *See also* satisficing
Communist Party: French (PCF), 251–52; German, former (PDS), 249–51, 256

competitive spatial location, 9–10, 20–27, 48, 92, 136, 183, 188, 191
Comparative Manifestos Project (CMP), 234–36
computational geometry, 9, 11, 22, 25
computer tournaments, 107–8
congruence, between party positions and voter ideal points, 47–48
Conservative Party: British, 246–48; Spanish (PP), 253–54
coordinate systems, 32–33
credibility, 208
Curry–Howard isomorphism, 7

decision costs, 136
DeMarchi, Scott, 36
demographic effects, 187
deterministic processes, 10, 62, 66, 71–72, 76, 87–88
deterrence, of new party entry, 220
dimensionality, 18–19
Downs, Anthony, 16, 20–21, 30, 41, 92, 95, 183, 188, 204, 206, 210–11
Downsian models. *See* Downs, Anthony

eccentricity: "net," 201–2; of party policy positions, 46–47, 69, 74–75, 89–95, 100–102, 125–27, 179–80; of voters' ideal points, 46–47, 91
effective number of decision rules (ENR), 49–50, 168–69, 172–76, 181
effective number of parties (ENP), 46, 74–75, 95–97, 122–23, 172–76, 240–41
Eguia, Jon, 38
electoral landscapes, 36
electoral systems, 131, 248
Empirical Implications of Theoretical Models (EITM), 13, 264–65
endogenous parties. *See* party birth; party death; party survival
equilibrium, 3–4, 64, 207, 263; dynamic, 13, 52, 263. *See also* stochastic steady state
ergodic process, 64, 67–69, 71–72, 88, 167, 171. *See also* Markov process

error tolerances, 243–46. *See also* tolerated predictions
estimation, of model outputs, 61–82
Euclidean metric, 30, 32, 34, 37–38, 42, 48, 114–15, 135, 186, 190–91, 211, 216
Eurobarometer, 3, 228, 231, 233–34, 236, 240–41
European Union (EU), 234
evolutionary dynamics, 123, 159–82
evolutionary shocks, 159, 167, 171
evolutionarily stable state (ESS), 162, 171
experimental design, 57–61
expert surveys, 20–21, 236–37, 239, 249, 251
exploration-exploitation tradeoff, 12, 154, 156
Explorer rule, 11–12, 133, 135–44, 147–49, 154–55, 172, 175–81, 193, 198–201, 210, 213, 222–26, 247, 250–52, 254–56, 261–62; relative frequency of, 254–56
expressive voting, 41

feedback, positive, 12, 159, 162, 166–71, 173–82, 262
fitness: of decision rules, 108, 161–67, 171, 194–95; of parties, 110–20, 123, 135, 137–38, 160–61, 194, 241
Fording, Richard, 236
Fowler, James, 107–9, 163
fractional polynomial plots, 101, 118
France, party competition in, 251–52
Free Democrats, German (FDP), 249–50
fundamentalists, 52–55

Gelman, Andrew, 70, 77
geometry. *See* Voronoi diagrams
Germany, party competition in, 17–18, 230–32, 249–51
Green Party: French (Verts), 252; German, 249
Golder, Matt, 47
Gonzalez, Felipe, 253, 256
grid sweeping, 10, 57–59, 79–81, 86, 99, 133, 140, 141, 150, 155, 165, 170, 194–95, 229
Grofman, Bernard, 39, 187, 204
Groseclose, Tim, 184–85

heuristics. *See* decision rules
hill-climbing rules, 12, 33, 133, 135–36, 148, 155, 251, 254–55
honesty, of politicians, 208

Hotelling, Harold, 16
Hue, Robert, 251
Humphreys, Macartan, 37–38
Hunt, W. Ben, 236–37
Hunter rule, 9, 11, 28–29, 42–43, 45, 58, 88–105, 113, 118–26, 130, 137–44, 149–51, 155–56, 162, 175–79, 193, 198–201, 210, 213, 147, 222–24, 250, 252, 254, 256; relative frequency of, 254, 256

ideal points, 10–13, 20–23, 30–37, 43–55, 85–93, 97–104, 117–29, 138–39, 142–45, 185–94, 203–4, 208–16, 221–27, 231–32, 237–39, 259–60, 265
imitation, 160, 162–63
intractability, 5, 20–26, 39–40, 220
intraparty politics, 28, 42, 114, 212
invasions, of rules, 168, 171–72, 176, 181
Ireland: political parties in, 21–23, 92–94; voter preferences in, 31–32

Kim, Heemin, 236
Kollman, Kenneth, 28, 33, 36, 135, 147

Labour Party, British, 246–48, 256
Laver, Michael, 9, 11, 17–18, 28–29, 37–38, 42–43, 107–11, 115, 133–34, 150, 163, 234–37
left–right dimension, 3–4, 17–18, 31, 231, 234–36, 239
liberal-conservative dimension, 17, 30, 231, 249
Liberal Democrats, British, 246–48
Lloyd's Algorithm, 11, 49, 90, 98–99
loss functions, 30, 38–39, 114, 190

Markov chain, 10, 62–66, 73–74
Markov process, 62–65, 82, 89; time homogenous, 63–64, 71
McKelvey, Richard, 19
mean. *See* average
Merrill, Samuel, 39, 187, 204
Michigan School, 266
Mikhaylov, Slava, 234–35
Miller, John, 28, 33, 36, 135, 147
Mitterrand, François, 251
Monte Carlo parameterization, 10, 57, 59–60, 86, 99–100, 111–12, 117–18, 141, 170, 195, 217, 242–45
Moore neighborhood, 135, 147
mutation, 108, 159, 162–66, 171, 174–77, 181, 262

NDP party, German, 249–50
NetLogo, xi, 51, 244, 265
Netherlands, party competition in, 1–2
nonergodic process, 10, 71–72, 76, 87–88
nonpolicy factors. *See* valence.
Northern Ireland, 129

Okabe, Atsuyuki, 22, 25, 49, 188–91,
optimal representation, 10–11, 42–43, 48, 99, 104, 255, 259

Page, Scott, 28, 33, 36, 135, 147
Palfrey, Thomas, 184–85
parameterization. *See* grid sweeping; Monte Carlo parameterization
parsimonious models, 26, 132, 210, 216, 258–59
Parti Socialiste (PS), 251–52
partisanship, 187
party birth, 11, 13, 29, 46, 110–18, 125–27, 131, 137, 159, 167, 180, 209, 211, 215, 219, 227, 237, 260–64; predicted, 245, 248, 249, 253, 255
party death, 11, 29, 46, 100, 110–13, 123–24, 137, 159–61, 180, 237, 241, 245, 260, 262
party survival, 11, 110–13, 123, 214–15, 241. *See also* survival thresholds; survival-of-the-fittest
path dependence, 166–67, 171
Pavlovian learning, 28, 45, 118, 150, 193, 199, 204
PDS party, German, 249–51, 256
polarization, of voter populations, 34–35, 59, 99–105, 119–21, 125–31, 141, 146, 170, 179–80, 201–4, 218, 221–27, 259–60
positive feedback. *See* feedback, positive
power diagrams, 188–91
power, of statistical tests, 79–81
precision, of estimates, x, 8, 14, 69, 75–82, 87–88, 232
Predator rule, 5, 11–12, 29, 42–43, 108, 133–35, 139–44, 149–51, 154–55, 162, 175–79, 191–92, 198–201, 204, 210, 213–14, 222–27, 247, 250, 252, 261–62; relative frequency of, 254–56
prediction experiment, 244–45
predictions, tolerated. *See* tolerated predictions
preferences: endogenous evolution of, 50–55, 265–66; of party leaders, 13, 41–43, 206–27, 263; of voters, ix–xii, 10, 16–19, 30–41, 47, 98, 186
Prisoner's Dilemma, 108
proportional representation, 40, 131
proximity voting, 20, 41, 188, 232, 238
pseudo-random numbers. *See* random seed

random seed, 56–57, 62, 68, 71, 76, 87, 167, 195
reneging, 207–8
replicator–mutator dynamics, 12, 160–82, 194–95, 216, 237, 262
replication errors. *See* mutation
representativeness, of party positions, 10–11, 47–49, 58, 61, 65, 97–99, 102–5, 127–31, 179–80, 201–3, 225–27, 255, 259–61
R-hat statistic, 68–70, 73–74, 77–78, 81
risk aversion, 39
robustness, 35
RPR party, French, 251–52, 256
Rubin, Donald, 70
Rubinstein, Ariel, 136
run size, 75–81

sample: representative, 68–70; run sample size, 75–81
satisficing, ix, 11–13, 133, 136–40, 151–56, 179, 217, 242, 262–63
scandals, 183
Schelling segregation model, 6
Schilperoord, Michel, 110–11, 115
Schofield, Norman, 19, 184–85, 187
Schroeder, Gerhard, 250, 256
serial correlation, 67
Snyder, James, 184
Social Democrats, German (SDP), 249–51
Socialist Party: French (PS), 251–52; Spanish (PSOE), 252–54, 256
Spain, party competition in, 252–55
spatial models, 15–27; multidimensional, 19–20
speed, of adaptation, 11, 133, 138–42, 149–51, 155–56, 165, 179, 195, 217, 240–42, 245, 247, 250, 252, 254
state space, 12, 62–68, 71–78, 81, 88–89, 143, 168
steady state, 4, 6, 11, 64–78, 81, 176; deterministic, 29, 71, 76, 87–88, 90, 97; stochastic, 52–55, 76, 89, 116–17, 167–68
Sticker rule, 9, 11, 28, 42–44, 58, 60–61, 65, 78, 86–88, 92, 96–98, 113, 118–19,

Sticker rule (*cont'd*)
  122–26, 137–44, 167, 175–78, 198–99, 210, 242, 246–54; relative frequency of, 254, 256
stochastic process, 10, 61–67, 71–76, 87–88, 116–17, 141, 166, 195
stochastic steady state. *See* steady state: stochastic
Stokes, Donald, 183–85
Stramski, Jacek, 47
strategic voting, 16, 40–41
subpopulations, of voters, 30, 32–35, 52–55, 59, 86, 90, 99–105, 117–21, 125–30, 141, 202, 231–32, 238–39, 260, 265
survival-of-the-fittest, 11–12, 138, 159, 178, 196–97, 218–19, 241, 262
survival threshold, 11, 100–113, 117–31, 141–44, 150–56, 160, 170, 173–79, 197–98, 215, 218–19, 222–29, 240–41, 260–61

tiling. *See* Voronoi diagrams
tolerated predictions, 244–57
transient state, 64, 66

transition probability, 63–64, 71, 168
traveling salesman problem (TSP), 25–26

utility, voter, 39

valence, 13, 97, 183–205, 208, 215–18, 237, 240–56, 263; activist, 185
volatility, of party policy positions, 215–16, 221–25
Voronoi boundaries. *See* Voronoi diagrams
Voronoi diagrams, 9–10, 20–25, 48–49, 92–98, 144–45, 148–50, 188–92, 197. *See also* centroidal Voronoi tessellations (CVTs)
Voronoi dynamics. *See* Voronoi diagrams.
Voronoi game, 23–24, 220
Voronoi tessellations. *See* Voronoi diagrams; centroidal Voronoi tessellations (CVTs)
voter centroid, 47, 91–94, 117, 126, 138
voter dissatisfaction, 114–15
voting cycles, 19

Wittman, Donald, 206–7, 211, 226

Zombies, 134